Science for All Children

Methods for Constructing Understanding

Science for All Children
Methods for Constructing Understanding

Ralph Martin
Ohio University

with

Colleen Sexton

Kay Wagner

Jack Gerlovich

Allyn and Bacon
Boston   London   Toronto   Sydney   Tokyo   Singapore

Senior Vice President and Editor-in-Chief, Education: Nancy Forsyth
Series Editor: Frances Helland
Editorial Assistant: Cheryl Ouellette
Senior Marketing Manager: Kathy Hunter
Cover Administrator: Linda Knowles
Composition Buyer: Linda Cox
Manufacturing Buyer: Suzanne Lareau
Production Coordinator: Deborah Brown
Editorial-Production Service: Anne Rebecca Starr
Text Designer: Glenna Collett
Photo Director: Susan Duane

The material in this book is based upon work supported by the National Science Foundation under grant number 91-47392. Any opinions, findings, conclusions, or recommendations expressed in this publication are those of the authors and do not necessarily reflect the views of the Foundation.

Portions of this book were published previously as *Teaching Science for All Children,* Second Edition.

Library of Congress Cataloging-in-Publication Data
Science for all children : methods for constructing understanding /
    Ralph Martin . . . [et al.].
        p.   cm.
    "This book is a condensed version of our popular Teaching science for all children"—Pref.
    Includes bibliographical references (p.) and index.
    ISBN (invalid) 0-205-27573-4 (pbk.)
    1. Science—Study and teaching—Methodology. 2. Science—Study and teaching (Elementary)—Methodology. 3. College students—Training of. 4. Teachers—Training of. 5. Constructivism (Education) I. Martin, Ralph E., 1951– . II. Teaching science for all children.
    Q181.S3737 1998   97–23185
    372.3'5044—dc21   CIP

Photo credits appear on p. xii, which represents a continuation of the copyright page.

Printed in the United States of America
10 9 8 7 6 5 4 3 2 1   02 01 00 99 98 97

DEDICATIONS

For Jerry DeBruin, who has long demonstrated creative methods for constructing understanding.

r.m.

I've been fortunate to have encountered many enthusiastic and energetic teachers as I sat in the classroom and as I work in classrooms. They have been constant sources of encouragement for my work. For their inspiration and the inspiration of other critical friends, I am deeply grateful.

c.s.

To my mentor and friend. Ditto.

k.w.

To the Elementary Science Methods students at Drake University who have been, and continue to be, inspirations for my science activity ideas, as well as enthusiastic supporters of hands-on, and often electronically delivered, quality science teaching.

j.g.

Contents

3 How Can You Teach Science for All Children? 66

4 What Goals Promote Scientific Literacy? 112

PART II   Preparing Science Lessons That Help Learners Construct Meaning 140

5 How Can You Plan Constructivist Science Lessons and Assess Student Performance? 140

How Can You Create a Safe, Efficient, Activity-Based Science Classroom? *190*

What Are the Characteristics of Effective Science Materials and Programs? *236*

How Can You Improve Your Science Instruction Through Human, Print, and Multimedia Resources? *276*

PART III   Teaching Science *298*

What Teaching Methods Help Learners to Construct Meaning? *298*

APPENDIXES

PHOTO CREDITS

Preface

The ancient Chinese left us a legacy of wisdom: "I hear and I forget, I see and I remember, but I *do* and I *understand*." This proverb suggests a number of things about teaching and learning. However, teaching and learning today are much more challenging than these three lines seem to imply. Today, teaching for science understanding means developing particular attitudes and skills, as well as conceptualizing several important ideas of physical, life, and earth/space science within the contexts of four new dimensions: the benefits and processes of scientific inquiry, the essential interplay of science and technology, the role of science in our personal lives and social perspectives, and the rich legacy left by the history and nature of science. According to the National Science Education Standards (NSES), all are essential for scientific literacy and present a formidable challenge for educators. How can we meet this challenge?

This book will help you to understand the new challenges and to develop particular skills that support a constructivist approach to learning. We ask you to construct science. What do we mean by "construction"? Perhaps our mission offers some insight: We believe that, as science teachers, we must find effective ways to help learners construct their own understanding by connecting their many ideas into a fabric of concepts, attitudes, and skills that carries meaning for them, both personally and academically. Understanding is constructed from experience, and this book strives to provide an array of experiences to help your understanding arise from what you do.

This book is a condensed version of our popular *Teaching Science for All Children*, Second Edition. In this book we apply the NSES content standards in many ways in order to stimulate among learners an awareness of the history and nature of science, and skills in using science inquiry processes, and to develop an understanding of the complex interrelationships among science, technology, and society.

The philosophy that guides our book is one of promoting the concept of *whole science* by making certain that the ideas, skills, and attitudes of science all are included in the experiences that teachers offer learners. Whole science is based on the *constructivist* belief that knowledge exists only in the minds of learners, and that they must create those understandings from their own experiences. All of the ideas and methods have been tested extensively at our universities and with many school-based science education projects; they can and do work. Success is evident in the significant and substantial gains in schoolchildren's science achievement, skills, and attitudes, and in the tremendous satisfaction and successes of preservice teachers in using the dominant teaching model of this text, as well as their achievements on national teaching examinations and performance evaluations.

We have constructed our book to help you connect the important parts of science, first by helping you to understand the holistic nature of science teaching and later by helping you to develop your own impression about how learners construct their understanding. The science goals, planning techniques, and teaching approaches provided in our book support this conception of constructivism. Dorothy Gabel, editor of the *Handbook of Research on Science Teaching and Learning* (Macmillan, 1994), recently identified the most promising and effective research-based teaching strategies and practices for science. Our textbook has incorporated those strategies and practices into its chapters. For example, in this edition you learn how to use *wait-time* and the strategies of a *learning cycle* and *cooperative learning*. *Analogies* are used within chapters to foster conceptual understanding, and the tool of *concept mapping* is illustrated and used as a lesson design, teaching, and assessment tool. Teaching for *conceptual understanding* is emphasized throughout, and *problem solving* is a common technique emphasized in the assessment tools for our science lessons. *Science-technology-society* is included in our example lessons, and the technique of using *discrepant events* is featured as a special teaching method. *Real-life situations* and uses are emphasized where they logically fit within chapters.

Each chapter begins with a *scenario*, a story that sets a visual context for the chapter's message. The scenarios, all factual, help to create a vicarious experience through a short story related to the chapter. This experience should give you an advanced *organizer* (a mental framework) for understanding parts of the chapter that may be new or difficult to you. We hope these features will help you to construct your own understanding of the material in our book.

Within each chapter we have added visual aids—figures, tables, exhibits, and photographs—to reinforce the ideas presented. Sometimes we include relevant exercises that you might want to try. The feature *What Research Says* supplements the chapters with a brief authoritative report taken from the recent research. Another feature we have added is *Teachers on Science Teaching*. These supplements are written by teachers to give an applied view on each chapter's topics, with classroom uses described by some of our country's finest teachers. Of course, we close each chapter with a customary summary. *Discussion questions* and ideas for class *projects* are included; many of these are field based to complement any early field experience or internship that instructors may prefer. *Additional readings* contain annotations for further study on the important topics of each chapter.

Experiment with how you use this book—we have written each chapter to stand alone, though we have organized this book in a linear way. In Part I we provide a foundation for science, learning, and literacy in four chapters. Then, in Part II, Chapters 5 through 8, we focus on preparing elementary and middle school lessons. In these chapters we explore constructivist lesson planning and assessment, ways to create and maintain a safe science classroom, the characteristics of effective science materials and programs, and ways to use a variety of resources (including technology) for science teaching. Safe science is featured in Chapter 6, but is also integrated throughout our textbook, and is included in each lesson.

Part III, Chapters 9 through 11, is devoted to a variety of teaching methods and teacher skills. These chapters include methods such as scientific inquiry, Suchman's inquiry, playful discovery, cooperative learning, and effective questioning techniques, as well as effective uses of traditional strategies and materials such as demonstrations, deduction, explicit teaching, and uses of science textbooks. However, the most potent and universal method that we promote is the 4-E learning cycle of *Exploration, Explanation, Expansion, and Evaluation*. The Exploration phase prepares students for science as an inquiry process, while the Explanation phase stimulates learners to construct conceptual understanding. This fundamental understanding is Expanded by addressing the new dimensions of the NSES content standards, such as the history and nature of science, the interrelationships of science and technology, and science in personal and social perspectives. Evaluation embeds assessment in the instruction throughout the cycle and uses performance-based techniques such as pictorial assessment, reflective questioning, and hands-on assessment. The lessons have been classroom tested many times.

All chapters are supported by several unique appendixes. These appendixes, which include the essential science concepts recommended by the NSES, are written for preservice and inservice teachers who wish to locate effective science resources or entire science curriculum projects, and/or to become involved in networks or alliances of science teachers through state or federal agencies.

Of course, at all times we encourage you to try our book's ideas your own way. If you do, you will be learning about teaching science as we advocate for the students you will teach: by constructing *your own* understanding. So you see we hope you will believe the ideas and information that you see in this book; more important, we hope that you will try each idea and learn to understand the complexity and rewards of effective science teaching from what you do.

ACKNOWLEDGMENTS

In addition to our author team, many important persons supported the project and turned the dreams and ideas into a reality. Indeed it is an understatement to say we are grateful to those many talented persons.

We are indebted to Nancy Forsyth, Senior Vice President and Editor-in-Chief, Education, whose vision shaped the project into a comprehensive product. Frances Helland, Series Editor, and her able Editorial Assistant, Cheryl Ouellette, ensured timelines and first-class treatment at every stage of the publishing process. Deborah Brown, as Production Administrator, steered us through the complexity of publishing. Anne Rebecca Starr functioned admirably and persistently as Production Editor. Beverly Miller earned the moniker of "Hawkeye" as copyeditor. Glenna Collett and Laurel Aiello delivered the nice touches that readers expect in design and illustration. Lois Oster created an extremely useful and comprehensive index.

Research support has been provided by Sara Busch, a dedicated and persistent assistant; Greg Hanek, a talented researcher; and Leah Wright, a skillful editor. Without them, the task would have much more difficult.

Our special thanks go to the reviewers who offered substantial suggestions that helped to shape this edition. They are:

Leonard Garigliano, Salisbury State University;
William Hughes, Ashland University;
Larry Kellerman, Bradley University;
Michael Leyden, Eastern Illinois University;
Robert Lonning, University of Connecticut;
J. Preston Prather, University of Virginia;
Mary Rubeck, Friends University.

Finally, we are grateful to our spouses and children for their encouragement, support, and understanding, especially during the tense moments that always accompany the deadlines for such a large project. Knowing that we could help our children's teachers gave inspiration and helped to shape our mission. There will always be a special place in our hearts for Marilyn, Jennifer, Jessica, Jonathan, Tim, Sarah, Celeste, Carl, Cade, Kara, Pat, Jacque, and Kelly.

About the Authors

Ralph Martin is Professor of Science Education and Director of the School of Curriculum and Instruction for Ohio University's College of Education. Throughout his years of teaching, he has received more than $1 million in grants for work in science and mathematics. He has served on Ohio commissions in science and vocational education to improve science education. He is an active member of the National Science Teachers Association and the School Science and Mathematics Association, as well as his state science organization, Science Education Council of Ohio (SECO), where he served four terms on the board of directors. Dr. Martin has earned the SECO Service Award in Science Education, Ohio's Outstanding Educator award for Project Learning Tree, and the Project Learning Tree national award. *Science for All Children: Methods for Constructing Understanding* is Dr. Martin's sixth book, including *Teaching Science for All Children,* Second Edition, (1997) and *Introduction to Teaching* (1988) with co-authors George Wood and Edward Stevens, also published by Allyn and Bacon.

Colleen Sexton is the State Administrator for Ohio's SchoolNet Plus Initiative through the Ohio Department of Education. This $400 million technology project is designed to provide one multimedia-capable computer workstation for every five children in grades K–4 in every school district in Ohio. Dr. Sexton's teaching experience includes high school biology, earth and physical sciences, and most recently, science education to preservice and practicing teachers at Ohio University in Athens, Ohio. Dr. Sexton served as director for the Appalachian Distance Learning Project—a project that utilizes a fiber optic network to link three third-grade classrooms separated by over 100 miles. This project led to the development of one of the Ohio Telecommunity Projects—The Learning Community Link—a venture that joins 84 urban and rural teachers and their students in an environmental project centered around rivers that covers four school districts across the state. Dr. Sexton currently serves on the state board for Project Learning Tree and state science teacher's organization, Science Education Council of Ohio.

Kay Wagner has over 26 years of experience in the education and information transfer field, including 18 years of public school teaching, 6 years as Ohio's state science education supervisor, and 12 years in project management related to public information and education programs, public information product development, resource curriculum production, public outreach program planning, and teacher and student activities. While employed as state science supervisor in Ohio, Ms. Wagner devised and implemented a statewide telecommunications network linking all school districts, vocational schools, and colleges and universities that provided teacher training. She served as the director of the Alliance Programs for the Triangle Coalition for Science and Technology Education, as President of the Science Education Council of Ohio, and on the Board of Directors for the National Science Teachers Association.

She currently is employed by Science Applications International Corporation (SAIC) as director of the U.S. Department of Energy's Center for Environmental Management Information, a nationwide information center for the Department's Environmental Management program.

Jack Gerlovich is Associate Professor of Science Education at Drake University. He was the state science consultant for the Iowa Department of Education for 11 years. He is also the president and founder of JaKel, Inc., a science education safety company. His 15 years of science teaching experience include elementary, junior high, high school, and college levels.

Dr. Gerlovich is a fellow at the American Association for the Advancement of Science and the Iowa Academy of Science. He is a member of the National Science Teachers Association (Board of Directors 1985–87), the Council of State Science Supervisors (National President 1985–87), and the National Academy of Applied Sciences (Board of Directors).

Dr. Gerlovich, a nationally renowned safety expert, has authored and coauthored 30 professional journal articles, eight state science publications, and developed books, software, and video products on the subject.

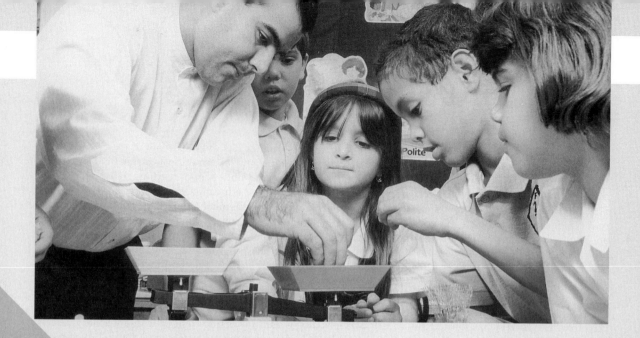

CHAPTER OUTLINE

CHAPTER 1 What Is Science?

"I'm not looking forward to this term," Jessica confided to a friend. When asked to explain, she shared her discomfort with science and all of its dreaded memories: difficult word lists, endless definitions, and reading, reading, reading during her elementary and middle school years—that is, when science was taught, and that didn't seem very often. In high school, Jessica remembered studying creepy things like insects and snakes. Other experiences stood out in Jessica's mind, too, like smelly, gooey dissections, memorization of the Periodic Table, and difficult metric and English measurement conversions. All her teachers had seemed to suggest that science was important, but Jessica had never understood why. "Why do I need to learn this?" Jessica had often asked.

Still, Jessica's friends, parents, and adviser urged her to give the science methods course a fair chance. "Maybe you'll learn something," they usually said. After a couple of classes in the methods course Jessica was about to believe they were correct.

The professor had begun with activities that had required some simple observations and predictions. Each prediction was tested by what had seemed like trial and error. Then a challenge had been given: Find several ways to light some small bulbs with minimal equipment. From there the class had moved on to building simple circuits. Any scientific terminology had always been introduced after Jessica was familiar with the equipment and its operation.

Today's class was her biggest challenge so far. Jessica had accumulated the odd assortment of materials: a cardboard tube, a bottle cap, paper fasteners, a paper clip, batteries, a couple of short wires, and a flashlight bulb. How would she ever figure out how to make a flashlight? Oh well, she would try—that was all her professor asked besides today's objective. That required practical application of what she had learned: Construct a flashlight and show him that it worked at least one time.

Minutes seemed like hours, and Jessica felt pressure that goes with being the last one to finish. "I did it!" She couldn't help herself. Her shout attracted the attention of the whole class, and now the professor was approaching her work station. His serious puckered concentration turned into a broad grin and his wink assured Jessica that he understood the sweet feeling of success.

"That's what science is all about," he whispered to Jessica as he turned to the class and asked, "What are your feelings, what caused them, and what have you learned?" Jessica's classmates offered comments that confirmed her own positive feelings. They agreed that the positive feelings were caused by the experiences of inquiry and discovery, and that it is important for children to have the same feelings about learning.

"In this course we are going to explore ways to offer the same types of experiences to children," Jessica's professor continued. "I think the best place to start is at the beginning, considering what you've told me about your prior experiences with science and your impressions of it. Think about what we have been doing and answer this question: 'What is science?' Once we know the answer to this question, we can make real progress in learning ways to teach science."   ◆

INTRODUCTION

Jessica's view of science influenced her initial performance in her classes. The same can happen to you. But there is more. Our perceptions influence our teaching decisions and what we expect from our students. This is why it is important to begin with a view of science in this course: It becomes a foundation for building our understanding about science and for determining our teaching mission.

This chapter helps to build a foundation for teaching science. To begin this foundation, we introduce you to:

1. Children's perceptions of science and scientists, as well as their achievements.
2. The nature of science.
3. The essential aspects of a holistic science experience and the importance of hands-on, minds-on experience.
4. The aims of modern science education.

HOW DO CHILDREN PERCEIVE SCIENCE?

One of Jessica's first class assignments was to interview children in the schools she had selected for her science field experience; she wanted to find out what they thought about science and scientists. Jessica's professor suggested that the insights she gained would help her understand the readiness and needs of the children and prepare her for the challenges that lay ahead.

Science Is . . .

Jessica obtained permission to visit several classes to ask children of different ages this question: "What is science?" Some children simply shrugged off the question or chose to talk about something else. Jessica presumed that was because they were unfamiliar with "real" science since she observed that little time seemed to be devoted to it. She reported to her professor a sample of her findings*:

"Real hard. Harder than reading. We aren't allowed to have it in kindergarten." (Antonio—kindergarten)

"The weatherman. He gets to choose the weather each day and he gets to color on the wall." (Mary Beth—kindergarten)

"After lunch sometimes when there is nothing else to do." (Shawna—grade 1)

"I don't think we have science yet. I'm not a good reader." (Jeremy—grade 1)

"Mostly rocks and leaves. We put them on a table." (Lyn—grade 1)

"Computers and moving things with buttons you push. Also, anything with batteries or that plugs in. Rockets are my favorite part of science." (Carl—grade 1)

"When you smoke cigarettes and get cancer it is because of science. (Nancy—grade 1)

"On TV sometimes. *NOVA* is my favorite." (Alex—grade 2)

"When you go up in the space shuttle and you are an astronaut. Girls can be astronauts too, you know. I'm going to be in science when I grow up. The only thing is—I don't know if I will have enough money to buy a space shuttle. You have to be rich to be an astronaut." (Andrea—grade 3)

"The opposite of social studies." (Luanne—grade 3)

"We just read a book. I think you get it in junior high. My brother is in junior high, and he has science." (William—grade 3)

"The same old stuff. I've seen the same filmstrip on erosion three years in a row." (Joshua—grade 4)

"It depends on what grade you're in and who your teacher is. If a teacher doesn't like science, then you don't get it very much. Once when the principal was

---

*These replies are direct quotations from a sample of children (distributed across race and socioeconomic status) in urban and surburban settings when asked the question: "What is science?" (Ohio Department of Education, 1988).

coming Mrs. ——— did this experiment with a tin can and a candle and a balloon—but that was the only time." (Greg—grade 5)

"Supposed to be about learning how we learn about the world and how to use the scientific method in thinking. I know because my dad is a scientist and he keeps asking me when we're going to learn that in science. I just tell him that we haven't gotten to it yet." (Doreen—grade 6)

Jessica pored over the messages and wrote a summary to report back to her methods class. Jessica was not certain how much she could generalize from the interviews, but nevertheless the children seemed to describe science as something that usually was not given much time in the primary grades, but rather was reserved for the more advanced grades, at least when the children could read well. Children also seemed to have several misconceptions about what science is and isn't; for example, one child opined that science is responsible for causing disease or illness. Overall, the children seemed not to value science much or perceive it as useful. Some thought it was repetitive or something to be watched, and implied that teachers used it as a time filler when nothing else more important was waiting to be done; or perhaps the teachers might not have felt comfortable or prepared to teach it adequately. On the positive side, Jessica noted that some children viewed science as a career opportunity for women, though access to science careers was believed to be limited, and that some parents expected the science curriculum to help the children develop important cognitive skills.

Scientists Are . . .

When Jessica's professor urged her to probe a bit more into the values and stereotypes that children might reveal, Jessica decided to try the Draw-A-Scientist Test (Chambers, 1983), which she had read about in several articles used in her classes. This test was simple; it required only that Jessica ask students to draw a picture of a scientist without prompting the students to do the drawing in any particular way. Judging that her earlier interview question could be considered a prompt, Jessica selected a new sample of students and hoped to get a fresh, unbiased perception. She collected dozens of drawings and compared them to find similarities. Then she selected two to put into her science methods class portfolio.

The first drawing (Figure 1.1) illustrated a rather common perception that most of the drawings seemed to share. She then wrote in her summary, "Scientists are middle-aged white males who wear lab coats and glasses. Their peculiar facial features are indicative of their generally deranged behavior. They work indoors, alone, perhaps underground, surrounded by smoking test tubes and other pieces of technology. An air of secrecy and danger surrounds their work" (Flick, 1989, p. 8).

Jessica based her summary on the fact that 86 percent of the girls pictured male scientists, while 99 percent of the boys portrayed scientists as male (Fort & Varney, 1989). Overall, only about 8 percent of the scientists were drawn as

◆**FIGURE 1.1 Children's Perception of a Scientist**

female—close to the reality of the 6 percent women in the engineering and scientific workforce (Kahle, 1983). Only 1 percent of the students drew minority scientists, mostly African Americans; in reality, Asians "make up 5 percent of the scientists and engineers (in comparison to 2 percent of the population)" (Fort & Varney, 1989, p. 9). When they drew the scientists, the children reached back into their own experiences. Some drew the scientist by race and gender as a self-image; some took their images from television and movies; some were honoring a significant person who had affected them; and, of course, some knew only the general stereotype that is perceived to fit the look of most scientists (Sumrall, 1995).

Jessica was now curious about why the children held these particular attitudes and beliefs about science and scientists and how the children's perceptions might reflect the beliefs of others, such as teachers. As she reflected on her findings, she decided to try to see a snapshot of the field of science teaching. Given all of the research and attention placed on improving science programs and teaching over the past several years, Jessica was motivated to ask . . .

WHERE IS ELEMENTARY SCIENCE?

"In the curriculum!" might be your answer to this seemingly silly question. Jessica, though, found that the proficiencies of school children make this question a serious one. Her snapshot of the field included information about achievement, teaching, teacher goals, time devoted to science, and diversity issues.

Achievement

In international comparisons, U.S. elementary (fourth-grade) youth rank ninth out of twelve countries. In biology, the most popular high school course, U.S. students rank last. The good news is that there are no substantial gender differences in the test scores for elementary children in the United States, although a gap appears and widens as children progress through school (ETS, 1989). For example, the 1990 National Assessment of Educational Progress (ETS, 1992) reports that, for both public and private schools:

- About two thirds of eighth graders and one third of fourth graders demonstrate an understanding of basic information in the physical sciences and ecological principles, with just a beginning ability to interpret experimental results.
- Across grades 4, 8, and 12 there are large differences in the proficiency levels between whites and minority students.
- Several factors in students' home environments are related to their science proficiencies, including the amounts and types of reading materials available, the presence of both parents in the home, and the amount of time spent watching television.
- At the fourth-grade level, fewer than half the schools give science priority status; science receives only slightly better treatment at the other grade levels in the study.
- Most fourth-grade students report that they like science, but interest declines as students progress through school.
- A national assessment of 6,500 students from grades 4, 8, and 12 revealed that students overall understood simple scientific principles but had great difficulty using that information to solve problems or design their own scientific investigations.

Science Teaching

- Science teachers rely on lectures and textbooks, although hands-on activities have increased since the mid-1980s. (Hands-on activities require students to

use firsthand experiences with science materials and phenomena to construct an understanding of science concepts and principles.)
- Seventy-five percent of the elementary classrooms and 95 percent of the middle school classrooms use commercially available textbooks or a single science program.
- A survey across all levels of science classes revealed that lecture and discussion consume 38 percent of class time, hands-on or laboratory work has 23 percent of class time, individual seatwork has a 19 percent share, and non-laboratory small-group work and noninstructional activities receive 10 percent each (Willis, 1995).

Goals

- The following percentages of teachers report that their teaching goals contain the these emphases: basic science concepts, 83 percent; awareness and important of science to daily life, 77 percent; and developing inquiry skills that are helpful for problem solving, 74 percent.
- Nearly 20 percent of the science classes in each grade put considerable emphasis on preparing students to take standardized tests.
- Teachers with high proportions of students who are minorities are more likely to emphasize preparation for standardized science tests rather than preparation for further study in science (Willis, 1995).

Time

- About 30 minutes is devoted to science each day in elementary schools, a slight increase over 15 years ago (Willis, 1995). (What does this seem to suggest about how much science is valued?)

Diversity

- Non-Asian minority students are most likely to discontinue taking science courses in high school.
- Only about 11 percent of the elementary and middle school science teachers belong to minority groups, whereas about 30 percent of students belong to such groups (Willis, 1995).

Jessica now turned her attention to the second drawing of a scientist that she put in her portfolio; it appealed to her for its special message (Figure 1.2) An older sister had drawn her younger brother and added this explanation: "This is my brother and I think he is a scientist. He is very curious, like this time when he threw our cat down the stairs. He always wants to know why things work and what will happen when he tries a new idea." Jessica doubted that the sister was advocating violence or cruelty toward animals. Rather, her remarks seem to suggest that the brother was following his natural curiosity. This caused Jessica to ponder what science is and what it means to "do" science.

FIGURE 1.2   **Children as Scientists**   Children are great examples of scientists. Their curiosity motivates them to act on their ideas.

THE NATURE OF SCIENCE

The word *science* originates from the Latin word *scientia,* meaning "knowledge," as in possessing knowledge instead of misunderstanding or being ignorant. In fact, one of us distinctly remembers having to memorize a definition from a junior high textbook (long since forgotten, along with almost everything else in it!) that defined science as an "organized body of knowledge." Following that were the steps of the scientific method, also to be memorized: (1) identify the problem, (2) examine the data, (3) form a hypothesis, (4) experiment, and (5) make a conclusion. Textbook definitions and memory exercises are helpful only to a point in learning *about* how some of the ideas of science were developed, a process that was often the subject of large posters adorning walls in science classrooms.

Eventually most science classrooms abandoned the posters and the scientific method as something to be memorized, perhaps because the mechanistic certainty of the steps did not reveal the true nature of science, its history, and its implications for society. For example, George deMestral did not set out to invent Velcro. However, his mind was specially prepared to be curious about why some burrs stuck so tightly to his clothing (Roberts, 1989). By recognizing that the commonplace provided an important insight, deMestral developed a product that has a wide range of uses. Charles Townes too saw the commonplace in a special way, and his vision helped him to invent the laser. He said: "The laser was born one beautiful spring morning on a park bench in Washington, D.C. As I sat in Franklin Square, musing and admiring the azaleas, an idea came to me for a practical way to obtain a very pure form of electromagnetic waves

Science naturally stimulates positive attitudes, enhances inquiry skills, and elevates understanding of our natural world.

from molecules" (Roberts, 1989, p. 82). Who among us does not use Velcro in some way? And consider how greatly the laser has changed whole fields: medicine, electronics, merchandising, and defense and warfare, among many others. These examples of serendipities—accidental discoveries made possible by a mind receptive to scientific thinking—are typical of many sudden breakthroughs in science and help us to understand that not all of what is learned through science is orderly and predictable. Robert Hazen and James Trefil help us to see this a bit more clearly:

> There is a temptation, when presenting a subject as complex as the natural sciences, to present topics in a rigid, mathematical outline. . . . In the first place, it does not reflect the way science is actually performed. Real science, like any human activity, tends to be a little messy around the edges. More important, the things you need to know to be scientifically literate tend to be a somewhat mixed bag. You need to know some facts, to be familiar with some general concepts, to know a little about how science works and how it comes to conclusions, and to know a little about scientists as people. All of these things may affect how you interpret the news of the day. . . . Finally, . . . [science] is just plain fun—not just "good for you" like some foul-tasting medicine. It grew out of observations of everyday experience by thousands of our ancestors, most of whom actually enjoyed what they were doing. (Hazen & Trefil, 1991, p. xix)

A definition or a description does not always help answer a question like Jessica's: "Why do *I* need to learn science?" Nor does it give a sufficient impression of what and how science should be taught for maximum effect. Consider Jessica's recollections of her classroom experiences with science and the influences made on her. It seems fair to assume that Jessica's teachers carried an image and feeling about science that contributed to their beliefs and affected their teaching of science. This teaching then influenced Jessica's beliefs. And when Jessica teaches, she will continue the cycle by influencing her own students' beliefs. Perhaps this is not a desirable picture when you consider the influence Jessica could have on children—that is, *before* she acquired new impressions about science.

How does a child receive information, construct knowledge, and gain meaning from what is experienced? Hazen and Trefil's view of science offers some useful clues for answering this question. From their description, we may infer that human curiosity is important and that certain types of mental and physical skills are needed for learning: skills for acquiring useful information that has practical value and carries real meaning for learners, meaning that is constructed from the learner's experiences.

Science is a human construct and a human activity. Children are naturally curious (remember the brother who threw the cat down the stairs). Their curiosity motivates them to discover new ways to use this powerful key for unlocking the mysteries of their world. Therefore, when we consider what science is and make decisions about what to teach children and how to teach them, three parts of what science actually is must be remembered and put to use:

1. *Attitudes.* Science encourages humans to develop positive attitudes, including their powerful curiosity;
2. *Skills.* Science stimulates humans to use their curiosity to construct new ways of investigating and understanding; and
3. *Knowledge.* Science consists of what humans learn—knowledge for practical learning and everyday living—the meaning humans construct for themselves (Flick, 1993, pp. 3–4).

The new things children learn tend to stimulate curiosity and motivate them to investigate further. When children are given a complete experience with all that science is—whole science—a cycle is established and continues to build under its own momentum (Figure 1.3). Whole science thus consists of three parts: development of children's *attitudes* and *skills* and children's construction of useful ideas—*knowledge.* Children's experiences can stimulate their curiosity (*attitudes*), which can motivate them to develop new ways of processing ideas or solving problems (*skills*); these are used to construct the *knowledge* of science. Successful learning enriches the experience universe of children and stimulates

FIGURE 1.3   The Science Cycle   Children receive a whole science experience when they are immersed in *all* of science's parts. The synergy among the parts makes science whole.

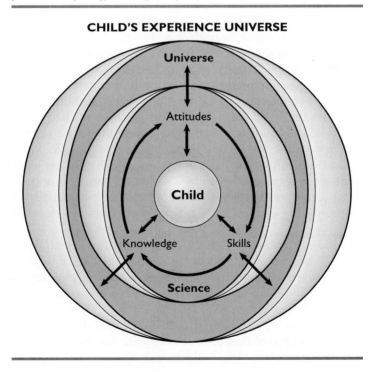

CHILD'S EXPERIENCE UNIVERSE

further inquiry. Teachers provide children with a whole science experience when they are immersed in all of science's parts.

THREE PARTS OF SCIENCE

All three aspects of science are necessary for a wholesome, productive learning experience: development of children's attitudes, development of their thinking and kinesthetic skills (gross, fine motor, and eye–hand coordination, as well as training of the senses), and development of knowledge that is constructed from experiences in natural settings.

Science Attitudes

What Are Attitudes?   Attitudes are mental predispositions toward people, objects, subjects, events, and so on. In science, attitudes are important because of three primary factors (Martin, 1984, pp. 13–14). First, a child's attitude carries a mental state of readiness with it. With a positive attitude, a child will perceive science objects, topics, activities, and people positively. A child who is unready or hesitant, for whatever reason, will be less willing to interact with people and things associated with science. Realize, though, that this readiness factor occurs unconsciously in a child, without prior thought or overt consent.

Second, attitudes are not innate or inborn. Contemporary psychologists maintain that attitudes are learned and are organized through experiences as children develop (Halloran, 1970; Oskamp, 1977). Furthermore, a child's attitude can be changed through experience.

Third, attitudes are dynamic results of experiences that act as directive factors when a child enters into new experiences. As a result, attitudes carry an emotional and an intellectual tone, both of which lead to making decisions and forming evaluations. These decisions and evaluations can cause a child to set priorities and hold different preferences. In our chapter scenario, Jessica is an example. Her attitude toward science and the way she values it appear to shift from a negative to a neutral or perhaps even a positive viewpoint. In time, with continued positive experiences and adjustments in her attitude, Jessica may become more open to science, think differently about it, and accumulate more useful ideas and skills—all products of her learning. But all of this begins with her attitude. Attitudes influence how people choose to respond.

Emotional Attitudes.   Young children's attitudes, so it seems, are more emotional than intellectual. Curiosity, the natural start of it all, may be accompanied by perseverance, a positive approach to failure (or accepting not getting one's own way all the time), and openness to new experiences or even other people's points of view (such as tolerance for other children's ways of playing a favorite game). These are fundamental attitudes, useful for building the other specific scientific attitudes that are necessary for success and the continuation of the science cycle.

Positive attitudes help children succeed in science.

Intellectual Attitudes.   Attitudes based on intellect or rational thought develop simultaneously with science process skill development (the second part of science) and with the discovery or construction of useful science ideas (the third part of science). Teacher guidance, learning materials that can be manipulated, and interactive teaching methods help encourage formation of intellectual attitudes. Examples include skepticism and the development of a desire to follow procedures that increase objectivity. (See Table 1.1.)

Importance of Attitudes.   Young children have positive attitudes toward science and display many of these attitudes as they explore and interact with agemates. However, over time these initial positive attitudes decline. For example, 67 percent of third graders in a study responded "Yes" to this question: "When you have science in school, do you like it?" The children also expressed considerable interest in science (78 percent), believed that what they learn in science is useful out of school (67 percent), and believed that knowing a lot about science would help them when they grow up (71 percent). This attitude declined when seventh graders (53 percent) and twelfth graders (49 percent) were asked about the usefulness of science (Mullins & Jenkins, 1988, pp. 126–127).

  Children can develop appreciation for the role science plays in their daily lives and realize its utility when attitudes and practical value become teaching goals. Consider, for example, the influence science has on the food we eat, the clothing we wear, our use of leisure time, the forms of entertainment we enjoy, and the higher quality of life its technology provides us. Is there any career that is unaffected by science? Appreciation for science and recognition of its value

TABLE I.I   Attitudes of Young Scientists

Emotional	Intellectual
From children's natural curiosity for learning and acquiring new experiences, we can encourage them to develop: • more curiosity • perseverance • a positive approach to failure • open-mindedness • cooperation with others	From children's positive learning experiences we can encourage them to develop: • a desire for reliable sources of information • skepticism; a desire to be shown or to have alternative points of view proven • avoidance of broad generalizations when evidence is limited • tolerance for other opinions, explanations, or points of view • willingness to withhold judgment until all evidence or information is found or examined • refusal to believe in superstitions or to accept claims without proof • openness to changing their minds when evidence for change is given and openness to questions about their own ideas

accumulate as the intellectual attitudes of science are emphasized. Guide children through the science process skills—ways of doing and learning science—to stimulate and develop the intellectual attitudes.

Science Process Skills

Perhaps you remember hearing about something called the "scientific method" in your science classes. Some people once believed that scientists used a specific, step-by-step method in their research. But when scientists were questioned about how they actually went about their work, it soon became clear that there were numerous ways that they approach problems. It was also obvious that there are several processes that are common to most forms of inquiry, and these soon became known as the *science process skills*. Those processes are applicable to other subjects of study as well as science, and you probably have been using some of them most of your life. What sets professional scientists aside from you might be little more than the skill with which they have learned to use those processes to solve problems. We think you will recognize the process skills as you review them, and we also think you will quickly realize how important it is that children learn to use them to solve their own problems.

The mission of elementary and middle school science is not to persuade all children to become scientists. The mission is to help make science more accessible to *all* children. One way this can be done is to help children discover how science can be important to them. Therefore, let us consider the process skills

WHAT RESEARCH SAYS ◆◆◆

Attitudes and Science Teaching

The importance of attitudes was recognized in science teaching and learning in the 1960s. The Educational Policies Commission issued a document titled *Education and the Spirit of Science*. The writers urged schools to promote "understanding of the values on which science is everywhere based. . . . We believe that the following values underlie science:

1. Longing to know and to understand
2. Questioning of all things
3. Search for data and their meaning
4. Demand for verification
5. Respect for logic
6. Consideration for premises
7. Consideration of consequences

"Commission members believed that the values of science are the most complete expression of one of the deepest of human values—the belief applies today, but assumes a lower level of rigor for elementary children, this is one way to justify the importance of developing a scientific attitude in children. Other reasons have been offered during more recent years: such attitudes help students have a better understanding of the nature of science by encouraging them to act out roles similar to those of scientists, and it is important for all students to become rational thinkers. What does this imply for science teachers?

"First, the science teacher is the key person for successful promotion of positive attitudes and affective attributes in children. Therefore, the science teacher must have a good knowledge of the nature of science and must be a good role model. Students must be enabled to perform experiments and solve problems that require use of the thinking skills involved in scientific inquiry."

Source: Compiled from Patricia Blosser, Bulletin Editor, Attitude Research in Science Education, Columbus, OH: ERIC/SMEAC, 1984, pp. 2–3.

rooted in science that young children must develop and the ways children can use these skills to solve their own problems of learning and life.

Learning How to Learn. Some people refer to developing process skills as "learning how to learn." Children learn how to learn by thinking critically and using information creatively. Children continue to learn how to learn

> when making discriminating observations, when organizing and analyzing facts and concepts, when giving reasons for expecting particular outcomes, when evaluating and interpreting the results of experiments, and when drawing justifiable conclusions. [Also, children]. . . should be able to predict what will happen when the conditions of a phenomenon in nature are changed. (Victor, 1985, p. 47)

Types of Process Skills. In science, the ways of thinking, measuring, solving problems, and using thoughts are called *processes. Process skills* describe the types of thinking and reasoning required. Science process skills may be divided into two types: basic skills and integrated skills (Funk et al., 1985). Table 1.2 suggests the grade levels at which these skills are appropriate.

TABLE 1.2   Science Process Skills

Basic skills can be emphasized at the primary grades and then serve as a foundation for using the integrated skills at the intermediate grades and higher.

	Grades								
Basic Skills	K	1	2	3	4	5	6	7	8
Observation	X	X	X	X	X	X	X	X	X
Classification	X	X	X	X	X	X	X	X	X
Communication	X	X	X	X	X	X	X	X	X
Measurement	X	X	X	X	X	X	X	X	X
Estimation	X	X	X	X	X	X	X	X	X
Prediction	X	X	X	X	X	X	X	X	X
Inference	X	X	X	X	X	X	X	X	X
Integrated Skills	K	1	2	3	4	5	6	7	8
Identifying				X	X	X	X	X	X
Controlling variables				X	X	X	X	X	X
Defining operationally				X	X	X	X	X	X
Hypothesizing				X	X	X	X	X	X
Experimenting				X	X	X	X	X	X
Graphing				X	X	X	X	X	X
Interpreting				X	X	X	X	X	X
Modeling				X	X	X	X	X	X
Investigating				X	X	X	X	X	X

Basic Skills.   If children show that they can observe, classify, communicate, measure, estimate, predict, and infer, they are showing understanding of basic science processes.

Observation is the primary way children obtain information. This does not mean that they benefit solely from watching someone else and listening to what others think. Children observe by using all their senses. For example, how do you observe a concert? Can you close your eyes now and recreate a concert you have attended by recalling how your senses were stimulated? Can you see the lights and special effects? Can you smell the odors unique to the crowd and those special effects? Can you feel the vibrations of the bass and drums? Can you hear the music and vocals—really hear them with all of their rhythm? Can you taste the popcorn or the Milk Duds? Teachers stimulate useful observation through the five senses when they ask children questions that cause them to identify properties of objects, changes, and similarities and differences; and to

Observation is a basic science process.

determine the difference between an observation and an inference. An example of an observation could be: *The object is hard, gray, round, and the size of a baseball.* Instruments such as thermometers, volt meters, balances, and computers help to add precision to observations.

Classification requires that children organize their observations in ways that carry special meaning. Teachers can encourage children to classify when they ask them to group objects by their observed properties and/or to arrange objects or events in a particular order. An example is: *Placing all rocks of the same size, color, and hardness into the same group.*

When *communication* is emphasized, children use language (spoken, written, and symbolic in many forms) to express their thoughts in ways that others can understand. Development of useful communication skills is encouraged by teachers who ask children to define words and terms operationally, to describe objects and events as they are perceived, and to record information and make data tables, graphs, and models to show what they have found. An example is: *Describing an observed change in a river over time by speaking, writing, or showing in a graph or data table.*

Measurement adds precision to observations, classifications, and communications. Children can be encouraged to measure by using standard tools like rulers, meter sticks, balances, graduated cylinders, calibrated liquid containers, clocks, calculators, computers, electrical instruments, and even arbitrary units such as marbles, paper clips, and so on to measure quantity or distance. An example is: *Using a meter stick to describe the height of a child.* (Note: The metric system is *the* measurement system in science.)

Estimation involves using judgment to approximate an amount or a value. The estimate is based on knowledge of measurement, but not direct measure. Estimation is useful for quick observations for which precision is not necessary. An example of an estimate could be: *I think the chair is about 1 meter high,* or *the glass looks as if it has about 300 milliliters of water in it.*

Predictions refer to types of thinking that require our best guesses based on the information available to us. Meteorologists, for example, predict the weather. Their predictions are made in advance of the weather's actual occurrence and are based on accumulated observations, analysis of information, and prior experience. Similarly, children can be encouraged to make predictions before they carry out an act, such as grouping different objects into classifications based on a prediction concerning whether they will float when placed in water. A teacher can stimulate predictive thinking by asking children to review the observed properties of objects or events and asking them to tell what they think will happen when a change of some sort is made, such as our sink-or-float example. Another example is: *Predicting the size and shape of an ice cube after heating it for 10 minutes.*

Inferences are conclusions about the cause of an observation. Consider the sink-or-float example again. Children may observe that all light-weight objects from their collections float in water and infer that light weight was the cause of floating. Of course, this could be disproved by items not included in the children's limited collection of objects. Therefore, it is necessary to help children make better inferences by guiding their thinking in ways that (1) help them make conclusions (2) about an observation (3) based on the prior knowledge they have. Another example of an inference is: *Saying a person is happy because she smiles and hums a song.*

Integrated Skills.   Integrated science process skills rely on the students' capabilities to think at a higher level and to consider more than one thought at a time. Just as the word *integrated* implies, several of the basic process skills can be combined for greater power to form the tools used to solve problems. The basic skills are prerequisites for integrated skills—those necessary to do science experiments. These skills consist of identifying and controlling variables, defining operationally, forming hypotheses, experimenting, interpreting data, forming models, making graphs, and investigating.

Identifying and controlling variables requires students to identify aspects of an experiment that can affect its outcome and to keep constant as many as possible, while manipulating only the aspects or factors (variables) that are independent. Example: *Varying only the amount of fertilizer used on similar plants while keeping soil type, amount of sunlight, water, and temperature the same.*

Defining operationally occurs when children use observations and other information gained through experience to describe or label an object or event. Example: *An acid is a substance that changes bromethymol blue indicator from blue to yellow.*

Forming hypotheses is important for designed investigations and is similar to prediction, but more controlled and formal. Hypothesizing is using information to make a best educated guess about the expected outcome of an experiment. An example could be: *The more fertilizer is added to plants, the greater their growth.*

Experimenting requires using many thinking skills to design and conduct a controlled scientific test. This consists of asking a research question, forming a hypothesis, identifying and controlling variables, using operational definitions, conducting the experiment, and interpreting the data. An example could be: *The entire operational process of investigating the effects of amounts of fertilizer added to plants of the same type.*

Graphing makes it necessary for students to convert measurements into a diagram to show the relationships among and between the measures. An example could be from the experiment above: *Constructing a graph to show the heights of the plants, experimental and control, for each day (or week) of the experiment.*

Interpreting data requires that students collect observations and measurements (data) in an organized way and that they draw conclusions from the information obtained by reading tables, graphs and diagrams. An example: *Reading information in a table or graph about the growth of plants in the experiment described above and forming conclusions based on the interpretation of the data.* The interpretation could help to "prove" that *more fertilizer added to plants causes greater growth.*

Forming models requires that students create an abstract (mental) or concrete (physical) illustration of an object or event. An example could be: *A model that shows the best amount of fertilizer to use on a plant and the consequences of using too litte or too much.*

Investigating is a complex process skill that requires students to use observations, to collect and analyze data, and to draw conclusions in order to solve a problem. Applying our plant experiment example further: *Complete an investigation to evaluate the fertilizer dosage model as a way of deciding on a plant feeding routine for the class's garden.*

Importance of Process Skills.   Basic science skills help children to expand their learning through experience. They begin with simple ideas, and then those ideas compound and form new, more complex ideas. All ideas are valuable because they have the potential to help children to become better decision makers, consumers, citizens, and problem solvers. Emphasis on science process skills helps them discover meaningful information and accumulate knowledge by constructing understanding within and beyond the science classroom.

The skills used in science are remarkably similar to those used in other subjects, especially reading (Table 1.3). When children are doing science, following scientific procedures, and thinking as scientists, they are developing skills that are necessary for effective reading and understanding (Padilla, Muth, & Lund Padilla, 1991). A creative lesson planner can have students working on science and developing the skills useful to other subjects simultaneously. Science experiences can help preschool children develop their intellect and get

TABLE 1.3   Relationship of Science and Reading Skills

Science Skills	Reading Skills	Examples
Observation	Discriminating shapes, sounds, syllables, and word accents	Break words in syllables and list on chalkboard. Class pronounces new words aloud. Teacher mispronounces some words and rewards students who make corrections.
Identification	Recognizing letters, words, prefixes, suffixes, and base words	Select a common science prefix, suffix, or base word, define it, and list several words in which it may be used. Example: *kilo* (1,000): *kilometer, kilogram, kiloliter.*
Description	Isolating important attributes and characteristics Enumerating ideas Using appropriate terminology and synonyms	Ask students to state the purpose of an activity. Construct keys for student rock collections, etc. Play vocabulary games. Use characteristics to identify an object or animal.
Classification	Comparing and contrasting characteristics Arranging ideas and ordering and sequencing information Considering multiple attributes	List in order the steps of a mealworm's metamorphosis. Construct charts that compare and contrast characteristics. Put concepts in order.
Investigation design	Question asking Investigating possible relationships Following organized procedures	Use library resources and design an experiment from an outline. Write original lab reports. Outline facts and concepts.

Source: The comparisons are drawn from Glenda S. Carter and Ronald D. Simpson's "Science and Reading: A Basic Duo," *Science Teacher* (March 1978): 20, and from Ronald Simpson and Norman Anderson's *Science, Students and Schools: A Guide for the Middle and Secondary School Teacher* (New York: Wiley, 1980).

an early start on fundamental reading and thinking skills. Primary students can become motivated through science activities and their natural interests to work on vocabulary development, word discrimination, and comprehension. Intermediate and middle school youth develop their abilities to identify and control variables, make meaningful conclusions, and communicate ideas clearly.

Science Knowledge

Importance of Science Knowledge.   Children construct important ideas and discover much for themselves when they use the skills of science. They gain knowledge by accumulating and processing information and by forming concepts

Science Skills	Reading Skills	Examples
Data collection	Note taking Using reference materials Using different parts of a book Recording information in an organized way Being precise and accurate	Prepare bibliographies from library information. Use tables of contents, indexes, and organizational features of chapters. Use quantitative skills in lab activities. Have students compare and discuss notes.
Interpretation of data	Recognizing cause-and-effect relationships Organizing facts Summarizing new information Varying reading rate Thinking inductively and deductively	Discuss matters that could affect the health of an animal. Teach students to preview and scan printed text. Have students organize notes in an outline. Have students construct concept maps, flowcharts, and new arrangements of facts.
Communication of results	Using graphs Arranging information logically Sequencing ideas Describing clearly	List discoveries through a time line. Ask for conclusions from graphed data or tables and figures. Describe chronological events.
Conclusion formation	Generalizing Critically analyzing Identifying main ideas Establishing relationships Using information in other situations	Ask "What if?" questions. Have students scrutinize conclusions for errors. Use case studies to develop conclusions through critical thinking.

about their natural world, human use of natural resources, and the impact of this use on society. Children also discover, in time, that knowledge provides power and carries with it a responsibility for its proper use. Perhaps most important, children can understand that much of science is tentative, has changed over time, and is subject to future change. Knowledge in science is not absolute, and research findings may be interpreted differently by different people, depending on their values and experiences.

Examples of Science Knowledge.   The information and ideas of science that compose its knowledge base are often referred to as *products*. That is because new discoveries that add to the base of scientific information are the products of curiosity and experimentation. An interesting thing about science knowledge is that new discoveries often lead to more questions, more experiments, and more new discoveries. Indeed, the solutions to scientific problems can create new problems. The science cycle moves under its own momentum, propelled initially and again later sustained by human curiosity and a desire to explain natural phenomena. The effect is an exploding accumulation of new information that is added to the knowledge base. Scientific knowledge consists primarily of facts, concepts, principles, and theories.

Facts are specific, verifiable pieces of information obtained through observation and measurement. For example, let us say that during a class project Jessica observes over the course of two weeks that she produces an average of 1 kilogram of solid waste each day: cans, bottles, paper, plastic, and so on—a fact of her living habits.

Concepts are abstract ideas that are generalized from facts or specific relevant experiences. Jessica's class project may help her form the concept that her habits of consumption yield considerable solid waste over time. Since she believes her habits are typical of other young adults, she also forms a conception of how much solid waste a number of people generate within a specific amount of time. Concepts are single ideas that may become linked to form more complex ideas.

Principles are more complex ideas based on several related concepts. To continue with Jessica's example, she might declare, "The reason people recycle solids is because they create a lot of waste." Jessica's principle is based on three concepts: creation, waste, and recycling.

Theories consist of broadly related principles that provide an explanation for a phenomenon. The purpose of a theory is to provide a best explanation based on evidence. Theories are used to explain, relate, and predict. After some added observation and consideration, Jessica may theorize that commercial marketing practices and convenience packaging are responsible for much of the eastern United States' landfill problems. She may use her theory to urge lawmakers to develop regulations and to persuade city leaders to establish recycling programs to ease the pressures on their landfills.

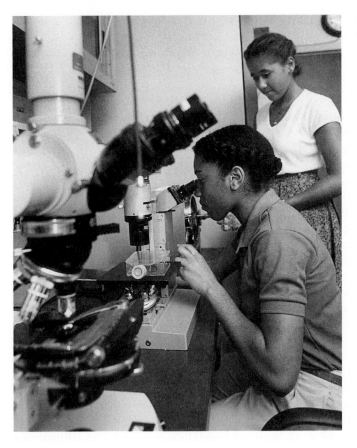

Children construct science knowledge for themselves.

Throughout history, scientific thinkers have found that the hierarchy of facts and ideas that they have accepted over the years cannot answer certain important questions. As scientists struggle to refine the theories and principles in an effort to answer those questions, they sometimes come up with a radical new idea that seems to solve the problem better. If the new idea appears to answer the old questions as well as the old way of thinking did, the scientific community will eventually throw out the old hierarchy of ideas in favor of what Thomas Kuhn (1970) called a *new paradigm*. The work of Copernicus is a good example of what Kuhn called a *scientific revolution*. Copernicus was trying to explain the orbit of Mars using Ptolemy's geocentric theory of the structure of the universe, but he was having no success. As he tried to refine Ptolemy's system, it occurred to him that it would be a much simpler problem to solve if only the sun were in the center rather than the Earth. In a moment of serendipity, he came up with an idea that, on further examination, seemed to explain the orbits of the other planets as well as Ptolemy's theory did, and a new paradigm was born. It was many years before Copernicus's heliocentric theory was widely accepted by the scientific community as the basis for a new hierarchy of theories about the relationship of the Earth to the sun and the other planets (Prather, 1991).

It is important for science teachers to help learners realize that scientific theories are based on the best information that scientists have been able to collect, but that many theories have been discarded as the result of new ideas that provide greater problem-solving power. Therefore, many of the theories and principles that scientists believe today may be discarded as new and better ideas are discovered in the future. At first, this concept may seem confusing to learners. They may ask why they should bother to learn about such things as Newton's laws or the theory of evolution if it might be imperfect and replaced by another view in the future. At this point, a teacher might use the history of science to help learners gain an appreciation of the nature of science and its worth. For example, Ptolemy's system was used for navigation for centuries, and Arabic camel drivers used it with confidence to navigate the otherwise intolerably hot deserts in the cool of night. Also, it was Ptolemy's astronomy that Magellan's sailors used to sail safely around the Earth—nearly a quarter of a century before Copernicus published his new astronomical theory (Prather, 1991).

Scientists are very aware of the limitations of their knowledge, but they are also aware that it represents the best information available to them at the time. Therefore, it is useful to learn about the theories of science, even if they might be replaced later. Theories are best explanations that scientists have, and they are based on the strength of evidence that is available to scientists at that time. Scientists possess a wholistic view of science: They use scientific attitudes to identify and define problems and scientific skills to inquire, and they contribute what they learn to the knowledge base of science, which makes it possible for the scientific community to attempt solutions to many important problems that can benefit us all.

THE AIMS OF MODERN SCIENCE EDUCATION

The aims of modern science education exceed the simplicity of understanding the three parts of science. The primary aim is to provide pupils with experiences that will help them become *scientifically literate*. Literacy is more than commanding a list of ideas and demonstrating selected skills. Modern views of scientific literacy include mathematics as well as technology and the social sciences as well as the natural sciences.

Science for All Americans–Project 2061 (Rutherford & Ahlgren, 1990) is a significant report, and *Benchmarks* (AAAS, 1993) is a curriculum effort based on many years of collaboration among several hundred scientists, mathematicians, engineers, physicians, philosophers, historians, and educators. These efforts offer a comprehensive and valid view of modern scientific literacy, the prime aim of science teaching. We learn from them that

> the scientifically literate person is one who is aware that science, mathematics, and technology are interdependent human enterprises with strengths and limitations; understands key concepts and principles of science; is familiar with the natural world and recognizes both its diversity and unity; and uses scientific knowledge and scientific ways of thinking for individual and social purposes. (Rutherford & Ahlgren, 1990, p. ix)

We must expand our vision of science when we take on this aim. Our national vision is to make our students first in the world in math and science achievement, and to develop a system of science education that prepares them to be informed and active participants in civic life, citizens who are productive workers and lifelong learners. The vision sees in the future a better informed citizenry that helps to maintain a strong democracy, strengthens our country's economy, and maintains excellent standing in science and technology.

The National Science Education Standards (NSES) (coordinated by the National Research Council of the National Academy of Sciences and the National Academy of Engineering) provides direction toward our national vision. NSES advocates a less-is-more philosophy for developing science curriculum, teaching approaches, and appropriate forms of assessment. These standards support practical learning experiences and problem-solving opportunities for children. The standards are based on a wholistic view of science. These standards can help us progress toward our national aims and to do our part, as teachers, to fulfill the national vision. Forthcoming chapters describe specific goals for science teaching and methods for the covering-less-but-doing-and-learning-more philosophy that undergirds the goals.

This chapter has introduced you to some of the problems observed in elementary and middle school science, described a wholistic view of science, and outlined the aims of modern elementary science. The remaining chapters will help you to understand and to practice *whole science*.

ABOUT THIS BOOK

We realize that these words are typically placed in a book's preface. We also realize that eager readers often skip the front material in favor of digging into the ideas quickly and we have added several words here to help you do just that. Let us consider two factors: (1) how we have designed this book and its features to assist your access to the ideas, and (2) an alternative route through the text.

Each chapter contains standard features. The text of each chapter begins with a *scenario,* all of them factual. The scenario helps to create a vicarious ex-

TEACHERS ON SCIENCE TEACHING

How Do Science and Real Life Connect?

by Phyllis Frysinger
Grades 7 and 8 Science Teacher, Miami View Elementary, South Charleston, Ohio

Remember the first time you learned that spiders have book lungs, sponges have spicules, oak trees have inadequate abscission layers, and two round bacteria existing together are called diplococci? I thought that was really interesting, too, and I couldn't wait to tell kids all of this neat stuff. Today I find myself presenting discovery lessons on the value of spiders, natural carnivores, as possible pest controllers in soybean fields; that strong sponge spicules will wreak havoc on populated beaches; that oak trees that keep their leaves longer will also lose more water in the fall; and I don't teach that diplococcus business, but rather demonstrate the subtlety of bacterial contamination.

Today's students are much more demanding that you as a teacher have a justification as to why you are teaching what you are. Be prepared: If you are using a text, don't try to cover all of Chapter 2 by Friday. Instead, sit down, read Chapter 2, and pretend that there is a student sitting beside you asking, "Why do we have to know this?" If you can't come up with an answer, then leave it out. Develop a list of outcomes or test objectives that you want to obtain from material to be studied. Give this list to the students at the beginning, de-

velop a way to teach each of your objectives, and show them how you plan to present each of these goals. If you cannot come up with a way to teach a particular goal or objective without standing in front of the class and telling them about it, then leave it out.

Once you have decided what is important and how you are going to teach it, sit down and write the evaluation for the chapter. Yes, right now, not the night before so that you only have time to reproduce it. This way you can justify in your own mind how you will evaluate an objective or your evaluation technique. Newer evaluation techniques are being proposed, and I have used all sorts of things through the years. You will, too, if you keep up with the times.

Oh yes, keeping up with the times. This does not mean doing the lambada while you are dissecting a frog, but developing viable alternatives to dissection in general. I still use dissecting and have even developed anatomy lessons to use with my eighth-grade earth science classes.

By promoting science as an important part of the life of students, you will promote a positive attitude toward science and encourage students to

perience through a short story; this should help you to construct a mental framework for understanding those parts of the chapter that may be new or difficult.

Within each chapter we have added figures, tables, and photographs to reinforce the ideas presented; sometimes we include relevant exercises that you might want to try. One unique feature is *What Research Says*. This material supplements the chapter's text with a brief authoritative report on recent research. Of course we close each chapter with the customary summary. *Discussion questions* and ideas for *class projects* are included; many of these are field develop science skills they will use for the rest of their lives.

To be more specific, I am now teaching in a multidisciplinary situation with a pod scheduled time in which three teachers have all of the seventh-grade students in the morning and all of the eighth-grade students in the afternoon. During this time we teach science, English, and literature.

Recently we presented a lesson in which the science classes had been working on chemical reactions. We had mixed together several chemicals including starch, sucrose, ovalbumin, ethyl buterate, and triglycerides to note a chemical reaction. The product was a cake. In literature class the students were reading *A Christmas Carol*, by Charles Dickens. In a combined class we mixed the ingredients for a traditional plum pudding, noting the chemical ingredients and the importance of accurate measurement, as in the science class. The English teacher made the point that there were no plums in the plum pudding and discussed the origin of the word. The literature teacher reflected Mrs. Cratchit's anxiety over the preparation.

After the concoction was properly steamed and the traditions closely followed, including the stirring and wish making by each student, the pudding was flamed with orange extract, and we all enjoyed the feast.

With this approach, the students were presented the opportunity of learning the importance and the interrelationship of each of the disciplines involved. There really was an answer to "Why do we have to know this?" We write journals each day, and it was certainly rewarding to note the number of times that we read, "I'm going to take this recipe home and make plum pudding for my family." When the students want to take your lesson home and share it with others, then you know that you have taught science.

One more thing: Don't forget to join all the professional organizations that are available, and participate in them. You will not only learn the latest that is available in your field but will also have a great deal of support in your professional years. That's how I ended up taking physics almost thirty years after I entered the classroom when I don't even teach physical science.

based to complement any early field experience or practice teaching your professor may ask you to do. *Additional readings* contain suggestions for further reading on the important topics of each chapter.

One other feature is *Teachers on Science Teaching*. This gives a practicing teacher's view on the chapter's topic, with real applications described.

This book also contains example *science lesson plans* that are constructed in a very powerful way—a way to encourage the highest level of student physical and mental activity and to stimulate high levels of pupil achievement. Our plans are consistent with how children construct their own understanding of science and may be used as a model for implementing the NSES goals.

Your instructor should have a copy of the *Instructor's Manual* for this text, which provides several masters that can be used as class handouts. Please ask for copies of the concept maps that we have developed for each chapter. A concept map is a picture of the main ideas we hope you will obtain from the chapter and the relationships among those ideas. Concept maps are explained more fully in Chapter 5, on planning. Please don't try to memorize a concept map. Although the map shows you the connections between ideas in the chapter as we see them, you should try to form your connections as you study the material in this textbook. As a suggestion, read our maps from box to box, noting the direction of the arrows and the linking words. Each map should tell a succinct story about the information in each chapter. The *Instructor's Manual* also contains transparency masters that may be copied and used as a study guide. Please ask your instructor for these materials.

We have written this book in a linear way, as suggested by those reviewers who use it. Part I provides a foundation for understanding science, learning, and literacy in four chapters as we discuss the nature of science and science inquiry, how science understanding is constructed, the challenges of teaching all children, and the special goals that drive the engine of science education reform.

Chapters 5 and 6, in Part II, examine specific techniques for preparing constructivist lessons and managing the active science classroom safely. Constructivism is the most recent theory about how children learn. Chapter 7 describes criteria for science education excellence that have arisen from the rich history of science reform efforts. Chapter 8 explores the tools of technology to identify and use effective materials in our instruction.

Part III is devoted to the action of science teaching. Constructivist teaching methods are explored, questioning skills are developed, and traditional teaching techniques are altered to support our quest for learner-centered, constructivist science education.

Often teachers and professors prefer a different approach, given the press of time and other factors:

1. Study Chapters 1 and 2 to understand the philosophy undergirding this textbook. Then explore the constructivist perspectives on how children learn science. Chapter 2 will also introduce you briefly to teaching approaches.
2. Prepare lessons using our planning model, and try teaching children or your peers. Specific teaching approaches can be studied and used from Chapters 9 and 11 as needed.
3. If planning becomes too challenging, you might jump back to Chapter 5, then perhaps Chapter 4, if you want to explore science goals that have influenced the lessons and teaching approaches we have recommended.

4. Questioning, covered in Chapter 10, is an important skill, which you may wish to develop as you teach.
5. As you encounter the need to understand and to promote student diversity, Chapter 3 should be helpful.
6. Also, as needed, Chapter 6 can provide ideas on managing safe science classrooms. Chapter 12, as well as our lesson plans, can help you to locate and select appropriate teaching materials.

Of course, at all times we encourage you to try the ideas your own way. If you do, you will be learning about teaching science as we advocate for the children you will teach: by constructing *your* own understanding.

CHAPTER SUMMARY

The nature of science must be viewed wholistically, and whole science is more than knowledge and scientific names and facts. This chapter has shown that assumptions about science that focus only on treating it as a body of knowledge are incomplete and incorrect. Science *is* possible because it is inherently human. Human *attitudes* provide the curiosity to begin its study, the perseverance to continue, and the necessary qualities for making informed judgments. Science *process skills* make it possible for children to accumulate the factual *information* they use to construct concepts, form scientific principles, and comprehend theories.

Children are able to construct their own understanding when encouraged to inquire by exploring, questioning, and seeking.

Science has the most impact on children when they value it and learn it wholistically. Children value science when they find uses for it and enjoy its pleasures. Science programs, science teaching practices, and assessment techniques must provide experiences that will help children to value and use science by making important discoveries for themselves. How children construct ideas and learn is a topic explored in Chapter 2.

DISCUSSION QUESTIONS AND PROJECTS

1. Think back to your elementary and middle school years. What do you remember about your science classes? How do your memories compare with those of your classmates? In what ways do your recollections represent whole science?

2. To what extent did your teachers teach science according to our definition? What do you remember about the emphasis given to attitudes, thinking skills, and science information? Why do you think your teachers emphasized (or did not emphasize) each of these parts?

3. Consider the case made for the science cycle in this chapter. Do you agree or disagree with it? State your reasons.

4. Think about developmental differences observed between first-, third-, and sixth-grade students. In each grade, how much emphasis do you think should be given to emotional and intellectual attitude development? Give reasons for your answer.

5. Review the differences between basic and integrated science process skills. Describe the connection between these skills and the types of science information children are expected to learn.

6. How much instructional time do you believe should be devoted to science? How should that time be used to emphasize attitudes, process skills, and information? Give reasons for your answers.

7. The attitudes we carry with us are linked to experiences we have accumulated over time. Both help us form images that we treat as our independent sense of reality. Sometimes these images represent widely recognized stereotypes. For example, when you hear the word *scientist*, what image comes to mind? Draw a picture of a scientist.

8. Compare your picture of a scientist with other class members' pictures. Classify them according to such features as age, gender, amount and types of hair, eyeglasses, lab coat, laboratory apparatus, appearance (weird, out of control, and so on), and other factors. Tally the features and compute percentages to develop a class profile of a scientist. Treat this as a pretest and do the exercise again at the end of the course to look for any possible differences in stereotypes.

9. Try a version of the projects described above with elementary school children. How do their pictures compare with your own or those of your college class? Develop a summary of the children's views and speculate about reasons.

ADDITIONAL READINGS

If you are interested in learning more about some of the topics raised in this chapter, consider the following sources.

Robert M. Hazen and James Trefil, *Science Matters: Achieving Scientific Literacy* (Garden City, NY: Doubleday, 1991). This is a unique source with a compelling introduction on scientific literacy. This book can be used as a primer to help you understand the most fundamental concepts the authors believe are necessary for modern science.

Stephen P. Kramer, *How To Think Like a Scientist* (New York: Thomas Y. Crowell, 1987). Will it really rain if you hang a dead snake over a tree branch? Speaking to children, this book illustrates the processes of science that are used to gather reliable information. This fun book helps children to think about why scientists ask questions and how they pursue the answers to those questions.

Carol Minnick and Donna Alvermann (eds.), *Science Learning Processes and Applications* (Newark, DE: International Reading Association, 1991); and Karen Ostlund, *Science Process Skills: Assessing Hands-On Student Performance* (Menlo Park, CA: Addison-Wesley, 1992). These are two fine sources for obtaining practical ideas to help you promote science process skills in your classroom.

The 1990 Science Report Card (or latest available version), prepared by the Educational Testing Service for the Office of Educational Research and Improvement of the U.S. Department of Education, March 1992. The wealth of demographic and example test items contained in this source is guaranteed to expand your vision of the conditions of science education and the means to determine what youth know and can do.

Royston M. Roberts, *Serendipity: Accidental Discoveries in Science* (New York: Wiley, 1989). This delightful book is filled with stories about the various accidental discoveries that scientists have made over the centuries. Roberts makes a case that the mind must be "prepared" to recognize what is important in order to make the discovery.

F. James Rutherford and Andrew Ahlgren, *Science for All Americans* (New York: Oxford University Press, 1990). This remake of the 1989 edition from the American Association for the Advancement of Science puts the complete vision of scientific literacy in terms the lay person can fully comprehend.

Carl J. Sindermann, *The Joy of Science* (New York: Plenum Press, 1985). The author accumulated many case histories from scientists over the years and used them to provide an inside look at the reasons for successful careers in science.

Although Thomas Edison is not usually thought of as a scientist, he did spend most of his life applying the work of scientists to his many inventions. *For information about Edison, his life, and his exciting experiences, consult the many books and articles written about him. In particular we recommend the following sources:*

Frank Lewis Dyer and Thomas Commerford Martin, *Edison: His Life and Inventions,* vols. I and II (New York: Harper & Row, 1929.) Written during Edi-son's lifetime, this massive collection of information digs deeply into his life and discusses many of Edison's inventions in detail.

Matthew Josephson, *Edison* (New York: McGraw-Hill, 1959.) This biography written for adults captures the excitement of science and the impact of Edison's inventions on a growing economy and an industrial society.

CHAPTER OUTLINE

How Do Children Learn Science?

W hen we revisit Jessica (of Chapter 1) after teaching for some years, we see that she has developed helpful routines to manage her classroom duties. Her teaching methods are consistent. In math, she presents the topic, demonstrates models, explains the functions and steps to follow by giving examples, and involves some of the children in board work. Drill and practice come next and are followed by assigned seatwork, which is reviewed at the start of math time the following day.

In science, Jessica explains the point, provides a demonstration, and gives her pupils step-by-step instructions for completing the corresponding activity. She always uses visual models to help students understand complicated concepts. Each learner follows her recipe, and her methods are similar for all subjects.

Jessica is regarded as an outstanding teacher and has received several commendations, yet although her students perform well on the school district's standardized tests, they do not fare as well as she would hope on the obligatory statewide performance assessments. Jessica is frustrated. Her fifth graders seem to do well only at memorization. In addition, they seem to return to their own ideas when confronted with problems or questions that are not an exact replica of what they have studied in class. Their learning appears to be superficial, and idea retention is elusive. What can Jessica do to develop deeper, lasting understanding?

Jessica was pondering this question during her vacation as she supervised the play of her two children. Her daughter, the older child, was experiencing some difficulty using a pump to inflate her bicycle tires. As her daughter struggled with the handle and plunger of the pump, she exclaimed: "Ouch! Why is this so hot?" She had touched the long plunger that she had been rapidly moving up and down to inflate the tire. Jessica's 9-year-old son, Jonathan, was close by, riding his skateboard, and stopped to offer an explanation: "It's hot because of friction."

"What's that?" inquired his sister.

Jonathan attempted to explain: "See the wheels on my skateboard? Listen as I turn them quickly. Hear this one squeak? Now let me put a little oil on it like Uncle Frank showed me." Jonathan retrieved the oil can from the garage workbench to put a few drops of oil on the bearings of the squeaking wheel. "What do you hear now?" he asked.

"I hear the wheel turning, but I don't hear the squeak," his sister replied.

"Exactly. The wheel squeaked because of too much friction. I put on some oil to take away some of it. I think there is still some friction here. That is why we hear this rolling sound of the little balls in the wheel," hypothesized Jonathan. "Let's try something. Feel the back wheel on your bike to see how hot it feels. Then hold up your bike so the back wheel is off the floor so I can turn the pedal really fast. Then hang on but drop it so the wheel hits the floor." This was done with a skidding sound and jerking motion that left a black mark on the concrete floor. "Now quick, feel the tire. How does it feel now?"

"I think its hotter, but I'm not sure," ventured his sister.

"Yes, that's because the tire rubbed against the floor and the friction heated it. Now try this. Press your hands together so the palms are flat. Press a little and then rub them back and forth. How do they feel now?"

"A little warm," replied his sister.

"Yes. Now press harder and move them faster. How do they feel now?" asked Jonathan.

"Hot!" exclaimed his sister.

Jessica was intrigued by this conversation and startled that her young son seemed to understand deeply the idea of friction, although he did not exactly define it. She knew this was a difficult concept and asked: "Jon, how do you know about friction? Did Ms. Glock teach you about it in school?"

"Well, I think she tried," offered Jonathan. "We studied machines in third grade, and I remember reading about friction in the book. Ms. Glock talked about it, but I couldn't remember much."

"Then how did you learn so much about friction?" persisted Jessica.

"Uncle Frank taught me."

Jessica encouraged Jonathan to explain and eventually uncovered his story. Jonathan had been helping his uncle to build a storage shed for lawn tools. His uncle had put a board in place with long screws as a temporary support, then rapidly removed the screws with his cordless drill when the support was no longer needed. Jonathan's job was to pick up the screws and put them away. His uncle had warned that the screws would be hot and that Jonathon should let them cool for a few moments. Jonathan did not understand. The screws had been cool to the touch when he had handed them to his uncle, *before* they were driven into the board. Instead of explaining, Jonathan's uncle had helped him to drive some cool screws into a board and then remove them quickly. They carefully touched the screws and noticed that they were quite warm. Uncle Frank then explained that the surface of the screw threads rubbed quickly against the wood and that the rubbing heated the screw. He showed Jonathan how to understand what happened by rubbing his hands together, as Jonathon had done with his sister.

Uncle Frank used the word *friction* to represent the idea they were investigating. He had also demonstrated the same idea with a sabre saw. Jonathan carefully touched the blade of the unplugged saw and felt that it was cool to the touch. Then Uncle Frank cut a board, unplugged the saw, and touched a piece of tissue paper to the blade. The hot saw blade scorched the paper. Uncle Frank asked Jonathan to explain what happened by using the idea of friction. He also asked Jonathan to get his Cub Scout book, and they looked at ways to make campfires with primitive methods that used a bow and friction. They continued their discussion of friction by trying to stand on marbles in a box and noticed that it was difficult to do since friction between their shoes and the floor was reduced, and they speculated what it would be like to try to run on slick, wet concrete with smooth-soled shoes. They discussed why oil and coolants are important to an automobile by reducing friction and removing excess heat from the motor that is caused by friction and why cars skid off rain-slicked highway curves or on snow and ice. Jonathan and his uncle worked together to identify times when friction is helpful, such as a fast-moving biker's trying to cycle around a sharp curve, or a basketball player's making a cut and driving to the basket. The firsthand experiences and discussions had helped Jonathan understand the basic idea of friction and expanded his understanding by applying the idea in new situations, such as with his sister and the bicycle pump.

The story was a serendipity for Jessica. Her prepared mind made a connection with her teaching. She decided to try a new learning opportunity for herself and developed a vision of how to present lessons during the upcoming school year. She changed her metaphor of learning from teacher-explainer/student-receiver to teacher-guide/student-constructor. Jessica was determined to view her learners through new eyes and considered different perspectives on how children learn. She resolved to try different teaching approaches that would help her guide her students' learning—helping them learn how to learn rather than telling them what they needed to know. ◆

INTRODUCTION

How did you learn science? Was it similar to Jessica's typical way of teaching it? Was your experience based on the teacher's instructions and explanations, vocabulary development, and memorization? Or was your experience more like an adventure, where the exact steps to follow were as unknown as the consequences of your decisions? Did your teachers emphasize the facts, symbols, labels, and formulas of science? Or were the general ideas—concepts—developed in a way that helped you to discover the connections among the many ideas and fields of science?

How you view science and how children learn share related consequences. If you view science as a discrete body of information to be learned, you will probably bring that assumption to your teaching, which will be much like Jessica's routine. If, after reading Chapter 1, you view science as a dynamic opportunity to help children develop essential attitudes, skills, and knowledge that can benefit each of them, you will likely bring that assumption to your teaching, which may resemble Jessica's new vision. Your view of how children learn has been shaped by your teachers, and in turn your beliefs will affect the children you teach. With a little imagination you can see the repeating cycle.

Jessica's routine methods did not produce the results she wanted. She decided to experiment with her methods and in doing so challenged and adapted her beliefs about learning. In this chapter we challenge you to:

1. Consider the role that children's prior ideas and miconceptions play in their learning.
2. Identify what children need to help them become self-motivated and to sustain independent learning.
3. Examine the dominant contemporary perspective on science learning.
4. Explore techniques important for constructivist teaching.

HOW DO CHILDREN'S IDEAS INFLUENCE THEIR LEARNING?

Rosalind Driver (1985) and her fellow researchers have studied this question extensively. Consider the following classroom example involving two 11-year-old students.

Tim and Ricky are studying the way a spring extends as they add ball bearings to a plastic drinking cup that is attached to and hangs from the spring, which is suspended from a clamp on a stand. Ricky carefully adds the bearings one at a time and measures the change in the length of the spring after each addition. Tim watches and inquires, "Wait a moment. What happens if we lift up the spring?" Ricky clamps the spring higher on the stand, measures its stretched length, and continues after he is satisfied that the length of the spring is the same as before the change in position. An observer asks Tim for the reasons behind his suggestion. Tim picks up two bearings, pretends they are pebbles, and explains his idea about weight changing as objects are lifted higher:

> This is farther up and gravity is pulling it down harder the farther away. The higher it gets the more effect gravity will have on it because if you just stood over there and someone dropped a pebble on him, it would just sting him, it wouldn't

Children form their own science ideas through direct experience.

hurt him. But if I dropped it from an aeroplane it would be accelerating faster and faster and when it hit someone on the head it would kill him. (Driver, Guensne, & Tiberghien, 1985, pp. 1–2)

Tim's idea is not scientifically correct. The object's weight decreases as height increases. However, the idea is not irrational if you consider Tim's reasoning: He seems to be referring to what scientists call gravitational potential energy. The ideas children bring with them often influence what and how they learn.

Preconceptions

The ideas from prior experiences that children bring with them have been called a variety of names: alternative frameworks, children's science, naive theories, and preconceptions. We prefer to call them *preconceptions* because children's ideas are often incomplete preliminary understandings of the fundamental science concepts that can be used to explain their everyday world. These preconceptions are influenced by hands-on, minds-on experiences, such as direct physical experiences, emotional experiences through social processes, and thoughtful efforts to make sense of the various things that exist in a child's world. These preconceptions that are brought to a new learning opportunity are important, even for adults, because the process of learning is a human activity, just as are the processes of science. Adults and children can be infected by a type of bias that is influenced by expectations. Bias is inherent in preconceptions and can influence concept formation. A well-known paleoanthropologist, Donald Johanson, recognized the importance of this when he wrote: "There is no such thing as total lack of bias. . . . The fossil hunter in the field has it. If he is interested in hippo teeth, that is what he is going to find, and that will bias his collection because he will walk right by other fossils without noticing them" (Kinnear, 1994, p. 3). Another scientist, David Pilbeam, illustrates this point by explaining how his original interpretation of a particular fossil was affected by his prior expectations: "I knew . . .[the fossil], being a hominid, would have a short face and rounded jaw—so that's what I saw" (Kinnear, 1994, p. 3). Additional discoveries and further investigation revealed that the fossil did not possess the features that Pilbeam described and that it was not a hominid.

Misconceptions

Misconceptions are alternative understandings about phenomena that learners have formed. They are scientifically incorrect interpretations that learners believe or responses to problems that learners provide. "Misconceptions do not simply signify a lack of knowledge, factual errors, or incorrect definitions. Instead, misconceptions represent explanations of phenomena constructed by a student in response to the student's prior knoweldge and experience" (Munson, 1994, pp. 30–31). For example, through reading and participation in class activities, including gamelike simulations, a learner may form the misconception that the top of a food chain has the most energy because it accumulates up the food chain (Adeniyi, 1985), whereas a correct scientific conception maintains the opposite: Available energy decreases as one progresses up a food chain (Munson, 1994).

William Philips, an earth science teacher, discovered some interesting but depressing facts about what his students knew about science—or rather, what they really did not understand. What was most troublesome was what his students thought they knew without realizing they were incorrect: their misconceptions. These are his words:

> Misconceptions are rarely expressed aloud or in writing and, therefore, often go undetected. Twenty years ago, shortly after I began teaching science, I encountered an outrageous misconception (or so it seemed at the time). While I was using a globe to explain seasonal changes, one very attentive eighth grader raised her hand and asked, "Where are we?" Thinking she wanted to know the location of our school, I pointed to Delaware and resumed my lecture. She immediately stopped me with another question. "No. I don't mean that. I mean, do we live inside the Earth or outside it?" The question caused several students to laugh, but most appeared to be waiting for an answer. It was all I could do to hide my astonishment. (Philips, 1991, p. 21)

Philips cites a survey in which second-grade teachers estimated that 95 percent of their students knew the earth is a sphere. Later the teachers conducted in-

Guided direct experiences help to reduce misconceptions.

terviews with the children and discovered that the students actually believed the earth is flat. Misconceptions are common, and once formed, they are held a long while. Misconceptions are linked to intuitive ideas, beliefs, or preconceptions. It is not unusual for students to progress through school providing correct answers when the teachers ask for them but believing otherwise, much like the second graders mentioned above. When students give science facts correctly to questions and on tests, it does not mean they have replaced the misconceptions they formed much earlier.

Examples of misconceptions Philips uncovered are given in Table 2.1. Misconceptions seem to occur as students construct knowledge; they may be linked to incomplete or insufficient experiences, faulty explanations, and misperceived meanings. Joseph Novak (1991), a professor of science and education, reminds us that students must construct new meaning from the foundation of the knowledge they already possess. This means that teachers cannot afford to overlook student misconceptions, because of the negative learning cycle caused

TABLE 2.1   Common Earth Science Misconceptions

More than ten years' worth of research on misconceptions yielded the following list for children. Adults often harbor the same misconceptions.

The earth is sitting on something.	Rain comes from holes in clouds.
The earth is larger than the sun.	Rain comes from clouds' sweating.
The earth is round like a pancake.	Rain falls from funnels in the clouds.
We live on the flat middle of a sphere.	Rain occurs when clouds are shaken.
There is a definite up and down in space.	God and angels cause thunder and lightning.
Astrology is able to predict the future.	Clouds move because we move.
Gravity increases with height.	Clouds come from somewhere above the sky.
Gravity cannot exist without air.	Empty clouds are refilled by the sea.
Any crystal that scratches glass is a diamond.	Clouds are formed by vapors from kettles.
Coral reefs exist throughout the Gulf of Mexico and the North Atlantic.	The sun boils the sea to create water vapor.
Dinosaurs and cavemen lived at the same time.	Clouds are made of cotton, wool, or smoke.
	Clouds are bags of water.

Source: Excerpted from the list provided by William C. Philips, "Earth Science Misconceptions," *Science Teacher* (February 1991): 21–23.

by misunderstanding the simplest point. Novak also states that students can create new meaning only by constructing new propositions, linked concepts that are usually formed through discovery learning.

What Do We Know About Children's Ideas?

Children bring many ideas to class. Their ideas represent the interpretations they have formed about the dilemmas and phenomena they have encountered, as in examples given earlier in this chapter. Many of these experiences occur out of school and are not connected to formal teaching. Children's ideas arise from everyday experiences, including play, conversations, and events observed through the media. The recent research on children's ideas reveals three important factors: (1) Children's ideas are very personal constructions, (2) the ideas may seem incomplete or contradictory, and (3) the ideas are often very stable and highly resistant to change (Driver et al., 1985).

Children's Ideas Are Personal.   Have you ever been with a group of your friends and witnessed a remarkable event such as a concert, athletic event, or auto accident? Or have you participated in a heated debate about a topic important to you? How did your perceptions of the facts or the event compare with those of your friends? Was there complete agreement on each detail? "No" is not an unusual answer. Consider the children in a class, each participating in the same science activity. It is likely that the children will report diverse perceptions of what happened during the activity. Each child has seen and experienced the activity, but each has internalized the experiences in his or her own way. Our perceptions and descriptions depend as much on our original ideas as they do on the nature of the new experience or lesson. All readers do not receive exactly the same message, even from written words.

Learners construct their own meanings. *Constructed meanings* are based on new experiences that are accumulated and compared with and processed from old ideas. The preexisting ideas are the basis for observing, classifying, and interpreting new experiences. In this way, each learner, even a very young one, continually forms and reforms hypotheses and theories about natural phenomena. We call on the mind's existing ideas to help us understand new experiences (Harlen, 1992, p. 11). What is remarkable is that although ideas are constructed independently, the general interpretations and conclusions are often shared by many (Driver, 1983).

A Child's Individual Ideas May Seem Contradictory. Natural science is blessed with many intriguing discrepancies. Touch the flat bottom of an uncoated paper cup with a candle flame, and predictably, the paper burns after a brief time. But add water to a cup and the cup will not burn even when heated by a stronger source for a much longer time. This result challenges the mature mind to identify a coherent reason that explains the behavior of the candle and cup under all circumstances. The younger mind may see no problem and simply use another, even contradictory, explanation, unconcerned that the explanation is inconsistent with what was previously said. As Driver (1983) reminds us:

> The same child may have different conceptions of a particular type of phenomenon, sometimes using different arguments leading to opposite predictions in situations which are equivalent from a scientist's point of view, and even switching from one sort of explanation to another for the same phenomenon. (p. 3)

A child does not have the same need for coherence as an adult or a scientist, nor does a child have a mental model to use to unify a range of different perceptions that relate to the same event. Furthermore, a child usually does not see the need for a consistent view. The constructed ideas work quite well for the child in his or her classroom practice, even though the ideas may be based on prior false conclusions.

Children's Ideas Often Resist Change. It is not simple for teachers to change children's incomplete or flawed ideas about scientific events and phenomena. Additional activities, comparative discussions, and even direct teacher explanations may not cause children to modify their ideas. Changing ideas is a slow process, and the necessary changes may never be complete. Children may simply realize that they are to provide a certain correct answer to a teacher's questions but choose to turn off the academically correct in favor of the previous independent ideas once the test is over. Counter evidence presented to the child seems to make no difference. Interpretations often are based on prior ideas. Personal, if contradictory, ideas have tremendous stability and endurance (Driver, 1983, p. 4).

WHAT DO CHILDREN NEED TO HELP THEM LEARN?

We must concern ourselves with more than what happens in the learner's mind. Stimulating learning in science, or any other subject, is a complex mission. Compare two age groups of children: primary and middle school. The physical, intellectual, social, and emotional differences are obvious. Younger children tend to be much smaller with less developed muscle structures, are less social, and are more prone to spontaneous emotional outbursts. As children become older and more experienced, their interest in their peers increases, they become less reliant on concrete objects and more capable of abstract reasoning, and their speech and language patterns become more complex.

Change and development happen over time. While their bodies are maturing and becoming stronger through exercise, children's minds, emotions, and self-confidence also develop through the exercise afforded by useful experiences. Children need experiences that will help develop their thinking, afford considerable activity, stimulate language, and help them develop social skills and self-confidence. Children need time for all of these changes to occur.

Thinking

Younger children benefit from using their five senses extensively. Talking about and showing children pictures of mammals, for example, provides less stimulation than giving them time to smell, touch, hear, and observe the movements of classroom pets. Imagine teaching children about foods that are salty, sweet, sour, or bitter without letting them taste! Stimulate many of the senses to overcome the limits imposed on children by just listening. Older youths benefit from the stimulation too, even though they are more capable of mental reasoning. Do you recall the difficulties prior ideas bring to new learning?

Physical Activity

Middle school children may be able to sit still for rather long periods of time, but young children cannot. Indeed, very young children may actually get more tired if they have to sit still for long. Martha Denckla (1989), a professor of neurology and pediatrics, explains that this difference is related to development of the brain: "The frontal lobe, the part of the brain that applies the brakes to children's natural energy and curiosity, is still maturing in 6–9 year olds. As the lobe develops, so does 'boredom tolerance' " (pp. 53–54). Purposeful physical activity helps to provide the experiences that are essential for thinking and language development.

Language

Children learn to develop and use language by talking, not by learning isolated skills. Reasoning and expression are developed through child–child and child–adult conversations. Encourage communication of ideas first; then worry over spelling and grammar. Again, class experience affords abundant opportunities to develop language and thinking patterns. Acquire the experience first; then develop the language from it.

Socialization

Social development is related to academic success. Children who are socially maladjusted and cannot get along with their peers often do poorly in school and may eventually drop out. Children tend to do better in school when they work in groups and cooperate with others. Some educators claim that *relationships* should be the first of the three Rs (Katz, 1989). Science provides abundant opportunities for children to cooperate and develop relationships through group activities and projects.

Self-Esteem

Younger and older children struggle to meet the teacher's adult expectations and in doing so learn to judge themselves in relation to others. The unfortunate aspect to this is that young children have not yet learned to distinguish between effort and ability. If trying hard to accomplish a task results in failure, a child is likely to conclude that he or she will never be able to succeed. Cooperation, rather than competition, may inflate self-esteem while it deflates feelings of incompetence.

Time

We cannot create more time. But we can decide how to allot the time we have. The fact is that young children need time to grow, mature, and develop the thinking and communication skills, socialization, and self-esteem they need for productive learning. Piling on more challenges for younger children or accelerating the classroom pace will not help them develop into well-adjusted, creative, and critically thinking youth. Developmental differences observed during the primary years often wash out around the fourth grade if the children have been exposed to useful experiences through heterogeneous groups during their early years.

The many needs of children are a part of their learning environment. Attend to the needs, and the learning will follow as children become self-motivated and confident and as they develop the capability to think more abstractly and to communicate their ideas. Successes that arise from fulfilled needs help children to develop and sustain the capability to learn more independently.

WHAT IS THE DOMINANT PERSPECTIVE ABOUT HOW CHILDREN LEARN SCIENCE?

Constructivism is the general name given to the dominant perspective on learning in science education. A constructivist perspective on teaching and learning is very different from traditional views that promote a teaching and learning

WHAT RESEARCH SAYS

Brain-Based Learning

Much has been written about hemispheric brain dominance, and these ideas have influenced our views on learning and teaching even though they do not apply to normal learners. While it is true that our brains benefit from abundant varieties of stimulation, prescriptions are difficult and risky because we are still learning how our brains function. Researchers Renate and Geoffrey Caine have summarized important principles from the brain-based research on teaching and learning that may help you to find effective ways to stimulate learning:

- Previous experiences and meaning affect how the brain processes new experiences and organizes new knowledge.
- Our emotions and our learning share an important relationship.
- Learning is more than exercising the brain like a muscle. It is a true physiological experience that involves a sophisticated set of systems.
- Our brain processes and organizes many stimuli and ideas at the same time, even though we may focus on only one thing at a time.

- The significance of subject matter content depends on how our experiences are arranged and fit into patterns.
- Our brains process peripheral stimuli consciously and unconsciously.
- Parts and wholes are processed simultaneously by our brains, not separately or in isolation in a particular hemisphere.
- We possess spatial memories that help us to retrieve experiences rapidly and easily; for example, we might have a detailed memory of an important event even though we made no special attempt to memorize details.
- We need more practice to recall facts and to establish a level of skill when these facts are not embedded in our spatial memories.
- Our brains respond positively to problems and challenges but are less effective under duress.

Sam Crowell, an educator, describes these principles of learning in a way that is closely compatible with our contemporary views on learning. He says that learning is complex, interrelated, unified, and emergent.

dialogue. A teacher who embraces constructivism supports a different view of science, regards the roles of teacher and learner very differently, and selects and organizes teaching materials with particular care. A constructivist perspective emphasizes the role of the learner, regarding the role as active—physically, mentally, and socially—rather than passive. The constructivist teacher seeks ways to enhance the active participation of learners in lessons and encourages learners to construct their own understanding from their sense of reality, which arises from their experiences. Let us visit Jessica again to see how her efforts toward change may illustrate a constructivist approach.

Jessica: A Constructivist Attempt

Based on her experience with her son, Jessica determined to avoid her usual demonstration and recipe instructions. Now she distributed the materials for

Ernst von Glaserfeld, philosopher and regarded leader of the constructivist movement in science education, provides the following implications for teaching and learning:

- Whatever a student provides as an answer to a question or problem is based on what made sense to the student at that time. The response must be taken seriously, regardless of how odd or "wrong" it might seem to the teacher. Otherwise the student will be discouraged and inhibited. Also, understand that the answer may be a good one depending on how the student interpreted the question.
- A teacher who wishes to modify a student's concepts and conceptual structures must try to build a mental model of the student's individual thinking. Never assume that a student's way of thinking is simple or transparent.
- Asking students how they arrived at their given answer is a good way of discovering something about their thinking, and it opens the way to explaining why a particular answer may not be useful under different circumstances.
- If you want to motivate students to delve further into questions that they say are of no particular interest to them, create situations where the students have an opportunity to experience the pleasure inherent in solving a problem. Simply being told "good" or "correct" does not help a learner's conceptual development.
- Successful thinking is more than "correct" answers; it should be rewarded even if it is based on unacceptable premises.
- A teacher must have an almost infinitely flexible mind to understand and appreciate students' thinking because students sometimes start from premises that seem inconceivable to teachers.
- Constructivist teachers can never justify what they teach by claiming it is true. In science, they cannot say more than that it is the best way of conceiving the situation because it is the most effective way at the moment of dealing with it.

Sources: Renate Nummela Caine and Geoffrey Caine, *Teaching and the Human Brain* (Alexandria, VA: Association for Supervision and Curriculum Development, 1991); Sam Crowell, "A New Way of Thinking: The Challenge of the Future," *Educational Leadership* (September 1989): 60–63; Ernst von Glaserfeld, "Questions and Answers about Radical Constructivism," in Kenneth Tobin (Ed.), *The Practice of Constructivism in Science Education* (Washington, DC: AAAS Press, 1993), pp. 32–33.

the science lesson *first*: clay, scissors, cardboard, rulers, string, and so on. She asked small groups of children to work together in teams to design and construct a landscape—any type of landscape *they* chose. Jessica wanted to avoid mimicry and to encourage the students not to get fixed on the definitions of a landscape, since that was not the point of the lesson. Therefore she did not define "landscape," nor did she show particular examples. When students questioned her about the task, she encouraged them to use their intuitive understanding about landscapes—their preconceptions—to think about their experiences and use what they already knew.

The groups did not begin smoothly, perhaps because the children were not accustomed to vague instructions. However, the puzzled expressions and occasional off-task behavior associated with the newfound freedom quickly subsided as Jessica maintained consistent contact with each group and asked guiding questions: "How else could you do that?" "What other features could you add?" "Where have you seen landscapes like this?" Jessica also lifted up the unique examples from single groups for all of the other groups to examine.

After a bit more exploration, Jessica challenged each group to draw two-dimensional maps of their three-dimensional landscapes. This proved difficult until the concepts of contour and interval were constructed. Jessica guided her class in defining what these words meant and figuring out how the ideas were important to the lesson. Soon each group was applying basic math and measurement skills to construct a contour map of their own landscapes to scale. Later, the children took actual contour maps and recreated different landscapes they had never visited, again to scale.

Jessica continued to use traditional testing methods and seemed to notice a deeper understanding of the children's learning. When she asked questions or when the children wrote answers to her tests, the responses were more detailed and appeared to be more thoughtful, and the children seemed able to use their ideas in new situations. The children seemed happier and excited about science, and this satisfied Jessica—for now.

Constructivism

Jessica appears to be guided by the notion of constructivism, an emerging consensus among psychologists, science educators, philosophers of science, scientists, and others who are interested in improving children's learning. This view of learning maintains that learners (young and old, and professionals such as scientists) must construct and reconstruct their own meaning for ideas about how the world works (Good, Wandersee, & St. Julien, 1993). In a very simplified way, an ancient Chinese proverb encapsulates the intent of constructivism: "I hear and I forget; I see and I remember; I *do* and I *understand*." A lot of wisdom is packed into these three phrases. One type of sensory experience alone is insufficient when we strive for understanding. Experience requires substantial stimulation of all senses and each child's mental processes if meaningful learning is to happen.

Childhood educators Connie Williams and Constance Kamii (1986) recommend that we strive to accomplish three things when we encourage children toward understanding:

1. Use or create learning circumstances that are indeed meaningful to the learners.
2. Encourage children to make real decisions.
3. Provide children opportunities to refine their thinking and deepen their understanding by exchanging views with their peers.

Williams and Kamii (1986) remind us that what is important is "the mental action that is encouraged when children act on objects themselves" (p. 26). The prevailing view of how children learn captures this intent: How can teachers stimulate the mental action necessary for children to construct ideas?

Constructivism enables each learner to build understanding.

Constructivism Defined. Constructivism is a theory that assumes knowledge cannot exist outside the minds of thinking persons. Joseph Novak (1986) defines constructivism as the notion that humans construct or build meaning into their ideas and experiences as a result of an effort to understand or to make sense of them. Novak explains that this construction

> involves at times recognition of new regularities in events or objects, inventing new concepts or extending old concepts, recognition of new relationships (propositions) between concepts, and . . . major restructuring of conceptual frameworks to see new higher order relationships. (p. 356)

Constructivism emphasizes the importance of each pupil's active construction of knowledge through the interplay of prior learning and newer learning. Connections are sought between the prior and newer learning; the connections are constructed by the learners for themselves. Researchers and theorists maintain that the key element of constructivist theory is that people learn by actively constructing their own knowledge, comparing new information with their previous understanding and using all of this to work through discrepancies to come to a new understanding (Loucks-Horsley, 1990; Harlen, 1992; Peterson & Knapp, 1993; Yager, 1991). For example:

> In their early experiences of the world, pupils develop ideas which enable them to make sense of the things that happen around them. They bring these informal

ideas into the classroom and the aim of science education is to give pupils more explanatory power so that their ideas can become useful concepts. Viewed from this perspective, it is important that we should take a pupil's initial ideas seriously so as to ensure that any change or development of these ideas . . . becomes "owned" by the pupil. (National Curriculum Council, 1989, p. 6.2)

Consider the possible vast difference between a scientist's ideas and those of a child. A scientist's perspective might be, "A plant is a producer." In contrast, a child's perspective might be:

A plant is something that grows in a garden. Carrots and cabbage from the garden are not plants; they are vegetables. Trees are not plants; they are plants when they are little, but when they grow up they are not plants. Seeds are not plants. Dandelions are not plants; they are weeds. Plants . . . have multiple sources of food. Photosynthesis is not important to plants. (Osborne & Freyberg, 1985, p. 49)

Some concepts are correct but not inclusive. Other concepts are incorrect and merit thoughtful attention and eventual correction.

Constructivism is a synthesis of several dominant perspectives on learning. It is not entirely new. Contemporary researchers from Great Britain, Australia, New Zealand, and the United States have updated the theories and methods to capture the synergy of legendary psychologists, philosophers, and researchers.

The constructivist perspective is grounded in the research and theories of Jean Piaget, Lev Vygotsky, the Gestalt psychologists, Jerome Bruner, and the philosophy of John Dewey. As you may imagine, the very nature and meaning of constructivism is open to interpretation; there is no one constructivist theory of learning. For example, some perspectives embrace the social nature of learning (Vygotsky); radical constructivists do not believe the world is knowable (Ernst von Glaserfeld); and more conservative views advocate using constructivist principles to help learners construct accurate and useful conceptions and webs of conceptual understanding. The continuum in Figure 2.1 implies degrees of difference in viewpoints among constructivists and positions the constructivist views respective to traditional views on teaching and learning (Shapiro, 1994). Radical constructivists place greater emphasis on the individual's active participation in knowledge construction and are located at the farthest point on the active/passive continuum. Conservative constructivists use activity-based and problem-based learning experiences and teacher intervention to promote conceptual constructions, yet they attempt to correct student misconceptions by helping learners construct understanding based on concepts embraced by the scientific community. Traditionalists, at the extreme right of the continuum, assume more passive learning roles for students.

Jean Piaget's research and cognitive development theory is regarded as the foundation of conservative constructivist's views. His contributions to the modern theory of constructivism are summarized for your convenience. Let us review some of his fundamental ideas.

◆ FIGURE 2.1　Teaching/Learning Continuum of Mental Operations

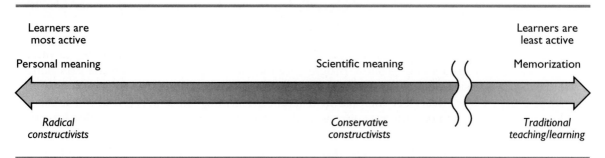

Learners are
most active

Learners are
least active

Personal meaning

Scientific meaning

Memorization

*Radical
constructivists*

*Conservative
constructivists*

*Traditional
teaching/learning*

Jean Piaget

Trained as a biologist, Jean Piaget (1896–1980) developed a theory of cognitive development that for several decades dominated our view of how children learn science. Not a learning theorist, Piaget described a process by which knowledge accumulates in a learner's mind when mental structures are formed.

If you have completed a course in educational psychology or child development, you may be familiar with Piaget's developmental stage theory. The stages are linked to probable age ranges and are labeled sensorimotor, preoperational, concrete operational, and formal operational. Young school children usually fit the preoperational stage description, while most elementary and middle school youngsters fit the descriptions of the concrete and formal operations stages, with many affected by the gradual transition between the two stages.

Preoperational Stage.　Children who think preoperationally may be 5 to 7 years old and not capable of reversing their thinking. In Piaget's classic experiment, a child believes that a ball of clay patted into a sausage shape has more or less clay than the original ball. Children have difficulty seeing that there is no difference in the amount. Young children tend to be intuitive, egocentric, not rational, and not logical; they may confuse play with reality.

Concrete Operations.　Thought becomes internal, rational, and reversible during this stage. Children at this stage interact well with real objects, not abstract ideas. Children who process events concretely develop the ability to classify and conserve, and they develop some ability to engage in if-then hypothetical thinking.

Formal Operations.　During early adolescence, perhaps from age 11 onward, children tend to develop the capability to think more formally, more abstractly.

They can consider many alternatives to a problem and can begin to identify the important variables that influence the outcomes of science activities and experiments. The ability to think about one's own thinking—*metacognition*—opens wonderful worlds of self-reliance and creativity.

The different stages are used to describe developmental differences among learners and to show progressive mental maturation through the experiences that each learner must process in his or her own mind. For educators, Piaget's work has been helpful in designing learning experiences that are most developmentally appropriate and that afford abundant opportunities for pupil success.

The stage progression portion of Piaget's theory implies that no person skips a stage and that learning is developmental; individuals may take different lengths of time and need different experiences to complete their development. Mental development does not merely click into place with a passing birthday. Indeed, learners differ in capability, most likely due to variations in their physical and mental experiences. Researchers in the United Kingdom and the United States report experimental results that cause them to question the absolute validity of the stage development and progression portion of Piaget's theory (Driver, 1983, pp. 52–58). Perhaps Piaget's most important contribution to our quest to understand learning is his description of a process through which each individual experiences stimuli and uses them to produce meaning.

Physical Knowledge.   Physical knowledge is formed from external observations and interactions with the physical world. Referring back to the Tim and Ricky scenario, each child observed a change in the length of the spring as each ball bearing was added to the cup. They could not have known the stretchiness of the spring and the firm, rolling weight of the bearings except through physical contact with the objects.

Logicomathematical Knowledge.   A more sophisticated type of knowledge, logicomathematical knowledge, is created when a learner establishes mental relationships between objects. Tim observed a type of cause-and-effect relationship about the length of the spring as more bearings were added; he formed a connection, albeit not completely correct, between the weight of the bearings and the distance the spring stretched away from the cup. Tim's mistake may have been due to a mental assumption that the bearing-and-spring experience was like pebbles being dropped first from the room's ceiling and then from an aircraft. The relationship existed in Tim's mind and was not based on direct physical knowledge.

External and Internal Knowledge.   In Piaget's theory, knowledge comes from two sources: external and internal. Physical knowledge is often external, and logicomathematical knowledge is internal. These sources of knowledge help each learner to form mental schemes or constructions: mental images constructed by organizing observations, behaviors, or thoughts into patterns. Piaget offers three other concepts to help us understand the complexity of forming schemes while learning: equilibration, assimilation, and accommodation.

Equilibration. According to Piaget's theory, learning is an active mental process in which each learner must construct knowledge by interacting with the environment and by resolving the cognitive conflicts that arise between what is expected and what is observed (Driver, 1983, p. 52). Each new interaction or conflict creates a dilemma in each learner's mind about how to maintain mental equilibrium.

Equilibration is a process by which each learner compensates mentally for each dilemma. Each new attempt at restoring equilibrium helps to create a higher level of functional equilibration; higher mental structures are formed. (See Figure 2.2.) However, equilibrium is not a static point at which the mind

FIGURE 2.2 Equilibrium Model Based on Piaget's Theory Disequilibrium occurs in each learner's universe of experiences and causes an attempt to restore equilibrium through assimilation and accommodation.

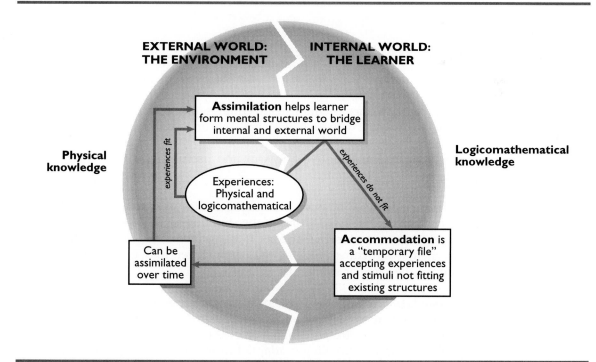

TEACHERS ON SCIENCE TEACHING

How Can You Teach Skills Now, Content Later?

by Charlotte Schartz
Grade 6 Mathematics and Science Teacher, Kingman Middle School, Kingman, Kansas

The year is 1977 and it's time for sixth-grade science class. There will be a unit on, let's say, the cell. We'll do lots of worksheets, with a large amount of reading. I'll lecture, assigning much vocabulary to memorize, and maybe I'll do a demonstration or two. The students are listening, I think. Individual seat work is the norm. Talking to your neighbor is out. I am on stage telling them what to learn, what to memorize. The emphasis is on content.

That was then, this is now, and I'm learning. My evolving theory on how an adolescent learns is based on a conglomeration of articles that I have read, behaviors that I have observed, and experiences that I have had. I believe that students learn in inconsistent surges. Their rate of content absorption is in proportion to their social, emotional, and hormonal situation at any given moment.

I am becoming more and more convinced that middle school students learned before they got to me, and they'll learn more at a later stage in their lives. But right now, they have more important things on their minds, like what to wear, who's going with who, why Susie didn't smile today, or why she smiled at someone else. They are distracted by the unpredictable changes associated with unstable families, economic conditions, and so on. The plant or animal cell just can't compete. And after visiting with the teachers at the senior high, I learned that when they introduce that same cell, they start from the beginning, assuming that most 15- to 16-year-olds will not remember too much from middle school anyway.

I used to spend so much time on content. That's what the experts said was right at the time, I guess. . . . That was then, this is now, and I'm learning.

rests as if on a balance beam. Instead, equilibration is like a cyclist's maintaining dynamic balance with each new challenge on the touring course. "The brain is continually seeking to impose order on incoming stimuli and to generate models that lead to adaptive behavior and useful predictions" (Yager, 1991, p. 54).

Assimilation.   Assimilation is one way the mind may adapt to the learning challenge and restore equilibrium. If the stimulus is not too different from previous experiences and mental actions, it may be combined with or added to existing mental structures, like filing a new letter into a preexisting folder containing the same or similar information.

Accommodation.   On those occasions when no preexisting mental structures (or file folders) are available to assimilate, the mind must adapt by changing or adding to its mental structures. This process of adaptation is called accommodation. The learner's thinking is adapted to accommodate the dilemma.

My teaching style has changed. I'm trying to match it to something unknown, unpredictable, inconsistent: a middle school student. If they aren't physically, emotionally, or socially able to learn and apply a bunch of big words mingled with abstract ideas and global concepts, then I must focus on something more concrete, like the skills that a scientist will need. In my classroom, we make observations, measure, keep records, analyze our data, make comparisons, predict based on patterns, and draw conclusions. During a project such as the design of a controlled experiment with bean seeds, my youngsters are expected to use all of the above. They work with their cooperative learning team to make their own observations, taking their own measurements, keeping their own records. They feel more of an ownership and involvement than if I had just told them about when someone else grew beans. (It's also safer to express an opinion, make a suggestion, or verbalize a revelation while working in a small group instead of in front of the whole class.) Now, are they ready to go out into the world as master bean growers? No, even though some relatively thorough content did get slipped in. But they will have practiced some useful scientific skills, constructed some important science concepts, and developed a greater ability to think, along with some critical social skills. They have a greater chance of remembering something they did rather than something they heard about. And who knows if there will even BE bean farms in fifty years?!? Look what happened to the four food groups! I do feel certain however, that the skills of doing science will endure. People will still have to observe, predict, compare, keep records, and so on; people will still have to think and solve problems.

In practice, assimilation and accommodation are related and do not occur in isolation; each process complements the other. A rational, thinking learner is mentally active. Always losing equilibrium and trying to restore it, the learner develops structures through the continuous interaction between the person and the external world. Again, rich, stimulating experiences—physical and mental—feed the learner's development.

Jessica: The Novelty Wore Off

Jessica used learning groups to undertake the class's new approach to science learning. The students were very excited and cooperative—for about a week. Soon what had been discussion, sharing and playing roles, and collective searches for meaning degenerated into arguments and stalemates over who would get materials and clean up. Normally the class time devoted to positive human relations, genuine regard, and time management would not concern Jessica. As the weeks passed, what bothered Jessica most was the growing number of students who seemed to have persistent ideas and misconceptions unchanged by the effort of problem- and project-based group work. Several individual students complained that they preferred to work by themselves rather than be a part of a group.

Concurrent reading that Jessica was doing as she experimented with her new class arrangements led her into a deeper investigation of cooperative group learning processes, constructivism, and learning models. Students wanted a flexible grouping arrangement and job assignments; they also wanted opportunities to leave a group structure. Poring over how to structure and manage all of the requests for changes, Jessica became mildly embarrassed by the sudden realization that the true spirit of constructivism would be for her to let the *students* decide how to solve their problem. The class decided to vary the number of persons in groups; some contained only two, while others usually consisted of three to five students. Most realized that working with others was a better way to form understandings because ideas and explanations always had to be tested; cases had to be presented and pass the scrutiny of other group members.

When ideas did not fit with existing conceptions, there seemed to be four options.

1. The uneasiness many group individuals experienced became a source of motivation as students attempted to create minitheories to help them include the new experiences into their conceptual structures.

2. When some fit was constructed, students achieved a level of learning that was meaningful to them by regaining their equilibrium and changing previous ideas by adjusting their schema through a process of accommodation; this was regarded as the preferred learning outcome (see Figure 2.3, Exit 2). Jessica realized that a single successful experience was not enough to cause major changes in student thinking. Recalling the story of her son, Jonathan, and his learning about friction, Jessica determined that multiple experiences in a variety of situations were helpful, and she used this notion to plan many opportunities for her students to expand their understanding of science concepts. She discovered that her role was important. At times she became the source of information and explanation, although she usually functioned as a guide and questioner.

3. Despite Jessica's best efforts, some learners preferred to wait for the answer to be given—by a book, a search on the Internet, other students, or Jessica. These few students seemed to prefer to learn the answer by rote (see Figure 2.3, Exit 3). As unsatisfying as this was to Jessica, she realized that it was a beginning for these youngsters, so she resolved to help them by challenging the students to use the answer in other contexts, much like Jonathan's uncle had encouraged him to do when constructing an understanding of friction.

FIGURE 2.3   Science Education Learning Model

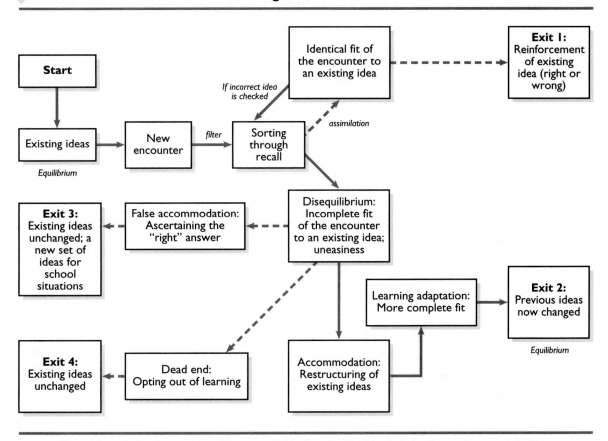

Source: Adapted from K. Appleton, "Using Theory to Guide Practice: Teaching Science from a Constructivist Perspective," *School Science and Mathematics* 93 (5) (1993): 270.

4. Jessica was most disappointed by the two or three children who opted out of the learning experience (see Figure 2.3, Exit 4). These learners were not only the isolated, surly types who did not consider the science topic interesting or the effort worthwhile; they also included the happy social types who were present in group activities, yet—perhaps because of prior poor experiences in science or repeated failures—chose to avoid further failure by opting out of the learning situation (Appleton, 1993, p. 270). This disconcerting student behavior motivated Jessica to seek teaching guidelines and intervention strategies that would serve all learners.

WHAT TECHNIQUES AND ROLES
SUPPORT CONSTRUCTIVIST LEARNING?

A Constructivist Learning and Teaching Model

A Constructivist Model.   Constructivism strives toward a deeper understanding. Frontal teaching—telling and showing students all kinds of things—is minimized. According to Eleanor Duckworth (1989), all people ever have is their own understanding, and you cannot make them believe anything unless they construct it for themselves. Some of the greatest gains from constructivist approaches have occurred in the teaching of mathematics. Martin Simon, a mathematics researcher and educator, maintains that giving students the ideas impairs "the robustness of what students learn, their depth and breadth of understanding, and their self-confidence" (1992, p. 4). As an alternative, students can be encouraged to learn by reinventing the wheel for themselves—not a particularly time-efficient approach, but it *is* effective: retention is greater and understanding is deeper. The learner does the discovering by forming mental connections; the teacher mediates the learning environment.

There is a downside of which we must be aware: Not all student conceptual constructions are correct, and simply voting on what is right does not make it so. At times like this, a teacher may feel compelled to step in and correct the record. This can be fine, but beware the tendency to do too much telling. Instead, try an approach like the one shown in Figure 2.4. Provide an opportunity for children to explore and be directly involved in manipulating objects; ask questions and encourage children to ask useful and productive questions themselves. Help children to construct best explanations from their direct experiences by finding out their ideas and encouraging them to reflect on similarities and differences, to construct connections among and between their ideas. Encourage children to expand on their ideas by using them in other settings, such as the natural world and technology, and to develop process skills to enhance their thinking. Try to evaluate children's thinking by assessing any change in their ideas and process skils. Also encourage children to evaluate ideas by helping them to become interested in the explanations of others.

Constructivist Teaching Roles

Constructivism is becoming a popular catchword in education. Teachers may mistakenly believe they are already using constructivism. (Try your hand at Figure 2.5 to be certain.) While it is true that hands-on science, mathematics manipulatives, and process writing share some common intentions with constructivism, applying constructivist research is much more difficult. The constructivist teacher must fill many roles but largely functions as a facilitator of knowledge construction. Young children can be encouraged to construct

FIGURE 2.4   A Constructivist Learning and Teaching Model

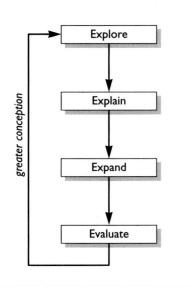

TEACHER'S ACTIVITY

Provide opportunities for students to explore through all appropriate senses and to be fully involved. Encourage group cooperation during investigations; encourage questions.

Interact with children to discover their ideas. Question to cause them to reflect. Help them use ideas formed from exploration to "construct" concepts and meaning sensible to them.

Help children develop their ideas further through additional physical and mental activity. Help them refine their ideas and expand their repertoire of science process skills. Encourage communication through group cooperation and broader experience of nature and technology.

Evaluate conception by examining changes in children's ideas and by their mastery of science process skills. Use hand-on assessment, pictorial problem solving, and reflective questioning. Encourage children's interest in the ideas and reasoning of others.

their own understanding if you perform these roles (Chaille & Britain, 1991, p. 54):

- *Presenter*—not a lecturer but one who demonstrates, models, and presents activities to groups of children and options to individuals so that direct pupil experiences are encouraged in an ongoing fashion.
- *Observer*—one who works in formal and informal ways to identify children's ideas, to interact appropriately, and to provide learning options.
- *Question asker and problem poser*—one who stimulates idea formation, idea testing, and concept construction by asking questions and posing problems that arise from observation.
- *Environment organizer*—one who organizes carefully and clearly what children are to do, while allowing sufficient freedom for true exploration; one who organizes from the child's perspective.
- *Public relations coordinator*—one who encourages cooperation, development of human relations, and patience with diversity within the class, and who defends this practice and educates others outside the class about the benefits for children of this approach.

FIGURE 2.5   Does Your Teaching Support Constructivism?   Use this continuum to determine the extent to which you are supporting constructivism.

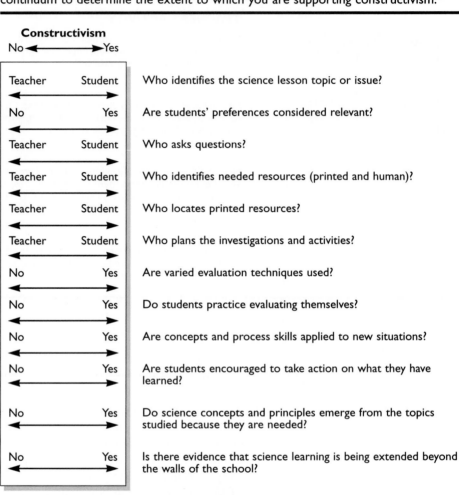

Constructivism		
No ⟵————⟶ Yes		
Teacher	Student	Who identifies the science lesson topic or issue?
No	Yes	Are students' preferences considered relevant?
Teacher	Student	Who asks questions?
Teacher	Student	Who identifies needed resources (printed and human)?
Teacher	Student	Who locates printed resources?
Teacher	Student	Who plans the investigations and activities?
No	Yes	Are varied evaluation techniques used?
No	Yes	Do students practice evaluating themselves?
No	Yes	Are concepts and process skills applied to new situations?
No	Yes	Are students encouraged to take action on what they have learned?
No	Yes	Do science concepts and principles emerge from the topics studied because they are needed?
No	Yes	Is there evidence that science learning is being extended beyond the walls of the school?

Source: Adapted from Robert E. Yager, "The Constructivist Learning Model," *Science Teacher* (September 1991): 56.

- *Documenter of learning*—one who satisfies the accountability expectations and gauges the impact of these practices on each learner in terms of knowledge construction and science skill development.
- *Theory builder*—one who helps children to form connections between and among their ideas and to construct meaningful patterns that represent their constructed knowledge.

Intermediate and middle school children can benefit from these same roles, particularly if cognition is elevated to a stimulating and challenging level that is developmentally appropriate.

Jessica's Knowledge Construction

Throughout this chapter we have seen how Jessica wrestled with her own learning as she attempted to reconceptualize learning and teaching. When this happens to a professional or even a student, there are often several recurring actions that are important to recognize. First, Jessica was dissatisfied with her teaching and what children were learning. This dissatisfaction perturbed her and motivated her to seek change. Shaw and Etchberger (1993) claim that change cannot occur without some *perturbation*. Jessica's perturbation stimulated considerable thought about how children learn and how she could teach more effectively. Students too must become perturbed in order to stimulate learning.

Perturbation often encourages *commitment*—a personal decision to make a change. Commitment and progress toward change often cause additional perturbations. If you commit to a course of constructivism in your science classroom, you are likely to encounter many such perturbations that disrupt your "mental state of equilibrium" (Shaw & Etchberger 1993, p. 264). When this happens, say Shaw and Jakubowski (1991), there are three likely pathways for you to deal with when experiencing this disequilibrium: (1) you may block the perturbation and reduce the opportunity for meaningful change; (2) you may rationalize excuses for not dealing with the perturbation; or (3) you will form an active plan for making a change. To which pathway are you likely to commit?

A *vision* may help you keep your commitments and steer the course toward meaningful change. This vision should be a clear, personal view of what the teaching and learning in your classroom should look like. You should be able to describe clearly to parents, supervisors, and visitors what you are trying to accomplish and the reasons for your choices. Figure 2.6 summarizes the differences between traditional and constructivist classrooms. Perhaps it will help you to construct and maintain your vision.

Reflection will help you to evaluate and improve your vision, strengthen your commitment, and construct options to overcome your perturbations. Thinking reflectively means to give serious and frequent consideration to the factors associated with your vision. The following questions illustrate a reflective process and can help bring congruence to your desires, beliefs, and teaching practices: "What do students know about this topic? How are students thinking about what I am presenting to them? How do they come to think this way? How can they learn to value new ways of thinking about things? How can I help them to grasp scientific ideas? How do learners feel uncomfortable with science?" (Shapiro, 1994, p. xv).

For successful constructivist teaching and learning to occur, the teacher must become perturbed, commit to change, envision the type of change pre-

◆ **FIGURE 2.6   Traditional versus Constructivist Classrooms**

TRADITIONAL CLASSROOMS	CONSTRUCTIVIST CLASSROOMS
Curriculum • Presented part to whole; emphasis on basic skills • Fixed curriculum • Relies heavily on textbooks and workbooks	• Presented whole to part; emphasis on big concepts and thinking skills • Responsive to student questions and interest • Relies heavily on primary sources of data and manipulative materials
Role of students • "Blank slates" onto which information is etched by the teacher • Work alone	• Thinkers with emerging theories about the world • Work in groups
Role of teacher • Generally behaves in a didactic manner; disseminates information to students • Seeks the correct answer to validate student learning	• Generally behaves in an interactive manner; mediates the environment for students • Seeks the students' point of view in order to understand students' present conceptions for use in subsequent lessons
Assessment • Viewed as separate from teaching; occurs almost entirely through testing	• Interwoven with teaching; occurs through teacher observations of students at work and through student exhibitions and portfolios

Source: Cantrell, D. C. & Barron, P. A. (Eds.). (1994). *Integrating environmental education and science.* Newark, OH: Environmental Education Council of Ohio, p. 148.

ferred, plan for change, garner the support for pursuing the vision, and reflect consistently about the progress and perturbations encountered along the path toward change. Change is a slow and deliberate process; for students, constructivist learning requires patience, persistence and respect for another's thinking (Shaw & Etchberger, 1993).

CHAPTER SUMMARY

Our approach in this chapter is different than what you might find in typical textbooks on teaching science. We assume you have completed a prior course in psychology or educational psychology, maybe even a course in child develop-

ment. Therefore, rather than revisit the depths of some theories you may have studied, we visit the fundamental ideas behind the dominant belief about learning science from the perspective of a practicing teacher. How can we take some of this dominant perspective on learning and use it to teach science better?

No perspective on learning is complete without considering the prior ideas of children. These ideas represent preconceptions—conceptual understanding in the early stages of development—and misconceptions—conceptual understandings that do not agree with the concepts of the scientific community. These ideas are personal, may be contradictory when examined under a variety of circumstances, and are stubbornly rooted in children's minds. That their ideas are resistant to change poses a big challenge for teachers.

Children's learning needs must be considered and assimilated into a perspective on learning. As children develop over time, their needs change, and their exact cognitive capabilities are dynamic rather than static. Children need extensive experiences to stimulate their senses and to affect thinking. Physical activity is especially important for younger children, with mental and physical activity being interrelated in learning. Language has no automatic meaning for children since words have no inherent value, making an emphasis on word recognition and memorization meaningless. However, language constructed from experience has meaning that represents the physical and mental action understood by children. A child's social development is related to academic success. Group work and tasks that require cooperation

help a child learn. Self-esteem is another need for effective learning. All of these needs must be attended to over time. The factor of time is variable for children since maturation and development occur at different rates.

Experience is the one factor that unites the dominant perspectives on how children learn science. But not all experiences are equivalent, and experience alone is insufficient. Constructivists advocate several approaches for stimulating mental action and learning in conjunction with experience.

Constructivism is the contemporary concept we use to think about a child's learning. This perspective focuses on the child and what the child does during learning. It holds that knowledge cannot exist outside the mind of a learner, it cannot be directly transferred, and it must be each learner's construction of reality. The teaching recommendations offered should help you construct appropriate roles for yourself. If you follow these recommendations, you will find yourself covering less and guiding more, and your students will learn more in the deepest sense of the word. The chapter ends with discussion of the relationship of dissatisfaction, commitment, vision, and reflection as a process for becoming the type of science teacher you wish to be. We challenge you to envision the type of learning you wish for children and to construct a classroom that supports this vision.

DISCUSSION QUESTIONS AND PROJECTS

1. In what ways do children benefit from learning through experience? What types of materials or problems do you think are developmentally appropriate for young children? for the intermediate grades? for middle school youth? What similarities and differences do you detect when you compare

the materials and problems you favor for each group?

2. As may be revealed by their prior ideas, how might children's science misconceptions affect how you teach? What could you do to learn about these prior ideas and to identify misconceptions?

3. Select several science concepts. Interview several children, perhaps from different age groups, to determine their ideas about the concepts. What are their misconceptions? What similarities or differences do you detect across the age groups you have selected? How do you think you could attempt to correct those misconceptions? What perspectives on learning could you use to help you with this task?

4. Prepare a lesson designed to teach a particular science concept. What teaching and learning recommendations do you plan to use to help your learners be successful? Videotape your lesson as you teach it. Analyze the tape. How consistent were you in using the recommendations you selected? What do you plan to do to become the type of science teacher you prefer? What are your specific goals and action plan for accomplishing your goals?

ADDITIONAL READINGS

If you are interested in learning more about some of the topics raised in this chapter, consider the following sources:

Charles Ault, "Intelligently Wrong: Some Comments on Children's Misconceptions," *Science and Children* (May 1984): pp. 22–24.

David Ausubel, *Education Psychology: A Cognitive View* (New York: Holt, Rinehart and Winston, 1968). In this classic study, Ausubel affords us a deeper look at his use of advance organizers for encouraging mental processing.

Patricia Blosser, *Science Misconceptions Research and Some Implications for the Teaching of Science to Elementary School Students,* a newsletter research report (No. 1, 1987) available through the ERIC Clearinghouse for Science, Mathematics, and Environmental Education, 1200 Chambers Road, Third Floor, Columbus, OH 43212.

Jerome Bruner and Helen Haste, *Making Sense: The Child's Construction of the World* (New York: Methuen, 1987). The authors take a detailed look at how children construct meaning.

Renate Nummela Caine and Geoffrey Caine, *Making Connections: Teaching and the Human Brain* (Alexandria, VA: ASCD, 1991). In this book for teachers, the authors describe the most recent synthesis from brain research.

Christine Chaille and Lory Britain, *The Young Child as Scientist* (New York: HarperCollins, 1991). This delightful, practical book for teachers of young children takes a constructivist perspective.

John Dewey, *Experience and Education* (originally published in 1938 by Kappa Delta Pi). This classic is a concise statement that describes Dewey's complex views on the nature and importance of experience and solving meaningful problems.

Joseph Novak and D. Bob Gown, *Learning How to Learn* (London: Cambridge University Press, 1984). This book explores in depth the ways to help learners develop mental structures through concept mapping and Vee-maps.

D. C. Phillips and Jonas F. Soltis, *Perspectives on Learning* (New York: Teachers College Press, 1991). This primer is especially reader friendly; the prime perspectives on learning from ancient Greece to modern times are reviewed in a contemporary context.

Jean Piaget, *To Understand Is to Invent* (New York: Penguin Books, reprinted from earlier translations in 1976). This is Piaget's essay on how the learner must invent meaning independently for understanding to occur.

Bonnie Shapiro, *What Children Bring to Light: A Constructivist Perspective on Children's Learning in Science* (New York: Teachers College Press, 1994). With an adequate review of the foundation of constructivism, Shapiro provides abundant case studies of children's concept formations and ways of knowing as they constructing understandings of light.

Joseph Stepans and Christine Kuehn, "What Research Says: Children's Conceptions of Weather," *Science and Children* (September 1985): pp. 44–47.

Kenneth Tobin (Ed.), *The Practice of Constructivism in Science Education* (Washington, DC: AAAS Press, 1993). This book of nineteen contributed chapters from experts in the field add depth to a reader's understanding of constructivism as a theory, a process for planning, an approach to teaching and learning, and a guide for appropriate assessment.

Anita Woolfolk, *Educational Psychology* (Boston: Allyn and Bacon, 1993). This is perhaps the most comprehensive text available on learning from an educational psychology perspective.

CHAPTER OUTLINE

CHAPTER 3

How Can You Teach Science for All Children?

Jeannie Rae Rice is an Indianapolis teacher of students with learning disabilities. She describes how her class began its trek toward a science fair, a project familiar to many children but unfamiliar to her students. While they worked on their projects, the students with learning disabilities learned more than anyone imagined they possibly could. They taught many other teachers and students an important lesson about the low expectations and unfair attitudes people often hold toward those with special needs.

It had been at least seven years since my school had a science fair. Late in the fall I asked my principal if I could organize and sponsor a school science fair for my class and the other students in grades four through six. My main concern would be to get as many students as possible to follow a project through to completion so they could experience the reward of displaying their work. She immediately gave her permission and support.

My sixteen boys and one girl, aged 11 to 13, have reading abilities ranging from beginning first grade to high third grade. Their math skills are somewhat higher, while handwriting and spelling skills vary but are generally low.

According to intelligence test scores, these students have at least average potential, but they have not achieved at the same rate as most of their peers. They have been placed in my class in order to receive special and individualized instruction.

The behavior and attitudes of children with learning disabilities have been described as impulsive, distractible, frustrated, stubborn, disruptive, defiant, obstinate, and extremely disorganized. One word I would never use to characterize my students, though, is "unmotivated." Of course their motivation varies according to the activity at hand, but when their interest has been roused, they really get into gear. Fortunately, my explanation of a science fair induced every member of the class to decide to enter a project.

During the three months our school was involved in the science fair, I noticed some important changes in my own students and in other students and the faculty.

Learning-disabled children have difficulty getting along with one another in group situations. They are easily frustrated and tend to argue and become angry. Much to my surprise, however, this did not occur when my students worked on their science fair projects. I must stress the significance of this change in behavior. Naturally it improved the quality of their work for the science fair, but it also demonstrated to me—and to them—that they could control themselves and cooperate to solve difficult problems.

While my students' perceptions of what they could do were changing, the attitudes of other students towards my class were also shifting. At the beginning, most of the other students in the school had little information about learning-disabled children. They only knew that my students were somehow different, and they usually called ours the "dummy class." I, of course, was the "dummies' teacher." But during preparations for the science fair, the perceptions of some of these other students began to change. They found it difficult to understand how a "dummy teacher" could run a science fair and why she'd want to. The fact that I seemed to be doing a good job created a halo effect that was important: As my image began to improve among students throughout the school, so did the image of my students. For the first time, members of my class began to develop friendships with other students.

Many teachers were as uninformed as their students about the limitations and the capabilities of learning-disabled children. These colleagues often viewed students in my class simply as behavior problems. This misapprehension is not necessarily the fault of the teachers, since many of them finished college before courses in special education and learning disabilities had become part of the curriculum.

I initiated our science fair with one goal—to have my students complete and display science projects. However, as preparations for the fair progressed, it became clear that my students were learning more than I had originally imagined possible. I was curious about their perceptions of what they were accomplishing, so I asked them.

My students had no doubt that they'd learned some valuable lessons by participating in the science fair and neither had I. In fact, it seems to me that several important academic and personal goals can be accomplished by involving learning-disabled children in a science fair.

> For me and my students, the school science fair was an extremely satisfy-
> ing experience. Of the nine winners chosen by outside judges, four were from
> my learning-disabled class. And while getting prizes was exciting, equally im-
> portant for my students were the intangible rewards of embarking on a joint
> enterprise with others, and discovering within themselves capabilities of which
> they had not been aware. (Rice, 1983, pp. 15–16)   ◆

INTRODUCTION

Have you ever heard someone reason like this: "If you can't walk, talk, or hear, or if you look or sound different, you must be intellectually and socially inferior." Most physical differences have no connection to one's intellect or mental capability. The biases of our hypothetical conversationalist are based on two important factors: stereotypes and a lack of information. Stereotypes caused the learners without disabilities in Ms. Rice's school to refer to her students as "dummies." The uninformed teacher can insufficiently stimulate the intellect by holding low expectations for children with learning disabilities. Without realizing just how unfairly their expectations may treat the children, teachers may actually reinforce the wider perception that learners who have disabilities or are different in some other way are dummies, and this type of teacher behavior may tend to reinforce the prejudices held by others.

Children with learning disabilities are only one example of students who have special needs. Each child is a special case and deserves special attention and encouragement. You will be in a better position to teach, to strike down unfair stereotypes, and to serve the needs of *all* learners if you become informed about the special needs many school children have. This will be a great service for all of your students and will especially benefit those who need special assistance.

This chapter is about teaching science to serve *all* children's needs. Technically, of course, all students are culturally different; each family is unique and has its own identity. The multicultural focus of this chapter explores the special needs of culturally diverse populations (groups of students with home environments very different from society's mainstream in terms of economics, ethnicity, religion, race, and/or language) and learners who have distinct exceptionalities (children with differences in vision, hearing, speech, emotions, giftedness, and so on). In both instances, the science teaching techniques we recommend to help the few students in your class who may have special needs will better serve the needs of all learners.

The chapter begins with an investigation of several general factors that impede science learning and provides teaching recommendations beneficial for all children. After reading the first part of this chapter, you should be able to:

1. Describe the special needs of children who are members of minority groups, culturally different, and/or multilingual.

2. Practice techniques that help meet their special needs.
3. Promote gender equality in your classroom.
4. Identify the different learning styles.
5. Discuss management and teaching practices that encourage all learners.

The second part of this chapter should help you to:

1. Identify characteristics of the exceptional students who will enrich your classes.
2. Practice classroom techniques that help meet these special needs.

The third part of this chapter explores ways to include parents in science teaching.

SCIENCE FOR ALL

Not all children come to school able to function effectively within a school's culture. Some children lack the skills necessary to cope with the routines or rigors of schooling. These children often feel hostile toward school and toward any authority figure, especially a teacher.

Being different carries liabilities. The price of being different may be exclusion from social groups at school and prejudiced treatment from those who appear not to be different. Cultural differences can contribute to the difficulties and problems of school children. The principles of multicultural education can help us meet the special needs of all children.

Multicultural Education

All children are culturally different. Multicultural education strives to promote the often-overlooked contributions made by less dominant cultures. Children who are culturally different may include those of minority races or children with special needs, as well as children who come from home environments out of the mainstream of society. Cultural differences include those of race, religion, economic level, ethnic background, the primary language used by the child, and in some instances gender. Different backgrounds often offer rich heritages beneficial to all. Cultural pluralism brings the perspectives of many cultures to our schools. The history of our nation is strong as a result of the contributions of this heritage.

The importance of cultural pluralism is recognized and supported in the 1991 Position Statement on Multicultural Science Education from the National Science Teachers Association. This statement encourages teachers to seek resources to ensure effective science learning for culturally diverse populations. The position statement urges that teachers

- provide access to high-quality science education experiences so that culturally diverse populations can become successful participants in our democratic society,

All children benefit from learning science.

- select and use curriculum materials and teaching strategies that reflect and incorporate diversity,
- become aware of children's learning styles and instructional preferences,
- expose culturally diverse children to career opportunities in science, engineering, and technology (NSTA, 1991).

Multicultural education advocates effective and appropriate schooling for all children, with subsequent acceptance by those who are part of the majority culture of the community. Multicultural education helps to enlighten the children of the majority about the value of the culture from which the minority or special-needs child comes, and it helps to boost the self-esteem of all children. It is easier for children to understand and accept cultural differences among people if they are exposed to and taught to accept differences of all sorts at an early age.

The many fields of science offer an enormous variety of topics for children to explore. Science teaches children to think more logically and reason about why things are as they are. It helps children learn to analyze and evaluate myths and stereotypes and to overcome prejudice. Science also provides important opportunities for children to study the contributions of scientists from culturally diverse backgrounds. If we are to promote multicultural education effectively, we must:

1. Stop believing in social assimilation, in which the minority group loses all its distinctive characteristics and is ultimately absorbed by the majority group.
2. Help minority and majority children maintain their distinct ethnic identities within the culture of the school's values, such as equal treatment, equal opportunity to participate fully in school, equal protection by law, and equal freedom of cultural and religious expression (Antonouris, 1989).

Who Makes Up Culturally Diverse Populations?   Often the African-American child who lives in poverty is envisioned as a typical example of one who is culturally different. This is an inaccurate stereotype of African Americans. Although the example does apply, culturally different children are as likely to come from the hills and mountains of Appalachia, Spanish-speaking communities of the Southwest, French settlements of the northernmost regions of Maine, or Asian communities of the West Coast. Let us not overlook the Native Americans who once were the majority on this land. They, too, are now culturally different from a changed mainstream society. In fact, each of us can become culturally different when we enter a community or region where our identity is not among the majority of the residents.

How Can You Use Cultural Differences to Promote Greater Science Understanding?   Your science classes can reflect greater cultural diversity if your instruction reflects contributions made by people all over the world. Often our print materials and media leave the impression that science is a recent white European construct. In fact this impression is very wrong. Consider that

> over 5000 years ago in Egypt and Mesopotamia copper was being extracted from its ores, glass was made, and fabrics were dyed with natural colours. . . . Iron swords are known to have been produced over 3000 years ago. . . . Distillation was used in Mesopotamia as far back as 1200 BC. for the production of perfumes. . . . Many of the techniques and much of the terminology of modern chemistry derives from ancient times; for example, *alkali* from the Arabic *al qality*—the roasted ashes; *soda* from Arabic *studa*—a splitting headache. (Williams, 1984, pp. 133–146)

You can promote multicultural education in your science class by:

- *Developing science themes related to conservation and pollution, disease, food and health, and population growth and teaching with consideration for humankind as a whole.* Develop an understanding among your students about the interdependence of people and unequal distribution of natural resources.

- *Selecting classroom teaching examples that address the contributions and participation of people from a range of backgrounds, cultures, and genders.*
- *Considering carefully any issues of race, gender, and human origins by exploring the myths that surround them* (Antonouris, 1989, p. 98).
- *Challenging inaccurate statements students make about ethnic minority communities and people.* Statements may refer to different physical features, countries of origin, religion, language, and customs (Antonouris, 1989). For example, we have all heard myths about the strengths and weaknesses of blacks, Asians, women, and so on. As educated adults, we understand that these alleged qualities cannot be applied to all members of a group and that beliefs like these arise from ignorance. We know that human beings are much more alike than they are different. Use science teaching as an opportunity to refute these myths when children repeat them.

A multicultural approach to education rejects the merely color-blind view that strives to treat all children the same. Advocates of multicultural education believe that the needs of all children differ and that these differences should be taken into account. Because all children *are* different, they should be treated differently, where appropriate. Special provisions can sometimes help children with language differences, minority status, or low-income backgrounds to develop positive self-images.

How Do You Meet the Needs of Children from Diverse Backgrounds? Although they come from different backgrounds and ways of life, culturally different children seem to share some characteristics. Here are some tips for meeting their needs:

Children with different experiences. What most of us take for granted may be completely lacking from the childhoods of children who are culturally different, minority, low income, or disabled. For example, herds of domestic animals, menageries of pets, and/or wild animals that roam at will may be as foreign to a city dweller as the piles of wind-tossed convenience packaging, crowds of densely packed people, and clouds of smog are to the rancher. Classroom activities, videos, and field trips with planned comparative discussions help to build awareness about and tolerance for differences by adding new experiences. Yet real experiences are a better choice. Activity-based science learning helps the student who is culturally different reach higher levels of science achievement, develop better process skills, and develop more logical thought processes (Bredderman, 1982).

Children with a desire for action rather than words. Few children who are multilingual or multicultural will be patient enough to listen to long instructions or descriptions. Get to the point. Provide simple, direct demonstrations and concrete experiences. Indeed, all children benefit from clarity and directness.

Children who need a better vocabulary. The rough, blunt street talk or backwoods language of some children can cause quite a culture shock. In the same way, the child with limited English proficiency who speaks haltingly may have difficulty following a normal conversation. Children need a vocabulary suited to the mainstream if they are to become competitive in the workplace. Science offers abundant opportunities for developing vocabulary and effective communication skills.

Disorganized children. Children can become frustrated and misunderstand the purpose of an activity if there are too many choices or if your instructions are too flexible. Some children may live in cultures in which they are not encouraged to make many of their own decisions. Be definite and clear with your instructions.

Children who need genuine (rather than patronizing) relationships. Be empathetic rather than sympathetic. Looking down on the students' different social or economic standing is demeaning despite your best intentions.

Children who cannot easily control their own destinies. Poverty tends to produce feelings of hopelessness and desperation. Children who are culturally different, minority, low income, or disabled may feel that they have little or no control over their lives and may look for immediate gratification. Fate control is defined as the belief that you can control what happens to you. Many children from culturally different backgrounds believe that what happens to them happens by chance or that their future lies in the hands of others who are more powerful and beyond influence. Science experiments help children to learn that variables can be manipulated to produce different outcomes. This understanding about variables can be applied to themselves and can be used eventually to help shift the locus of fate control to a point where they perceive the power to control their own lives (Rowe, 1974).

How Can You Help Non-English-Speaking Students?

Lack of familiarity with the dominant spoken language can cause students to believe their fate is beyond their control. Bruce Reichert (1989), a science teacher with the American Cooperative School in Tunis, has taught students who speak several different languages. He offers the following tips for assisting non-English speakers in your classes.

Helping Students Help Themselves.   Ideally, students should learn to help themselves learn. Try these approaches:

Distribute a vocabulary list and/or copy of the curriculum guide at the beginning of each unit. This material helps students know exactly what will be expected of them and will give them additional time to master the difficult terms.

Ask students who are readers of their native language to carry pocket dictionaries (English-to-native language and vice versa). At times simple words create communication barriers. Pocket dictionaries can solve the problem and help create the self-sufficient habit of looking up unfamiliar words. English-speaking students can be encouraged to do the same as a way of learning words in another language.

Invite the students who are uncomfortable with English to ask questions. This personal invitation, in a nonthreatening environment, will help students to overcome fear of using the new language. The joy of being successful at expressing opinions or asking questions becomes a positive reinforcer.

Be patient. Wait-time is particularly important for multilingual speakers, to allow them to form their questions or answers.

Encourage the children to write their own translations of words in their notes. As you examine lab notebooks and see translations, you will be aware that the student has looked up the words and probably understands them better.

Encourage students to read science articles and books in their own languages. Additional supplemental readings such as those available from *Scholastic* provide brief, popular articles and photographs that encourage additional practice with the language.

I Hear and I Forget. For those times when you feel you must lecture, try the following to help students remember:

Speak slowly and enunciate clearly. All students benefit from this because the technical words of science at times seem like a foreign language.

On the chalkboard or overhead projector, display an outline or definitions, descriptions, or figures to add meaning to your spoken words.

Add emphasis to the main ideas. Underline concepts or highlight the important meanings. Non-English speakers will remember to look them up later, while other students will treat the emphasis as a study cue.

I See and I Remember. A picture really is worth a thousand words. It provides another mode for learning, and it is helpful for memory retention. Try these suggestions:

Use visual aids as often as possible. The problem in science education is deciding what to teach and what materials to use, not the availability of interesting, useful materials. Check the school district's resource center or curriculum library or the education resource co-op that serves your school. There is a wealth of films, videos, film strips, bulletin board ideas, computer programs, models, posters, and charts. Old, discarded science textbooks or magazines can be salvaged for useful visual aids.

Nurture animals and plants. They add excitement and can also make superior visual aids.

Use artwork. Add your own artwork and invite talented student artists to contribute to your notes, transparencies, learning activity illustrations, and lab activities. Stick figures with details are fine too.

I Do and I Understand. All three learning approaches—hearing, seeing, and doing—are important, especially when all five senses are stimulated. Combined approaches provide better opportunities for understanding than a single approach. The power of activity learning stimulates improved communication as well as greater levels of science achievement, process skill development, scientific attitudes, and logical thinking than traditional teaching, in which teacher talk and student reading dominate (Shymansky, Kyle & Alport, 1982). Keep these suggestions in mind while working with non-English speakers:

Try the "demonstrate–group investigate–individual investigate" teaching model. You can demonstrate the concept and create interest as well as stimulate curiosity. A demonstration also gives students an opportunity to listen and observe before having to produce any language. Group investigation can help learners comprehend and practice communication skills with peers. Language skills are developed naturally as students observe and communicate with others. Independent individual investigation helps students to explore questions that are related to the concept but already familiar to them. Table 3.1 provides some examples of this teaching and learning model.

TABLE 3.1   Language Development Model

Teacher Demonstration	Group Investigation	Individual Investigation
Concept: **Electrical energy causes motion.**		
Use an inflated balloon to pick up small pieces of paper.	Use an inflated balloon to cause another balloon to move.	Use an inflated balloon to test what objects it will pick up.
Concept: **Rapid motion causes the temperature of objects to rise.**		
Rub a wooden block over sandpaper to show how the temperature of the block goes up.	Bend paper clip rapidly back and forth, and use cheeks to test for temperature change.	Find other objects (e.g., saw, chisel, file) outside the classroom that change temperature after rapid motion, and test them for temperature change.
Concept: **Animals move in different ways; some animals move by stretching.**		
Use earthworms to show how they move by stretching because they have no legs.	Observe earthworm activity when these are placed in a carton of soil.	Find examples of other animals without legs outside the classroom or in pictures. Name and classify them according to how they move.
Concept: **Rapidly moving air causes some objects to rise.**		
Hold a long piece of paper to the bottom lip and blow hard across the top of the paper to show how it moves up.	Blow hard across the top of a balloon, and then try to explain why it rises and what makes airplanes rise into the air.	Use a fan to see what objects you can lift up into the air.

Source: A. K. Fathman, M. E. Quinn, and C. Kessler, *Teaching Science to English Learners, Grades 4–8* (Washington, DC: National Clearinghouse for Bilingual Education, 1992), p. 13 (ERIC Document Reproduction Service No. ED 349 844).

Have students do hands-on, lab-type learning activities often. The minds-on experiences that accompany hands-on learning can contribute to language and reading development. Some non-English-speaking students may not understand a lecture, discussion, or teacher demonstration, but once they have done it themselves, the experience is easier for them to link with the language. You can assist language development by focusing on one or two language functions that are particularly appropriate for the planned activities. "Language functions are specific uses of language for accomplishing certain functions. . . . For example, *directing* (giving and following directions) may be emphasized in an activity where the teacher first gives directions on how to build a rocket" (Fathman, Quinn, & Kessler, 1992, p. 16) and then has students work in groups to direct each other in building their own paper rockets. Table 3.2 shows several language functions that are commonly used in science classrooms.

Coordinate your teaching with the English as a Second Language (ESL) teacher. Blend the grammar and vocabulary used in both classes so the students have a double exposure to the science vocabulary.

Link science concepts with the students' background experiences. Learn what you can about the children's countries of origin and refer to geographical locations, climate conditions, fauna and flora, and so on to link the new science concepts with what the students already know. Why is it always necessary to mention the Rocky Mountains or the Mississippi? The rest of the class will benefit from the geography enrichment.

Use guest speakers and field trips. These are good ways to help multilingual students become more accepted and feel at home in their new environment and with science. Be aware of the linguistic and cultural differences and include all children in the full range of activities. Invite speakers from the students'

TABLE 3.2 Language Functions

Language functions are specific uses of language for accomplishing certain purposes. Teachers can help students develop an understanding of these functions by building them into their lessons. Verbal ("What to Discuss") and written ("What to Record") exercises can be included in teacher demonstrations and student group and individual investigations.

Directing	Requesting	Questioning
Praising	Cautioning	Encouraging
Advising	Suggesting	Disagreeing
Agreeing	Describing	Expressing opinions
Refusing	Accepting	Defining

Source: A. K. Fathman, M. E. Quinn, C. Kessler, *Teaching Science to English Learners, Grades 4–8* (Washington, DC: National Clearinghouse for Bilingual Education, 1992), p. 13 (ERIC Document Reproduction Service No. ED 349 844).

countries of origin to help classmates become familiar with people from other cultures.

Try to Reduce Test Anxiety.   Children from other countries often attach more importance to testing and achievement than native-born American children might. The mere mention of a test can evoke much anxiety because of its importance in determining children's academic futures in other countries, and a test in the English language can pump anxiety to counterproductive levels. The following suggestions offer some ideas for reducing test anxiety:

Try puzzles. Crossword puzzles assist spelling and provide additional cues for correct answers. Students seem to do better when they know how many letters to expect in an answer. A list of words helps, too, for crosswords and fill-in-the-blank questions.

Encourage children to draw. Invite children to draw answers rather than write. This is a good way to communicate ideas as the child gets around the temporary language barriers.

Encourage students to check their work. At the end of each test, consider allotting 3 to 5 minutes for students to check answers. Permit them to use books, notes, and class handouts.

Try bonus points for extra credit. Offer bonus points for student creations. Science-oriented jokes, riddles, poems, and songs that use the concepts and vocabulary being studied can be a great way to encourage review and creativity. Permitted as homework, this can also be a good way to promote language study between the child and parents.

Is Gender Equality a Special Need?

Females do not have equal access to or receive equal encouragement for careers in science. This appears to be a cultural problem linked to how females are socialized in the mainstream of society; it is not a women's problem. Both males and females, by age 11, have developed strong sex-stereotyped attitudes concerning socially appropriate behavior and gender roles in society (Chivers, 1986). Although improvements have been made, many people still attribute cultural differences to gender. Cultural gender differences play an important role in career selection.

How Does Culture Affect Females in Science?   There are cultural disincentives for women to pursue careers in science, technology, and mathematics. Proportionally fewer women and minorities have sufficient background for scientific careers, and they are underrepresented in these careers. While our country's population is 51 percent female, and 43.2 percent of our workforce is composed of women, women represent only 3 percent of our nation's engineers (Elfner, 1988) and about 6 percent of our scientists (Jones & Wheatley, 1988). In addition, the U.S. Senate Report on the Education for Economic Security Act of 1984

Females deserve equal encouragement and access to science.

reports that many young women score lower on standardized achievement tests in mathematics and science than their male classmates. The report from a recent National Assessment of Education Progress illustrates this fact: In fourth grade, the average science proficiency for males and females was approximately the same; a small, but significant, performance gap was evident by eighth grade; the gap widened to ten scale points by twelfth grade. At age 17, roughly 50 percent of the males demonstrated the ability to analyze scientific procedures and data, but only 33 percent of the females could do the same (Jones et al., 1992).

Some of the achievement differences can be traced to low enrollment of women in advanced science courses. Generally there are equal numbers of males and females enrolled in high school general or physical science, biology, and chemistry courses, but only 5.6 percent of physics students are female (Jones & Wheatley, 1988). Encouraging females to take more science courses is not always the way to reduce the achievement deficit. The large difference in science achievement performance by gender cannot be explained entirely by the number of courses taken. In some cases, the proficiency gap between high-school-aged males and females actually increases as more science courses are taken (Mullis & Jenkins, 1988). It appears that in some cases, taking more science courses could actually do more harm to females than good, particularly if the extra courses give them negative experiences (Mullis & Jenkins, 1988).

Other aspects of the gender inequality problem can include the following factors:

- Parents, teachers, school counselors, and peers discourage females from pursuing scientific careers (Elfner, 1988).
- Most elementary teachers are women and lack strong background in science; their lack of confidence can reinforce children's beliefs that women are not supposed to like science (Chivers, 1986; Shepardson & Pizzini, 1992).
- A shortage of appropriate female science and engineering role models reinforces the belief that science is a male domain (Jones & Wheatley, 1988).
- Young males report more positive attitudes toward science and young females less positive attitudes; females report less confidence and more fear of success in careers like engineering; females report that physics courses are too difficult (Jones & Whetley, 1988; Kahle & Rennie, 1993).
- Females may not be socialized at home or at school to develop and demonstrate scientific skills and may not be encouraged to develop practical ability, independence, and self-confidence. Several studies reveal that skills and characteristics associated with scientists are those often attributed to masculine characters: high intellectual ability, persistence at work, extreme independence, and apartness from others. Females may be hesitant to pursue science because they fear that they will be considered unfeminine (Jones & Wheatley, 1988; Shepardson & Pizzini, 1992). Even the toys typically given to boys require more assembly and manipulation than the toys given to girls.
- When women have problems, they tend to blame themselves for the problems or the inability to solve them, whereas when men have difficulties, they tend to place the blame outside themselves. These differences can tend to develop female feelings of learned helplessness and may cause females to believe that they are not intellectually capable (Jones & Wheatley, 1988).
- Teachers reflect the values and expectations thrust upon them by the dominant society and can unintentionally perpetuate sex stereotypes in science. In addition, sex bias can be observed in the practices of teachers and the assignments of science teachers. Female science teachers usually are assigned to introductory science classes and biology, whereas males more often are high school department chairmen and are assigned to teach such advanced science classes as chemistry and physics (Jones & Wheatley, 1988; Kahle & Rennie, 1993).

How Do Teachers Contribute to Gender Problems in Science?   While the role of teachers perpetuating sex-role stereotypes has not been fully explored, the literature indicates that teachers are not consciously and intentionally sex stereotyping students. Many teachers do try to treat males and females fairly and equally. Often teachers tell us that they want all children to develop to their full potential. But some effects are larger than life. We were all raised in a society where gender differences are prevalent. Parents, school counselors, other teachers, social workers, books, and television have taught teachers (even you!) that certain behaviors are appropriate for females and others are appropriate for males (Sadker, Sadker, and Thomas, 1981; Shepardson & Pizzini, 1992). Bias by gender will begin to change only when you are able to recognize the subtle messages that steer males and females toward particular behaviors and career choices.

Considerable evidence indicates that teachers' expectations affect students' performances. Elementary teachers often perceive males to have higher scientific ability than females. This perception usually sends a negative message to females, influences the self-perceptions of females, and determines the tasks and responsibilities that teachers assign to students during scientific activities (Shepardson & Pizzini, 1992). More likely, females are given passive roles to perform during group activities (Baker, 1988; Kahle, 1990), which reinforce teachers' perceptions that females are less interested and less capable in science (Shepardson & Pizzini, 1992). Cooper's model (1979) is based on this evidence and explains how sex differences in achievement may stem from differences in teacher expectations (see Figure 3.1). The model, which consists of the following steps, can be useful for overcoming gender stereotypes:

Step 1. Form different expectations for students.

Regardless of gender, hold high but realistic expectations for all students.

Step 2. Believe that females are as capable in science as males.

Do not be tempted to assign class roles or jobs based on flawed beliefs that females are better note takers and writers and males are better handlers of equipment.

Step 3. Encourage females to take the lead in activities, to make lab decisions, to take measurements and handle equipment.

Do the same for males, but without leading them to believe they are better at it than females.

Step 4. Strive for equal amounts and types of nurturant contact with females and males.

Several studies in preschool and elementary classrooms indicate that males often receive more attention from teachers and more feedback about their performance (Jones & Wheatley, 1988; Shepardson & Pizzini, 1992). Added atten-

FIGURE 3.1 **Overcoming Gender Stereotypes**

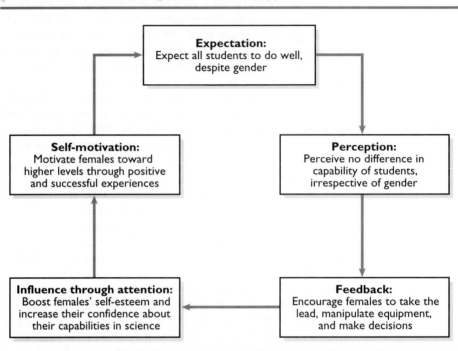

tion can bolster student beliefs about the importance of their effort and encourage them to work harder.

Step 5. Provide opportunities for success.

As children master classroom tasks, they become more motivated to strive for even higher quality. Females will undertake and excel at physical science study instead of achieving dramatically less than males do by the seventh grade.

What Can You Do to Overcome Gender Inequality in Science? Realize that gender bias begins at an early age. The younger the child when you begin to address the issue, the better your chances of having an impact. From early childhood, males are expected to be more independent, creative, and manipulative. These early experiences may affect their development of spatial and verbal abilities (Levin & Ornstein, 1983). Males have many more opportunities to experience science-oriented activities than females, although females have the interest to become more involved in science, if given the opportunity (Kahle & Lakes, 1983; Kahle & Rennie, 1993). Some things you can do to help promote gender equality in your science class include the following:

Strengthen your science preparation. Particularly if you are a female, strive to strengthen your experience with science and project the importance of science to your students. You do not want to suggest that science is not for women. Your attitude toward the subject will have a powerful effect on all the children.

Strive to become aware of your own subtle biases and different expectations for students. Examine how you assign classroom tasks and the daily life examples you use of science at work for evidence of subtle gender bias.

Experiment with single-sex class groups. Until you develop more skills at creating and maintaining a nonsexist learning environment, females may receive less biased treatment if they are not paired with males for small-group activities. Females in mixed groups have been found to spend more time than males watching and listening, whereas in same-sex groups females spend the same amount of time as males in same-sex groups on hands-on science processes and experimental tasks (Rennie & Parker, 1983; Shepardson & Pizzini, 1992).

Expect the same from females as from males. Examine your reinforcement for equality, fairness in discipline, and encouraging nonverbal behavior toward females, especially during science class. Ensure that females participate fully in all science activities.

Be aware of the difficulties some females experience when using equipment unfamiliar to them. Differences in social expectations often lead parents to give different types of toys to boys and girls and encourage different types of social interactions through games and sports. Young males are often encouraged to manipulate objects that are very similar to the tools and equipment of science. Young females may not have the same opportunities and therefore could have some initial difficulty with science equipment. A little extra time and encouragement early on will help females build their confidence so they can cope easily.

Hands-on learning is a great equalizer. Science process-oriented learning tasks help females to acquire manipulative experiences that put them on par with males, making access to science learning more equal (Humrich, 1988; Shepardson & Pizzini, 1992).

Treat science as gender free. Do not always refer to scientists as males.

Screen teaching materials. Examine all print materials and media for gender bias. Posters, textbooks, filmstrips, and other media should have equal representations of males and females.

Invite female science role models. Males will be well served too, because they will see new opportunities for females.

Help female students develop personal characteristics that are associated with success in science. Encourage them to break away from any submissive behavior patterns and encourage them to become more independent and self-reliant. Also encourage females to explore new topics and materials and to test out their new ideas and interests (Kahle & Jennie, 1993; Shepardson & Pizzini, 1992).

Anna Pollina (1995) offers specific actions in Table 3.3 to help you bring gender balance to your science lessons.

TABLE 3.3   **Bringing Gender Balance to Your Science Lessons**

Despite change efforts for more than a decade, females are greatly underrepresented in fields such as physical sciences, engineering, and technology. Past efforts that have attempted to increase female involvement in the sciences ranged from awareness programs in elementary schools to direct intervention at the collegiate level. Often the change efforts attempted to "masculinize" the females—to help them participate in the sciences by becoming more aggressive, more analytical, emotionally tougher, and more competitive. These efforts yielded spurious results; decreases in female self-esteem were recorded. Anna Pollina reports ten recent successful and proven strategies, based on research, that celebrate the characteristics that many females bring to science, which are vital to science and science education.

1. *Connect science and technology to the real world.* Connecting any subject to the lives of real people and the good of the world is a powerful hook for females.

2. *Choose metaphors carefully, and have students develop their own.* In the past we have asked females to "tackle" problems, used "batting averages" to illustrate points, and have used the "paths of rockets" to demonstrate principles of physics. Use images of science that are more comfortable for females. This is more than political correctness—it is essential.

3. *Foster an atmosphere of collaboration.* Turn taking in small groups of circled students is not collaboration. Small groups work for females if all group members are taught to listen, be respectful, be noncompetitive, and are held responsible for one another's learning.

4. *Encourage females to act as experts.* Females begin to see themselves as scientists when the group is responsible for verifying its own logic, and when the students are responsible for critiquing their own work as well as the work of their peers.

5. *Give females the opportunity to be in control of technology.* Expect females to share in the uses of technology, to demonstrate its uses to others, to complete basic repairs, and to deal with simple emergencies.

6. *Portray technology as a way to solve problems.* Females most often use technology as a tool rather than as a toy. One way to help them see that technology is relevant to their lives is to emphasize the networking and communications capabilities. Pairing females can help to create a comfortable, supportive way to use the technology.

7. *Capitalize on females' verbal strengths.* Encourage all students to express the logic for their choices and solutions in spoken, written, or picture form. Proofs should be well-constructed, complete arguments.

8. *Experiment with testing and evaluation.* Embedded assessments work well for females. These are alternatives to right/wrong choices and make use of females' abilities to synthesize material, make connections, and use their practical intelligence. Some examples could be working in groups to perform experiments, identify patterns, hypothesize outcomes.

9. *Give frequent feedback, and keep expectations high.* Females may tend to need more encouragement than males in science. You can do this by giving frequent feedback such as homework checks, quizzes, and comments that reinforce the students' beliefs in their control over the material.

10. *Experiment with note-taking techniques.* Females are dutiful learners who can become so absorbed in the task of note taking that they miss opportunities to become involved in important discussions. Try "no-note-taking-allowed" times, distribute written summaries, or have diagrams and figures on file for learners to access when they are needed.

Source: A. Pollina, "Gender Balance: Lessons from Girls in Science and Mathematics," *Educational Leadership 53,* 1 (1995): 30–33.

Similarities in Learning

Children from other cultures or who are not English speakers benefit from specific management and teaching techniques. The recommendations we have offered reveal some similarities. Indeed, most children can benefit from the suggestions recommended for special groups of learners. Children benefit when they are taught with the learning styles they prefer.

Learning Styles.   The concept of learning styles arises from the general acceptance that we all learn in a variety of ways, that those ways can be identified, and that teachers can teach in ways that capitalize on student preferences. If they begin from a position of strength (preferred learning style), learners can be exposed to other ways of learning and expand their repertoires as they overcome weaknesses.

Teaching to accommodate different learning styles helps teachers reach each individual. Students who need special assistance receive instruction through their preferred learning style during the intervention process. Children learn about how they learn and are encouraged to use their strengths. All benefit from the variety of approaches. Teachers also plan instruction carefully to make certain that all children have an opportunity to learn through their own preferred styles.

Types of Styles.   Learning styles are often classified by function. As learners, we have different modes of perception, we prefer various environments, we are motivated by different things, we express ourselves uniquely, we think differently, and we prefer various levels of mobility as we learn. True individualiza-

Children perceive in different ways and prefer various learning environments.

tion is a challenge. At least nine learning styles can be identified by function (Dunn & Dunn, 1975):

1. *Visual*—prefer to perceive by seeing words, numbers, charts, models, objects, and so on.
2. *Auditory*—prefer to perceive meaning by hearing.
3. *Bodily kinesthetic*—prefer to be involved, hands on.
4. *Individual learners*—prefer to work alone. This type of student may be more confident in his or her own opinion than in the ideas of others.
5. *Group learners*—prefer to learn with at least one other child.
6. *Oral expressive*—can easily tell or explain their ideas and opinions. They may know more than they can reveal on a test.
7. *Written expressive*—write fluent essays or good answers on tests. Their thoughts are organized better on paper than they are presented orally.
8. *Sequential*—have the ability to arrange thoughts and ideas in a linear, organized fashion.
9. *Global*—have the ability to be spontaneous, flexible thinkers. These learners may be quiet and intuitive and order their thoughts randomly, preferring to do things their own way.

All learners do not fit exclusively into one style. Many may share strong preferences among several styles. All students can be served better when learning opportunities are provided in multisensory, multiexpressive, and multienvironmental modes. The following suggestions can help a wide variety of learners, particularly those who have special needs.

Establish classroom and study routines. Many children are unable to organize unaided, and traditional school learning cannot occur until organization is established. You can provide a helpful model for children if you are well organized and consistent in your classroom. Children will then know what to do and how to do it.

Limit choices. Democratic learning and cooperative learning encourage choices, but this approach may not help children who get confused easily. Asking "Would you like to . . ." implies choice. As an example, if your intention is to have a child put science equipment back on the storage shelf or follow a specific instruction, it is better for the child if your instructions are explicit and/or provide limited choices.

Make certain the children are attending to what is going on. Asking students to repeat instructions or information, requesting a response to a specific question, requiring that a child complete a specific motor task, and maintaining eye contact are some ways to determine the extent to which a child may be attending to what is going on around him or her. Focus on each child often.

Give clues to help remembering. Use mnemonic devices, rhymes, auditory associations, linking associations, and visual clues to help the child remember. Help the children construct personal memory devices.

Sequence instruction carefully. Concept mapping and task analysis can help you to find the most logical sequence of any task. The four Ws help to begin a task analysis: *what* to teach, *where* to begin, *when* the objective has been met, and *what* to teach next. Figure 3.2 provides a more detailed model for analyzing and determining the sequence for science concepts.

Separate teaching and testing. Worksheet assignments may seem to the students more like a test than the type of reinforcement activity you may intend. Provide instructional assistance to encourage learning and to help lower the failure rate. An example at the top of a worksheet or a list of guiding questions can transform the assignment from a test into a learning task. Also provide models, cues, verbal and written prompts, and correct answers as feedback.

Be specific with criticism and praise. Tell the child exactly why the response is correct or wrong. Telling the child to try number two again will cause him or her to change an answer, but he or she will not know what to change. When part of the answer is correct, tell the child; also identify what is not correct.

Provide time clues. Some children may have difficulty remembering time sequences, estimating time intervals, and determining the amount of time needed to complete tasks. By routinely displaying schedules in prominent places and referring to time in the classroom, you can help students learn to structure their school work.

Confer with special education teachers, second-language teachers, and gifted and talented coordinators. Continuity of content and consistency of management and routines help many children. Coordinate your classroom activities with those of other classes the child attends.

Show empathy, encouragement, sensitivity, and understanding for each child's attempts to learn, to remember, and to conform to your routines. Point out the child's abilities and respect the child as a human being.

Provide kinesthetic experiences, practical hands-on learning activities with concrete, relevant materials. Children who are experience-deficient will benefit, as will children who prefer this type of learning. Hands-on experiences stimulate minds-on learning.

Identify desired behaviors, set clear expectations, and reduce distractions.

Simplify. Break each task down into its simplest steps; assist the students with step-by-step instructions.

Give frequent feedback. Small improvements deserve praise, and precise direction helps children continue to improve.

Use the preferred learning mode. If the child has a dominant mode of learning (visual, tactile, auditory), use it. Regard the preference as a strength and try to build success on it. Then use this preference to help build self-esteem on successes before tackling learning weaknesses.

SCIENCE FOR EXCEPTIONAL CHILDREN

Public Law 94–142 of 1975 (the Education for All Handicapped Children Act) is part of a federal law (Individuals with Disabilities Education Act, IDEA) that helps ensure a place for students with disabilities in American public schools. The law requires that every student with a disability must be provided an

FIGURE 3.2   Concept Analysis Model for Teaching Children with Special Needs

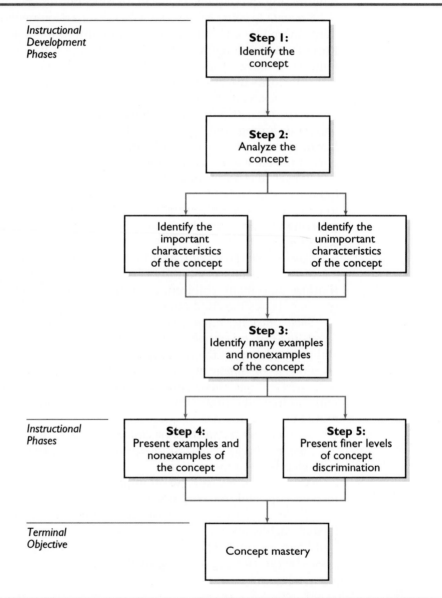

Source: Adapted from "Concept Analysis: A Model for Teaching Basic Science Concepts to Intellectually Handicapped Students" by Jack T. Cole, Margie K. Kitano, and Lewis M. Brown in Marshall E. Corrick, Jr. (Ed.), *Teaching Handicapped Students* (Washington, DC: NEA, 1981), p. 52. Reprinted with permission.

appropriate education in the least restrictive environment possible. The law includes nine specific categories of disability: deafness, hearing impairment, mental retardation, orthopedic impairment, other health impairment, serious emotional disturbance, specific learning disability, speech impairment, and visual impairment.

The "least restrictive environment" provision requires that whenever possible students with disabilities be educated in regular classrooms. Students with disabilities who are included in regular classrooms are placed there because it has been determined to be the most appropriate environment for them. These decisions are based on extensive assessment, parental consent, and decision making among school personnel that must follow due process of law.

The presence of students with disabilities in regular classrooms does not mean that the curriculum must be the same for all children. Federal law states that the schooling of children with disabilities must be differentiated according to their special needs and provided with necessary support. This may require a degree of individualized education not usually found in typical classrooms. The Individualized Education Program (IEP) prescribes goals for the school year based on present performance levels, specific educational services the school must provide, the extent to which the student participates in the regular classroom, and schedules and procedures for evaluation. Indeed, many educators believe the intent of the IEP benefits all children. Table 3.4 provides a brief description of adaptations that help students who have special needs.

Teaching Children Who Have Learning Disabilities

A child with a learning disability has the intellectual potential to succeed in school. But for some reason, the child's academic achievements are significantly below the expected level of performance in a specific subject such as reading or mathematics.

What Is a Learning Disability?

A child can be identified as having a learning disability if a school evaluation team finds a severe discrepancy between the child's achievement and intellectual ability in one or more of seven areas: oral expression, listening comprehension, written expression, basic reading skill, reading comprehension, mathematics calculation, and mathematics reasoning (U.S. Office of Education, 1975). The child may perform at or above the expected level in some school subjects but poorly in others. When this happens it is especially frustrating for the child and makes identification of the disability difficult. The child may develop failure-avoidance techniques that surface as behavior problems to draw attention away from areas of academic failure.

Nearly 5 percent of school-age children have learning disabilities. Perhaps 5 to 10 million children today may have some type of learning disability. The numbers have increased over time, in part because of greater sensitivity in assessment and diagnosis and teacher alertness for possible learning disabilities.

◆ **TABLE 3.4   Teaching Children Who Have Special Needs**

Special Need	Environmental Adaptation	Materials Adaptation	Teaching Adaptation	Assessment Adaptation
Cultural	Carefully select visuals and non-print materials for cultural inclusion. Represent plural culture. Maintain clear classroom organization. Establish empathic relationships.	Use culturally representative materials. Avoid cultural stereotypes. Use broad themes to include all cultures.	Set explicit expectations, and give explicit instructions. Use divergent questions to encourage pluralism and inclusion. Challenge inaccurate statements. Include careful consideration of issues. Use experience-rich methods.	Provide and accept diverse contexts for assessment activities.
Non-English–speaking	Be patient. Use visual aids to help communicate. Provide direct experience. Encourage high levels of activity.	Maintain a conceptual focus. Enrich vocabulary development.	Be verbally clear. Maintain written clarity; use outlines. Emphasize concepts. Link concepts to experiences. Use guest speakers and field trips. Reduce test anxiety.	Encourage the use of pocket translators and dictionaries. Use pictorial assessment devices, puzzles, and performance tasks.
Gender	Nurture independence and self-confidence. Use hands-on learning activities. Use female role models in the sciences.	Identify and eliminate gender bias in materials. Use a wide variety of manipulatives.	Experiment with heterogeneous and single-sex grouping. Use cooperative learning techniques. Maintain high but realistic expectations for all. Provide frequent progress feedback.	None
Learning style preferences	Include all styles.	Select a balance of visual, auditory, kinesthetic, oral, and written materials.	Provide activities to match preference for individual, group, sequential, visual, verbal, auditory, and global learners.	Assess concepts through verbal, written, kinesthetic, individual, and group opportunities.

Special Need	Environmental Adaptation	Materials Adaptation	Teaching Adaptation	Assessment Adaptation
Learning disability	Show empathy. Focus attention. Seat away from distractions.	Use concrete manipulatives. Screen out irrelevant materials and distractions.	Show clear expectations. Simplify; give cues and specific praise. Use dominant learning mode and multisensory activities. Use concept analysis.	Provide specific criticism and praise. Try oral tests. Modify reading and writing exercises if needed.
Intellectual	Limit visual and verbal distractions.	Select appropriate reading level. Use concrete, relevant manipulatives.	Use concept analysis. Simplify. Praise. Use repetition. Maintain eye contact. Engage in physical activity. Give feedback, use cues, cooperative learning. Use examples and nonexamples. Use brief periods of direct instruction.	Verbal tests. Provide assistance with written tests. Provide small-step progress checks.
Visual	Provide clear, predictable traffic pathways. Maintain organized, predictable locations for materials and storage. Provide good lighting. Seat student near activity. Sighted student tutor can assist.	Use voice tapes and audiotapes. Print materials should be large, clear, and uncluttered with numerous colors and geometric designs. Adapt materials to special equipment students may have to use.	Emphasize uses of other senses. Taped instructions or science information can be provided. Pair with sighted students.	More verbal assessment. Assist with written assessment. Assist with physical manipulation of objects during performance assessment.

(continued)

TABLE 3.4 *(continued)*

Special Need	Environmental Adaptation	Materials Adaptation	Teaching Adaptation	Assessment Adaptation
Hearing	Seat so vision is not obstructed. Seat away from distracting background noises.	Modify for making observations through other senses. Use captioned films and videos. Use printed text to accompany audiotapes. Model or illustrate spoken instructions.	Face the child when speaking. Speak distinctly; do not shout. Use written outlines.	Avoid spoken forms of assessment.
Orthopedic	Identify and remove physical barriers. Provide adequate space for movement. Seat near exits for safety. Check tables and desks for proper height.	Identify devices that assist handling of objects, such as spring-loaded tongs, accountant's pencil grips, test tube racks.	Encourage physical manipulation of objects. Pair with nonimpaired student peer. Provide student training time with equipment prior to use.	Provide assistance with writing and manipulation of materials.
Behavior	Seat away from distractions. Provide well-lighted quiet space for study.	Train in use prior to providing special equipment.	Use brief activities. Give praise and cues. Reinforce desired behaviors. Obtain attention and establish eye contact prior to discussion or giving instructions.	None
Gifted	None	Advanced reading materials. Greater application of technology.	Emphasize problem solving. Accelerate pace. Arrange mentorships. Emphasize processes, mathematics, and uses of technology.	Increase expectations for analysis, application, and hypotheses. Use open-ended assessment devices.

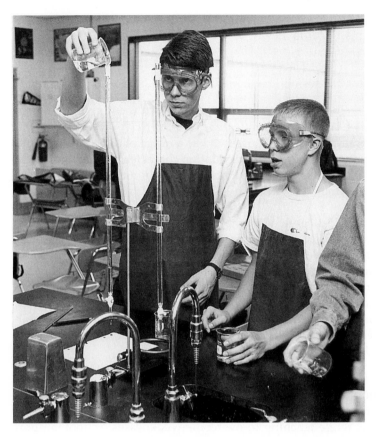

Exceptional children learn science with the proper type of support and encouragement.

Nationwide, nearly 30 percent of the students who receive special education services attend regular classrooms (Smith & Luckasson, 1992).

Learning disabilities are not diseases. There is no single learning disability. Disabilities include dysgraphia, disorders in written language; dyscalculia, disorders in arithmetic; dyslexia, disorders in receptive and expressive language and reading; and difficulties in perception of spatial relations and organization. Some famous people who have had learning disabilities include Thomas Edison, Albert Einstein, Winston Churchill, Cher, and Tom Cruise.

How Can You Help a Child with Learning Disabilities? Structure is the most important concept when teaching children with learning disabilities. These children have perceptual and cognitive difficulties that may make it impossible for children to mask out unnecessary stimuli such as sights and sounds in the background of the classroom. Ways to promote structure include class and study routines, limited choices, focused attention, memory clues, sequenced instruction, clear distinctions between instruction and testing, specific criticism and praise, time clues, conferences with special education teachers, and empathy and encouragement (Coble, Levey, & Mattheis, 1985).

Teaching Children Who Have Intellectual Disabilities

Some children in your classes will have intellectual disabilities, also referred to as *mental retardation.*

Who Are the Children Who Have Intellectual Disabilities?

There are different categories of mental retardation, and each has a range of different functions the child is expected to achieve. Mental retardation characterizes approximately 25 percent of the total population of students with disabilities, and of that portion nearly one third may be successful in regular classrooms (Charles & Malian, 1980).

Children with a mild degree of mental retardation may be mainstreamed into your classroom. Their IQs can range from 52 to 67 on the Stanford-Binet test. *Educable mentally retarded* (EMR) is the term used to describe this level of intelligence. The American Association of Mental Deficiency describes children who have mental retardation as having subaverage intelligence and being deficient in behavior and responsibility for their age-related cultural group. These limitations affect academic and motor skills. Children with intellectual disabilities are capable of learning some academics, acquiring social skills, and developing occupational skills.

How Can You Teach Children Who Have Intellectual Disabilities?

Peer acceptance is very important for the child with an intellectual disability. By acquiring as much information as you can about the child, you can prepare to emphasize strengths while teaching to overcome weaknesses. School support services and special education personnel can make situation-specific suggestions to assist any particular child. However, the recommendations in Table 3.4 can help you enhance the child's academic skills.

Concept analysis is a strategy that has great potential for teaching science to children who have intellectual or learning disabilities as well as children who are not disabled. See Figure 3.2 for a visual guide to the five distinct steps of concept analysis (Cole, Kitano, & Brown, 1981).

Step 1. Identify the concept.

Select the main idea to be taught.

Step 2. Analyze the concept.

Identify the concept's critical attributes (characteristics that make the concept different from others) and its noncritical attributes.

Step 3. Identify several examples and nonexamples of the concept.

Examples illustrate the critical attributes, and nonexamples do not contain the attributes.

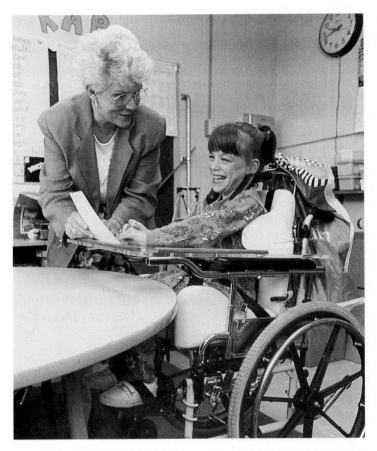

Help children to overcome barriers to learning science.

Step 4. Present the examples and nonexamples of the concept.

Use a variety of media and hands-on experiences to present the examples of the concept and to expose the children to nonexamples as well. The examples should be used to help children identify other examples that you have not identified for them. Comparisons with the nonexamples help to identify the attributes and nonattributes and help children transfer their learning to other situations.

Step 5. Present finer levels of discrimination.

A funnel approach can be used to move the children from making simple discriminations to more difficult comparisons.

Teaching Children Who Have Physical Disabilities

Physical disabilities include visual, hearing, and orthopedic impairments. Conservative estimates suggest that 1 percent of school children may have visual impairments, and hearing and orthopedic impairments may affect 6 and 5 percent, respectively (Charles & Malian, 1980).

What Barriers Do Children with Physical Disabilities Face?   Although few in number, children with physical disabilities carry huge burdens that limit their access to science education. Most of these burdens arise from the barriers the children encounter, such as

- parents and school advisers who limit the children through stereotypes and low expectations,
- classroom structures that limit accessibility and reduce exposure to tactile manipulative experiences that are critical to basic learning in science,
- science programs that have not been modified or adapted to meet the needs of children who have physical impairments,
- teachers who may harbor fearful or negative attitudes or who may treat the children in an overly protective or cautious manner (Stefanich, 1985, pp. 8–9).

Why Is Science Important for Children Who Are Physically Disabled?   Science instruction should begin at an early age and continue throughout schooling for physically disabled children. The National Science Board Commission on Precollege Education in Mathematics, Science, and Technology (1983, p. 27) offers three reasons for this early and sustained education in science:

1. Science emphasizes hands-on experience and exploration of the environment. It can help to fill some experiential gaps that may have evolved because of extensive hospital stays and/or overprotectiveness of schools or parents. Science can help to develop the individual's independence and overall positive self-image.

2. Recent scientific and technological advances have provided tools such as computers, talking calculators, control systems, versabraille hook-ups to computers, and special telephone systems. These advances can help to mitigate the limitations imposed by a physical disability and can enable the individuals to become independent, contributing members of society. Science instruction that emphasizes making observations, collecting and organizing information, and making conclusions can help develop the individual's mental and manipulative readiness for using new technology.

3. Job opportunities in the future will require greater knowledge and understanding of technological devices. Computers will continue to be an important part of many jobs. Advances in technology have helped children with physical disabilities learn and provide new employment opportunities for them. Children with physical disabilities will need the background, training, and self-confidence to seek these opportunities.

Visual Impairments.   Children who are *educationally blind* and *partially sighted* are increasingly benefiting from regular education experiences. The educationally blind cannot read printed materials and must learn from voice, audio tapes, braille reading, and other forms of nonprinted materials. They may have residual vision and should be encouraged to use it as widely as possible. Children who are partially sighted can read printed materials, but that material must be larger than standard school print. Magnifying devices can also be used to enlarge standard print.

Children with severe vision problems are identified at an early age. However, less severe problems often go undetected for years. Regular classroom teachers may be the first to notice sight problems. Some behaviors that may indicate vision loss include squinting at the chalkboard, holding a book closer or farther away than most other children, blinking or otherwise distorting the eyes, holding the head at an odd angle, and unusual sensitivity to light. Refer all children who demonstrate any of these behaviors to the school official who can arrange a vision screening. Parents and children appreciate early notification.

Teaching Children with Visual Impairments. An audio-tactile teaching approach helps children who have visual impairments. Verbal lessons can be audiotaped for later playback, written assignments and tests can be tape-recorded, and a personal recorder with headphones can be used by children who are educationally blind without disturbing the rest of the class. (Be certain to provide verbal or tape-recorded feedback about answers too.) Magnified print materials and visual aids with high contrast can help children who are partially sighted.

Science process skills (Chapter 1) can provide helpful tactile experiences for the student with a visual impairment. Tactile experiences that require more than passive participation include:

- modeling various birds and habitats with clay
- illustrating the carbon cycle of a forest with papier maché
- constructing leaf print books from old newspapers
- designing constellations by constructing paper stars
- illustrating a food chain by using natural objects
- designing cloud formations from cotton balls
- building bridges and other structures using drinking straws
- building a replica of a coral reef
- illustrating an electromagnetic wave by using iron filings and magnets
- constructing replicas of prehistoric tools (Harris, 1981, p. 40).

Instruction that stimulates the greatest range of senses (multimodal instruction) is vital for children with physical impairments. Commercial materials exist and may be modified to assist the student who is visually impaired. Programs such as the Elementary Science Study and Science: A Process Approach II have been used with over 3 million students. Teacher supplements are available with suggestions for modifications for students with disabilities.

Adapting Science Materials for the Blind (ASMB) was developed from two Science Curriculum Improvement Study units for use with visually impaired children in mainstreamed classrooms. Science Activities for the Visually Impaired (SAVI) have been designed especially for middle-level children.

Pair children with visual disabilities with sighted children. Several researchers have found that this approach enables the child with a visual impairment to achieve on par with their nondisabled peers. The sighted member of a team can translate the class experiences to the child with a visual disability, who can obtain an understanding through other senses. Together both can report the results of an experiment or activity. The team pairing approach has shown outstanding promise (Brown, 1979).

Hearing Impairments.   *Deaf* and *hard of hearing* are two types of hearing impairments. Regular classroom teachers occasionally work with children who have profound hearing losses, but more often have students with some lesser degree of hearing loss. Common types of hearing impairments concern volume and pitch. Another type is intelligibility—the volume of a sound may be adequate, but it is garbled. Hearing aids, lipreading, expressions, and gestures help the child with a hearing disability succeed in the regular classroom.

Deafness is often identified early in childhood, but mild hearing losses frequently go undetected. The following behaviors may signal a hearing impairment that should be referred to school personnel for screening: odd positioning of the head while listening, inattention during discussions, often asking the speaker to repeat, and asking classmates for instructions.

Teaching Children Who Have Hearing Impairments.   Language development is one of the major problems for the hearing impaired. Direct experience with objects is essential if children are to develop language sufficiently, and objects from a child's environment enhance learning of scientific concepts. When we provide rich experiences, children who have hearing impairments can improve

> language performance, observing and listening skills, vocabulary, the learning of science concepts and development of cognitive skills through direct experiential experiences in science. In order for this learning to occur, students must have the opportunity of "doing science" by hands-on, inquiry, real-life experiences through direct physical manipulation of objects that focus attention on patterns of interaction in physical and biological systems. The pairing or coupling of handicapped and nonhandicapped children also seems to be an effective means for students to learn science (Brown, 1979, p. 89).

Observations students must make can be adapted. For example, auditory observations may be changed to visual observations, as in the case of the sounds made by different sizes of tuning forks. Have the child transfer the sound wave to water or sand and compare what happens as an alternative to hearing. Other techniques teachers can use are similar to those used for multilingual children, including seating the child near the front of the room so vision is not obstructed, looking directly at the child and obtaining his or her attention before speaking, shaving beards or mustaches so lips are visible for the student's lipreading, speaking loudly and distinctly without shouting, pairing students, and using a written outline for activities that require several steps.

Orthopedic Impairments.   Orthopedic impairments are disabilities caused by diseases and deformities of the muscles, joints, and skeletal system. Examples include cerebral palsy, spina bifida, amputations, birth defects, arthritis, and muscular dystrophy. Temporary injuries are not addressed by Public Law 94-142 because they can be corrected. A child with an orthopedic impairment may require an appliance such as a wheel chair, walker, crutches, or skeletal braces.

Teaching Children with Orthopedic Disabilities.   Generally, the way an orthopedically disabled child learns is not affected. Adjustments are more physical than educational. Be aware of and attempt to remove physical and psychological barriers in your classroom. Examine the curriculum materials and activities and modify them to include the child with a disability without sacrificing their purpose or science content. Do not underestimate the capabilities of the child. Become familiar with the function and maintenance of any appliance the child uses.

Teaching Learners Who Are Gifted and Talented

Children who are gifted or talented are not protected by Public Law 94-142. However, gifted or talented children do have special needs that are not usually served well by the instruction given to most children. Gifted and talented children are included in this chapter because most teachers have children of this type in their classrooms, and authorities have questioned the wisdom of pulling gifted children out of the regular classroom for special instruction. Like children with disabilities or cultural differences, gifted and talented children

> require a balanced view of humanity, and they must prepare to work and live in the greater society. This preparation can best be accomplished within the regular classroom. This does not imply that curriculum, materials, and instruction for the gifted should be the same as for the nongifted. What it does imply is that the gifted, like everyone else, should be considered individuals, with unique needs and abilities. Their education should attend specifically to those needs and abilities (Charles & Malian, 1980, p. 181).

Who Are Gifted and Talented Learners?   Children who are gifted and/or talented show promise of making superior progress in school. These children may demonstrate advanced progress in academic achievement in a school subject or exceptional ability and creativity in the arts. Their special talents are observed and may be verified by achievement and IQ tests or superior performance in a

What Is Science Integration through Inclusion?

by Najwa Abdul Tawwab
Grade 2 Teacher, Oliver Wendell Holmes School, Dorchester, MA

The integration model of the newly opened Oliver Wendell Homes School in Boston promises an exciting, creative, inclusive model to teaching science and integrating special-need children who have mild to moderate learning and behavior difficulties. These twenty children attend full-day classes. Fourteen of the children receive regular education, and six have special needs. Each child has strengths and weaknesses that must be addressed in this classroom setting for optimal learning to occur.

Oliver Wendell Holmes is a science-based school. For me, science on the primary level of instruction is not a complicated process. Imagination, enthusiasm, excitement, and clear and logical thinking are crucial. I look at science instruction as basic as reading, writing, and mathematics. For my special education students it is one of the few ways in which their varied disabilities now become a strength. Science-based instruction allows all of our students to consider themselves observers, experimenters, investigators, and questioners. Most of all they become risk takers.

The process of scientific thinking mandated that one must ask questions and develop hypotheses through repeated practice or experiments or by just looking at something over time. When we made rock crystals, we expected the solution to harden in three weeks. We clearly learned the value of patience and perseverance as it took our solutions three months to solidify. Those of us who shook the solution or stuck our fingers in it quickly found out how variables affect the scientific process.

My focus is not one specific area of science. It is my job to prepare my student to love and be curious about all branches of science as they move up the ladder of education. In time, answers come, and they come from everyone, not just the teacher. Through this process I have found that the weak links in my special education students now have become their strengths. An observer of these twenty children would find it hard to determine who is or is not special education. My children have begun to develop consistency, patience and perseverance. Most important, I see the light of self-confidence, which was ever so dim, now growing brighter and stronger. They are prepared to believe in their own ability to grasp and understand new concepts. They are also discovering techniques that help them see their own problems, claim ownership of them, and move on to solve them. Could there be a better approach to problem solving?

A Team Approach to Developing Units

Our philosophy is based on inclusion in the broadest sense. Once I have determined my theme, I call a team meeting. I invite parents, the educational team leader, an occupational therapist, an adaptive physical education specialist, a speech therapist, and art and music teachers. I also approach faculty from colleges that have partnerships with our school. All of these people are invaluable assets to the development and exe-

subject or artistic area. In addition, gifted children may demonstrate other traits such as sensitivity to the needs of other children, a need for independence, a predisposition for expression, a capacity for social leadership, broad interests in different school areas, apparent natural talents in the arts, and such noticeable behaviors as intensity, persistence, self-assured introversion, or detachment from what they believe are mundane topics.

cution of a project. We explore discussions, activities, and materials that will allow all students to discover the connections between what they already know and the various science topics to be studied. We plan how I can integrate science with other areas of the curriculum.

Each participant recommends resources, approaches, and projects that will address objectives outlined in the individualized education programs. All team participants spend time in the class observing and taking ethnographic notes that will be discussed later during planning periods. The service providers bring their skills into the classroom. They work in small groups as well as with the entire class. This integration model does not support pull-out programs. Inclusion is the number-one priority. These team members are all part of my class in spirit, content, and approach. Our school motto is, "It takes an entire community to educate our children."

Are the Connections Being Made?

I believe this is a question that remains with all educators. We don't need to look at process, assessment, learning styles, and inclusion. These are areas that I have attempted to address. Any strong school of education's science department can give you content. How do you as an educator know that you are reaching and serving the diverse children in front of you?

My science themes are based on the seasons. That leaves a lot of territory to be covered. The children sitting in front of me have an abundance of academic, social and behavioral needs. My neediest child requires the services of all the itinerant people assigned to the school. His short attention span, weak muscle tone, poor social skills, and limited writing ability force me to provide lessons that are intellectually challenging, require minimum writing, coloring, or sitting, and allow lots of movement about the room. For those children who have cultural, ethnic, and geographical ties around the world, our approach to the seasons transcends typical gender and race stereotypes. Our school librarian helps by reading and providing books that meet our needs. Our public librarian will make visits to share cultural and seasonal activities. Science is all about learning, questioning, discovering, and sharing. It's also about brainstorming and taking these ideas, experiments, and observations and writing and publishing our own chapter in the biggest science book in the world: the creation and nature.

Last but not least, for those children who have volcanic, eruptive behaviors periodically because they don't feel they are equal to their peers, a science discovery assisted by a caring parent, an inquisitive college professor, or the calmest child in the class often proves to be a remedy. Science points out to them that there are many beautiful, positive ways for them to be discovered or noticed. It gives them a chance to say, "Look at me—notice and discover the wonders in me too."

Children who are gifted and talented have a wide range of possible characteristics. This range makes it difficult to generalize about all gifted children. Gifted and talented children can represent a tremendous challenge to the elementary science teacher.

Academically gifted children may appear to become easily bored with instruction offered to the rest of the class. If you have not majored in science, you may have some anxiety about having a scientifically gifted child in your class. Fear not. Feeling unprepared in science should not stop you from teaching gifted children. Perhaps your anxiety will be eased if you can keep the issue in perspective. Remember that you are an adult who teaches children, and the experiences of adulthood provide advantages when working with the student who is gifted. Despite all the knowledge a young gifted learner may have, he or she is still an elementary or middle school student, and the student's social, emotional, physical, psychological, and cognitive development is not complete. As an adult, you still have much to offer. All learners enjoy seeing their teacher get excited about their students' work. Having a gifted child in your science class is reason to rejoice and will give you a wonderful opportunity to become a real facilitator and guide rather than a messenger.

Teaching Learners Who Are Gifted and Talented   Children who are gifted in science often are capable of accelerated and more detailed learning. You can en-

When encouraged and supported, exceptional children can overcome exceptional challenges.

rich their experiences by encouraging them to pursue the subject to a greater depth. You may also accelerate their instruction by drawing on topics from advanced grades or by arranging for the child to work with a mentor (perhaps an older student, another teacher, or a science career professional) on special science topics. It is not uncommon for gifted students to perform two or three years above grade level in the subject or area where they show talent (Piburn & Enyeart, 1985). Therefore, more flexibility in written assignments and higher expectations for verbal communication are necessary. Try having gifted learners engage in more speculation about scientific events, hypothesize, and develop arguments and counterarguments that pertain to scientific/social issues. Have gifted learners demonstrate the application of science as well as the relationships between science and material learned in other subjects. The following teaching strategies are often appropriate for gifted learners.

Develop open-ended learning activities. Whereas children who have learning and intellectual disabilities benefit from narrowly focused, sequential activities, children who are gifted should be challenged to develop their intellectual reasoning through open-ended activities that have many possible outcomes. These activities avoid step-by-step recipe procedures and do not have predetermined results. Several of the cooperative inquiry teaching methods of Chapter 9 and the tools of questioning in Chapter 10 are useful when working with gifted learners.

Use the gifted students as classroom leaders. These children may become reliable informal teachers of their peers who can greatly enhance the classroom atmosphere. Children who are gifted can also be used as resource persons, researchers, science assistants, and community ambassadors for exciting school programs.

Use technology, science processes, and mathematics. Scientific observation can be enhanced through mathematics. Encourage gifted children to use higher forms of mathematics and statistics as often as possible. Engage them in more precise measures and more extensive uses of science process skills. Technology will challenge gifted students to expand research capabilities as well as quantify and communicate their scientific findings.

Reinforce and reward superior efforts. Some school programs for gifted and talented children use pull-out approaches: learners are placed in special programs or given accelerated instruction. Mainstreaming can also benefit children who are gifted. Adaptations of science content and changes in instruction with more options for the gifted learners can provide suitable instruction in the regular classroom. Science content adaptations could include emphasizing higher levels of thinking, abstraction, and independent thinking. The challenge is fundamentally the same as with any other child: Help the child learn how to learn. Reinforcement and rewards for effort and work well done are usually all that is necessary to help gifted children keep their high level of motivation for learning. Some suggestions for reinforcing and rewarding superior effort include

WHAT RESEARCH SAYS

Teaching Exceptional Students

Who has the wisdom and ability to predict which of our students will succeed and which will not? People with disabilities are often erroneously thought to be mentally deficient, but the prevailing social attitude is slowly changing. Thanks to federal laws, inclusion, and local school efforts to service better the special needs of children are greater than at any time in the history of schooling. All children are given more encouragement and are provided with more opportunities to achieve their full potential.

After decades of turning away students with disabilities, universities are now accepting them for scientific career training. A three-year survey by the American Association for the Advancement of Science reported a resource group of more than 700 scientists with disabilities. People with disabilities *can* do science. But our schools still must do more. Robert Menchel, a senior physicist for the Xerox Corporation who has been deaf since the age of 7, has visited many schools. He says:

> The lack of development of a basic science curriculum from kindergarten to the twelfth grade is a national disgrace and one that puts the deaf child at a disadvantage in comparison to the nonhandicapped child.

Furthermore, these students are still being pushed into stereotyped job roles and dead-end jobs. For the female students it is even worse.

Robert Hoffman, a researcher who has cerebral palsy, speaks about the effects of isolation due to a disability:

> When one is born with a disability severe enough so society shoves him into a special program (which non-handicapped people develop), one becomes separated from "normal" persons. All through his school years, he learns from other disabled students, and the teachers design studies to fit the limitations of his physical handicap.

John Gavin, a research scientist with a physical impairment, cautions those who have no apparent disability:

> One of the least desirable traits of the human condition is our propensity to avoid those among us who are afflicted with overt physical disabilities. While this may be an inherent psychological carryover from those days of survival of the fittest, it is more likely we do not wish to have a reminder that we are potentially and continually eligible to join them.

---

public recognition for effort, extra credit or waiver of standard assignments, positive teacher comments, extra leadership opportunities and/or classroom responsibilities, and encouraging students to do real research projects.

Provide extra- or cocurricular learning opportunities. Your classroom will have limited teaching resources, and your time will also have limits. Out-of-class or out-of-school learning options may also help the gifted student continue to learn science. Use community library resources or make arrangements for the child to do special work at a community college or nearby university. Develop and utilize community resource personnel: Construct a network of science-related resource people and arrange mentor-intern relationships. Start a science club for students with special interests. Begin an after-school science lab—encourage the learners to design and pursue experiments. Student teachers or field experience interns from a nearby university may be able to assist with the science lab instruction and programming.

Teachers become the key. A caring teacher with a positive can-do attitude is consistently ranked highly by children with disabilities. Teachers who care seem to expect that their students can learn at a high level. These teachers try to see that all children fulfill the high expectations held for them.

Language development is one of the major problems of children with hearing impairments. Researchers report that direct experience with objects is essential and that utilization of objects from a child's environment enhances his or her learning of concepts.

The most significant changes needed for teaching children who have visual impairments are related to the adaptation of educational materials and equipment to take advantage of each child's residual vision.

Children who are orthopedically disabled are a heterogeneous group, and it is difficult to prescribe general methods and adaptations that will serve *each* child well. However, pairing a child with an orthopedic impairment with a child with no disabilities helps both. The child who is impaired still needs direct physical experience with the science phenomena to the greatest extent possible. For example,

> a magnet can be taped to the arm or leg. Another student can bring objects in contact with the magnets. The child should be able to feel and see which objects interact with the magnet and which do not. In this way, the child [with a disability] is involved in the decision making and discovery that is the major emphasis of [the] lesson.

Dean Brown's research shows that children with physical disabilities can learn to understand science concepts and that they can develop higher levels of reasoning skills if given the opportunity. Children with disabilities need direct, experiential, sensory experiences in science. Many researchers repeatedly express the need for doing science through hands-on, inquiry-based, real-life experiences.

Source: Adapted from the literature review by Dean R. Brown, "Helping Handicapped Youngsters Learn by 'Doing,' " in Mary Budd Rowe (Ed.), *What Research Says to the Science Teacher*, Washington, D.C.: National Science Teachers Association (1979), 2: 80–100.

HOW CAN PARENTS HELP MEET CHILDREN'S SPECIAL NEEDS?

More parents are realizing the importance of science. Reinforce its importance often with those parents who are already aware of it. For parents who are unaware, share these ideas through school or class newsletters and during conferences with parents.

Science Is Important to Their Children's Future

Children will have a much better chance of finding a job if they have a good background in mathematics, science, and computers. The College Board of New York, for example, estimates the unemployment rate of African-American scientists and engineers at 2.5 percent. This compares with an overall unemployment rate of 14.5 percent for African-American adults. Unemployment for Hispanic adults is 11.5 percent, but for Hispanics who are scientists and

Science is found in all aspects of life and is important to children's successful futures.

engineers it is only 2.1 percent. Unemployment statistics are inexact for Native Americans, but they show the same trends for those with a background in science (College Board, 1987).

Skills in mathematics and science will help children earn more money when they enter careers. A scientist or engineer from a minority background earns well over twice the annual salary of the average person from the same background (College Board, 1987).

Science can help break the cycle of unemployment, underemployment, and poverty in culturally different and special-needs populations. Scientific careers command higher levels of pay, and demands for personnel are increasing.

Science skills develop over time, and development builds on older skills. "If you don't use it, you'll lose it" applies here. The science foundation begun during childhood will increase each individual's potential for later success. Also, science depends on mathematics. Students should be encouraged to study mathematics every school year.

All students learn science through hands-on, minds-on experiences. Children should be encouraged to handle physical objects, make measurements and direct comparisons, and ask frequent questions about what they observe and experience.

How Can Parents Help Their Children Study and Prepare for Science?

Parents are invaluable when it comes to educating children. They are closest to the special needs their children may have and are naturally protective of their children's best interests. Parents can help their children succeed in science by following these suggestions:

Stimulate interest in and foster feelings for science. Parents can help their children realize that science can be fun and help them experience success, with its feelings of excitement, discovery, and mastery.

Include science in the child's everyday experiences. Children can be asked to count and form sets of utensils at dinner time and can help to measure ingredients. Include them also in repairing broken appliances or building a model airplane.

Establish a regular study time and provide a designated space for study away from distractions. Work with the teachers to develop effective ways to communicate with children who have vision and hearing disabilities. Equipment modifications can be developed for children who have physical disabilities, and these can be shared with the school.

Check with their children every day to make sure homework and special projects are completed. They should ask to see completed homework and any tests or projects that have been graded or returned.

Offer to read assignment questions. Even if the parents do not know the answers, a stronger academic bond will be formed between parent and child. The child will benefit from an interested adult role model, forming the impression that school, homework, and effort are important.

Ask if their children have any difficulties with science or mathematics. Suggest that parents talk with their children at least once per week about this and then follow up by communicating with you if there appear to be problems.

Use a homework hot-line if the school has one. This may be school based or supported by individual teachers for their classes during designated hours.

What Are Some Extra Science Activities Parents Can Do to Help Their Children?

Some teachers, even entire schools, arrange home-based science activities to supplement school instruction. Parents become enthusiastic and develop a stronger bond with the school. They often say, "Let's have parent involvement programs more often." "It helps me keep in touch with my child." "The activities didn't take too much time, so it was simple to include them into our busy evening schedule." "I think it's great to get the parents involved. Each activity we did benefited our older child and the younger child who is not even in school!" (Williams-Norton, Reisdorf, & Spees, 1990, pp. 13–15).

The rich variety of science teaching resources makes it easy to suggest home study extensions. Giving parents options to choose from helps them overcome limits of time and materials. When selecting options and making suggestions to parents, keep these criteria in mind (Williams-Norton, Reisdorf, & Spees, 1990, p. 14):

The activities should be at grade level and developmentally appropriate for the child. Select options with the special needs of the children in mind.

Activities should require materials that are available at home. No parent will welcome traveling to gather together materials, and many cannot afford the expense.

The activities should supplement what is taught in school, not duplicate it. Do not expect parental teaching to be a substitute for your own responsibility.

The activities should require only a brief amount of time. There are many simple, inexpensive activities that require only 10 or 20 minutes. (See Table 3.5.)

TABLE 3.5   Science Resources for Home Activities

J. Barber, *Bubble-ology* (Berkeley, CA: Great Explorations in Math and Science, Lawrence Hall of Science, 1986).

F. Barhydt, *Science Discovery Activities Kit* (West Nyack, NY: Center for Applied Research in Education, 1989).

J. DeBruin, *Creative, Hands-On Science Experiences* (Carthage, IL: Good Apple, 1986).

J. Echols, *Buzzing a Hive* (Berkeley, CA: Great Explorations in Math and Science, Lawrence Hall of Science, 1986).

J. Hassard, *Science Experiences* (Menlo Park, CA: Addison-Wesley, 1990).

D. Herbert, *Mr. Wizard's Supermarket Science* (New York: Random House, 1980).

D. Herbert and H. Ruchlis, *Mr. Wizard's 400 Experiments in Science* (North Bergen, NJ: Book Lab, 1983).

N. Paulu and M. Martin, *Helping Your Child Learn Science* (Washington D.C.: U.S. Department of Education, 1992).

C. Shaffer and E. Fielder, *City Safaris* (San Francisco: Sierra Club Books, 1987).

J. VanCleave, *Astronomy for Every Kid* (New York: John Wiley, 1991).

———. *Biology for Every Kid* (New York: John Wiley, 1990).

———. *Chemistry for Every Kid* (New York: John Wiley, 1989).

———. *Earth Science for Every Kid* (New York: John Wiley, 1991).

———. *Physics for Every Kid* (New York: John Wiley, 1991).

W. Willnitz, *Be a Kid Physicist* (Blue Ridge Summit, PA: TAB Books, 1993).

Provide complete and accurate instructions. Try the activities yourself before sending them home. Do they work? Are the instructions clear? Are they safe? Can a child do the activity with minimal adult guidance? Revise the instructions as necessary for the children you teach, again being mindful of the special needs of the children.

Select activities that emphasize simple and accurate concepts. Cross-check the concepts of the activity with those of your textbook or science program. Are they consistent? Or are there differences in terminology and accuracy of information? If they are different, modify them or select another activity. Choose activities that emphasize a main science idea, and encourage the parents to continue emphasizing this main idea.

The activities should be fun. Parents and children will enjoy a special time together when the activity is fun. No one, not even an adult, will do something that is not enjoyable if it can be avoided. Encourage parents to share the joys and mysteries of science with their children. Scientific attitudes and positive values parents give to science at home also will benefit school science.

Table 3.5 provides a brief list of science resources useful for home learning activities. Ideas similar to the following may be selected from sources such as those shown in the table (College Board, 1987):

Develop the concepts of sink or float and density by floating common objects such as straws and plastic buttons in plain water and in salt water. Because the density of salt water is greater, objects that sink in plain water often float in salt water. Try adding different amounts of salt to water to explore the effects of salt concentration on density and floating.

Explore primary and secondary colors. Following the directions on food coloring packages, prepare different colors and arrange them in glass jars. Dye macaroni or paper to represent the colors of a rainbow. Combine the three primary colors to produce every color.

Demonstrate magnetism by having children compare the effects of magnets on different objects in the kitchen. Let the children predict which objects will and will not be attracted to the magnets.

Use building blocks to develop the concepts of set and order. Lay a foundation of three blocks; then place two blocks on the next layer and one on the top layer. Ask the children to count the blocks and to estimate how many blocks would be necessary to build towers six and ten blocks high.

CHAPTER SUMMARY

A single science teaching method by itself is insufficient. Each hands-on science lesson must be accompanied by adaptations to suit the needs of each special student. Nothing is so unequal as equal treatment without exception.

There is no single method or science program that can be used to teach all children fairly and equally all the time. However, one single factor does benefit *all* children: hands-on science— where all children have abundant opportunities to benefit from multisensory stimulation in co-operative settings. This approach has the potential to become the great equalizer. Children who are culturally different may acquire missing experiences through hands-on science. Non-English-speaking children can use science to learn and develop language skills. Young females can overcome skill deficits, gender stereotypes, and career limitations through hands-on, minds-on science. Exceptional children are given new opportunities because of hands-on science and its ability to include all children in minds-on experiences. Gifted and talented children also benefit as they are introduced to new experiences and are motivated to process those experiences at an advanced intellectual level.

Parents play a vital role with students who have special needs. Teachers should inform parents about the importance of science and offer activities to strengthen the school-home learning connection.

DISCUSSION QUESTIONS AND PROJECTS

1. Cultural differences can have a positive impact on the social climate of a classroom. What are some ways you can encourage the expression of differences and make a positive impact on all children?

2. Take the picture of a scientist you drew in Chapter 1, and draw another one now. How do the pictures compare? What features are similar? How many of these features do you observe: male, middle aged, bald, glasses, facial hair, lab coat with pocket protector, test tubes? How can these features reflect bias, attitudes, stereotypes, and values? Where did the impressions portrayed in the pictures come from? What types of multicultural education concepts are reflected in the picture? How can social context and media influence impressions? How are the impressions you have of science and scientists likely to influence young children?

3. Blindfold yourself or attend a class while wearing earplugs. How is your ability to function impaired? What long-term cumulative effects could result from your temporary disability if it were to become permanent? How could those effects influence your ability to function in a regular classroom?

4. Brainstorm ideas suitable for teaching science to gifted students. What differences are found on your list according to grade level? How would you work with a youngster who is gifted and who also has a cultural or language difference and/or a disability?

5. Brainstorm ideas related to classroom organization. How can a typical self-contained room be converted to better suit the needs of special students? Look especially for barriers that might limit the inclusion of children who have physical disabilities. What complications might a teacher encounter? What are some ways to overcome these complications?

6. Interview a teacher whose students are culturally different from himself or herself. Inquire about how the science program or instruction has been modified to recognize and use cultural differences in a positive way. What effects have the teacher's efforts had on all of the children?

7. Peruse several science textbooks from different publishers. Report observations about possible gender bias, omitted discussion of cultural differences, and potential for adaptation for non-English-speaking, disabled, and/or gifted children. What suggestions are provided in the teacher's guide?

8. Choose any lesson from a science textbook or hands-on program. Demonstrate how you would adapt it to provide special instruction for female students or children with learning disabilities, intellectual disabilities, impaired vision, hearing loss, or orthopedic impairment.

9. Sketch the floor plan of an elementary classroom. Examine the floor plan carefully and make changes to show adaptations that would assist children with orthopedic impairments.

10. Use the concept analysis model presented in this chapter (Figure 3.2) to make changes in a science lesson plan. How would you use the model to instruct children who are learning disabled or intellectually disabled? How could the model be used with all children? What are the possible benefits and limits?

ADDITIONAL READINGS

If you are interested in learning more about some of the topics raised in this chapter consider the following sources:

Patricia B. Campbell has written a series of brochures (published by the U.S. Department of Education, 1991) about females in mathematics and science. The brochures cover such topics as appropriate ways to evaluate programs for girls in math, science, and engineering; designing effective programs; working in and out of school to encourage young females; and the kinds of things parents can do.

Michael E. Corrick, Jr. (Ed.), *Teaching Handicapped Students Science* (Washington, DC: National Education Association, 1981). This concise collection of essays addresses goals, approaches, materials, barriers, and evaluation practices. This is a worthy personal reference for any science teacher.

William L. Heward and Michael D. Orlansky, *Exceptional Children*, 3d ed. (Columbus, OH: Merrill, 1988). This is one of many fine texts that delve deeper into the characteristics of special children. Included is extensive coverage of federal law, the philosophy of special education, and specific detailed descriptions of exceptionalities. Teaching and educational service alternatives are offered.

William D. Romey and Mary L. Hibert, *Teaching the Gifted and Talented in the Science Classroom* (Washington, DC: national Education Association, 1988). This guide offers practical suggestions for creating a learning environment that nurtures giftedness. It includes several science activity ideas.

Deborah Deutsch Smith and Ruth Luckasson, *Introduction to Special Education* (Boston: Allyn and Bacon, 1992). This text provides interesting descriptions of students who are members of minority groups, non–English speaking, and who also have mental, learning, or physical impairments.

Francis Sutman, *Teaching Science Effectively to Limited English Proficient Students* (ERIC Clearinghouse ED 357113, 1993). A brief practical set of guidelines to help teachers teach science to students with limited English proficiency. The paper contains dozens of references and identifies suitable instructional materials.

Francis X. Sutman, Virginia French Allen, and Francis Shoemaker, *Learning English Through Science* (Washington, DC: NSTA, 1986). A guide to collaboration for science teachers, English teachers, and teachers of English as a second language, this book offers practical suggestions for setting up classrooms and science programs as models for cultural pluralism through multilingual efforts.

Some sources of information for science for students with special needs are:

Center for Multisensory Learning
   Lawrence Hall of Science
   University of California
   Berkeley, CA 94720

Exceptional Children Science Education Project (ECSEP)
   Science for the Learning Disabled
   Charlotte-Mecklenburg Schools
   P.O. Box 140
   Charlotte, NC 28230

The Project on the Handicapped in Science American Association for the Advancement of Science
   1776 Massachusetts Avenue, NW
   Washington, DC 20036

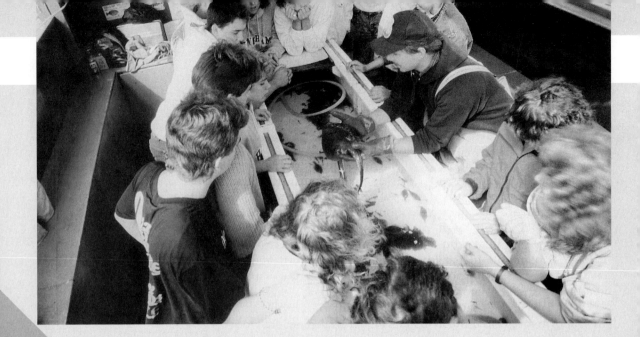

CHAPTER OUTLINE

CHAPTER 4

What Goals Promote Scientific Literacy?

Being an experienced principal did not make this part of his job any easier. Mr. Emerson always felt some personal loss when any one of "his" teachers left for other opportunities. However, the chance to interview new teacher candidates always encouraged him because teachers were becoming more sophisticated, with new teaching methods and emphasis on activity learning. Mr. Emerson had invested much time and energy to help teachers find their school an exciting place. To call their school a zoo was a compliment, not an insult. All of the classrooms and offices had plants and animals, and each hallway pronounced a different science theme. Science was emphasized and was used as a way of promoting social studies, mathematics, reading, and language. Indeed, education was alive in the school and made as real as possible. Pride ran high, and it was important to maintain the proper mix of teachers to support the school's vision. Mr. Emerson was hopeful the next candidate would be a good fit, especially for the science program. Everyone in the school was proud of the progress made toward new science program standards. After a brief guided tour and warm-up session of chatting, the interview began.

"Jennifer, would you please tell me what you think your most important goals should be for science, and how you could meet them."

"Well," replied Jennifer, "as you know I am not a science specialist."

"The position does not call for a specialist, Jennifer. We are proud of our science program and want all teachers to support it. So what do you think you would try to accomplish in science if we hire you?"

Jennifer thought briefly, then responded. "I think a good science program should be more than science. Its focus should be broader than science facts. Don't get me wrong. Facts are important, but they should not drive the entire program. I like to think in terms of what I would like children to be able to understand and be able to do."

"Such as . . .?"

"I would like children to understand that even they are responsible, in some small way, for what happens to our environment. That even they should think about it. So I guess that means they should be able to think and solve problems. In addition, they should understand that something like science is both good and can be bad if misused." As she continued, Jennifer spoke with more ease: "I would like the children in my class to be curious, aware, and even skeptical from time to time. I don't want them to depend on me for the answer; I want them to learn how to figure out some things for themselves. I think this is important, especially when they grow up and have to solve their own serious problems. I think that what they do in science should carry over to other subjects. As an example, technology is all around us, and children usually adapt very quickly to new technology with enthusiasm. At the same time, I would like the children to have some awareness of the historical relationship between science and technology and how that history affects our society, especially our daily lives. This might seem to you as if I am talking about teaching college-level courses to children or avoiding science by teaching social studies. That's not what I mean. I would try to put all of this on the children's level, to connect with what they know and have experienced. I would try to make my science teaching practical by connecting the children's experiences with essential science concepts."

"How would you teach, Jennifer, to make your goals happen?" asked Mr. Emerson.

"Obviously the children need to *do* science. I think hands-on science is more than a slogan. I want children to get their minds involved in what they are doing. Conceptual learning should be emphasized over memorizing science facts. Facts are certainly necessary; they help to build a base for understanding the concept of a lesson. But students must have concrete experiences before an abstract concept is introduced. Ideally, the students would be able to construct the concept, with my guidance, by thinking about their own experiences. This means that my teaching would include inquiry teaching, so I would introduce new science words or technical terms only after the students and I have thoroughly experienced the concept. Also, I think it is important to be selective. I would focus on fewer concepts than most textbooks introduce but attempt to go into greater depth and help students apply what they learn to real life. I would try to connect new learning with the students' prior learning. I also think it is important to expose the students to all of the science disciplines, to try for a good balance between earth, life, and physical science."

Mr. Emerson asked, "Would you please describe an example of some topic where you might be able to do these things as you just described?"

"One way is to make the learning real. For example, I would try to help the children develop a knowledge of the working world—how their clothes are constructed, what the differences are among fabrics and comfort, and how those are connected to science and new technologies. A theme that might guide this type of study could be "Form and Function." We would examine the function of particular fabrics and how they vary and how their constructed forms differ, such as differences between polyester and cotton or wool. Studying the source of these materials permits us to integrate earth and life science. The construction and function help us apply physical science concepts. Another example is to examine why it is important to cook certain foods in particular ways and to brush our teeth, and why some plants grow better in certain environments than others. I would want the students to see examples of how science is used by society and the problems as well as the good that causes. I would also like children to understand that science offers important career opportunities, that it is also important to many other careers, and that no one has to become a scientist to benefit from science."

"Jennifer," said Mr. Emerson, "what you have described sounds much like what many educators would call a literacy education, where you would attempt to overcome the unfortunate perceptions of narrow boundaries that many believe exist between the subject areas. Instead you would attempt teach for connections among and between all subjects. Is this what you really mean?" ◆

INTRODUCTION

Mr. Emerson raises a fair question. Does any one subject in the elementary or middle school curriculum hold dominion over the others, and can it lay claim to being more important than others in the development of literacy? Or, as in Jennifer's description of her preferred goals in science, is it realistic for science to appear broad enough to cover so much? We try to respond to these questions in this chapter by dividing it into three parts:

1. an examination of scientific literacy,
2. a review of several recent and influential reform efforts in science education, and
3. a synthesis of goals from those reform efforts that are designed to promote scientific literacy in elementary and middle schools.

WHAT IS SCIENTIFIC LITERACY?

A literate person has a fundamental command of the essentials: what one needs to know and be able to do in order to function as a contributing member of society. Not long ago the standard refrain in education was that a literate person commanded the basics of reading, writing, and arithmetic. But this view is too narrow to provide an education that helps our youngsters survive in a complex world with its wonders of technology and sophisticated social, economic, and political problems. Tomorrow's leaders and policy makers must know more, have a different worldview, and possess an impressive array of skills. What does a scientifically literate person know, and what is that person able to do in a modern society?

In this time of change and challenge, many definitions of scientific literacy have been written. We refer to that promulgated by the organization that set the national standards in science education, the National Research Council (NRC):

> Scientific literacy means that a person can ask and find or determine answers to questions derived from curiosity about everyday experiences. It means the ability to describe, explain, and predict natural phenomena. It means the ability to read with understanding articles about science in the popular press and engage in so-

Science helps improve our lives.

cial conversation about the validity of the conclusions. Scientific literacy implies that a person can identify scientific issues underlying national and local decisions and express positions that are scientifically and technologically informed. A literate citizen should be able to evaluate the quality of scientific information on the basis of its sources and the methods used to generate it. Scientific literacy also implies the capacity to pose and evaluate arguments based on evidence and to apply conclusions from such arguments appropriately. (NRC, 1996, p. 22)

The NRC also reminds us that scientific literacy is not an all-or-nothing happening; a person may be scientifically literate in some fields or topics of study but not in others. Furthermore, scientific literacy is developed over a lifetime. Schooling is important, but literacy continues to develop during the adult years. The development of scientific literacy is influenced, as the details of its description suggest, by the attitudes and values of the individual, as well as the habits of mind and conceptual understandings that the individual uses and knows. Very broadly, then, a scientifically literate person has a capacity to use essential scientific attitudes, processes, and reasoning skills, and science types of information to reach reasoned conclusions and use the ideas of science in meaningful ways. This is representative of an ancient proverb's wisdom: "Teach a person how to fish, feed the person for a lifetime." Various reform efforts in science education pursue lifelong learning through efforts that strive to develop attitudes, skills, and knowledge. In other words, educators are encouraged to believe that if they teach a person how to learn, the person will learn for a lifetime.

Positive scientific attitudes—persistence, curiosity, humility, a healthy dose of skepticism—motivate learners to approach a task or problem with enough interest to find out for themselves. There is a relationship between attitudes, interest, achievement, and perception of one's successes, summed up by the saying, "success breeds success." Anyone who has ever persisted with a problem long enough to solve it knows the sweet feeling of achievement and that "can-do" perception that accompanies success. Figure 4.1 demonstrates the interactions of these attitudinal factors. The relationship appears to be cumulative and conveys the notion that as children develop more positive attitudes and more interest in science (as well as other subjects), their achievement increases. As achievement increases, motivation and desire stimulate the development of new learning skills, and that leads to greater understanding of the information, which is accumulating at a dizzying pace. Therefore, the processes of science are the skills by which observations are acquired and meaning is constructed by the learner. Processes can provide the type and quality of the science experience desired for children where thinking is expanded and improved.

Process skills, as literacy-building tools, have tremendous carry-over value in and out of school. They are also vital to adult living. They are the mechanisms by which problems are identified, explored, and solved. Whether the adult mission is to improve or improvise on a recipe; determine the cause of a blown fuse (or tripped circuit breaker); troubleshoot the cause of a car's failure

FIGURE 4.1   Importance of Basic Science Attitudes: Building a Learner's Self-Esteem

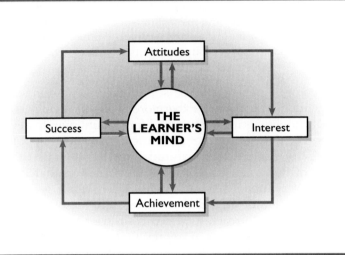

Source: Adapted from Benjamin Bloom, *Human Characteristics and School Learning* (New York: McGraw-Hill, 1979).

to start; plan the best route to run a new line for an extension telephone; identify evidence and separate it from opinion while listening to a political candidate; or determine how to thread a sewing machine, the processes of science contribute to solving the problem.

Children are naturally interested in science and associated science topics. Surveys done in elementary schools show that children choose science a majority of the time when given lists of school topics from which they can choose. Parents report, too, that their children list science as one of their favored school subjects (Mechling & Oliver, 1983).

Like you, children cannot escape the importance of science; it affects every aspect of their lives. However, the intent of scientific information is that it be a means, not an end. Science content can help children become responsible consumers and personally learn how to benefit more from learning science. If science content is applied to real circumstances, scientific information and areas of study provide meaningful contexts for developing literacy skills. Recommendations from science organizations, such as the National Science Teachers Association, urge that children have daily opportunities to relate science to their own lives and that science study not be limited to science time. Other organizations, such as the American Association for the Advancement of Science and the National Research Council, urge that science content be used to organize meaningful standards that address the historical, social, technological, and interdisciplinary nature of science. The information, attitudes, and skills of science can be used to enrich other school experiences, and times of reading, art, music, social studies, writing, mathematics, discussion, physical education, and so on, can be used to deepen an understanding of science. Science is central to the education of literate citizens.

WHAT REFORM EFFORTS HAVE SOUGHT TO PROVIDE GOALS FOR SCIENTIFIC LITERACY?

Science teaching goals may be provided by your state curriculum or by major science improvement efforts, such as those offered by the National Science Foundation (NSF), the American Association for the Advancement of Science (AAAS), the National Science Teachers Association (NSTA), or the NRC. Modern goals respond to urgent needs and are based on the knowledge of what works. We describe four reform efforts important for their contemporary breadth and depth: Project Synthesis of the NSF, the Scope, Sequence, and Coordination Project of the NSTA, Project 2061 of the American Association for the Advance of Science, and the National Science Education Standards of the NRC Committee on Science Education and Assessment.

EXERCISE 4.1

What Is the Relationship Between Science and Other School Subjects?

We have listed some common topics in science that you may be asked to teach. Science has considerable potential for integration with other subject or skill areas. How could you help make this integration work for you as you attempt to educate scientifically literate learners? List several subjects into which the science topics could be integrated, and exchange your ideas with your classmates to develop a resource file of ideas.

Science Topic	Related School Subject/Topic/Skill	Science Topic	Related School Subject/Topic/Skill
simple machines		energy	
growth		plants	
nutrition		animals	
weather		space	
electricity		life cycles	
sound		senses	
color		adaptations	

Project Synthesis

The NSF supported $2 billion worth of programs and courses developed in mathematics and science during the 1960s and 1970s. Major social and political pressures removed adequate levels of funding for science education during the mid-to-late 1970s, much as pressures to reduce the national deficit caused the Congress to review support for education in the mid-1990s. Teachers and citizens concluded that federal funds had been wasted and, in the wake of mixed research reports, that the programs had not accomplished what they were designed to do. It was in this setting that the NSF responded to congressional pressure and awarded contracts in 1976 for several landmark studies of science education (Harms, 1981).

Consensus within and among the Project Synthesis research groups yielded several general conclusions about the status of science education. For the most part, these conclusions are still accurate today and contribute much of the knowledge base that recent reform efforts are built upon. These conclusions are:

1. Science education at all levels is given a low priority when compared with the importance of language arts, mathematics, and social studies. School systems generally do not support science.
2. Textbooks dominate science teaching and learning and limit what can be accomplished.
3. School science programs generally emphasize preparing students for the next grade level of study or for college.
4. Teachers become the curriculum to the extent that they decide what will be taught or studied. Therefore, teachers determine many of the goals of science education. These goals are often incongruent with the national agenda and with what works in elementary science education. (Weiss, 1978; Holdzkom & Lutz, 1984)

These general conclusions led researchers and science educators to proclaim that existing science programs did not serve the majority of children well. In fact, many existing programs served only about one out of every ten pupils well. Their primary goal was to recruit students into science careers. These conclusions helped to set a new goal for science literacy for the 1980s. This goal had four outcomes.

Outcome I: Science Enhances Each Learner's Personal Development.   Science education should help learners use science to improve their own lives and to learn how to cope with an increasingly technological world.

This outcome focused on ways to enhance each student's curiosity, honesty, imagination, self-confidence, and ability to be persistent, make decisions, cope with changes, examine values, reason logically, and practice the ethics of science. This outcome reflected the many ways science and technology affect one's life. Included were the attitudes and abilities one needs to become a responsible consumer, to maintain a healthy body, and to use science in making daily decisions and solving daily problems.

Outcome II: Learners Understand the Interrelationships of Science, Technology, and Society. The science curriculum must prepare students to function as informed citizens and to deal responsibly with science-related social and technological issues. Opportunities must be provided for students to develop a greater ability to understand the impact science has on social issues and the way science shapes our expectations about responsible citizenship: personal interaction with the environment, responsible consumerism, respect for environmental order and aesthetics, and so on.

In addition, this outcome taught that technology and science are worthy human endeavors, that there are distinctions between them, and that students must recognize their impact on the future of society.

Outcome III: Science Develops Each Learner's Academic and Process Skills. The science curriculum must provide all students opportunities to acquire the academic knowledge and skills they need to solve personal problems and to continue lifelong learning. Therefore, emphasis was given to improving children's thinking skills. The science program attempted to prepare students who were likely to pursue science and science-related careers with the fundamental knowledge and skills necessary to support further education in their career fields.

This outcome concentrated on what children needed to become scientifically literate and urged that the curriculum include the knowledge, concepts, principles, and ideas of science, as well as the attitudes, values, and ethics of science and critical thinking and problem-solving skills.

Outcome IV: Science Helps to Expand Each Learner's Career Awareness. Science education must give *all* students an awareness of the nature and scope of the science- and technology-related careers that exist. The science curriculum must provide opportunities for children to develop an awareness of how important science is to different occupations and professions. This outcome helped students realize that science is relevant to all fields of employment. It also included development of positive attitudes toward science-related careers and an awareness that these careers provide occupational opportunities for women, minorities, and the disabled. Some examples include the many careers in research, engineering, laboratory technology, equipment design, and computer programming; they include jobs in which people apply scientific knowledge, in such fields as agriculture, nutrition, medicine, sanitation, conservation, and so on. Students became informed about the contributions people in such careers make to society as well as the specific educational preparation, interests, attitudes, and abilities associated with each career. Students realized

TEACHERS ON SCIENCE TEACHING

What Are the Goals of Middle School Science?

by Terry L. Kluesner
Erin Elementary School, Hartford, Wisconsin

"Thank you for making science interesting," was a comment I heard this past fall during parent/ teacher conferences from a mother of a sixth grader. It was especially gratifying for me to hear because I feel the most important goal of a middle school science program is to develop and maintain within students an interest in the field and study of science. My hope is that this interest is carried into high school, where they will take more than the required science courses. This kind of preparation would not only give students a broader choice in their higher education goals, but ultimately, if the interest is carried into adulthood, produce more scientifically literate adults able to make knowledgeable decisions in this increasingly technological world.

How does a teacher develop interest in science? In the past, many people interpreted this as making science fun. *Hands-on* became the catchphrase, and students began manipulating just about anything the teacher could get his or her hands on

without any real information being gained. I do believe my classes are often fun, but when fun becomes the priority, it is possible that the thought process of science get abandoned. I believe students will be interested in science only when they see it as worthwhile to them, when they feel a part of the learning, and when the information gained holds some meaning for them. The key to this is to have students actively involved, not only with their hands but with their minds as well.

Before conducting any investigation or hands-on experiment, students must be given enough pertinent background knowledge about a subject so they can generate informed hypotheses. They must have a reason to carry out the experiment: Why would the students need to or want to find out the kind of information you're asking them to find? Once the experiment is completed, students must be asked to organize the data into tables and graphs as well as to make some sort of meaningful interpretation or conclusion from

that science, mathematics, language arts, and social studies are interrelated, and they understood the interrelationships of science, technology, and society.

Scope, Sequence, and Coordination of Secondary School Science (SS&C)

The NSTA supports an effort to reform science programs in grades 7 through 12. A brief description is provided here for the middle school teachers who may be affected by such school curricula and for elementary teachers who must strive to prepare learners for the advanced grades. SS&C encourages all learners to study each science discipline every year for six years, from seventh through twelfth grades. This means that science programs that follow SS&C recommendations include the study of biology, chemistry, physics, and earth and space sciences within the parameters of each year's science course. This is a radical change from the layer-cake approach, where students typically study earth science in the ninth grade, biology in the tenth grade, chemistry in the

the data. Only when students are asked to engage in scientific reasoning will they see how the information they collected is relevant to them.

Problem solving is intertwined throughout this whole learning process. Students must not only be able to perform canned experiments the teacher sets up, but must be able to figure out how to answer questions and solve problems of their own. What variables would they manipulate, control, and measure? Students need to be given opportunities to practice designing their own experiments. These may be formal written plans on topics such as plant propagation or more spontaneous, creative experiments, such as trying to design a catapult that is capable of flinging a 2 cm by 2 cm piece of potato into a 1 meter square target from a distance of 4 meters.

One of the things I do in my classroom throughout the year to maintain interest is to run contests. These contests most often require the use of problem solving. The contests range from the very simple, such as the egg drop contest and the mealworm race, to the complex, such as the straw bridge contest and the hot-air balloon contest. Toward the end of the year I hold a science fair in which students in grades 6, 7, and 8 compete for gold, silver, and bronze medals at each grade level. I realize there is controversy over the competition aspect of contests and a science fair but I find that when it is not used excessively, it is a great motivator as well as a lesson on the competitive nature of scientists in the business world.

In summary, I believe the major outcomes of any school science program must be to develop and maintain interest in science programs and include:

- the learning of basic science knowledge and concepts,
- active participation by students,
- opportunities for hands-on learning,
- opportunities for problem solving,
- scientific reasoning development.

eleventh, and physics in the twelfth grade, although more than half of the secondary school students in the United States do not take a science course beyond the tenth grade.

Curricula based on SS&C spread the study of each science discipline over several years, using inquiry teaching and discovery learning approaches that are consistent with how students learn. Each student learns from each discipline first without complex mathematics, while encountering the major concepts of science in an interdisciplinary fashion without the artificial barriers of the separate disciplines. The curriculum is designed so that teachers can help learners make conceptual connections that span the science disciplines. These connections often are coordinated through science themes, such as changes in biological organisms that are influenced by changes in biochemistry. A theme, such as change, can be used as an organizer for examining differences over geologic time, as well as change within the concepts of cause and effect in physical sciences. This approach provides a substantial opportunity for

Modern science includes all children.

students to learn chemistry and physics when more than half of the student population never takes those separate courses. From the pilot efforts in middle schools, students seem to be developing an affinity for science rather than a fear of it (Willis, 1995).

Project 2061

The AAAS commissioned a comprehensive initiative to improve science education, *Project 2061*—named for the year Halley's Comet will next reappear (Rutherford & Ahlgren, 1990). Project 2061 recommends several principles for effective science instruction. Guided by the National Council on Science and Technology Education, the project relies on scientists, engineers, and mathematicians to provide ideas for the project staff and consultants. Teams of consultants and reviewers consist of scientists, teachers, educators, historians, philosophers, and others who use science and reflect on its place in human affairs. Project 2061 is built upon several important guiding principles. Each principle suggests some elements that should be included in the new goals for science instruction. They address the following ideas:

- What science students should know must be carefully identified.
- Effective science instruction must encourage student diversity and serve the needs and interests of all students with a common core of knowledge and experiences.
- Students should learn science concepts rather than a list of science topics.

- Learning outcomes should be accomplished through appropriate teaching practices that begin with questions and phenomena that interest children and should be directed toward helping them find out how things work.
- The science curriculum should be selective and relevant and should not try to cover the full spectrum of the sciences.
- Science should be integrated with other subjects (such as mathematics and the humanities) when integration will *not* make learning science substantially more difficult.
- Science learning goals should be more generic without reference to a specific science course.
- Students must learn that science is tentative, not absolute, and that it is evidence oriented, speculative, and creative.
- Science curricula should include content that deals with social issues and technology when possible.
- Science taught in school should be based on explicitly stated educational criteria (Rutherford & Ahlgren, 1988, pp. 75–90).

The principles of Project 2061 stimulated efforts to develop science programs that emphasized fewer science concepts but strived to explore concepts in more depth. The boundaries between traditional science subjects and content topics are softened, and stronger conceptual linkages are emphasized; "teaching for connections" captures the intent of the curriculum. In addition, nontraditional topics are included in the curriculum, such as the nature of science and mathematics and important episodes in the history of science and technology.

Themes identify some ways of thinking that help make conceptual connections across the fields of science, mathematics and technology. Project 2061 urges that a curriculum be designed and used to help students gradually learn and use the ideas of the themes. Themes help learners construct meaning from their experiences and ideas. Therefore, some teachers and curriculum developers use themes as conceptual organizers to teach and write curriculum. Project 2061 recommends that teachers see that themes arise naturally from the science content that is built into a curriculum rather than impose themes on the content. Some themes that seem to arise naturally from typical science content are systems, models, constancy and change, and scale. Project 2061 claims that these themes "pervade science, mathematics, and technology and appear over and over again, whether we are looking at an ancient civilization, the human body, or a comet. [The ideas connected by themes] transcend disciplinary boundaries and prove fruitful in explanation, in theory, in observation, and in design" (AAAS, 1993, p. 261).

As an example, let us consider the theme of systems. The meaning envisioned for this theme is described and supported by particular outcomes as benchmarks for grades 2, 5, and 8.

One of the essential components of higher-order thinking is the ability to think about a whole in terms of its parts and, alternatively, about parts in terms of how they relate to one another and to the whole. People are accustomed to speak of political systems, sewage systems, transportation systems, the respiratory system, the solar system, and so on. . . . [M]ost people would probably say that a system is a collection of things and processes (and often people) that interact to perform some function. The scientific idea of a system implies detailed attention to inputs and outputs and to interactions among the system components. If these can be specified quantitatively, a computer simulation of the system might be run to study its theoretical behavior, and so provide a way to define problems and investigate complex phenomena. But a system need not have a "purpose" (e.g., an ecosystem or the solar system) and what a system includes can be imagined in any way that is interesting or useful. (AAAS, 1993, p. 262)

Table 4.1 provides examples of the outcomes recommended by Project 2061 for this theme for grade levels from kindergarten through high school. Curriculum developers and schools use these outcomes to design experiences for students that encourage the long-term development of scientific literacy among learners; teachers use them to keep daily lessons focused on meaningful grade-level outcomes that contribute to long-term literacy.

National Science Education Standards

The NRC coordinated the development of the national standards for K–12 science education. Diverse working groups from professional organizations, states, and other countries offered ideas that the NRC examined and transformed into draft standards. More than 40,000 copies of the draft were reviewed by individuals and focus groups of teachers, scientists, and businesspersons. The standards are based on goals that strive to prepare students who are able to:

- use scientific information and processes appropriately in making personal decisions;
- experience the attitudes and excitement of knowing about and understanding the natural world;
- increase their economic productivity;
- engage intelligently in public discourse and debate about matters of scientific and technological concern (NRC, 1996).

These broad goals may be addressed through school science programs that provide experiences that:

- are personally and socially relevant to the child;
- include a wide range of knowledge, methods, and approaches so that students can analyze personal and societal issues critically;
- encourage students to think and act in ways that reflect their understanding of the impact science has on their lives, society, and the world;
- encourage students to appreciate science;
- helps student develop an appreciation for the beauty and order of the natural world (NRC, 1996).

TABLE 4.1   Example Benchmark Outcomes for a Theme of Systems, Project 2061

Primary grades

Experiences with a variety of dissectable and rearrangeable objects, such as gear trains and toy vehicles and animals, as well as conventional blocks, dolls, and doll houses in order for children to learn how to predict the effects of removing or changing parts. By the end of the second grade, students should know the following concepts:

• Most things are made of parts.
• Something may not work if some of its parts are missing.
• When parts are put together, they can do things that they could not do by themselves.

Intermediate grades

A variety of experiences with mechanical systems that include familiar hardware devices that can be taken apart and reassembled with familiar hand tools. By the end of the fifth grade, students should know the following concepts:

• In something that consists of many parts, the parts usually influence each other.
• Something may not work as well (or at all) if a part of it is missing, broken, worn out, mismatched, or disconnected.

Middle school

Analyses of parts, subsystems, and interactions; to move beyond calling everything a system. Students should work cooperatively on projects to design, assemble, and trouble-shoot systems, such as bicycles, clocks, mechanical toys, battery-powered circuits, aquariums, and gardens. By the end of the eighth grade, students should know the following concepts:

• A system can include processes as well as things.
• Thinking about things as systems means looking for how every part is related to others. The output from one part of a system (which can include material, energy, or information) can become the input to other parts. Such feedback can serve to control what goes on in the system as a whole.
• Any system is usually connected to other systems, both internally and externally. Thus, a system may be thought of as containing subsystems and as being a sub-system of a larger system.

Source: Adapted from AAAS, *Benchmarks for Scientific Literacy* (New York: Oxford University Press, 1993), pp. 264–265.

The standards are based on a belief that a systemic approach to reform is necessary for meaningful change to occur. Although many of the goals focus on improving student learning, the standards describe important science content to be learned, teaching approaches, professional development needs for teachers, and broad-based assessment techniques that must be used to chart progress. In total, the standards describe the overall science program expectations that educators should strive to achieve. Table 4.2 describes briefly the expectations for each standard area. The systemic nature of the National Science Education

Teaching Standards

Teachers of science must:

- Plan an inquiry-based program for their students.
- Guide and facilitate learning.
- Engage in ongoing assessment of their teaching and of student learning.
- Design and manage learning environments that provide students with the time, space, and resources needed for learning science.
- Develop communities of science learners that reflect the intellectual rigor of scientific inquiry and the attitudes and social values conducive to science learning.
- Actively participate in the ongoing planning and development of the school science program.

Professional Teacher Development Standards

The professional development of science teachers:

- Requires learning science content through the perspectives and methods of inquiry.
- Requires integrating knowledge of science, learning, pedagogy, and students and applying that understanding to science teaching.
- Enables teachers to build the knowledge, skills, and attitudes needed to engage in lifelong learning.
- Requires preservice and inservice programs that are coherent and integrated.

Assessment in Science Education Standards

Assessments require:

- Designs and procedures that are consistent with the decisions they are to inform.
- Assessment of both student achievement and the opportunity to learn science.
- A good fit between the type and quality of data collected and the consequences of the decisions and actions taken.
- Fair, unbiased practices and uses.
- Sound inferences about student achievement and the opportunity to learn.

Science Content Standards

All students in kindergarten through eighth grade should:

- Develop abilities necessary to do and understand scientific inquiry.
- Understand fundamental physical science concepts about properties and changes of materials; position and motion of objects; light, heat, electricity, and magnetism; motions and forces; and transformations of energy.
- Understand fundamental life science concepts about characteristics of organisms; life cycles of organisms; environments; structure and function of living systems; reproduction and heredity; regulation and behavior; populations and ecosystems; and diversity and adaptations of organisms.
- Understand fundamental earth and space science concepts about properties of earth materials; objects in the sky; structure of the earth's system; earth's history; and earth's position and role in the solar system.
- Understand fundamental science and technology concepts, such as distinguishing between natural and human-made objects; abilities of technological design; and the relationship of science and technology.

Source: National Research Council, *National Science Education Standards* (Washington, DC: National Academy Press, 1996).

Science Content Standards (continued)

- Understand fundamental personal and social perspectives in science, such as health; characteristics and changes in populations; types of resources; changes in environments; science and technology in a local context; natural hazards; risks and benefits; and science and technology in society.
- Understand science as a human endeavor; the nature of science and scientific knowledge; and the history of science.
- Construct conceptual connections among science experiences through unifying concepts and processes such as order and organization; evidence, models, and explanation; change, constancy, and measurement; evolution and equilibrium; and form and function.

Science Education Program Standards

All science programs in kindergarten through eighth grade should:

- Be consistently articulated within and across all grade levels to encompass clearly stated goals, curriculum framework, teaching practices, assessment policies, support systems, and leadership for supporting and maintaining these elements.
- Contain all of the content standards embedded in a variety of curriculum patterns that are developmentally appropriate, interesting, and relevant to students' lives. Emphasize inquiry as a learning tool, and the curriculum should connect with other school subjects.
- Be coordinated with the mathematics program in order to improve students' understanding of science and mathematics overall.
- Give students access to appropriate and sufficient resources that include time, materials and equipment, space, teachers, and the community.
- Provide all students equitable access to opportunities that help them meet the standards.
- Help schools become communities that encourage, support, and sustain teachers as they implement an effective science program.

Science Education System Standards

The overlapping systems that affect science education include professional societies, the government judiciary, and the private sector. These systems must:

- Use a common vision to set policies that influence the practice of science education at the program level, while allowing for adaptations to local circumstances.
- Coordinate policies within and across agencies, institutions, and organizations.
- Provide continuity for reform efforts by sustaining policies over sufficient time.
- Support new policies with adequate resources.
- Provide equitable support for all students.
- Be reviewed frequently for possible unintended effects on the classroom practice of science education.
- Encourage individuals to take responsibility for making changes described by the standards.

FIGURE 4.2   National Science Education Standards for Systemic Reform

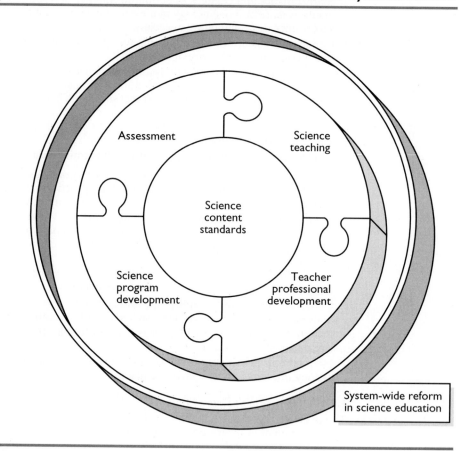

Standards is shown in Figure 4.2. Note that system-wide reform for scientific literacy requires a coordinated effort across all of the five interrelated standards.

GOALS PROMOTING SCIENTIFIC LITERACY

The extensive bases of research and recommendations from these significant reform efforts help us to set new goals for effective science instruction. These goals provide a foundation for planning and influence the science improvement initiatives that arise from national organizations, states, and school districts. All of these goals intend to help educators pursue scientific literacy for learners. However, as the National Science Education Standards make clear, focusing only on student improvements and new standards for teachers falls short of repairing the systemic support structures that are necessary for broad and sweeping changes. The necessary systemic changes fall beyond what a single teacher can do. Still, there is reason for hope and perseverance. The goals toward literacy that each teacher can pursue are focused on learners: what we would have all learners know and be able to do in science.

The science content standards make clear the science subject matter expectations we should have for all learners across various levels of schooling. These standards are detailed and help us set clear learning outcomes—the kinds of changes that teachers can pursue in classrooms in the name of scientific literacy. The standards describe conceptual content outcomes that are distributed across the three science domains typically found in elementary and middle school science programs: physical, life, and earth/space science. (These outcomes are lengthy and are set out in Appendix A.) In brief, the content standards make it possible to identify essential science topics that all children should learn, such as characteristics and life cycles of organisms; properties, position, and motion of objects; and structure and history of the earth and solar system. The science content standards describe a foundation, not a ceiling for learning.

The standards and specific outcomes provide a context for scientific literacy that strives to provide students with powerful ideas that help them understand the natural world. The standards recommend concepts and processes that can be used as integrative mechanisms to unify students' science experiences, first by helping to establish meaning during the early grades, then later to enhance learning in the middle grades by providing students with the big picture that cuts across scientific ideas.

Themes are recommended tools for teaching and learning that are described by the standards. They help us unify the science concepts and processes by organizing the instruction and providing a context for connection among various student learning experiences. Potential science themes are: order and organization; evidence, models, and explanation; change, constancy, and measurement; evolution and equilibrium; and form and function.

The standards recommend four other content factors that intend to make science appealing and meaningful learning for all students and offer new learning outcomes that add depth and breadth to the subject matter content of science. Figure 4.3 illustrates the relationships and interrelationships of the seven factors that compose the content standards for students.

Several of the content factors cluster conveniently around four new dimensions for science teaching: science as inquiry, science and technology, science in personal and social perspectives, and history and nature of science. These new dimensions should complement all science lessons that have conceptual targets in the physical, life, and earth and space sciences. The functions of these dimensions and the learning outcomes are outlined in Table 4.3.

Science as Inquiry

Inquiry means the use of the processes of science, scientific knowledge, and attitudes to reason and to think critically. As described by the standards, inquiry

FIGURE 4.3   Relationships and Interrelationships of the National Science Education Content Standards   An appropriate theme provides an organizing mechanism for designing instruction drawn from the areas of physical, earth/space, and life sciences. Each lesson is shaped by the new dimensions of science education.

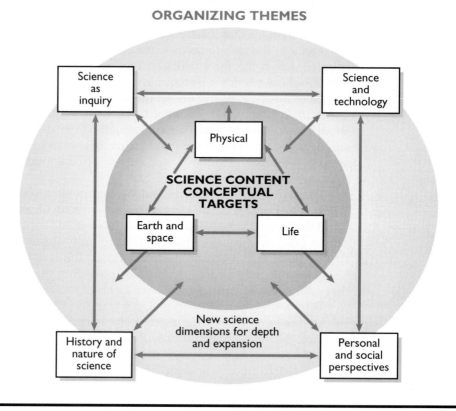

assists in constructing an understanding of scientific concepts, learning how to learn, becoming an independent and life-long learner, and further developing the habits of mind associated with science. Learning outcomes for the inquiry dimension require students to be able to understand inquiry and do a variety of types of science activities in order to learn the uses and skills of inquiry and develop a greater capacity to inquire.

Inquiry is the process that students should use to learn science. They should be able to ask questions, use their questions to plan and conduct a scientific investigation, use appropriate science tools and scientific techniques, evaluate evidence and use it logically to construct several alternative explanations, and communicate (argue) their conclusions scientifically (NRC, 1994, p. V-4-6).

TABLE 4.3   Four New Dimensions of Science Content Standards and Outcomes

Dimension 1. Science as Inquiry Standard
The students will:

1.1   Develop abilities necessary to do scientific inquiry.

- Ask questions about objects, organisms, and events in their natural environment.
- Plan and conduct simple science investigations.
- Use simple science equipment and other appropriate tools that extend their senses in order to gather, analyze, and interpret data.
- Use data to construct descriptions, explanations, predictions, and models.
- Identify relationships between evidence and explanations.
- Communicate, critique, and analyze the work of other students and recognize and analyze alternative explanations and predictions.

1.2   Understand about scientific inquiry.

- Ask and answer questions and compare answers to what scientists already know about the world.
- Select the kind of investigation that fits the questions they are trying to answer.
- Realize the instruments provide more information than a scientist can obtain only by using his or her senses, and enhance the accuracy of that information.
- Develop explanations that are based on observation, evidence, and scientific concepts.
- Describe investigations in ways that make it possible for others to repeat the same investigation.
- Review and ask questions about the results of others' work and realize that science advances through legitimate skepticism.

Dimension 2. Science and Technology Standard
The students will:

2.1   Develop an ability to distinguish between natural objects and objects made by humans.

- Realize that some objects occur in nature and that other objects have been designed by people to solve human problems.
- Categorize objects into two groups, natural and designed.

2.2   Develop an ability to understand and produce a technological design.

- Identify an age-appropriate problem for technological design, propose a solution, and design it, perhaps by collaborating with others.
- Evaluate a product or design and communicate the results to others by describing the process of technological design.

2.3   Understand about science and technology.

- Realize that science and technological design often have similarities and differences that make it necessary for scientists and engineers to work together, often in teams with other professionals, in order to solve problems.

(continued)

TABLE 4.3   *(continued)*

- Understand that science and technology provide opportunities to women and men of all ages, groups, backgrounds, races, religions, and abilities to do various scientific and technological work and that a person's appearance, gender, race, or national origin should not influence acceptance or rejection of his or her contributions to science or technology.
- Understand that tools help scientists to make better observations, measurements, and equipment for investigations and that science helps drive technology.
- Understand that people have always had questions about the natural world and that scientists have invented tools and techniques to help answer those questions.
- Understand that technological designs have constraints and that the technological solutions may have intended benefits and unintended consequences, some of which may not be predictable.

Dimension 3. Science in Personal and Social Perspectives Standard
The students will:

3.1 Develop an understanding of personal health.

- Understand that safety and security are basic needs of humans.
- Demonstrate responsibility for their own health through regular exercise routines.
- Understand that good nutrition is essential to health, develop nutritious eating habits, and recognize that nutritional needs vary with age, sex, weight, activity, and body functions.
- Recognize and avoid substances that can damage the human body, including environmental hazards (e.g., lead, radon), and recognize that prescription drugs can be beneficial if taken as directed.
- Recognize the potential for accidents, identify safety hazards, and take precautions for safe living.
- Understand that the sex drive is a natural human instinct; the consequences of new life and disease must be understood.

3.2 Identify characteristics and describe changes in populations.

- Understand that human populations include groups of persons who live in a particular location.
- Understand that density refers to the number of individual of a population who can live in a particular amount of space.
- Realize that the size of a human and animal population can increase or decrease and that populations will increase unless factors such as disease, insufficient food, or disasters limit it. Overpopulation increases the consumption of resources.

3.3 Identify types of resources.

- Understand resources are materials we get from the living and nonliving environment to meet the needs of a population.

TABLE 4.3 *(continued)*

- Identify examples of resources such as air, water, soil, food, fuel, building materials, and the nonmaterial such as quiet places, beauty, security, and safety.
- Understand that the supply of resources is limited but that recycling and reduced use can extend the length of time that resources are available; over-consumption and overpopulation deplete resources.

3.4 Identify environments and changes.

- Understand that the concept of environment includes the space, conditions, and factors that affect an individual's or an entire population's quality of life and ability to survive.
- Realize that environmental changes can be caused by natural or human causes and that some changes are good, some bad, other neither good nor bad.
- Understand that internal and external changes in the earth's system cause natural hazards and destruction of life.
- Understand that pollution is a change in the environment that can influence health and survival or limit the activities of organisms, including humans; pollution can be caused by natural occurrences and human activity.
- Comprehend that some environmental changes occur slowly and other rapidly and describe examples of each (e.g., weather, climate, erosion, movements of large geologic masses).

3.5 Recognize the benefits and challenges of science and technology.

- Understand that inventions and problem solutions can affect other people in helpful and harmful ways.
- Recognize that science influences society through its knowledge and world-view and that technology influences society through its products and processes.
- Identify risks and analyze the potential benefits and consequences and understand that risks and benefits relate directly to personal and social decisions.
- Describe how science and technology have improved transportation, health, sanitation, and communication and realize that the benefits of science and technology are not always available to all people.
- Understand that science and technology have advanced through the contributions of many different people, different cultures, and at different times throughout history.
- Realize that scientists and engineers have codes of ethics that require humans who are part of their research to be fully informed about the risks and benefits associated with the research.
- Understand that science cannot answer all questions and that technology cannot solve all human problems or meet all human needs.

Dimension 4. History and Nature of Science Standard
The students will:

4.1 Understand that science is a human endeavor.

- Realize that science and technology have been used for a long time. *(continued)*

▸ **TABLE 4.3**   *(continued)*

- Understand that women and men have made important contributions to science and technology throughout history.
- Understand that there is still much to learn about science.
- Understand that doing science requires persons of different abilities and talents.

4.2 Understand the nature of science.

- Realize that scientists use consistent procedures to test explanations and to form ideas.
- Understand that scientists do not always agree, particularly when active research is pursued in new experimental areas, but that science ideas are supported by considerable observation and confirmation, even though the nature of science is tentative.
- Understand that scientists expect their ideas and research to be evaluated by other scientists and that while scientists may disagree over conclusions, they agree that skepticism, questioning, and open communication are essential to progress in science.

4.3 Understand the importance of history to science.

- Realize that studying the lives and times of important scientists provides further understanding about the nature of scientific inquiry and the relationships between science and society.
- Realize that the history of science reveals that the scientists and engineers of high achievement are considered to be among the most valued contributors of any culture.
- Trace the history of science to understand how difficult it was for innovators to break through the dominant scientific preconceptions of their times and to reach conclusions that seem obvious today.

Source: Adapted from National Research Council, *National Science Education Standards* (Washington, DC: National Academy Press, 1996), pp. 121–171.

Science and Technology

Science and technology complements the inquiry standard. This standard places emphasis on helping students develop scientific abilities and science understandings and to understand connections between the natural world and the human-designed world. Decision making is an important student outcome that arises from student activity associated with the process of identifying scientific problems, determining risks and benefits, designing solutions, and evaluating solutions (NRC, 1996).

Science in Personal and Social Perspectives

Meeting this standard ensures that learners understand that science is a part of personal and social issues. This dimension encourages teachers to help learners achieve outcomes that will help them develop decision-making skills to solve

WHAT RESEARCH **SAYS**   ◆◆◆

What Are Teachers' Attitudes Toward Reform?

To what extent do experienced teachers support and participate in the new spirit of science education reform? Scott Willis (1995) reports the results of a survey of 6,000 teachers from grades 1 through 12 were asked about their preparation, teaching beliefs, and teaching methods. Following are some of the highlights from the report:

- Nearly all teachers believe that hands-on student activities should be part of science education.
- Ninety percent of the elementary and middle school teachers believe that students should receive direct concrete experiences before they are exposed to abstract science concepts and technical terminology.
- Ninety percent of the elementary and middle school teachers believe that students learn best when science is connected to a personal context or to social issues.
- More than 90 percent of the elementary and middle school teachers support some form of cooperative group learning.
- Seventy percent of the elementary and middle school teachers believe it is a good idea to emphasize depth over breadth—covering fewer science concepts but going into greater depth.

- Almost one-third of the grades 1 through 4 teachers disagree with the recommendation to teach science concepts *before* the terminology associated with those concepts.
- Although the reform literature urges less emphasis on science facts, half of the elementary teachers and almost two-thirds of the middle school teachers put heavy emphasis on having their students learn "important terms and facts in science."
- Thirty percent of the teachers of grades 1 through 4 believe that students learn best in groups with peers of similar abilities. Most doubt that heterogeneous grouping is best for all students.
- Seventy-five percent of the elementary and middle school teachers rate their science textbooks as "good" or better, although most reform advocates are critical of these books.
- Elementary teachers are confident in their ability to use recommendations offered by the science reform movements, such as cooperative learning.
- Many elementary teachers do not feel confident in their ability to teach some of the science concepts recommended by the reform movements.

Source: Adapted from S. Willis, "Reinventing Science Education: Reformers Promote Hands-On, Inquiry-Based Learning," ASCD *Curriculum Update* (Summer 1995).

---

personal and community problems. The standard provides ideas to help expose students to matters of making personal health choices, help students understand changes in populations and the complications of resource usage, and become aware of science and society issues on local, national, and global levels (NRC, 1996).

History and Nature of Science

Science is ongoing, and the ideas change over time. The history and nature of science standard encourages teachers to provide learning experiences that use the history of science to inform the present, predict likely changes in the future, and appreciate that science is not a static or absolute discipline. This dimension of scientific literacy helps students appreciate the human role in science and how that role has helped shape various cultures (NRC, 1996).

Science goals focus on the interrelationships of learners, their inquiry processes, society, technology, and the history of science.

CHAPTER SUMMARY

Part of the answer to the question, "What are the goals for science teaching?" lies in the belief that science is an essential component of literacy and must achieve its proper place in the school curriculum. If science is regarded as a single subject to be focused upon only in itself, this defeats the conception of the basics that are necessary for an effective education. Science can help learners develop important attitudes that foster desired habits of the mind and positive levels of self-esteem. The attitudes typically arise from successes experienced while developing many skills. In science we call these *process skills* (they were described in Chapter 1). The processes are ways in which important outcomes are achieved, such as increases in language skills, social skills improvements, and advances in reading, in addition to new levels of knowledge. Acquiring knowledge is typically the focus of many subjects. In science, this is one desired outcome. Even so, the knowledge gained in science is viewed as a pathway or route to other destinations. The content of science may be integrated with other subject and skill areas; it fills the many interests of children and can have a tremendous impact on chidren's lives.

Various reform efforts inform us as we change science programs, adjust expectations for learners, and modify teaching habits. The National Science Education Standards describe seven essential parts that are necessary for systemic reform. As teachers we cannot meet the standards by ourselves, but we can focus on the content standards that fall within our responsibility as teachers. The content standards require further study. While understanding fundamental science content concepts is important, some may misperceive that the standards are concerned only with the physical, life, and earth/space science concepts and learning activities for children. This is not true; to focus only on those topics shortchanges students, depriving them of additional essential experiences.

The physical, life, and earth/space science content is an important context for developing scientific literacy. The standards require four new dimensions of science learning to ensure that real progress is made toward helping students achieve literacy in science. These new dimensions challenge us to help students understand science as a process of inquiry, understand the interrelationships between science and technology, benefit from science personally and understand the social perspective of science, and understand and appreciate the history and nature of science. Parts of the many outcomes for these new dimensions predictably overlap and complement learning. The challenge will be to find a way to link all of these dimensions of science learning and literacy to the content context.

DISCUSSION QUESTIONS AND PROJECTS

1. What principles guide your views on teaching and learning? Combine your beliefs into a philosophy statement, and write it down. How does your philosophy compare with the goals and standards of science education given in this chapter? How do your ideas compare with those of others in your class? Which of the reform efforts do you embrace philosophically?

2. Imagine that you are preparing for an interview with a school principal or a director of personnel. You have heard that this question will be asked: "What are your top four or five goals for teaching science in _____ grade" [your choice of grade level]? How would you answer this question?

3. Survey your state department of education, school district, and science professionals to compile a list of the main goals for elementary or middle school science education. How does this list compare to the recommendations of the National Science Education Standards, Project 2061, Scope, Sequence, and Coordination Project, and Project Synthesis?

4. Examine several popular elementary science textbooks or school science programs, or both. How do these materials attempt to meet the new standards and dimensions of scientific literacy?

5. How can you act on the science standards by building them into your lessons? Examine how we use the goals in our lesson plans located in the last part of this book. What other suggestions do you have for using the standards?

ADDITIONAL READINGS

If you are interested in learning more about some of the topics raised in this chapter, consider the following sources.

American Association for the Advancement of Science, *Benchmarks for Scientific Literacy* (New York: Oxford University Press, 1993). You will gain an understanding of the changing outcomes that are recommended for modern scientific literacy.

Carol Minnick and Donna Alvermann, *Science Learning* (Newark, DE: International Reading Association, 1991). This book emphasizes the basic and integrated science process skills, an important aspect of learning to read.

National Research Council, *National Science Education Standards* (Washington, DC: National Academy Press, 1996). This is must reading. The content standards section contains rich classroom vignettes and detailed examples of how the various standards may be met. These descriptions stimulate many practical ideas about selecting appropriate materials and planning lessons that will promote scientific literacy.

F. James Rutherford and Andrew Ahlgren, *Science for All Americans* (New York: Oxford University Press, 1990). This book contains a complete description of the content and type of science teaching envisioned. It is written in lay language.

2061 Today newsletter, from 2061 Today, American Association for the Advancement of Science, 1333 H Street, NW, Washington, DC 20005.

CHAPTER OUTLINE

CHAPTER 5

How Can You Plan Constructivist Science Lessons and Assess Student Performance?

It was spring, and Jennifer was near the end of her first year of the fourth-grade teaching position that she had won over forty-two applicants. Jennifer was astounded to learn that the competition had been so keen; she could not believe that she was better prepared for the position than the other applicants, especially since some had several years of teaching experience. When she politely inquired during casual conversation midway through her first semester, Jennifer learned that she had impressed Mr. Emerson, the principal, and the teaching staff with her views on teaching and that the science demonstration lesson that she taught was perceived by the staff as being on the cutting edge of the movement stimulated by the National Science Education Standards. Mr. Emerson and her fourth-grade teaching team of three other teachers had high expectations for Jennifer. The fact that she was a first-year teacher did not tempt them to make excuses for her; the school's staff had its focus on providing what was best for the students.

Jennifer did not disappoint anyone. She proved her value among her teammates, and her humble, self-effacing ways made her a joy to collaborate with. Jennifer read widely, eagerly collected teaching ideas, and was genuinely grateful for suggestions. She was flattered when other teachers indicated interest in her science lessons and how those lessons could interface with some of the topics taught by her teammates who, among themselves, chose to specialize in one subject, which was taught to all fourth-grade students who rotated through the mod. Jennifer thought her teammates were only being kind, but they recognized considerable skill and potential for teacher leadership and recommended that Mr. Emerson appoint her to the Professional Development Council (PDC).

Jennifer accepted her appointment to the school PDC, although she was surprised by the offer, thinking the appointment should be given to someone with more experience. Science was the topic for next year's PDC agenda. The school had a recent curriculum revision that attempted to fulfill the National Science Education Standards. Curriculum decisions for her school district were made by a local control process and site-based management. The state recommended a general curriculum model and materials that schools might use but let the schools determine how best to devise and implement the curriculum. The standards made it difficult to select a single textbook and still be able to prepare students well for the statewide mandatory proficiency test, given to students each year at each grade level. The test was designed to measure progress toward fulfilling the standards. The PDC was concerned with the teachers' needs that were identified on a survey they had taken. The survey spoke of high frustration levels and a desire for extensive inservice in teaching toward the standards.

Coincidentally, the school's student proficiency test scores were received the same day as Jennifer's first meeting with the council. Teacher comparisons were discouraged but were unavoidable. Jennifer's students were the only ones who scored above the norm. Was this a fluke, or did this first-year teacher do something different to encourage higher student performance?

Jennifer felt somewhat defensive at first but soon realized that her colleagues' questions were professional and were asked in the spirit of schoolwide collaboration. Did she feel overwhelmed by the standards? What science concepts did she teach, and how did she decide when to teach them? Was there an order that worked best? How did she bring some balance from the science disciplines into her lessons? What did she do with the four new dimensions of science: science as inquiry, science and technology, science in personal and social perspectives, and history and nature of science? How could she possibly fit them into science lessons?

Jennifer described the frustrated feelings she too experienced at first. The standards advocated covering fewer concepts but actually seemed to expect teachers and students to do more in science than had ever before been attempted. Jennifer explained that desperation motivated her to think back to some of her experiences during teacher preparation. She found a way to connect certain experiences and use them as tools for dealing with the expectations that the standards seemed to bring.

Jennifer described a tool called *concept mapping* that helped her to sort and organize the science content concepts into story lines that were supported by themes. One of the other teachers thought that the concept mapping technique seemed like brainstorming and webbing used in language arts, but Jennifer demonstrated that mapping was much more than that and explained how the techniques helped her to find a focus for the lessons. Jennifer designed each of her lessons for a single concept but planned comprehensively to help students construct their understanding of the concept and to connect it with other concepts from other lessons. Over time, students seemed to be able to make many connections among what they learned. Students even learned to make their own concept maps to illustrate their understanding.

Jennifer also described a *learning cycle model* that she used to plan the sequence of student activities, in order to ensure that the concept was built from direct student activity and then expanded in order to connect with the new content outcomes given by the National Science Education Standards.

She shared some of her lesson plans with the other PDC members. Some members asked her to explain what she meant by *explore, explain, expand,* and *evaluate*. They were curious why Jennifer had students do activities first without explaining the point of the lesson and why she did not always test students at the end of her lessons, although the "evaluate" part of her planning model seemed to indicate that she would assess student learning at the end of each lesson.

Her lesson plans seemed to contain several activities that were related to each other, in a sequence over several days, sometimes requiring that almost a whole day be devoted to science. Of course, these special occasions were supported by Jennifer's teammates and at times they helped her teach science to all of the 100 fourth graders whom they shared. The PDC concluded that the ideas that Jennifer learned and used might help other teachers, and they decided to plan next year's professional development agenda around concept mapping, learning cycle planning, and teaching techniques. Jennifer was consulted often about how to do this and to suggest where the PDC might find assistance.   ◆

INTRODUCTION

You say that this scenario is too far-fetched? Rest assured, it is not. We find that many of our new teacher graduates experience situations very much like this one. They have skills that are different—in some ways more sophisticated—than more experienced teacher professionals have and that make them in demand when schools and teachers find themselves facing the challenges afforded by change. New science standards and rising expectations for students and teachers require new ways of thinking and doing business. One new challenge is to convert typical planning processes into an approach that supports constructivist teaching and learning. In this chapter we:

1. explore the use of concept mapping as a planning and assessment tool.
2. investigate a constructivist model for planning lessons that unifies the National Science Education (content) Standards.
3. explore several assessment techniques that are appropriate for constructivist learning.

CONCEPT MAPPING

"Outcomes are high quality, culminating demonstrations of significant learning in context" (Spady, 1994, p. 18). William Spady reminds us that the operative word is *demonstration*. Outcomes identify in general terms the end product that we expect students to develop or achieve. The National Science Education Standards, and other reform movements, identify the essential contexts and the types of high-quality end products that we should expect from scientifically literate students. Sometimes these end products—outcomes—are described for a particular grade level, but most often they are listed for a cluster of school grades. The grade-level placement, order, fit, and process of the steps required for successful demonstration of these end products is not defined. This planning chore is the duty of the curriculum developers or, more likely, each teacher. Several of the questions asked of Jennifer in our chapter scenario sound anxious and imply the uncertainty that this chore can cause for teachers.

There is a tool that can help teachers and curriculum developers to face the challenge of planning: *concept mapping.* Concept maps are essential tools for planning and teaching, and they can help improve student concept constructions, while helping to avoid misconceptions. Concept mapping is a more recent development that is becoming widely used as constructivist learning models are more accepted in science education.

Concept mapping helps students fulfill high-quality and meaningful learning outcomes in science. Maps provide concrete visual aids to help organize information before it is learned. Many science textbooks are beginning to use concept maps among their end-of-chapter activities. Teachers who have used them have found that they provide a logical basis for deciding what main ideas to include in (or delete from) their lesson plans and science teaching. Concept maps can be developed for an entire course, one or more units, or even a single lesson. We have developed concept maps for each chapter of this book. These maps introduce you to the dominant ideas and illustrate the relationships among the chapter's concepts and are available in the instructor's manual. Please ask your instructor for copies.

A concept map is a tool that illustrates the conceptual connections understood by the map's creator. Each person may construct a different map, depending on how he or she understands the subject of the map. Never try to memorize a concept map. Instead, study it for the conceptual story that it tells, paying attention to the main ideas and the relationships among them.

Necessary Definitions

Some definitions must be provided before we can proceed. Bear in mind the fundamental purpose of education: to help students find new meaning in what they learn. We refer to this as *meaningful learning.* David Ausubel (1968) contrasts meaningful learning with rote learning, which is the result of many disjointed lessons. Concept maps use three types of knowledge: facts, concepts, and generalizations.

Meaningful Learning.   Meaningful learning implies that as a result of instruction, individuals are able to relate new material to previously acquired learning. This means that learners see new knowledge in the light of what they already know and understand; hence they find new meaning. Knowledge continually grows, but in a fashion that encourages connections with what learners already know. If these connections are missing, learners may regard the ideas they are taught as useless abstractions that only need to be memorized for a test.

As an example, learning that electricity flows through a circuit can be meaningful for children if they are able to see (with a teacher's guidance) that this idea applies to their previous understanding about how and where electricity is used (Figure 5.1). Children may have previously believed that electricity comes from the wall where an electric switch or outlet is located. When someone turns the switch on or plugs an appliance into the outlet, the electricity flows to a lamp or an appliance. A teacher would facilitate learning by helping children understand that electricity indeed flows through the switch or comes out of the outlet, but also that there are continuous electric wires between the electric pole outside the house and the switch or outlet inside the house, and between the switch or outlet and the appliance. Unless children are able to see these connections between the existing knowledge and the new, they are likely to regard this generalization about electricity as an abstraction, or something to memorize without exactly knowing its importance.

FIGURE 5.1   Example Concept Map

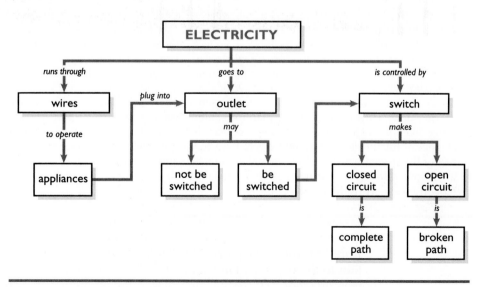

<TEACHERS ON SCIENCE TEACHING>

How Can You Create Learning Opportunities?

by Mike Roberts
Grade 1 Teacher, Hollister School District, Hollister, CA

When I was a student teacher, my master teacher made available to me a space in which to save some of the materials I used in her second-grade classroom. Here I saved all the odds and ends for which I had no other place. Eventually this collection included many objects that were useful for creating science activities.

One day a boy brought an old fifth-grade science textbook into school. He had found many activities in it that he desperately wanted to do. I told him to select one we could do with the things we had on hand. He selected a wind speed indicator made from a paper plate, paper cups, a pin, tape, and a pencil—all readily available from the box of extra materials. We constructed it, and he made many more with his friends.

There were several lessons here for me. First, children have a very good idea of what they want to learn about. Second, they can figure out how to create something from the available material. Third and most important, it is very important to keep a significant amount of stuff around for children to use.

Since then I have tried to ensure that somewhere in the room there are materials that students can use in their own fashion. I collect everyday materials because science is a curricular area that requires that students investigate their everyday world and inquire about its workings. That's all well and good, but there are also practical questions. How does a teacher plan for something like this? How does a teacher set up a classroom for this kind of activity? What are the rest of the students doing while several are messing about with a box of interesting materials? How do we meet students' needs?

Here are some of the ways I dealt with these issues, and I am sure other teachers are inventing different ways also. First, collect things that you suspect may be useful: paper tubes, plates, cups, string, wire, batteries, lights, switches—the list goes on and on. These things are supposed to be in your science kits, but in my experience they have been used up and not replaced. If you do have a pristine kit, then you will be expected to replace what is used. I found it best to collect my own. I don't spend a lot of money. Most of this can be salvaged from the refuse of daily life.

Second, I arranged my school day to accommodate a free time that allows activities that give the students a chance to use materials with my supervision. I try to encourage, question, and challenge. I try not to direct. I know everyone won't choose every activity every day. The material at hand will allow the students to negotiate and discuss the use of whatever is available.

The goal of our educational system is to engage young minds in activities that lead them to experiment. As they become more aware of their world, they are encouraged to explore and then use their new knowledge to construct a more complete understanding. More understanding means more use of the knowledge and more questions.

I haven't written a lesson plan here, but I've described a plan for creating learning opportunities. This is how I as a teacher place the materials in the room and how I build in opportunities for students to explore them. This way they learn to question each other and me and to experiment and thereby construct a better understanding of their world.

Rote Learning.   Memorization without understanding and without a connection to the previous knowledge is called *rote learning*. Rote learning promotes memorization of facts; meaningful learning promotes conceptual understanding.

Facts. A *fact* is a singular occurrence that happens in the past or present and that has no predictive value for the future. Thus, the information that you are now reading in this book at a specific time of day is a fact, just as a statement about what you ate for lunch or dinner yesterday is a fact. These facts may be completely isolated events that give no indications about your study or eating habits. On the other hand, if you regularly read your science methods book at the same time, or if you consistently eat salad for lunch and chicken or fish for dinner, then these seemingly isolated facts have much in common with your similar actions at other times.

Concepts. Common attributes between facts can be described and named. The name given represents a *concept*. Interestingly, your behavior today or yesterday can be described by a single word or brief phrase. Words such as *preparation* and *follow-up* or a phrase like *nutritious diet* are examples of concepts based on an accumulation of facts. The definitions of these concepts may include descriptions such as "you read your textbook before and after the science methods class," or "you try to eat foods that are low in calories, fat, and cholesterol." A concept covers a broader set of events than a singular occurrence that might happen at random. Therefore, concepts by their nature are abstract. Other examples of concepts are computer, animal, mineral, vegetable, food chain, magnets, solution, conservation, and buoyancy. All require that we know the definition to understand the meaning. In fact, most words in the dictionary represent concepts. All learners, especially young children, need to experience many examples of singular occurrences or facts before they can develop the abstract understanding necessary for conceptualization. But once they learn the concept, they do not need to learn isolated facts that are subsumed in it. They can reconstruct these facts when they need them.

Generalizations. *Generalizations* are broad patterns between two or more concepts that have predictive value. Generalizations are rules or principles that contain more than one concept and that have predictive value. Thus, a statement such as "like poles in magnets repel each other and opposite poles attract" is a generalization, and it can predict what would happen if two magnets were brought next to each other. Learners must know the concepts of *magnets, poles, attraction,* and *repel* before they can fully understand the meaning of the generalization.

What Are Concept Maps?

Concepts are abstract ideas. Concept maps, on the other hand, are concrete graphic illustrations that indicate how a single concept is related to other concepts in the same category (see Figure 5.2). As you begin to learn about concept maps, you may prefer to think of them as sophisticated planning webs that reveal what concepts children must learn and how the concepts must be related. Curricula are primarily designed to teach concepts that students do not already know. Therefore, teaching and learning will be greatly enhanced if we know

FIGURE 5.2   Concept Map for Air

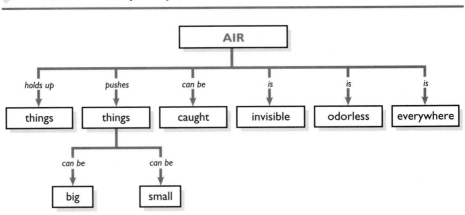

Source: This figure represents concepts found in the first-grade text (Addison-Wesley, publisher) described by John R. Staver and Mary Bay in "Analysis of the Conceptual Structure and Reasoning Demands of Elementary Science Texts at the Primary (K–3) Level," *Journal of Research in Science Teaching* 26, no. 4 (1989): 334.

which concepts should be included and which need to be excluded from instructional programs.

Concept maps show relationships among different smaller and larger concepts. By looking at a concept map and considering the level of the children's abilities and other instructional factors, you can make a decision about the scope of the concepts you need to cover in an instructional program. Joseph Novak states that

> a good curriculum design requires an analysis first of the concepts in a field of knowledge and, second, consideration of some relationships between these concepts that can serve to illustrate which concepts are most general and superordinate and which are more specific and subordinate. (Novak, 1979, p. 86)

A concept map's visual illustration of main ideas is the primary advantage it provides over other ways of planning instruction. A concept map shows hierarchical relationships: how various subordinate concepts are related to the superordinate concepts. A relationship can descend several levels deep in the hierarchy of concepts. The relationship between superordinate and subordinate concepts is shown in Figure 5.3.

A concept map is different in several ways from the outline or table of contents generally found at the beginning of a book. First, outlines do not show any definite relationships between concepts; they simply show how the material is organized. Concept maps, on the other hand, show a definite relationship between big ideas and small ideas, thus clarifying the difference between details

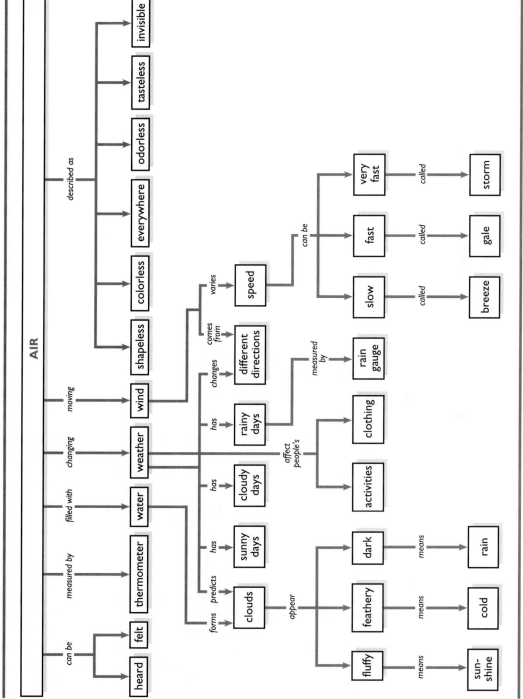

Source: The figure shows the relationship of several levels of subordinate concepts as provided by John R. Staver and Mary Bay, in "Analysis of the Conceptual Structure and Reasoning Demands of Elementary Science Texts at the Primary (K–3) Level," *Journal of Research in Science Teaching* 26, no. 4 (1989): 339. The researchers examined the contents of the Merrill first-grade science text.

or specifics and the big idea or superordinate concept. This can be helpful when a teacher must decide how much emphasis to give to specific facts as compared to concepts in a lesson.

The second difference is that concept maps provide visual imagery that can help students recall information and see relationships between concepts. Outlines do not provide such imagery. Outlines do serve a useful function: They indicate a sequence of different steps. Concept maps, on the other hand, show hierarchies of ideas that suggest psychologically valid sequences. These hierarchies may not match the linear sequence, or outline, that a teacher has decided to use for a presentation.

Third, concept maps can show interrelationships between ideas, or *cross-links*. These help to "tie it all together," as students often remark.

Why Should Concept Maps Be Developed?

Concept maps help teachers understand the various concepts that are embedded in the larger topic they are to teach. This understanding improves teacher planning and instruction. Since the science knowledge domain is vast, and most of us have acquired it in pieces at different stages, we are not likely to see the important connections between the separate ideas we teach. As an exercise, mapping provides an opportunity to express our understanding about various concepts and to show relationships with other similar and dissimilar concepts. Ultimately, the larger topic or unit (superordinate concept) is hierarchically arranged. This arrangement shows facts at the bottom and subordinate concepts arranged in relationships with each other in the body of the map (see, for example, the details of Figures 5.1 through 5.3). Our experience with hundreds of teachers and students has convinced us that they gain new insight from developing concept maps when they structure what they know around a superordinate concept. This observation is also supported by Novak and Gowin (1986): "Students and teachers often remark that they recognize new relationships among concepts that they did not before" (p. 17).

Concept mapping is one of the most crucial steps to take while deciding what to include in a curriculum, unit, or lesson plan. Clear mapping may help to avoid student-formed misconceptions. Without concept maps, teachers choose to teach what they can remember or what they prefer. The topics they select in this manner may be appropriate at times, especially for teachers who have had previous successful experiences with the material, but this process opens a major psychological flaw in the process of curricuum development and lesson planning. The concepts or topics chosen may be so disconnected from each other that learners are baffled and see no connections. Learners may also fail to receive new meaning because they cannot link the new material with what they have previously learned. As a result, learners may resort to memorizing isolated facts, treating the experiences and ideas with less thought than we prefer. This mental inaction would defeat the modern science goal of developing new habits of the mind.

While some material must be memorized, sustained memorization has questionable value in science. Taking the time to identify concepts yields clear science topics and helps to determine which topics are worth learning. Mapping concepts suggests specific objectives that teachers must establish for pupils. Concept maps can help you see the logic of the relationships among specific concepts. Once you see this logic, you can decide how much depth or breadth to include in lessons so that students will see the same conceptual relationships. These decisions consist of choosing the proper activities and learning aids, as well as selecting the appropriate type of pupil evaluation.

You can also use concept maps to organize the flow of the classroom lessons. We have used concept maps as advance organizers to focus students' attention and guide them along to seeing a bigger picture and for use as a mental scaffolding for organizing their thoughts and discoveries. You can use concept maps as road maps to indicate the direction in which instruction is to proceed in your classroom—up, down, and across the map. Students can be shown concept maps several times during instruction so that they can see what has been covered and how it fits with the rest.

Another way you can use concept maps is for student evaluations. For example, display large pieces of newsprint in a conspicuous place and use them daily to show the science ideas students have learned and how these ideas interrelate. This daily effort is an example of formative evaluation. You could ask intermediate and middle school children to develop maps at the end of instruction to reflect what they understand, a process called *summative evaluation*.

Steps for Developing a Concept Map

A concept map can be developed for the entire course for a year or semester, or for a single unit, or even for a single lesson. Figure 5.4 shows the relationship of concepts in a concept map. The following steps work for all concept maps:

1. List on paper all of the concepts (names of topics) that pertain to a general area you will teach. Only the names are needed at this stage. No descriptions are necessary. For example, let us say you have examined your next science chapter or module and have listed the following topics: air, weather, clouds, storms, and effects of weather.

2. Note any specific facts (examples) that are either essential for students to learn or that you find especially interesting. The facts and examples you list might include: air moves, measurements are used to track air movement, moving air causes weather, weather can be helpful or harmful, and weather helps us decide what clothes to wear.

3. From the list of concepts, choose what you find as an overarching concept (superordinate), and place it at the top of the paper. (You may want to use a large sheet of newsprint or other suitable drawing paper.) You decide that the overarching concept is *weather*. It seems that all other ideas relate to it. Satisfied, you now line up the other concepts by going to Step 4.

4. Arrange the first level of subordinate concepts underneath the superordinate concept. Generally, this stage requires the use of propositions or linking words like *provides, types, contains, can be,* and so on to develop the appropriate connections between subordinate concepts. Refer to the second line of boxes in Figure 5.4. (The first level of subordinate concepts is known by another term, *coordinate concepts,* because they link or coordinate the superordinate concept and the subordinate concepts found lower in the hierarchy. Each coordinate concept is related to the same superordinate concept, but it is distinctly different from other concepts arranged at that level of the hierarchy.)

5. After the first level of coordinate concepts has been identified, start arranging other subordinate concepts that are directly related to the level above.

FIGURE 5.4   Concept Map for Concept Maps

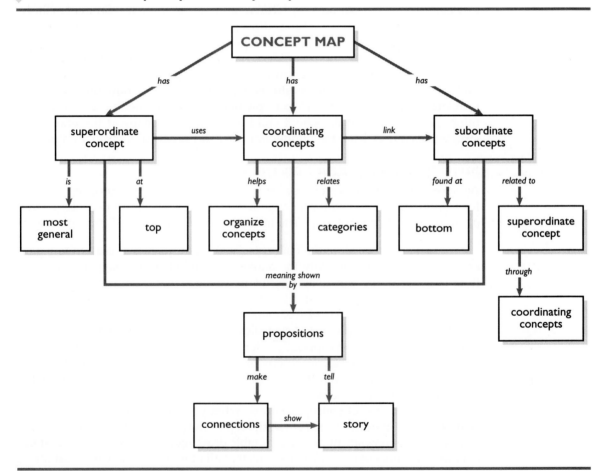

Similarly, you can develop further hierarchies by going down several levels. You will find that specific facts will be examples of certain individual subordinate concepts that will most likely be at the bottom of the hierarchy. See, for example, in Figure 5.3 that *clouds* is a subordinate concept connected to coordinate concepts of *water* and *weather,* and the concepts *fluffy, feathery,* and *dark* are connected to *clouds* to show other subordinate concepts in the hierarchy; each concept relates back to the superordinate concept, *air.*

6. Draw lines to show relationships among the subordinate, coordinate, and superordinate concepts. The entire hierarchy should resemble a pyramid. Write linking words (propositions) on the lines to show relationships among concepts. These relationships form principles. Refer to Figure 5.4 and notice the connecting lines with propositions—for example, *has, uses,* and *through.*

7. After the entire map has been developed, mark or circle certain subordinate concepts that are particularly appealing for your students or are at the appropriate difficulty level. These would generally constitute your course or unit for the given time period.

There are two more important points. First, try to minimize jumping around the entire map; try not to select topics without a strong rationale. The strongest reason for selecting a topic should rest on the knowledge the children acquired earlier. During the appropriate phases of your instruction (called *concept invention* and *expansion,* which are explained later in this chapter), you need to help children link the new concept with previous learning.

Second, balance the number of specific details you teach in terms of how well they contribute to overall conceptual development. Remember, the factual information sits at the bottom of the map, and your purpose is to have children understand what rests at higher levels of the map. Teaching factual information alone does not help children to develop concepts at a higher level unless you make specific attempts to move up the hierarchical ladder.

PLANNING CONSTRUCTIVIST SCIENCE LESSONS

Reform efforts, such as the National Science Education Standards, direct our attention toward teaching for the goal of scientific literacy. Standards identify numerous outcomes that we attempt to help students achieve. Embedded in the outcomes are dozens of essential science concepts, skills, values, and cross-disciplinary science knowledge that students are expected to demonstrate. Constructivist learning theory cautions us against attempting the futile effort of frontal teaching. How can we address the new expectations held aloft for science teachers and students?

Selecting or Developing Unit Activities

Concept maps illustrate clusters of concepts that share relationships with other science concepts. These relationships make it possible to identify a unifying theme that can help us construct units of science experiences for learners. The standards content outcomes help to provide parameters that are useful for selecting or developing units of science study that encourage full, active participation and student conceptual constructions. The standards, outcomes, and concept maps are tools for making prudent selections to avoid the "fill-up-the-empty-time" approach. Unfortunately, this approach may be chosen in order to fill a certain amount of time that has been set aside for science—just to keep the learners busy and orderly. Used appropriately, mapping and planning can help to make wise choices so lessons have clear expectations, abundant opportunities for students to inquire in order to construct understanding, and expanded contact with science in many contexts. Some general planning principles can help us help students develop their thinking skills and learn meaningful science:

1. *Provide a variety of activities for learning.* Activities that provide children opportunities to experience and manipulate real objects are essential. Stress direct physical and mental involvement for children in primary and intermediate grades. All children must be given opportunities to explain what they experience and to communicate to others in written and spoken language. All learning activities should be expanded to address as many of the goal clusters as possible.

2. *Use specialized vocabulary and introduce concepts after children have gained first-hand experiences with the object or concept.* As a general rule, teachers should talk less and involve students more. One way of doing this is to tell less and ask more. Questions are devices for encouraging children to use their minds. Chapter 10 is devoted to the uses of questions.

3. *Interact with children and have them interact with each other.* Questions stimulate interaction, and interaction encourages thinking. Ask children to describe what they have done or observed. Encourage children to ask each other questions about their experiences and to ask *why* questions.

4. *Focus learning experiences so that children are encouraged to discover concepts.* Focusing on concepts, the main ideas behind learning, helps children learn connections more easily and removes the learning barrier of disconnected facts.

A unit plan consists of goals, objectives, and learning activities. Two types of goals are included: global goals or outcomes selected from visionary science groups and national recommendations that guide the elementary science program (such as those provided here and in Chapter 4) and goals set by the teacher or the school that guide the unit itself. Objectives are smaller, specific statements of what students will do. Learning activities consist of descriptions of what teachers and students will do; they are selected to fulfill the objectives. When the learning activities have been completed, the objectives will have been met, and when the objectives have been met, the unit goals will have been achieved. In turn, when the unit goals have been achieved, meaningful progress will have been made toward accomplishing the science program goals.

Developing Objectives

Objectives are more narrowly focused than goals and consist of the many smaller steps you take to accomplish a goal. Objectives are descriptions of what you, the teacher, expect your students to *do*. This last word is important. Objectives make clear the particular expectations teachers have for their students; objectives use key *action words*—verbs—to describe what students will do to satisfy the teacher that they are meeting the goals. Objectives are beneficial because they help sequence instruction properly, suggest appropriate learning activities and resources, and specify the appropriate evaluation procedures.

Different kinds of objectives exist. The type recommended in this chapter may be called a *performance* or an *instructional objective.* Named after its intention, this objective is a statement that describes what students are expected to be able to do. This type of objective has four parts and can be remembered by the letters A, B, C, and D.

A is the **audience** (class, group, or child) for whom the objective is intended.

B is the **behavior** that a teacher expects from the children.

C is the **conditions** that are necessary for the learning to take place (such as the prerequisites, prior activity, arrangements, or support materials that are needed).

D is the **degree** or minimum level of student performance that shows that the children have completed the objective satisfactorily.

For example, "Given plastic drinking straws, straight pins, thread, tape, modeling clay, paper clips, and metal washers (*conditions*), each fourth-grade child (*audience*) will build (*behavior*) a structure that is at least 30 centimeters tall, uses at least three triangles, and supports at least ten washers without falling down (*degree*)."

The behavior stated in a goal must follow a precise rule: The behavior must be observable or detectable. Verbs like *appreciate, desire, feel, know, like,* and *understand* are too general to use in an objective, yet these verbs are fine when used in a goal, because a goal *is* more general. Verbs like *build, classify, measure,* and *match* are much more precise, and the teacher can measure or observe accomplishment; there is no need to make assumptions about whether a child has done them. Lists of science process skills are rich sources of verbs for your objectives.

Planning the Lesson

Effective science lessons have a central focus and clear expectations for student performance. The *lesson concept*—the main science idea—is the central focus. Lesson objectives help define the expected types and levels of performance, or what and how the students are to demonstrate that they understand the concept and can apply their understanding to useful matters. Conceptual understanding, to have lasting value, must be applied to the student's world. This

Effective science lessons stimulate learners' minds, shape attitudes, and provide learning opportunities for physical manipulation of learning materials.

application expands the depth of learning and helps fulfill the new dimensions of science outcomes: experiencing science as inquiry, understanding the interrelationships of science and technology, using personal and social perspectives to understand science, and comprehending the nature of science throughout its history.

The planning model presented here uses a conceptual focus, helps learners to construct meaning, encourages students to expand understanding of that fundamental meaning, and evaluates student performance in authentic ways. Called a *learning cycle* (see Figure 5.5), this series of planning and teaching steps helps teachers to encourage learners to construct meaning from direct experiences, then expand that understanding through direct treatment of the new dimensions of science. The lesson planning model in this chapter closely follows the original format of the Science Curriculum Improvement Study (SCIS, see Chapter 7), which is credited with the greatest student achievement gains in

FIGURE 5.5   The Planning and Learning Cycle

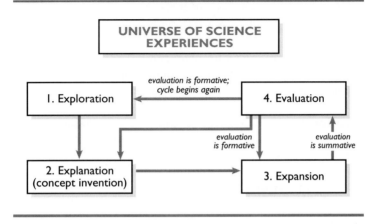

major research studies and significant improvements in student science attitudes and inquiry skills, when compared to similar experimental science programs and traditional science curricula (Shymansky et al., 1982; Bredderman, 1982). Our planning model has been modified to reflect constructivist learning expectations and to emphasize appropriate student evaluation. This approach is simple and thorough, and has considerable potential to effect improvements in students' learning. The planning model also becomes the teaching method. A detailed description of the teaching method is given in Chapter 9. The elements of planning are given here.

The four phases of the science planning and learning cycle provide most of the structure for planning an effective science lesson. Once you identify the concept that is to be learned, you can structure the learning activity to take advantage of the learning cycle. Then you can add descriptions of the proper ways to evaluate what the children learn.

The *4 E approach* is recommended: exploration, explanation, expansion, and evaluation. The following questions should help you plan for each step of the learning cycle as you write the lesson plan. The parenthetical remarks suggest the aspects of science and teaching strategies that may be used. A sample science learning cycle lesson plan is shown in Exhibit 5.1.

Step 1. Planning for student exploration

Children must have concrete materials and experiences if they are to learn concrete concepts. Abstract concepts are largely inappropriate, even with concrete materials, until around age 15 for most pupils. Use these guiding questions:

- What do I want the children to learn? (goals, objectives, attitudes, processes, products)

GRADE
3–4
DISCIPLINE
Physical
Science

Simple Circuits (NSES K–4 Physical Science Outcomes)

Concept statement to be invented

A *circuit* is a pathway that electricity follows from the power source, through the bulb, and back to the power source.

Additional concepts that are important for expansion

Open or closed circuit, series circuit, parallel circuit, switch, filament, insulation, conductor.

Attitudes to emphasize

Curiosity, open-mindedness, perseverance, positive approach to failure, cooperation.

Materials needed

Dry cells, wires, flashlight bulbs, bulb holders, switches, wire strippers, screwdrivers, scissors, aluminum foil, paper clips, paper fasteners, masking tape, small pieces of cardboard.

➡ **Safety precautions:** Have students use not more than five dry cells in the same circuit to limit shock potential and to preserve light bulbs.

EXPLORATION: What process skills will the students use?

(Observation, predictions, classification)

What will the students do?

Teacher's instructions to students: "Using only the three pieces of equipment given to you, light the bulb. Once you are successful, find three other ways to light the bulb. You can use only the three pieces of equipment you have been given. Carefully draw a picture of each method you use to try to light the bulb. Label your drawings *will light* and *will not light.* Be certain to show exactly where your wire is touching and how your bulb is positioned with the battery."

EXHIBIT 5.1   A Sample Lesson Plan Based on the Planning and Learning Cycle

EXPLANATION: What is the concept? How will the concept be constructed?

Concept: *circuit.*

Have students draw their pictures on the chalkboard. Use your finger to trace the pathway that electricity from the battery flows through when the bulb lights and when it does not light. This path is called a *circuit.* Using the students' own ideas and words, construct an explanation that a *circuit* is a pathway electricity follows from the power source to the bulb and back to the power source. Show the students that contact with the bulb must be made in two specific places. The path must be complete from the battery, through the bulb, and back to the battery for the bulb to light. A key question to ask: "In how many places must metal touch the bulb for it to light?" The answer is "two": the side and bottom conductors of the bulb must be included in the circuit.

EXPANSION: What process skills will the students use?

(Making predictions, classifying, controlling variables)

How will the concept be applied and expanded?

Challenge the students to light more than one bulb, combine batteries for more power, and add equipment such as a bulb holder, a switch, and more wires. Ask what happens to other bulbs when one is unscrewed. Make a circuit so all bulbs go out when one is unscrewed: a series circuit. Make a circuit so the other bulbs remain lighted when one bulb is unscrewed: a parallel circuit or a separate series circuit; look carefully. Construct a paper clip switch and demonstrate its function.

Science in Personal and Social Perspectives

1. Name some devices you use that require an electrical circuit.
2. What type of circuit is needed?
3. What would your life be like without electricity controlled by circuits?
4. How is electricity "made"? What resources are necessary? How has demand for electricity changed with population growth?

Science and Technology

A set of car headlights is one example of a specific circuit used for safety purposes. When one light burns out or is broken, the others remain lighted.

1. What are other examples in which the type of circuit used is important for safety or convenience?

(continued)

2. A flashlight uses a simple series circuit and is an example of technology. How has the simple flashlight improved or affected your life? your community? the world?

3. Use the idea of a circuit to make a flashlight out of these materials: cardboard tube, wire, two D-cell batteries, flashlight bulb, paper clip, two paper fasteners, bottle cap, tape.

Science as Inquiry

Plan, conduct, and explain investigations that illustrate: short circuits, open and closed circuits, series and parallel circuits. Identify new concepts in new lessons, such as resistance, cell versus battery, and electromagnetism. Use the concept of open and closed circuit to solve circuit puzzles.

History and Nature of Science

1. Thomas Edison experimented thousands of times before he successfully found a material suitable as a filament that could be used to complete the circuit in a light bulb. How would our world be different today if Edison had never succeeded?

2. Who needs to know about circuits? Name careers, and have students identify those careers that they previously did not know about that rely on some knowledge of electrical circuits. Some possibilities include electrician, appliance repair person, architect, city planner, electric power producer, computer engineer, car/truck repair person.

3. How have the expectations changed over time for persons in these careers?

EVALUATION: How will the students show what they have learned?

(The lesson's performance objectives go here.)

1. Given a prediction sheet containing different circuit diagrams, the students will correctly identify all of the circuits as complete or incomplete by marking them *will light* or *will not light*.

2. The students will construct a working switch from cardboard, two paper fasteners, a paper clip, and two wires.

3. The students will construct and demonstrate the operation of a series circuit and a parallel circuit. Each circuit must include at least two bulbs and be controlled by the paper clip switch.

4. Students will accurately draw a diagram and correctly label the parts of the circuit they use to make their flashlights.

EXHIBIT 5.1   *(continued)*

5. Each student must construct a flashlight that functions properly. Students must show the teacher that the switch turns the light on and off.
6. Each student will cooperate with group partners, volunteer to assist those who request help, and demonstrate a positive approach when having difficulty with manipulative tasks.
7. Each student will describe three ways to use circuits and identify at least two different inventions that control the flow of electricity through those circuits.
8. Each student will describe at least three safety precautions that they take to avoid accidents with electricity.
9. Each student will use inquiry skills to solve correctly four circuit puzzles.

- What concepts will be invented? (science products)
- What activities must the children do to find and to construct the needed data? (processes, information, answers to questions)
- What kinds of records should the children keep? (process skills)
- What kinds of instructions and encouragement will the children need? (attitudes)

Teachers need to direct the children's activities and suggest what kinds of records they should keep. *They should not tell or explain the concept.* State the instructions succinctly, even in the form of objectives. Plan this step carefully so that it is student centered and student-activity based.

Step 2. Planning for explanation

The main purpose of this phase is to reach mental equilibrium through accommodation, as described in the theory of Jean Piaget (see Chapter 2). Equilibrium is reached when a new concept is formed and/or linked to previously understood related concepts. Here students must focus on their primary findings from exploration, and the teacher must help them by introducing proper language or concept labels. This step was originally called *concept invention*. The teacher's task is to lead students through a discussion so that students can discover the concept by inventing it for themselves. The teacher's technique is to question skillfully so that students use the experiences of their explorations to construct scientific meaning. The teacher acts as a facilitator and introduces any special vocabulary that must accompany the concept. Plan this step carefully so that it does not become completely teacher centered; your lectures must be minimal. Use these questions as you plan for this part of your lesson:

- What kinds of information or findings are students expected to provide? (products, process skills)
- How will the students' findings from the exploration phase be reviewed and summarized? (teacher questioning, pupil discussion, graphing, board work)

Effective science lessons stimulate unique learner products.

- How can I use the students' findings and refrain from telling them what they should have found, even if they are incorrect or incomplete? (teacher questioning, guided construction, attitudes)
- What are the proper concept labels or terms that must be attached to the concept? (products)
- What reasons can I give the students if they ask me why the concept is important? (teacher exposition, lesson expansion)

The last question automatically leads to the next phase: Expansion.

Step 3. Planning for expansion

The purpose of this phase is to help students organize their thinking by applying what they have just learned to other ideas or experiences that relate to the lesson's concept and to help the students to expand their ideas. It is very important to use the language of the concept during the expansion-of-the-idea phase. Plan this phase for student involvement. Consider using these questions:

- What previous experiences have the children had that are related to the concept? How can I connect the concept to these experiences? (new activities, questioning)
- What are some examples of how the concept and the activities encourage the students' science inquiry skills? (learning activities, questioning)

- What examples can be used to illustrate the interrelationship of science and technology and the contributions of each to society and the quality (or problems) of life? (discussion, readings, uses of multimedia, class projects)
- In what ways has science benefited the students personally? (class projects, reflective questioning)
- What are examples of how science has influenced our society, policies, and laws? (linkages with social studies, current events)
- What have been the dominant ideas of science throughout recorded history, and how have those ideas and the nature of science changed over time? (linkages with social studies, documentaries, class projects, discussion, biographies)
- What new experiences do the children need in order to expand on the concept? (processes, attitudes, activities)
- What is the next concept related to the present one? How can I encourage exploration of the next concept? (products, processes)

Step 4. Planning for evaluation

The purpose of this phase is to go beyond standard forms of testing. Learning must occur in small increments before larger leaps of insight are possible. Your evaluation can be planned in terms of outcomes and pupil performances. Several types of records are necessary to form a holistic evaluation of the students' learning and to encourage conceptual understanding as well as process skill development. Table 5.1 reflects the need for continual evaluation, not just end-of-chapter or end-of-unit testing. Evaluation can occur at any point in the lesson. Consistent evaluation can help to reveal misconceptions before they become deeply rooted. Ask yourself:

- What key questions should I ask to encourage deep exploration? (processes, attitudes)
- What questions can I ask to help students think about their data in an effort to construct realistic concepts? (processes)
- What questions will expand conception and achieve several science goals? (processes, products)
- What behavior (mental, physical, attitudinal) can I expect from the students? (attitudes, processes)
- What hands-on assessments can the students do to demonstrate the basic skills of observation, classification, communication, measurement, prediction, and inference? (processes)
- What assessments can students do to demonstrate the integrated skills of identifying and controlling variables, defining operationally, forming hypotheses, experimenting, interpreting data, and forming models?
- What pictorial assessments can students do to demonstrate how well they can think through problems that require both knowledge and the integration of ideas? (products)

◢**TABLE 5.1   Types of Appropriate Evaluations for the Learning Cycles**

Phase	Purpose of Evaluation	Type of Evaluation
Explore	Determine possible misconceptions	Questioning and student answers, pictorial assessment
	Document students' uses of process skills	Process skills checklists
	Encourage exploration	Record observations, make predictions, ask observation questions
	Improve social skills and interactions	Teacher observations, checklists
Explain	Clarify concept constructions	Group discussions, data processing, picture drawing, constructing models, reflective questioning
	Document conceptual change	Concept mapping, interviews, pictorial assessment
Expand	Document ability to use integrated process skills	Reflective questioning, hands-on assessment
	Determine students' abilities to transfer learning to new situations	Inventions, writing activities, presentations
	Stimulate new interests, make connections to previous learning	Projects and activities that address standards outcomes, portfolios

- What reflective question assessments will indicate how well the students recall and use what has been learned? (products)

HOW CAN YOU EVALUATE STUDENT LEARNING?

Children learn more and better when we focus clearly on the learning outcomes and objectives we want them to achieve, because planning, teaching, and evaluation go hand in hand. Next we explore these connections.

Limits and Purposes of Tests

Typical forms of evaluation, such as standardized tests and teacher-prepared paper-and-pencil multiple choice or true-false tests, have severe limits. True, they are easy to use and grade. However, their formats limit what they can evaluate; their almost exclusive focus on facts inhibits inductive reasoning, scientific process skills, and affective factors of learning. Indeed, facts are necessary, and children cannot do much science or effectively reason scientifically without a solid factual base. Children may be able to memorize the facts, however, without having any idea about how to apply them. Being able to identify or describe a scientific procedure or apparatus on paper does not mean a child knows when that procedure is appropriate or how to use the apparatus properly. Consider the following test items, which are similar to those used by a recent National Assessment of Education Progress (Raizen & Kaser, 1989):

1. [The child is given a picture of four animals; one is a bird and the other three are mammals.] Which one of these animals is not a mammal?
2. Which of the following is used to measure temperature: feet, degrees, centimeters, minutes, calories?
3. Mary and Jane each bought the same kind of rubber ball. Mary said, "My ball bounces better than yours." Jane replied, "I'd like to see you prove that." What should Mary do?
   (a) Drop both balls from the same height and notice which bounces higher.
   (b) Throw both balls against a wall and see how far each ball bounces off the wall.
   (c) Drop the two balls from different heights and notice which bounces higher.
   (d) Throw the balls down against the floor and see how high they bounce.
   (e) Feel the balls to see which is harder.

The first item asks for a factual answer that could be memorized. The second item also requires a factual answer, but a student could answer correctly without ever having had science, since everyday experience could prevail. Although the third item is more complex, as a teacher you could find it difficult to determine why a pupil gave a wrong answer, since there is no way to evaluate the child's reasoning with this format. Benjamin Bloom sums up the emphasis of traditional testing practices: "Teacher-made [and standardized] tests are largely tests of remembered information. . . . [It] is estimated that over 90 percent of test questions the U.S. public school students are now expected to answer deal with little more than information" (Bloom, 1984, pp. 4–16). Bloom claims that instructional material and classroom teaching rarely rise above the lowest level of his taxonomy for the cognitive domain: the *knowledge level.* In response, science testing is receiving a great deal of attention, and alternate forms of elementary and middle school science assessments are being developed.

Selecting the Tool for the Task

Evaluation, testing, assessment, performance assessment, and *authentic assessment* are terms frequently used by educators interchangeably, but they are not the same. In the Evaluation phase of the learning cycle lesson, we intend for the evaluation to remind us to select the most appropriate tool for determining what students understand and can do so that modifications can be made to instruction or appropriate intervention can be given to correct possible misconceptions among students. Our intention fits Nancy Murphy's (1994) definition of *authentic assessment*: "the determination and documentation of students' current understandings so that teachers might better address students' immediate needs" (p. 14). Therefore, teacher evaluation of student understanding and performance should be ongoing and cumulative, rather than have a summative function—that is, done only at the end of units or chapters. Periodic, focused assessments become the tools of evaluation.

Anne Grall Reichel (1994) offers several questions for planning appropriate assessment tools and placing those tools within the proper scope of teaching:

- Have I determined the skills I want to assess?
- Have I focused on key conceptual ideas and problem solving?
- Have I established criteria to assess student learning?
- Have I made my expectations clear to my students?
- Have I designed instructional tasks with opportunities to create, perform, or produce an end product?
- Am I beginning to make assessment an integral part of my teaching rather than an end point?
- Have I involved students in the evaluation of their own work (Reichel, 1994, p. 25)?

The learning cycle planning and teaching model described in this chapter requires timely and continual teacher assessment of student understanding and skills. Table 5.1 lists several appropriate assessment types that support the expectations for students during each phase of the learning cycle. Most of the effects offered by these assessment types cluster into three types of teacher-designed assessment devices: pictorial assessment, reflective questioning, and hands-on assessment. These approaches were invented by the Full Option Science System (FOSS) of the Lawrence Hall of Science in Berkeley, California, as special techniques to support constructivist teaching and learning through authentic assessment. We used FOSS as a model for designing authentic assessments for the lesson that is featured in this chapter.

Pictorial Assessment.   Pictorial assessment requires students to complete reasoning tasks that differ from traditional fill-in, multiple-choice, and one-answer tasks. The nature of the analysis depends on the types of pictures (or illustrations) used and the context associated with the pictures. Pictorial assessment encourages students to demonstrate their capability to use science process skills appropriately. Some tasks that students may be asked to do could include estimating, predicting, comparing, classifying, identifying properties, determining sequences of events, or designing an experiment.

Pictorial assessment uses pictures that represent familiar objects and events. The assessment device couples well with learning activities and can be completed concurrently. Students are required to apply what they have learned and to communicate what they understand. Often more than one correct answer or solution is possible an assessment task. Some tasks encourage students to estimate their answers, then do a hands-on task that permits them to check their estimations. Other assessments may ask students to complete a pretest

WHAT RESEARCH SAYS   ◆◆◆

Questions to Ask About Tests

Here are some questions the National Center for Improving Science Education suggests that teachers ask when they evaluate the quality of a science test:

1. Are there problems that require students to think about and analyze situations?
2. Are the levels of thinking and analysis developmentally appropriate for the children?
3. Does the test feature sets of problems that call for more than one step in arriving at a solution?
4. Are problems with more than one correct solution included?
5. Are there opportunities for students to use their own data and create their own problems?
6. Are the students encouraged to use a variety of approaches to solve a problem?
7. Are there assessment exercises that encourage students to estimate their answers and check their results?

8. Is the science information that is given in the story problem and elicited in the answer accurate?
9. Is there an opportunity for assessing skills (both in the use of science tools and in science thinking) through some exercises that call for hands-on activities?
10. Are there exercises included in the overall assessment strategy that need to be carried out over time?
11. Are there problems with purposely missing or mistaken information that ask students to find errors or critique the way the problem is set up?
12. Are there opportunities for students to make up their own questions, problems, or designs?

Source: Adapted from Senta A. Raizen and Joyce S. Kaser, "Assessing Science Learning in Elementary School: Why, What, and How?" *Phi Delta Kappan* (May 1989): 721.

and then use a similar activity as a pictorial assessment post-test, such as those shown in Figure 5.6. Figure 5.7 is another type of pictorial assessment; both complement the learning cycle plan in Exhibit 5.1.

Reflective Questioning. This type of assessment consists of written tasks that expect students to respond to a wide range of intellectual tasks. Use of basic and integrated science process skills may be necessary. For example, students may have to recall essential information, analyze information that is provided, apply what they have learned to new but related circumstances, and integrate information in order to construct answers to unusual situations. Students will find it necessary to read instructions carefully, then follow the directions. Students may list responses, construct illustrations, select the best response from choices given, defend their choices, or write extensive responses that can be evaluated for language arts concepts and skills, as well as science.

Reflective questioning assessments require students to reflect on the lesson's content and to use their knowledge in a way that is different from the way it was experienced in the lesson. This type of assessment encourages students

FIGURE 5.6   Pictorial Assessment of Simple Circuits

Pre-test

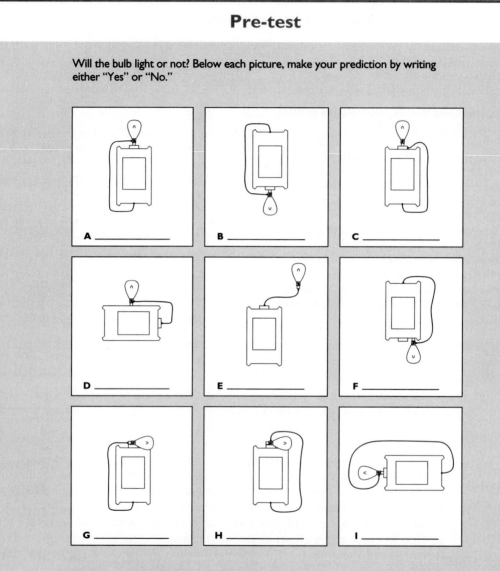

Will the bulb light or not? Below each picture, make your prediction by writing either "Yes" or "No."

Now, use your materials to try each prediction.
Which of your predictions were correct?
Which picture diagrams do not work? Why do you think they might not work? What do they seem to have in common?
What do the pictures that worked have in common?

Post-test

Will the bulb light or not? Write "Yes" or "No" on
the prediction line under each picture.

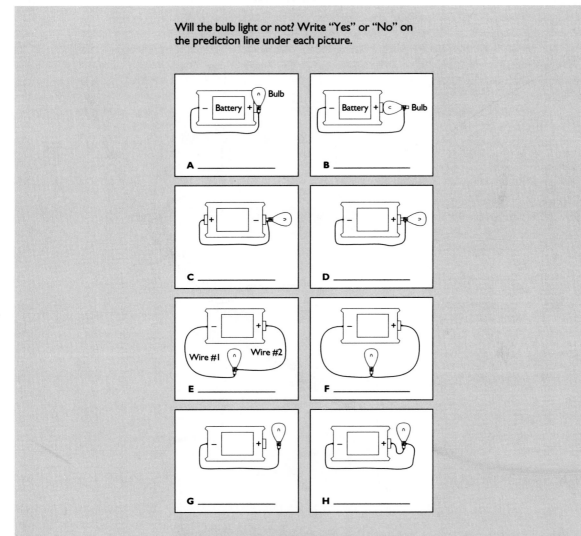

Which picture diagrams will *not* light?
What would you do to each one to make it light?

FIGURE 5.7   Pictorial Assessment

Please examine the pictures carefully. These objects were used in class and contain some parts that relate to concepts that we studied in earlier classes: *insulation* and *conduction*. Other parts and functions represent concepts that we are now studying.

Use the word list to identify the parts shown by the arrows. Words may be used more than once, or not at all. Write your answers on the blank line by each arrow.

Word Bank
open
closed
series
parallel
switch
insulator
conductor
short circuit

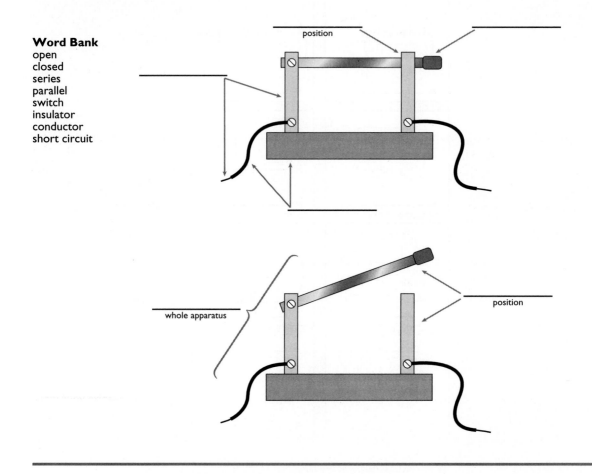

position

whole apparatus

position

---

to use a variety of approaches to solve a problem. Problems often require more than one step in arriving at a solution, and teachers must be prepared to accept all reasonable and correct answers. We have been delighted to observe students discover creative or unique answers and solutions that we did not have in mind when devising the reflective questioning assessment. Figures 5.8 and 5.9 illustrate this type of assessment tool; both complement the learning cycle plan in Exhibit 5.1.

FIGURE 5.8   Reflective Questioning Assessment of Simple Circuits

Pictures A, B, C, and D show batteries, bulbs, wires, and sockets. These pictures represent some of the circuits that we constructed in class. Examine each carefully and answer the questions below the pictures.

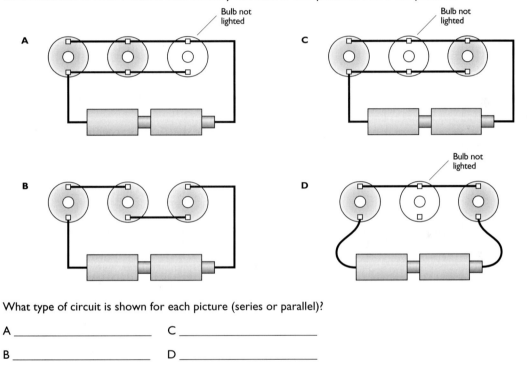

What type of circuit is shown for each picture (series or parallel)?

A _____   C _____

B _____   D _____

Why do you think the bulbs do not light in A, C, and D? There might be many reasons, so please organize your work and explain completely.

What would you do to make the unlit bulbs light in circuits A and C? Please describe all possibilities you can think of.

Go back to circuit D and trace a pathway to show how you would rewire it to make the bulb light. You may remove some wires or add extra wires if you need them.

FIGURE 5.9   Reflective Questioning Assessment of Safety, Circuits, and Electrical Uses

Imagine that a storm has passed, it is nighttime, and you are walking down the street with a flashlight. The street lights are not working and many houses are dark, but you do notice light coming from some houses. You see a loose electrical wire with one end on the ground and the other end attached to a utility pole. What are three safe things you might do?

1. _____

2. _____

3. _____

What are three electrical devices that you use regularly? List them below and identify the types of circuits that they have (series, parallel, or both). Also for each, list inventions that control the flow of electricity to or within the device. You must identify at least two different inventions overall.

Electrical devices	Type of circuit used	Invention that controls
_____	_____	_____
_____	_____	_____
_____	_____	_____

Imagine the our community has a power failure for one week. Life must go on, including school! What things would change in your daily routine in which you usually use electricity, but now cannot? Describe your day without electricity, beginning with your morning wake-up and preparation for school, time spent getting to and from school, and your evening until you go to sleep.

_____

_____

_____

_____

Hands-On Assessment.   Hands-on assessment requires what the term implies: Students must manipulate materials from the lesson in order to complete tasks that enable them to demonstrate what they understand. Hands-on assessment permits a teacher to observe how well a student can perform. (*Performance assessment* is another name for this tool.) Students must use their knowledge and skill in a practical way to solve a problem. Students often must use integrated process skills to identify variables, design investigations, gather information, and demonstrate outcomes of their investigations.

Hands-on assessment gives a teacher opportunities to determine how well students use science tools and science thinking. This type of performance assessment directly pursues the "science as inquiry" and the "nature of science" dimensions of the National Science Education Standards. Students are encouraged to create their own problems and use their own data in identifying solutions. They are required to think about and analyze science in a practical context; the context can be the physical, life, and earth/space science content standards. Hands-on assessment is easily expanded through the complementary technique of reflective questioning. Figures 5.10, 5.11, and 5.12 illustrate the tools of hands-on assessment and complement the learning cycle plan in Exhibit 5.1.

Teacher Records and Observations. Tangible records can reveal a lot about what students know and can and cannot do. Useful records can include the successes and difficulties a child has with homework assignments and notations

FIGURE 5.10 Hands-On Assessment: Electricity Mystery Boxes

Find out what is in the six mystery boxes A, B, C, D, E, and F. They have five different things inside, shown below. Two of the boxes will have the same thing. All of the others will have something different inside.

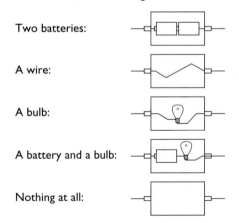

Two batteries:

A wire:

A bulb:

A battery and a bulb:

Nothing at all:

You can use your bulbs, batteries, and wires any way you like. Connect them in a circuit to help you figure out what is inside.

When you find out what is in a box, fill in the spaces on the following pages.

Box A: Has _____ inside.

Draw a picture of the circuit that told you what was inside Box A.

How could you tell from your circuit what was inside Box A?

Do the same for Boxes B, C, D, E, and F.

FIGURE 5.11   Hands-On Assessment: Electric Circuit Boards

Below are the pictures of four circuit boards you will find in your science center. Design a simple circuit tester from a battery, bulb, socket, and wires. Test the four boards to determine which points (A, B, C, and so on) are wired into the same circuit. Draw lines on the circuit picture showing where you believe the wires make a connection between the points. Show your teacher your work, and then open the circuit folder and check the results. Were you correct?

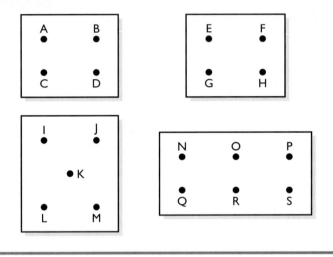

about the quality of a completed science project, written report, class notes, activity data sheets, and so on. Your teacher records are important because they can reveal the interplay among memorizing, understanding, and using scientific concepts. Emphasis on practical application encourages hands-on, minds-on interaction and helps to address the various dimensions of the science program. Figure 5.13 shows a record-keeping system a teacher might use to complement the sample lesson plan on basic electricity. This type of record keeping is useful because it helps to focus a teacher's observations of a child on the concepts and processes to be learned. Figure 5.14 shows a generic form suitable for an entire class. It may be used as a checklist to keep track of who has and has not demonstrated mastery of the concepts or preferred science skills. This format can be used to record student progress on the pictorial, reflective questioning, and hands-on assessment techniques.

Rubrics.   Not all student performances can be classified with simple systems, numbers, or letter grades. The sheer volume of a teacher's work load can limit the types of written or verbal comments offered to students. Therefore, many

FIGURE 5.12   Hands-On Assessment: Help MacGyver!

MacGyver is in a jam! Lost in a cave, he is using a small candle that is about to burn out. What he really needs is a flashlight—one that can withstand the drafty and damp cave—to help him find his way out. All he has is:

2 size "D" dry cells
1 small 3-volt bulb
1 thin piece of insulated wire, 30 centimeters long (about 12 inches)
1 metal paper clip
2 metal paper fasteners
1 cardboard tube, 15 centimeters long (about 6 inches)
1 roll of masking tape
1 plastic bottle cap
1 small knife

1. Use the materials to sketch a picture of how these things could be assembled to make a temporary flashlight. Make certain you draw your circuit carefully. (Draw your picture here.)

2. Now help MacGyver. Follow your plan. Did the light work? Keep trying! Now show MacGyver his new light and explain to him how it works.

teachers use rubrics to assess the quality of student work. *Rubrics* are devices, such as checklists, scales, or descriptions, that identify the criteria used to evaluate a student's work. Paul Smith (1995), a middle school science teacher, recommends using rubrics that have been created by the students for students, with teacher guidance. Since students are part of the design process, they

◆ **FIGURE 5.13   Student Progress Report**

Student's Name: Raul
Lesson or Unit: Basic Electricity

Concept Number	Description of Activity or Skill	Teacher Rating Low 1 2 3 4 5 High	Teacher Comments
1	Open circuit using one bulb, wire, and dry cell	5	Was the first to do it in group
2	Closed circuit using same materials	3	Had difficulty, needed my help
3	Closed circuit with bulb socket	4	Easily done after I helped with clips
4	Series circuit, 2 or more bulbs	5	Done independently
5	Parallel circuit	2	Having difficulty, made 2 series circuits
6	Short circuit	4	
7	Use a knife switch	5	Easily done
8	Make a paper clip switch	5	Concept easily shown
9	Construct a flashlight	4	No circuit trouble, difficulty with bulb connections only

◆ **FIGURE 5.14   Class Record-Keeping System**

Unit: Basic Electricity

Children's Names	Objective, Concept, Skill, or Activity Number											Comments
	1	2	3	4	5	6	7	8	9	10	11	
Emerson												
Frankie												
Jaclyn												
Jana												
Jay												
Julie												
Joy												
Marilyn												

Note: This format is easily managed by a spreadsheet program available for all popular microcomputers, if a value number is assigned to each object. Some teachers prefer a coding system that shows progress, such as: + for entirely correct, *n* for partially correct, *u* for mostly incorrect, or − for entirely incorrect.

clearly understand the expectations and use this understanding to improve their work. The creation of the rubrics also affords additional teaching opporunties.

For written work, Smith (1995) asks students to consider two questions: "What information should go into the written response?" and "How should the information be presented?" He uses a peer and parental review system that encourages students to prepare and improve written drafts. Parents and caregivers appreciate the rubrics because they help them to improve guidance offered while helping with homework. Smith claims that students are able to make better sense of what they learn and that student satisfaction is very high with his participatory approach.

Rubrics can help a teacher encourage students to give better responses to reflective questioning assessments. The rubric shown in Figure 5.15 has been generalized for use with reflective questioning assessments. It illustrates Smith's recommendations. Figure 5.16 provides a general rubric that you may use for a variety of science tasks.

Systematic Observation. The types of records shown in Figures 5.17 and 5.18 require systematic teacher observation. Systematic observation is another source of information that is helpful to meaningful evaluation. Teachers always make observations, but systematic observation goes beyond being aware that Emily is interested in birds, Joel asks questions all the time, and David creates messes. Systematic observation is illustrated in this example:

> A teacher divides the class into working groups to figure out a way to test the strength of different brands of paper towels. As the children work on the problem, the teacher walks about the room, listens carefully to the questions the children ask each other, and observes how they approach the task. The teacher notes who does nothing, who appears to have difficulty, who has trouble measuring, who asks the most interesting questions, and who offers the most interesting ideas.

Systematic observation is guided by a structure; the teacher's observations are focused on specific tasks. These tasks include trying to determine how well the children demonstrate their understanding of the science ideas, how well the children use the science process skills, and what types of scientific attitudes the children demonstrate. Figure 5.17 illustrates an observation form for science skills. Table 5.2 defines the attributes of the skills.

Science learning improves when student attitudes are positive (Yager & Penick, 1987). There are dramatic differences between traditional science classrooms and exemplary ones where teaching and assessment involve all aspects of science. Positive attitudes about science greatly influence students' achievement levels and process skills, as is shown by research on exemplary science classrooms (Yager & Penick, 1987). These results are now prompting teachers to question the traditional view that attitudes are inconsequential. Figure 5.18 shows one way you can evaluate and record the levels of your students' science attitudes.

▶ **FIGURE 5.15**   **Reflective Questioning Assessment Rubric**

This is a scoring rubric for a learning-cycle lesson on simple circuits. A score of three indicates what the class believes all students should be able to do. A score of four indicates that the students exceeded expectations.

Content scale

0	1	2	3	4
• No work completed	• Few concepts • Models not used in explanation • Some awareness of safety • Some awareness of technology uses	• Some concepts explained • Three common safety examples • Three common technology examples	• Uses circuit model to explain differences • Identifies differences in series, parallel, open, closed circuits • Uses concepts from previous lessons, e.g., conductor, insulator, etc. • Uses additional concepts to explain differences, e.g., switch, resistance, energy flow • Unusual safety and/or technology examples	

Style scale

0	1	2	3	4
• No work completed	• Poor organization • Many misspellings • Punctuation missing or inappropriate	• Clear organization • Very few misspellings	• Appropriate punctuation	• Extremely clear, concise writing

First reviewer's name: _____

Score for content: _____   Score for style: _____

Comments:

Second reviewer's name: _____

Score for content: _____   Score for style: _____

Comments:

FIGURE 5.16 General Scoring Rubric

This scoring rubric may be used for a variety of science activities or to offer guidance for developing expectations for activity-specific rubrics. The number in parentheses could be correlated with a scoring scale.

Poor (0): The student did not do the task, did not complete the assignment, or did not show comprehension of the activity.

Inadequate (1): The product or performance does not satisfy a significant number of the criteria, does not accomplish what was asked, contains errors, or is of poor quality.

Fair (2): The performance or product meets most of the criteria and does not contain gross errors or fundamental omissions.

Good (3): The performance or product completely meets the expectations described by the criteria.

Outstanding (4): All of the criteria are met, and the performance or product exceeds the expectations for the task; additional effort or outstanding features are shown.

Source: Adapted from S. Price and G. E. Hein, "Scoring active assessments," *Science and Children* (October 1994): 26–29.

FIGURE 5.17 Recording Science Process Skills

Directions: Circle the number that best represents the skill level you have observed. Number 1 means *having difficulty*, 2 means *fair*, 3 means *good*, 4 means *outstanding*.

Name	Observation	Classification	Communication	Measurement	Prediction
Sam	1 2 3 4	1 2 3 4	1 2 3 4	1 2 3 4	1 2 3 4
Wanda	1 2 3 4	1 2 3 4	1 2 3 4	1 2 3 4	1 2 3 4
Herman	1 2 3 4	1 2 3 4	1 2 3 4	1 2 3 4	1 2 3 4
Kara	1 2 3 4	1 2 3 4	1 2 3 4	1 2 3 4	1 2 3 4

Note: The process skills can be changed and the form expanded to address better the science skills your lessons emphasize.

TABLE 5.2   Definitions and Indicators of Basic and Integrated Process Skills

Basic Processes

Observation: involves active engagement with the manipulation of objects and the use of the senses, directly or indirectly, with simple or complex instruments. This process:

- describes objects' attributes
- describes changes in terms of actions
- describes changes with accuracy in terms of patterns and relationships.

Classification: systematically imposing order to data based on observational relationships. This process:

- creates groups by using a single attribute and expresses linear relationships
- creates groups and subgroups using one attribute to express symmetrical relationships
- creates groups using several attributes together to express symmetrical relationships among different groups.

Communication: exchanging information through a variety of media. This process involves:

- expressing opinions
- explaining using sense data (touch, taste, hearing, sight, and smell)
- explaining causal relationships

Measurement: describing an event by using instruments to quantify observations. This process:

- uses nonstandard instruments, such as paper clips, hands, and feet
- uses standard instruments, such as rulers, balance scales, and graduated cylinders
- uses standard instruments with precision, such as measuring within tenths or hundredths when using the metric system.

Prediction: stating future cause-and-effect relationships through manipulation of objects. Accuracy of prediction is based on information gathered through observations. This process includes:

- guesses from minimal supportive evidence
- guesses based on limited observable facts
- guesses based on an accurate understanding of cause-and-effect relationships.

Questioning: raising uncertainty. This process:

- focuses on the attributes of objects
- focuses on relationships and patterns within an experiment
- focuses on events and patterns abstracted from an experiment

◆ **TABLE 5.2** *(continued)*

Using numbers: expressing ideas, observations, and relationships in figures rather than words. This process:

- uses numbers to express ideas without relating them
- uses numbers to express relationships
- uses numbers to express relationships in precise terms

Integrated Processes

Interpreting data: finding patterns or meaning not immediately apparent among sets of data that lead to the construction of inferences, predictions, and hypotheses. This process:

- identifies a single pattern among objects within an experiment
- uses accuracy to identify a single pattern among objects within an experiment
- uses accuracy to identify multiple patterns among objects

Controlling variables: identifying and selecting factors from variables that are to be held constant and those that are to be manipulated in order to carry out a proposed investigation. This process involves managing:

- one manipulative variable without holding others constant
- several manipulative variables and holds at least one variable constant
- several manipulative and constant variables at the same time

Designing experiments: planning data-gathering operations to determine results. This process involves:

- collecting data through trial-and-error processes
- testing questions and hypothesizing with an attempt to identify and control variables
- using organized, sequential plans to test hypotheses and interpret results in measurable terms

Inferring: providing explanations, reasons, or causes for events based on limited facts. Inferences are of questionable validity because they rely heavily on personal judgment. This process:

- explains by making guesses
- explains using observable data
- explains using quantifiable observable data

Defining operationally: describing what works. This process:

- explains how to measure variables in an experiment
- states relationships between observed actions to explain phenomena
- explains relationships by generalizing to other events not observed

(continued)

◆ **TABLE 5.2** *(continued)*

Hypothesizing: tentatively accepting an explanation as a basis for further investigation. Constructing generalizations that include all objects or events of the same class. The hypothesis must be tested if credibility is to be established. This process involves making:

- statements based on opinions
- statement based on simple sensory observations without explanations
- statements used to create concepts through explanations

Formulating models: describing or constructing physical, verbal, or mathematical explanations of systems and phenomena that cannot be observed directly. Models may be used in predicting outcomes and planned investigations. This process:

- creates one-dimensional explanations
- creates multidimensional models
- creates scalar multidimensional explanations

Source: G. W. Foster & W. A. Heiting, "Embedded Assessment," *Science and Children* 32, 2 (1994): 30–33. Reprinted with permission from NSTA Publications, copyright 1994 from *Science and Children,* National Science Teachers Association, 1840 Wilson Boulevard, Arlington, VA 22201-3000.

Social skills are important to science learning. Karen Ostlund (1992) tells us that we are not born with a set of instinctive behaviors that help us to interact well in social settings. Social skills are learned. If we expect students to work together in cooperative science activity groups or on science projects in smaller teams, then we must assess the extent to which the learners develop those skills. Table 5.3 lists important social skills that students can learn if we encourage them. Systematic record-keeping formats (similar to those shown in Figures 5.17 and 5.18) can help us to monitor the status of students' social skills.

◆ **FIGURE 5.18   Evaluating and Recording Science Attitudes**

Check those attitudes or record the number of times each student demonstrates the desired scientific attitudes during the observation period.

Name	Is curious	Cooperates	Persists	Is open-minded	Safely uses materials
Celeste	✓✓✓	✓✓	✓	✓	✓
Jen	✓	✓✓✓✓✓	✓	✓✓✓✓	✓✓✓
Tikara	✓✓✓✓	✓✓✓	✓✓✓✓✓	✓✓	✓✓✓
Jon	✓	✓✓✓	✓✓	✓✓	✓✓
Sara	✓✓	✓✓	✓✓✓	✓✓✓✓	✓✓✓✓

According to Ostlund (1992), science social skills group into three types:

1. *Cluster skills*—behaviors that involve a student's ability to move into a science learning group quickly and quietly and to get the task started.
2. *Camaraderie skills*—which help all learners feel better about themselves and about each other as they work together. These skills help build a sense of cohesiveness and encourage stable operation of the science group.
3. *Task skills*—pertaining to management chores and ranging from the skills that are necessary for mastering a task to those that use critical thinking to construct a deeper level of understanding.

Student Self-Assessments. Student self-assessments are an important part of the authenticity found in constructivist science teaching. Self-assessments can range from the informal collections of reflective tape-recorded (for nonreaders) or written journal notes, to more formal efforts, such as those revealed through self-evaluation ratings. A student portfolio is a common technique that is used to organize and present the self-assessment.

A *portfolio* is a selection of student work that is collected over a period of time (Hein & Price, 1994). A portfolio's purpose is often to tell a story about the student's science activities. The contents of a portfolio may be focused on illustrating a student's abilities to solve problems, show thinking and understanding, illustrate content and capability of written communication, and reveal science connections that a student is able to make across many lessons and the views that students have of themselves in science (Glencoe, 1994).

Teachers decide in various ways who has the responsibility for selecting the work and the criteria it is to fulfill. At times, students may make the selection "according to criteria established collaboratively between themselves and their teacher. Criteria might be the 'piece that was hardest for me to do,' 'my best piece of work,' 'the project I learned most from doing,' 'a piece that shows important science learning' " (Hein & Price, 1994, p. 48).

Whatever the work selected, the process of reflection assists the selection and presentation process. Students must reflect and show the depth of their reflection when they explain why they made their selections. Explanations may be verbal or written and may be encouraged through teacher and student interviews.

A student *journal* is a type of self-assessment. A journal can assist the reflective process when students are encouraged to record what they have done and what they have learned. A journal may provide a written summary that is helpful for planning and constructing a portfolio. The following examples are appropriate for a portfolio:

- written report of a project or investigation
- responses to open-ended questions
- examples of problems that have been formed or solved
- journal excerpts
- science art

TABLE 5.3 Science Social Skills

Science social skills can be observed and recorded by a teacher, or used as a part of a student self-evaluation. As an example, for student self-evaluation you could ask students to rate how often or how well they do the following.

Cluster skills: How often do you:

- move into groups quietly?
- stay with your group?
- use a quiet voice to speak within your group?
- call the people in your group by their names?
- look at the person in your group who is talking?
- keep your hands and feet to yourself?
- share materials with your group mates?
- wait and take your turn?
- share your ideas?

Camaraderie skills: How often do you:

- avoid saying "put-downs"?
- encourage others in your group to participate?
- give each person in your group a compliment?
- show your support to others with words or actions?
- describe how you feel when it is appropriate?
- try humor or enthusiasm to help energize your group?
- criticize the idea, not the person?
- allow each person in the group to talk before you talk again?

Task skills: How often do you:

- ask questions of your group members about the task?
- ask for help from group members?
- ask group members to explain what you do not understand?
- offer to explain things to another group member?
- check for understanding with group members?
- state the purpose of the task and make certain others understand it?
- watch time and let others know when time is short?
- offer ideas about how best to do the task?
- value other group members' contributions?
- summarize the material to help others in your group?
- develop ways to help the group remember important details?
- encourage other group members to share their thinking?
- ask others to plan out loud how they would solve a problem?
- compare viewpoints when there is a disagreement and try to reach agreement?
- combine parts of different persons ideas into a single point of view?
- ask others to explain their reasons?
- help other group members reach a conclusion?
- check your group's work against the instructions?

Source: Adapted from K. L. Ostlund, "Sizing Up Social Skills," *Science Scope* (March 1992): 31–33.

FIGURE 5.19 Portfolio Evaluation Form

Portfolio Topic _____

Student: _____

Teacher: _____

Date: _____

1. Concepts, procedures, process skills explored: _____

    _____

    _____

2. Areas of growth in understanding: _____

    _____

    _____

3. Unfinished work or work needing revision: _____

    _____

    _____

4. Assessment of the following areas:

    (a) Problem-solving work: _____

    _____

    _____

    (b) Reasoning and critical thinking: _____

    _____

    _____

    (c) Use of language: _____

    _____

    _____

    (d) Other: _____

    _____

    _____

Source: Glencoe Science Professional Series, *Alternative Assessment in the Science Classroom,* (1994). (ERIC Document Reproduction Service No. ED 370 778), p. 37.

FIGURE 5.20   Student Self-Evaluation Checklist

Student Self-Evaluation Checklist

Name: _____

Date: _____

Did the circuit problems
Finished some   Finished them all

┼───┼───┼───┼───┼───┼───┼───┼───┼───┼

Worked with the materials
Messy   Always careful

┼───┼───┼───┼───┼───┼───┼───┼───┼───┼

Recorded and described in my journal
Wrote a little   Wrote a lot

┼───┼───┼───┼───┼───┼───┼───┼───┼───┼

Practiced important safety rules
Some of the time   All of the time

┼───┼───┼───┼───┼───┼───┼───┼───┼───┼

Discussed ideas and results with the class
Some of the time   All of the time

┼───┼───┼───┼───┼───┼───┼───┼───┼───┼

Worked well with classmates
Some of the time   All of the time

┼───┼───┼───┼───┼───┼───┼───┼───┼───┼

Used time well
Wasted time   Worked hard

┼───┼───┼───┼───┼───┼───┼───┼───┼───┼

Learned from the lesson
Learned a little   Learned a lot

┼───┼───┼───┼───┼───┼───┼───┼───┼───┼

Things I liked or did well: _____

_____

Things I did not like: _____

_____

Source: Adapted from G. E. Hein and S. Price, *Active Assessment for Active Science: A Guide for Elementary School Teachers* (Portsmouth, NH: Heinemann, 1994).

FIGURE 5.21   Student Self-Evaluation Rating Scale

Self-Evaluation Rating Scale

Name: _____

Date: _____

Directions: Rate yourself. On a scale of one (low) to ten (high), how well did you do each of the following activities?

Making a switch
Didn't understand what to do   Made a great one

| I | 2 | 3 | 4 | 5 | 6 | 7 | 8 | 9 | 10 |

Making circuits
Had trouble   Easy to do

| I | 2 | 3 | 4 | 5 | 6 | 7 | 8 | 9 | 10 |

Solving circuit puzzles
Had trouble   Easy to solve

| I | 2 | 3 | 4 | 5 | 6 | 7 | 8 | 9 | 10 |

Electricity mystery boxes
Did some   Did all

| I | 2 | 3 | 4 | 5 | 6 | 7 | 8 | 9 | 10 |

Making the flashlight
Could have tried harder   Did my best

| I | 2 | 3 | 4 | 5 | 6 | 7 | 8 | 9 | 10 |

Overall feeling about the electricity lessons
Liked them a little   Liked them a lot

| I | 2 | 3 | 4 | 5 | 6 | 7 | 8 | 9 | 10 |

Things I liked or did well: _____

_____

Things I did not like: _____

_____

Source: Adapted from G. E. Hein and S. Price, *Active Assessment for Active Science: A Guide for Elementary School Teachers* (Portsmouth, NH: Heinemann, 1994).

- individual student's contribution to a group report or project
- photographs or drawings of science models
- teacher check-sheets and recorded observations of student performance
- uses of science tools, equipment, and suitable technologies to solve problems or to complete an activity
- examples of how science is important to the student
- descriptions of safe science practices learned and applied in another setting, such as at home
- linkages of science history and how views have changed as a result of study
- examples of how science is used in the community and careers that use the science topics that have been studied

Portions of a portfolio may be evaluated by the teacher individually or collectively within the portfolio package. Items in the portfolio should invite student self-evaluation. Figure 5.19 on page 185 provides a format that invites students and teachers to have input into the evaluation in an open-ended way. Figures 5.20 and 5.21 on pages 186 and 187 illustrate more specific student self-evaluation approaches that may be used to inform teachers and caregivers about how students perceive their own learning.

CHAPTER SUMMARY

The National Science Education Standards have ushered in a new era of exciting learning opportunities for students and new instructional challenges for teachers. Constructivist teaching and learning requires careful planning that places conceptual focus, acts of created understanding, essential experiences, and authentic assessment in a carefully balanced dynamic system. In this chapter we have described and illustrated a planning model that will help you meet the new challenges.

Concept mapping is a tool that helps teachers identify essential concepts and the relationships among concepts. The tool is helpful for making fundamental planning decisions in order to fulfill the outcomes of the content standards. Concept mapping is also a useful evaluation tool.

The 4-E learning cycle provides a dynamic planning system that balances student-centered exploration with teacher-guided conceptual construction. Expansion nurtures understanding as the new dimensions of science learning are fulfilled. Evaluation is continual and is fit to the task. Tools for authentic assessment include pictorial analysis, hands-on performance tasks, reflective questioning, and systematic observation. Many illustrations show various types of teacher records and student products, including portfolios, that verify the types and levels of understanding. These techniques are pragmatically illustrated by supporting a central lesson throughout the chapter.

DISCUSSION QUESTIONS AND PROJECTS

1. Contemporary movements in education usually embrace the preference for students to demonstrate learning outcomes. Performance or behavioral objectives may be used for this purpose. What advantages or disadvantages do you see with this type of objective?

2. Examine a textbook or science module and teacher's manual for any grade level you choose. Construct a concept map for the material you select. State your opinion about how the printed materials' organization helps make connections between associated concepts.

3. Prepare several plans for science teaching. First map the concepts you wish to teach, and then use the learning cycle planning format demonstrated in this chapter. What new dimensions of science education are you able to address?

4. Prepare a lesson plan using the 4-E approach. How many learning activities do you have, and where do they fit into the cycle? What science dimensions do you pursue? How do you evaluate student's learning?

5. Construct appropriate ways to evaluate the children's science knowledge, skills, and attitudes for your plans in projects 3 and 4.

6. Prepare the rubrics you will need for project 5.

7. How could you use rubrics to help you evaluate a student's portfolio?

ADDITIONAL READINGS

If you are interested in learning more about some of the topics raised in this chapter, consider the following sources:

Charles Ault, "Intelligently Wrong: Some Comments on Children's Misconceptions," *Science and Children*, (May 1984): 22–24.

Patricia Blosser, *Science Misconceptions Research and Some Implications for the Teaching of Science to Elementary School Students*, a newsletter research report (No. 1, 1987) available through the ERIC Clearinghouse for Science, Mathematics, and Environmental Education, 1200 Chambers Road, Third Floor, Columbus, OH 43212.

George Hein and Sabra Price, *Active Assessment for Active Science: A Guide for Elementary School Teachers* (Portsmouth, NH: Heineman, 1994). This practical book illustrates several forms of assessment and management techniques, including techniques for assessing educational values.

John W. Renner and Edmund A. Marek, *The Learning Cycle and Elementary School Science Teaching* (Portsmouth, NH: Heinemann, 1988). This book is organized around three phases of the learning cycle. Detailed sample learning cycle plans are given for grades K–6. Examples include lessons in the biological, earth, and physical sciences, as well as special lessons for kindergarten children.

Science and Children 32, no. 2 (October 1994). This feature issue on assessment contains practical classroom-tested approaches that include video quizzes, performance assessments, scoring devices, embedded assessment techniques, and descriptions of systemic approaches used by the state of California.

Science Scope 15, no. 6 (March 1992). This issue provides a special supplement on science assessment. Numerous ways to evaluate student learning are amply illustrated and include classroom-tested examples of portfolios, group assessment, concept mapping, performance-based assessment, and scoring rubrics.

Debra L. Seabury and Susan L. Peeples, *Ready-to-Use Science Activities for the Elementary Classroom* (West Nyack, NY: Center for Applied Research in Education, 1987). Included are more than 175 reproducible activity pages that cover six interdisciplinary teaching units: plants, animals, the human body, geology, weather, and space. Activities can accommodate many of the science goals encouraged in this chapter and can be adapted to the learning cycle lesson planning format.

Joseph Stepans and Christine Kuehn, "What Research Says: Children's Conceptions of Weather," *Science and Children* (September 1985): 44–47.

Marvin N. Tolman and James O. Morton, *Life Science Activities for Grades 2–8, Earth Science Activities for Grades 2–8*, and *Physical Science Activities for Grades 2–8* (West Nyack, NY: Parker Publishing, 1986). Nearly 500 science activities are included in these three books. The concept/skills index in each book makes it simple to identify the science concepts for each activity and to see the big picture necessary for concept mapping a course or unit. Each activity may be easily adapted for the learning cycle.

CHAPTER OUTLINE

How Can You Create a Safe, Efficient, Activity-Based Science Classroom?

Nine-year-old Celeste sat reading her current issue of *3-2-1 Contact Magazine*. She was intrigued by an article about volcanoes. At the end of the article was an activity on making a volcano. She read over the list of materials she needed. "Let's see," she said half out loud, "the water I can get from the sink; in the bottom cupboard I can find the large baking pan; in the upper cabinet there's the white vinegar, red food coloring, baking soda, and dishwashing liquid; in the first drawer on the right I should find the glue, masking tape, and scissors; and in the drawer on the left I can find the tin foil and teaspoons." Celeste collected the materials from their storage areas and found the clay flower pot and the potting soil stored with the garden supplies. She checked over the materials list once again. "I think I have just about everything I need to make my own volcano," she announced to Sarah, who was passing by.

Ten-year-old Sarah looked over Celeste's shoulder at the magazine, then took a quick inventory of the materials Celeste had collected. "You forgot an empty tuna can," Sarah proclaimed. Celeste looked pensive for a moment and then shouted, "I know. I can go to the recycling bin, I'll probably find just what I need in there!"

In a few moments Celeste was back with an empty tuna can. The two girls arranged the materials according to the directions in the magazine. They dumped the baking soda down the vent of their newly formed volcano. They mixed the vinegar, dishwashing liquid, water, and food coloring together. They were just about to pour the vinegar mixture into the vent when they were startled by a command from an adult: "STOP! What do you think will happen to you if you continue to look down that vent as you pour in the liquid? How are you going to protect your eyes and your clothing? And do you think it's a good idea to do that on the carpet?"

A surprised look came over their faces. "Oh, I'm sorry! I forgot about that," exclaimed Celeste. "I guess I was so excited after reading this article, I really wanted to try it out as quickly as possible. Come on, Sarah. Let's move this off the carpet and then go get our goggles and put some old sweatshirts on before we make our volcano erupt."

Twanna returned from the supply table of the second-grade classroom with her hands full of materials. "Did you get the paper, iron filings, hand lens, and magnets?" asked José.

"Yes I did," responded Twanna. "Let's get going."

"First, we need to be sure that we have plenty of room to perform this activity," stated José, who was the manager and recorder for the science activity. "Are you sure that you have all the materials now, Twanna?"

Twanna, the materials manager for the activity, ran off to get a box. In a few minutes she returned from the supply table with a shoebox with one end cut out of it.

"Now," stated José, "lay the shoebox flat on the table and place the white paper over it. While I am doing that, Twanna, you need to pour some iron filings onto the second sheet of paper and examine them with your hand lens."

José went about his work while Twanna poured the filings from the glass jar onto the paper. "Wow!" she squealed. "Look at these things! They look like baby fish hooks and spears. Why are they so jagged?"

"Maybe they were simply made using a file on an old piece of pipe," said José. "My father makes them all the time when he puts new pipes in people's houses."

"Okay," said Twanna. "Are you ready for the filings now?"

"Sí," replied José. "Put them on the paper covering the shoebox now."

Twanna poured half her filings onto the paper and leaned forward to watch José, who picked up the large bar magnet and reached under the paper with it. "Watch to see what happens to the iron filings as I move the magnet around under the paper," he stated.

Both students were peering at the shoebox from opposite sides, their eyes on the same level as the filings. Just as José touched the lower right edge of the paper with the magnet, Twanna sneezed. Several of the iron filings sprayed into José's face, with a few of them entering his right eye. "Oowww!" shrieked José as he twirled from his chair, eyes buried in his hands. "Help me, please!!!"

How could this accident have been prevented? Were there any oversights that you noticed?

The Roosevelt sixth-grade class finally arrived at its destination, the old Wilson farm. As the bus rolled to a stop, Mr. J arose and addressed the class: "Please remember our purpose here today. We are visitors to these animals' homes, so do not disturb them or the plants. In science we observe, measure, and record; we don't destroy or disrupt. Let's review our lesson plans for today's environmental science."

Following a five-minute clarification of the outcomes and precautions for the activity, Mr. J answered student questions. "Now for our safety guidelines," he stated. "Are there any questions concerning the safety items on your activity page such as equipment operation, accident procedures, and the buddy system? Remember to stay with your buddy and never allow yourself to be separated from myself, Mr. P, Mrs. M, or Ms. O by more than 50 meters in this pasture area. If you need help in an emergency, please use your whistles. We adults were here earlier this morning checking out the area and found no hazards to worry about during this mapping exercise. But please be careful, just in case."

Mark and Alicia filed off the bus, confident of their purpose.

"Let's see," said Alicia. "We need to proceed 50 meters to the northeast to pick up our first marker, then 60 meters to the east for our second one. Do you have the map, compass, and whistle ready, Mark?"

"Yes, I do," replied Mark. "Put on your helmet."

As the students proceeded about 20 meters into the trees, they noticed that the terrain became more rugged and difficult to negotiate.

"See these little lines, Alicia?" remarked Mark, looking at the map. "They are the little hills we are walking over now. Another 30 meters and we should spot the first marker."

Just as they came over the next hillock, they both spotted a green plastic lid, partially hidden in the leaves.

"What is that?" asked Mark.

"I don't know. Let's check it out," replied Alicia.

As they cautiously lifted the lid, it broke into several pieces. Revealed before them was a deep hole about 1 meter in diameter. It did not appear to have a bottom, although there was water down about 2 meters.

"Let's explore it," suggested Alicia.

"No way! Let's get help!" replied Mark.

"Don't be silly," said Alicia. "We can check it out, finish our assignment and return before anyone knows. It could be our secret."

"What if that water is over your head?" persisted Mark. "How long could you stay afloat? I say we get help before some animal or another person falls into it."

"I guess you are right," agreed Alicia. "Use that whistle!"

What was the difference between the safety emphasis in this scenario and those in the first two? Could you credit the judgment simply to the older age of the students? ◆

INTRODUCTION

The first scenario could have taken place in any activity-based science class where the teacher gives the students time to engage in different kinds of inquiry at a science learning center. The girls were able to create the volcano immediately to satisfy their natural curiosity because they knew where the materials were stored and could easily obtain them. The person who reminded them of basic safety rules, however, was not their teacher. It was their mother.

The sisters know where everything is kept in their home. When they want materials for a project, such as building a volcano, they know where to get them. This same familiarity with materials storage that children feel in their homes, including what things they are allowed to touch and those they are to avoid, should occur in the classroom. Teaching children safe science practices and instilling in them a basic safety philosophy, as emphasized in the third scenario, are important for a safe and efficient activity-based science classroom.

This chapter uses two organizing questions: *What are the foreseeable hazards associated with valued educational activities?* and *What materials are necessary for the activities?* The chapter helps you construct answers for these questions by:

1. encouraging you to develop a philosophy of safe science teaching,
2. helping you understand your legal responsibilities,
3. helping you understand when and how to use safety equipment,
4. encouraging you to perform safety assessments of your classroom, lab, field site, or working space,
5. examining the tasks necessary for safe and efficient storage of equipment and materials,
6. suggesting methods for distributing, maintaining, and inventorying science materials.

WHAT FORESEEABLE HAZARDS ARE ASSOCIATED WITH VALUED EDUCATIONAL ACTIVITIES?

Children are natural scientists because they are curious about everything in their physical world. Given the opportunity, they will investigate events and objects of all types and see beauty and intrigue in events that adults accept as mundane. Sometimes it is difficult for children to separate danger from fascination. The teacher's responsibility is to balance these two factors, with information from publishers, science experts, peers, and consideration of their own teaching environment (student abilities and maturities, equipment available) in order to ensure that science learning is effective yet safe.

Natural events provide effective learning opportunities for elementary students. Ice storms, tornadoes, thunderstorms, floods, the first snowfall, a gentle rain, and the changes of the seasons are all natural phenomena about which elementary students are curious. When these events happen around them, students become even more curious about their cause and thus receptive to learning what causes the events.

In order to keep students safe while attempting to construct an understanding of science concepts through hands-on science activities, the teacher must have a simple yet effective safety philosophy that guides the students. It is important to identify appropriate grade-level concepts and worthwhile explorations in order to enact an effective safety philosophy. Once those are clearly identified then the teacher must ask, "What are the foreseeable hazards associated with valued educational activities?" Ask yourself, "Would a respected peer use the same materials or activity I have selected? What adjustments might another teacher make to fit the needs of students according to their emotional, social, and academic abilities? What group size or class setting would a reasonable teacher use to make the activity effective and safe?"

You must think about any foreseeable hazards your students may encounter as they participate in your activities. Be sensitive to such issues as chemical problems about which you may have insufficient knowledge, fire hazards, potential eye injuries from sharp objects or flying projectiles, and overcrowding. If the foreseeable hazards exceed the educational value of the knowledge or experience students could gain from their direct participation in them, you have some choices to make:

1. Provide additional safety parameters, such as safety goggles, fire blankets, eyewashes, and additional supervision.
2. Limit the activity to a teacher demonstration, in which you are the only one who manipulates the equipment, and students become active observers. (In many instances this is the most logical and educationally responsible choice.)
3. Eliminate the activity entirely from the curriculum. Unless you have recently performed a detailed assessment of the entire science curriculum across grades, you might be surprised at how many duplicate activities of little value exist in science classes that may be taught primarily because of tradition (Gerlovich & Hartman, 1990).

WHAT ARE YOUR LEGAL RESPONSIBILITIES?

Although this section focuses on tort law as it relates to science teaching, the principles and philosophy apply to all school subjects. There are several legal concepts you must be familiar with in order to understand your legal responsibilities.

Tort

A *tort* is a wrong, or injury, that someone has committed against someone else. The injured party generally wants restitution for the injury or damages. The resolution of such conflicts between litigants (*plaintiffs* being those who bring the claim and *defendants* being those whom the claim has been filed against) generally occurs in a court, involving lawyers, a judge, possibly jurors, and witnesses, and is referred to as a *lawsuit*.

Reasonable and Prudent Judgment

The U.S. legal system does not require educators to be superhuman in the performance of their duties. It is expected only that they be *reasonable and prudent* in their judgment when performing their duties with students. Educators need only do what reasonable persons with comparable training and experience would do in similar situations. They must ask themselves if their peers would endorse the activities being performed with students. Proceed with confidence only if these questions are answered affirmatively. If not, add more safety features, limit the activity to a teacher demonstration, or eliminate it entirely. As

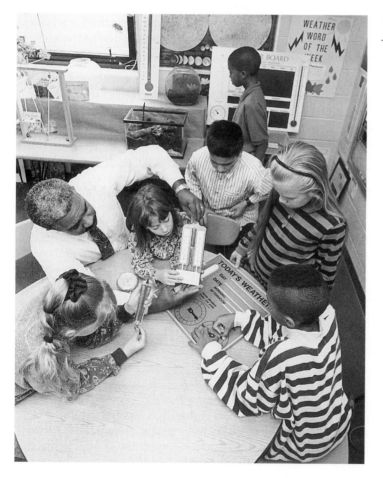

Prudent judgment and proper supervision fulfill most legal responsibilities.

science teachers, we must attempt to anticipate reasonable hazards, eliminate them, or be confidently prepared to address them.

Foreseeability

If you discover something amiss in your teaching environment, you should request corrections, preferably in writing, as soon as possible (see Figure 6.1). Essential items such as fire extinguishers, fire blankets, eyewashes, or safety goggles need to be obtained or repaired immediately; less important items, like nonskid floor wax, could be discussed with administrators for future correction. All known hazards and appropriate emergency measures should be explained to students as well.

The foreseeable hazards of all activities, as well as appropriate emergency reactions, should be completely explained to students *prior* to an activity. Field trip sites should be reviewed very carefully by the teacher before students arrive. Ask the owner or proprietor of the field site about any known hazards or

FIGURE 6.1　Request for Correction of Safety Concern

Date filed with administrator: _____

Secretary's initials: _____

Request for Correction of Safety Concern

Date: _____　　　　　Room: _____

The following is a safety concern in the science area:

_____　　_____
　　(Teacher name)　　　　　　　　(Signature)

CC: Teacher, Dept. Chair

Determine the educational value of an activity before doing it.

potential hazards to students. Any sensitivities to foods the class might be working with should be ascertained before the activity begins. Any phobias should be known before students are placed in potentially frightening situations. The teacher *must* know about any medical problems that students may have—for example, medication schedules, allergies, fears, and anxieties. Before ever involving students in activities, ask yourself, "What could go wrong with this activity, and am I prepared to address the problem?" If you can answer the questions affirmatively, proceed with confidence.

Negligence

Before you can be held accountable for personal injury accidents, it must be proven that you were negligent. *Negligence* has been defined as "conduct that falls below a standard established by law or profession to protect others from harm" (School Code of Iowa, 1988). It is sometimes described as failure to exercise due care.

Due Care

Due care may be defined as your duty to protect your students (School Code of Iowa, 1988). For younger or disabled students, the degree of care provided must be increased. You must remember that you are the authority in the classroom. You, or an equally qualified adult substitute, must be with students at all times, especially when the potential for injury exists. During science activities, when materials and chemicals are being manipulated, your presence is essential. If you need to leave the room during such activities, you must make certain that an equally qualified person assumes this responsibility. Due care is often summarized in three teacher duties: instruction, supervision, and maintenance (School Code of Iowa, 1988).

Instruction.   You must ensure that the instruction is appropriate for the physical and mental development levels of your students. Since textbooks form the basis of many science programs, you would be wise to ensure that safety is an integral and conspicuous component. Strive to select textbooks that parallel your safe science teaching philosophy.

All activities in which students are involved should be weighed for their educational value versus the hazards involved in having students perform them. If the foreseeable dangers outweigh the educational value of the activity, it must be limited to teacher demonstration, have more safety features added, or be eliminated from the science experience (Gerlovich & Hartman, 1992). As a service to teachers, newsletters are supplied by safety-conscious scientific supply companies. Many such equipment supplier newsletters include safety columns and hints, as well as more effective safety equipment ideas for young students.

Rules should be clearly written and explained to students. Copies of the most important rules should be posted conspicuously throughout the room. Serious consideration should be given to developing and implementing a *student safety contract* (see Figure 6.2) for students in the upper grades (4–6). The contract should identify all foreseeable hazards and appropriate actions to be taken, describe the location and proper use of safety equipment items, and explain essential rules. At this level, students should sign a contract that indicates their understanding. It is best to explain and have students initial only a couple of items each day. Teachers should collect these forms between each event and retain them for dissemination at the next safety discussion session. Teachers may wish to administer safety tests to determine the degree of student understanding.

Discipline during science activities should be fair, consistent, and firmly enforced. Safety is so important that no one should be exempt. The only exceptions should be based on a student's obvious physical or mental limitations. Students will support teachers in their activities a great deal more if they feel that everyone is treated fairly. You may also wish to involve students in the safe science and discipline rules for the class.

You are a role model. You set the safety expectations for your class by example. Students cannot be expected to take safety seriously if you do not observe all guidelines. Be especially careful to wear safety equipment items

◆FIGURE 6.2   **Student Safety Contract**

Student Safety Contract

My teacher told me, _____, about these
(student name)
safety items in my science class.

1. Safety rules   _____

2. How to find and use these:

   (a) Fire extinguisher   _____

   (b) Fire blanket   _____

   (c) Goggles   _____

   (d) Eyewash   _____

   (e) Drench shower   _____

   (f) Safety can   _____

   (g) Heat sources (bunsen burner, alcohol
       lamp, microwave oven, etc.)   _____

   (h) Electrical equipment   _____

   (i) Telephone or intercom   _____

3. What to do during:

   (a) Fire   _____

   (b) Chemical splash to the body   _____

   (c) Eye emergency   _____

   (d) Chemical spill   _____

   (e) Electrical emergency   _____

Date: _____   Teacher: _____

(goggles) and observe all safety rules. Explain all safety considerations and have all safety equipment items available before beginning any activity. Safety should be something that students expect you to enforce.

Consider simulating foreseeable emergencies—for example, a student who receives a chemical splash on his clothing, face, or eyes; a classroom or clothing fire caused by science items; finding another adult to give emergency assistance; evacuating the room—and proper safety responses as part of your daily teaching. Following instruction, you might evaluate students on their proper and expeditious performances. Accent the positive; emphasize what you want students to *do.* Be careful to protect students from any hazards during the simulations.

Should an accident or incident occur, collect as much information as possible from witnesses (student and staff). An accident or incident report (see Figure 6.3) can help focus the report should legal repercussions arise from the

FIGURE 6.3　Teacher Accident/Incident Report

1. Staff member completing the report: _____

2. Date of accident/incident: _____

3. Time of the accident/incident: _____

4. Location of the accident/incident:

5. Staff/student(s) involved in the accident/incident:

    (a) Staff (report attached)　　　　　　　　(b) Student (report attached)

    _____　　　　　_____

    _____　　　　　_____

    _____　　　　　_____

    _____　　　　　_____

6. Teacher description of the accident/incident:

7. Immediate action taken to deal with the emergency:

8. Corrective action taken to avoid a repeat of the accident/incident in the future:

_____　　　　　_____
(Date report completed)　　　　　　　(Signature of person completing report)

incident. These accounts are powerful, firsthand evidence of what actions were taken and the teacher's commitment to safety. Some states set limits on the length of time after an incident occurs wherein legal action can be taken. When this statute of limitations for legal actions passes for the incident, dispose of the materials. These reports can also be very effective learning tools when used with other classes.

Supervision.   The duty of supervision, as part of due care, can be a significant challenge. Teachers should always be in the classroom when scientific equipment or chemicals are accessible to students. The only exceptions to this rule are times of extreme emergencies or when the supervision has been delegated to another equally qualified person. Overcrowding, class size, and field trips are matters that require specific supervisory attention.

There is increasing evidence that *overcrowding* is the root cause of accidents in science settings. Supervision should increase when the danger level of the activity increases, the number of students with disabilities in the class increases, and the learning environment differs from the conventional classroom setting. Teachers must be aware of overcrowding and initiate corrections as soon as possible. The Texas Education Agency recommends at least 30 square feet of floor space for each student (including storage and teacher preparation area) in elementary school science classes.

The National Science Teachers Association (and numerous other professional science teaching organizations) recommends that the teacher-to-student ratio never exceed 1:24 during science labs and activities (National Science Teachers Association, 1983). The classroom teaching environment has a significant influence on the safety that can be provided to students. In its 1989 safety guide, the Texas Education Agency recommended two types of floor plans for teaching elementary school science that may provide a model for the nation. Emphasis was placed on safety equipment, a maximum of twenty-four students during science activities, and extensive open space leading to at least two exits. There is adequate room for students to move about without bumping into each other or equipment. Students can also be readily supervised by the teacher from any point in the room. There must be no blind spots.

For field trips, you should obtain parent or guardian release forms or waivers for all students and apprise the administration of the event (Figure 6.4). The activity should be an integral part of the course. Teachers should use only school-sanctioned and insured vehicles. Supervision should generally be increased to one teacher or other qualified adult to ten students. It is imperative that teachers and other assisting adults preview the field site for hazards *before* students are involved. Students should be apprised of any known hazards and appropriate reactions in an emergency, such as described in this chapter's third scenario. Be careful to consider poisonous plants and plants with thorns or other irritating parts, and check for poisonous or biting animals. On the school grounds, look for broken glass, holes, drug paraphernalia, and other unexpected items.

FIGURE 6.4   Safety Considerations for Field Trips

1. The teacher has visited the field trip site prior to involving students there. _____
2. The activity is a well-planned part of the science course. _____
3. The activity is appropriate for the mental and physical age of the students taking the trip. _____
4. Transportation is via school or school-sanctioned vehicles only. _____
5. Clear, appropriate rules of behavior are established, and the students understand them. _____
6. All field trip dangers are pointed out to students in advance and again when students arrive at the site. _____
7. Students are dressed according to the demands of the environment and weather. _____
8. Supervision is increased according to the novelty and danger inherent in the field trip environment. _____
9. Equipment is in a proper state of repair. _____
10. Equipment is designed for the mental and physical ages of the students using it. _____
11. Students know how to use the equipment properly. _____
12. If students are to be separated from the teacher at any time, prearranged meetings are planned. _____
13. The buddy system of pairing students in teams is used to help ensure safety and mutual responsibility. _____
14. The teacher is aware of any student medical needs (allergies, medication schedules, phobias). _____
15. Signed parent or guardian permission forms have been received and processed. _____
16. For extended-length field trips, appropriate medical and liability insurance policies have been obtained. _____
17. First-aid kits appropriate for the environment are available. _____
18. All safety procedures have been demonstrated and are understood by students. _____
19. The teacher has talked with the landowner or proprietor concerning hazards and special points of interest before involving students at the site. _____

Source: Jack Gerlovich, *Safe Science Teaching: A Diskette for Elementary Educators,* computer program (Waukee, IA: JaKel, 1990).

Implement the buddy system on field trips, pairing students and holding them responsible for each other (Rakow, 1989). Buddies can apprise adults of any problem. Of course, very young students (grades K–3) should not be separated from adult supervision at any time. The teacher should arrange for upper elementary students to meet at prearranged times and these times should be adhered to explicitly. Increase the adult supervision for young learners.

Maintenance.   Maintaining the educational environment is the third teacher duty. It is imperative that you attempt to foresee hazards and expedite their correction. You are not expected to be superhuman in your identification or make

What must a teacher do to ensure safe field trips?

the repairs yourself. However, a logical, regular review of the teaching environment is a reasonable expectation. The information available in the safety equipment and safety assessment sections of this chapter can help you with maintenance.

Federal and State Legislation

A vital state law or statute about which you should instruct students relates to eye protective equipment (safety goggles) (School Code of Iowa, 1988). You must insist that appropriate eyewear approved by the American National Standards Institute (ANSI) (School Code of Iowa, 1988) is provided to all students whenever the potential for eye injury exists. These federal equipment criteria were established to ensure minimum quality standards. You must insist that such eyewear meets ANSI standards and that you and your students wear them.

Compliance with these federal equipment standards is ensured when you see "Z87" printed on the goggle. The faceplate will not shatter, splinter, or fall backward into the face of the wearer if hit by a 1-inch ball bearing dropped from 50 inches, or by a quarter-inch ball bearing traveling at 150 feet per second. In addition, the frame will not burn. The teacher is responsible for insisting that the purchasing agent order only goggles that conform to these standards. Goggles that do not meet ANSI Z87 standards, that do not fit the students, or that

Safety goggles

have scratched faceplates, missing vent plugs, or damaged rubber moldings or headbands should not be used.

Require students to wear the goggles whenever there is the slightest chance that someone could sustain an eye injury in your classroom. Remember that injuries can happen even when students are walking about the room while others are performing science activities. Think also about injuries that could happen with such simple chemicals as salt or vinegar or with flying objects like rubber bands or balloons. Attempt to foresee such problems and act accordingly.

Most state statutes require that goggles be cleaned before students wear them. Such equipment should be stored in a relatively dust-free environment such as a box or a cabinet. (Secure a copy of your state's eye protective equipment legislation from the state department of education or school administration, and check for specific details.) Remember, in many states this is the law.

You need to understand and comply with applicable federal and state legislation as another way of ensuring proper and safe science teaching. Contact the state science consultant at your state department of education to secure copies of relevant science education legislation. Examples of such legislation include goggle laws, chemical right-to-know laws, bloodborne pathogen legislation, and other applicable Occupational Safety and Health Association (OSHA) regulations.

SAFETY EQUIPMENT

Certain safety equipment items are essential when teaching science activities. You should be confident that such items are immediately accessible when needed, that you and students can operate them, and that the items are appropriate for your students. Students should also be taught proper operation and location of all safety equipment items they might need to use, including fire extinguishers, fire blankets, eyewashes, safety goggles, and a telephone or intercom, if available. You might need duplicate safety items in more than one location in the room. Every student should have a set of goggles during science activities when eye protection is needed.

Electrical Equipment

Whenever possible, hot plates with on-off indicator lights should replace open flames. This simple change could eliminate many fire situations from science rooms. You should not have to use extension cords for hot plates, since the room

Alcohol lamp

should have sufficient electrical outlets. Extension cords on the floor create tripping hazards unless they are in cord protectors. Do not allow cords to be draped across desks or other work areas in order to prevent students from inadvertently upsetting apparatus. Electrical outlet caps should be in place when the outlets are not in use. In primary grades, outlets should be covered at all times so students cannot stick metal items in the plug holes, which could cause electrocution or burns.

Heating Equipment

If open flames are periodically necessary, be certain that emergency fire equipment is functioning properly and is immediately available. If alcohol lamps, sterno cans, or candles must be used, place them in pie pans filled with damp sand. Should a spill occur, the pie pan will prevent flaming liquids from spreading to clothing, tables, and other items. Alcohol looks like water; be sure to keep it off items where it might be treated like water. If you put alcohol in lamps, add a small amount of table salt so that the flame burns a bright orange color. Large quantities (½ liter or more) of alcohol or other flammable liquids should never be brought into the room, and students should never have access to quantities of these liquids.

Flammable Liquid Storage

If you are storing flammable liquids, such as alcohol, do so only in small quantities in the manufacturer's original container or in an approved safety can. A safety can is made of heavy-gauge steel or polyethylene. It has a spring-loaded lid to prevent spilling and to vent during vapor expansion caused by a heat source. It also has a flame arrester or heat sump in the throat of the spout to help prevent explosions.

Safety can

Loose Clothing and Long Hair

Loose clothing (especially sweaters) and long hair should be restricted when students are working with open flames. This seems obvious, yet clothing and hair commonly cause accidents. Be careful to pull long hair back so that it does not hang down over the flame, and restrict loose clothing

Fire blanket

by pushing up sleeves and securing them with pins or elastic (non-restricting rubber bands) to keep clothing from falling into open flames.

Fire Blankets

Fire blankets should be of the proper type and size and in the proper location. They should not be so large that students could not use them in an emergency. Check to be certain that they are placed in conspicuous locations and easily retrievable by all students and staff, including those with disabilities. Unless otherwise recommended by your fire marshal, these blankets should be made of wool. Fire blanket display and storage containers should be carefully checked for proper function. Be sure to eliminate containers with rusted hinges and latches, blankets still stored in plastic wrappers, and blankets made with asbestos fiber. Six-foot vertical standing fire blanket tubes should be avoided since they can result in facial burns. Do not attempt to extinguish torso fires by wrapping a student in the fire blanket. Because of the chimney effect, heat is pushed across the student's face, causing facial burns. The stop-drop-and-roll procedure endorsed by fire departments appears to be most effective at extinguishing body fires and presents the fewest drawbacks.

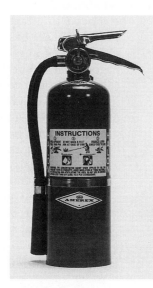

Fire extinguisher

Fire Extinguishers

ABC triclass fire extinguishers are usually preferred by fire departments because they can extinguish most foreseeable fires, such as fires from paper products, electrical items, and grease, that are likely to happen in elementary science. In settings where microcomputers are used regularly, it might be wise to investigate halon extinguisher types. These have been used in aviation for years because their fire-extinguishing chemicals do not foul contacts as dry chemical types will in delicate electronic navigation, communications equipment, and microcomputers.

Halon has also been preferred over carbon dioxide for extinguishing fires within electronic equipment, such as computers, because they do not cause the cold thermal shock to sensitive electronic microcircuits. Teachers should confirm such suggestions with their local or state fire marshal. The major disadvantage to halon is its harmful effect on the earth's ozone layer. Since such small quantities of this ingredient are in the halon and such emergency tools are used so infrequently, we believe that the benefits outweigh the drawbacks.

It is a good idea to have fire department personnel come into your classroom to demonstrate appropriate fire procedures and equipment to students. You should be confident and comfortable in using fire equipment items. You should also establish the habit of checking the pressure valve on fire extinguishers in or near your room to ensure that they are still adequately pressurized. It would also be wise for students to heft extinguishers, unfold and use a fire blanket, and rehearse foreseeable emergencies involving fire.

Eyewash and Shower

It is recommended that 15 minutes (2.5 gallons per minute) of aerated, tempered (60–90 degrees Fahrenheit), running water be deliverable from an eyewash to flush the eyes of a person who has suffered a chemical splash. At the elementary and middle school level, eye irritants could include salt, vinegar, sand, alcohol, and other chemicals. You should explore the installation of the fountain fixture type eyewash station (Sargent-Welch Scientific Company). It is not expensive ($60–70) and is easy to install by screwing it into an existing gooseneck faucet. The fixture allows the plumbing to be used as both an eyewash and a faucet simply by pushing a diverter valve. Should traffic patterns or room designs change, fountain fixtures can be moved to other faucets easily. On a temporary basis, you can stretch a piece of surgical tubing over a gooseneck faucet in order to deliver aerated, cool, running water to the eyes of a chemical splash victim. In the event of chemical spills on other and/or larger parts of the body, drench showers are recommended. Again, it is critical that such equipment be easily accessible to all staff and students. Be certain that the hot water faucet handle has been removed from any sink eyewash to prevent accidental burns that could be caused by hot water.

Eyewash station

Bottled water stations are not recommended because they can become contaminated, and they cannot deliver 15 minutes of aerated running water. They should be used only when there is no alternative, such as in field settings, and where you maintain strict control of them.

Critical safety equipment such as fire blankets, fire extinguishers, eyewashes, and drench showers should be located within thirty steps or 15 seconds of any location in the science room. These vital equipment items should be checked for proper operation every three to six months.

Teachers who work with chemicals must understand the properties, hazards, and appropriate emergency procedures to follow in the event of an accident. Material Safety Data Sheets (MSDS) (*CHRIS: Hazardous Chemical Data*) and the Merck Index (Budavari et al., 1989) provide such comprehensive information from chemical manufacturers. They identify the material, listing hazardous ingredients, physical and chemical characteristics, fire and explosion hazards, reactivity with other substances, health hazards, precautions for safe handling and use, as well as control measures. You can secure MSDSs from the U.S. Government Printing Office or directly from the manufacturers or suppliers from which schools purchase their chemicals.

We also recommend that you secure a copy of *School Science Laboratories: A Guide to Some Hazardous Chemicals* (1984) or *The Total Science Safety System* (Gerlovich & Hartman, 1992). Both encompass chemical management systems. Check the Additional Readings section of this chapter for addresses.

PERFORMING SAFETY ASSESSMENTS

You must be prepared to assess the safety situation within your teaching environment (classroom or field trips) regularly and accurately. The best way to accomplish this task is to develop and use safety software checklists regularly. The Total Science Safety System–Elementary (Gerlovich & Hartman, 1990) is available in Macintosh, Apple, and IBM formats and is cited in the Additional Readings section of this chapter. This software will help you develop a customized assessment system that fits your academic and facility needs. In addition, you can create complete and easily accessible records that can be updated regularly and printed as needed. These records could provide a defense in the case of an unforeseeable accident or injury lawsuit.

Elementary and middle school science safety checklists should include but not be limited to the components outlined in Figure 6.5. The assessments should be performed every semester in order to ensure that safety items are identified and corrected in a timely fashion.

Any safety problems should be corrected as soon as practical. This is best accomplished by informing the administration of the problem in writing. State the facts of the problem without explanation. Request an answer within ten days.

◆FIGURE 6.5   **Science Safety Checklist**

This listing is only representative of teachers' safety duties. Check off those items you are well informed about or prepared for and ask you instructor for more information about the remaining items.

Item	Well Prepared or Informed	Item	Well Prepared or Informed
Teachers understand their teaching duties of		Teachers ensure that all safety equipment is functioning and available	_____
Instruction	_____	Teachers ensure that all science equipment is of the right size and is appropriate for their students	_____
Supervision	_____		
Maintenance of the environment, equipment	_____	Teachers ensure that students know how to use safety and other science equipment items	_____
Teachers attempt to foresee hazards and correct them	_____	Teachers ensure that the following fire safety equipment is available whenever they are using open flames:	
Teachers' activities are consistent with those recommended by their textbooks, professional organizations, state agencies, federal standards	_____	Fire blanket	_____
		Fire extinguisher	_____
		Fire alarm	_____
Teachers use student safety contracts with upper elementary students	_____	Teachers ensure that loose clothing and long hair are confined when students are using open flames	_____
Teachers use only ANSI Z87–approved safety goggles	_____		
Teachers insist that students wear safety goggles whenever the potential for an eye injury exists	_____	Teachers ensure that an eyewash is available and functioning whenever the potential for an eye injury exists	_____
Teachers ensure that classes are not overcrowded (fewer than twenty-four students per teacher)	_____	Teachers use only chemicals for which they have MSDS sheets that they have reviewed for hazards	_____
Teachers ensure that field trips are not overcrowded (fewer than ten students per adult)	_____	Teachers ensure that extension cords are used only when absolutely necessary, and then only grounded types	_____
Teachers review the field trip site before taking students	_____	Teachers ensure that all electrical outlets are capped when not in use	_____
Teachers use the buddy system on field trips	_____		

Source: Jack Gerlovich and Kenneth Hartman, *The Total Science Safety System—Elementary* (Waukee, IA: JaKel, 1995).

The Total Science Safety System (Gerlovich & Hartman, 1992) provides checklists concerning life, earth, and physical science activities and procedures, and forms such as a student safety contract, an accident/incident report, and request for safety correction.

WHAT MATERIALS ARE NECESSARY FOR THE ACTIVITIES?

As the foreseeable hazards are addressed, you should determine materials that are needed for the activity. Identify readily available items, and determine

A variety of materials is necessary for effective science instruction.

where any additional items can be obtained. A good suggestion is to divide the remaining items into categories: items to be purchased through a scientific supplier, items that can be purchased locally through a discount or hardware store, and items that can be made for little or no cost from recycled materials.

A Science Activity Planner form (Figure 6.6) will facilitate your ordering needs. Fill out this sheet at least six weeks before you teach the lesson to allow time for vendor shipping and/or the steps your order must go through for approval of purchase and appropriation of funds in your school district. Figure 6.7 provides an example of how this form can be used.

Items Purchased Through a Scientific Supplier

Microscopes, slides, cover slips, thermometers, magnets, and electrical bulbs are the typical kinds of materials supplied by many reputable science equipment vendors. Science teachers in your school may already have suppliers they regularly deal with. Talk with fellow teachers about companies they have used in the past. If you are uncertain, request supply catalogs from companies.

Do not be quick to order from the vendor. Be a wise shopper, and compare prices and quality. Ask questions of others who may have previously ordered materials from a particular vendor. "How good is their service? Are they willing to meet needs quickly or slow in processing orders? What type of return policy do they have? Are they willing to take a purchase order or do they need to be paid up front?" A complete listing of science vendors, updated yearly, is available from the National Science Teachers Association.

◄ **FIGURE 6.6   Form for Science Activity Planner**

Concept to be taught: _____

_____

Material needs: _____

_____

Items available through school inventory: _____

_____

Items available at no cost/recycle: _____

_____

Scientific supplier (indicate vendor name, catalog number, description, number needed, cost per unit, total cost):

Local store (indicate store name and exact cost):

◄ **FIGURE 6.7   Science Activity Planner Example**

Concept to be taught: The circular path electrons follow is called a *circuit.*

Material needs: *For each student:* Battery, flashlight bulb, insulated copper wire, switch, bulb socket, cardboard tube (toilet paper tube), paper clip, two brass fasteners, plastic cap from a gallon milk container or a 35mm film can.

Items available through:

School inventory	Bulbs, switches, wire
No cost/recycle	Cardboard tubes, milk caps, film canister caps
Scientific supplier	Delta Supply, Nashua, New Hampshire
	57–020–9769, Bucket of Batteries, 30, $29.95, $29.95
	57–020–5644, Bulb Sockets, 30, $4.85/pkg. of 6, $24.25
Local store	John's Dollar Store on Main Street
	1 box of paper clips, 79¢
	2 boxes of brass fasteners, $1.45

Does your current textbook publisher supply prepackaged kits that go along with their activities? If so, will it be necessary to replenish materials in those kits? Is there a specific supplier you should order those kits from? If your answers to these questions are "yes," then determine which items need to be replaced and if it is possible to replace only the used items or necessary to order a new kit. You may often come across prepackaged general science kits, such as one that supplies all materials you will need to do a unit on electricity. Under both circumstances, you must determine your needs. Will you use all of the materials provided in the kit? Will it be less expensive to order the items individually?

Carefully examine the supply catalogs. You may spot items that could enhance a lesson—an item you did not even think of in your original materials list. Perhaps you found the item in two different catalogs, each at a different price. As you gain experience in ordering, you will find that companies differ in prices on equivalent items. If you are placing a big order with one company, it is usually more economical to purchase the higher-priced item from it along with the rest of your order. The money you may save on the price of the item with a different vendor could be spent on shipping charges.

Local restaurants, grocery stores, or discount stores are usually willing to donate items such as paper cups, containers, or straws to meet your science activity needs.

The task of ordering supplies with school money may appear overwhelming. But if you follow a few easy steps, the work is painless. First, plan ahead. Avoid waiting until the last minute to order supplies. Often district paperwork or supply availability may delay shipment. Live plant or animal specimens can be ordered several months in advance with an indication of when you want them shipped. Once you have determined what items you will need and from which suppliers, you probably will have to obtain a purchase order. Check with the principal or school district treasurer about the proper procedure. Most often this involves filling out the purchase order completely. *Completely* means not only names of items but catalog numbers, quantities, prices, shipping charges, complete name, address, and phone and/or fax number of vendor. Remember that you need only one purchase order per vendor. Once it is completed, you will need to obtain the authorized signatures before you can mail it. If the purchase order form has duplicates, mail the original to the vendor. If it is a single copy, make a copy for the administration and one for yourself.

If you phone in the order, be sure to provide the vendor with all information included on the purchase order, especially the purchase order number. After the initial order is placed, it is customary to write on the purchase order the date and time the order was phoned in. You may be required to send the vendor a copy of that purchase order. If so, make sure to write on the purchase order, "This is a copy of a phone order."

Items Purchased Locally

Consumable items—paper cups, bags, straws—are some of the common items purchased from local vendors. If you teach in a community that is very supportive of its local schools, you may be able to get donations of consumable items from local restaurants, grocery stores, or discount stores. Even the local lumber yard may be willing to supply a class with yard or meter sticks or scrap lumber.

Discount stores that specialize in overruns are an excellent source for science supplies. As you walk up and down the aisles, scan the shelves thinking about science concepts you could teach with various items. You may be surprised at what you come up with. Simple toys like yo-yos, ball and jacks, paddle balls, and rubber balls can be used to teach a variety of scientific concepts. Paper clips, masking tape, batteries, or wire can start you on the way to a terrific electricity unit. Inexpensive bubble gums or chocolate chip cookies can lead to exciting lessons that focus on the scientific method. Never underestimate the science possibilities in a discount store.

Local stores may already have agreements with your school district, such as charge accounts or cash credit accounts. Check with the school district treasurer. You may be able to charge the items at those stores. Other stores may take purchase orders. Occasionally you may have to provide your own money. If this is the case, find out the procedure for reimbursement in your school. Does the principal have a fund from which you can immediately be reimbursed upon turning in your receipt? Is a receipt necessary? Do you need a petty cash voucher from the school before you make a purchase? What kind of information does the vendor need to supply on that voucher? Do you need to supply the vendor with a tax-exempt number from the school so that you are not charged sales tax? Ask all of these questions *before* you go out and spend your own money. You do not want to find out after the fact that since you did not complete the proper paper trail, you will not be reimbursed.

Items Made from Recycled Materials

You've been caught again rummaging through the bin at the local recycling center. Embarrassed? There is no need to be when it's done in the name of science! What was it this time? Looking for cans to paint black for a unit on heat? Was it a plastic soda bottle to make another Cartesian diver? Do you need various size jars for a sound unit? Whatever the science topic, usually one or two items can be found in a recycling bin. Of course, you can avoid those embarrassing moments by encouraging your students to bring in materials they ordinarily throw away. Setting up a recycling area in your classroom will provide a quick source for those necessary items and teach students the importance of recycling.

In the scenario at the beginning of this chapter, Celeste needed a tuna can so she went to the area in her home where recyclables were stored; thus she did not have to hold off creating the volcano for lack of a tuna can. Cans are not the only useful recyclable item. Styrofoam plates from prepackaged meats are useful in many activities. They make great placemats for messy activities that involve liquids. Styrofoam egg cartons can be turned into charcoal crystal gardens in no time, or they can be used to stack small items like rock collections. Toilet paper and paper towel tubes can be used in making flashlights, and aluminum pie plates are useful for heating water. Plastic containers with lids, such as the ones that food comes in at the grocery store, can be used for storage. Your imagination is your only limit when it comes to deciding what to do with recycled materials.

STORAGE

Central or Classroom Storage Access

The biggest task is over—or so you think. The materials have been ordered and are beginning to arrive. So where do they go? Does your school have a central storage area for science materials? Are the materials you ordered solely for your classroom use, or will you be sharing them with other teachers? Who will be allowed access to the materials? Do you have space in your classroom to store materials? Before you begin stocking your classroom shelves, find the answers to these questions.

Central Storage Area.   Some schools designate one room or area in the school to keep all science materials. If this is the case at your school, find out who is

Proper materials storage makes preparation and replacement easier.

responsible for maintaining that area. Careful inventory should be maintained of the items stored there. It is best if one person is responsible for keeping the inventory current. Teachers who borrow materials should be held responsible for their return. One person should have the authority to request the return of borrowed materials after a reasonable time period. Sign-out sheets (see Figure 6.8) should be completed by any staff member who uses materials from the central storage.

The teachers should determine who will have access to the central storage area:

- Will only science teachers be allowed to use it?
- Will other teachers have access?
- Will students be allowed to borrow items from central storage?
- Who will be responsible for disseminating the materials? Will it be done on an honor system?

These questions may appear trivial, but once you count on items for a particular activity only to find that someone has borrowed them without signing

◆FIGURE 6.8   Science Equipment Checkout Form

Science Equipment Checkout Form

Name: _____

Grade and/or subject area: _____

Room number: _____

Date of checkout: Expected date of return:

_____   _____

Items borrowed:

_____

_____

_____

Signature: _____

---

them out, you will not be too happy. Often it becomes a wild-goose chase to find out who used the materials last. If the search comes up short, you may end up omitting a valuable lesson for lack of supplies. Some ground rules can avoid any unnecessary searches or hard feelings.

Classroom Storage.   If you store materials in your classroom, plan where the materials will be located. The first consideration is who will have access to those materials. Will the students be allowed access to everything, or will safety reasons prohibit total access? Where can you store materials that you consider dangerous to students? Ideally any hazardous materials should be stored in locked cabinets.

Think about the storage of live specimens. If plants are brought into the classroom, is an area available near windows to facilitate plant growth? Is shelf space available near a window, or will you have to appropriate a table or bookshelf to set up near a window? Can artificial lights be used on the plant? If window space is minimal, where will this designated artificial light be? Should the students have access to these plants? Do they present any potential harm to the students if ingested?

What about live animals? Are adequate cages or containers available for the animals' safety? What about your students' safety near the animals? Is a water source available for the animals? What are their food requirements? How and where will their food be stored? Take care to ensure that through proper storage of animal food, pests will not be drawn to your classroom. If you keep a live animal in the classroom, you should be aware of your responsibility to the animal and to the students' health and safety. Learn the school's policy on live animals in the classroom. Find out if any of your students have allergies to certain animals. Learn what kind of insurance coverage you need should a student become injured while handling the animal. Make sure that any animal kept around children is not a carrier of infectious diseases. And make sure the animal is cared for on weekends and during vacations.

Animals brought into the classroom should be used to increase the students' understanding and respect for the animal. Of course, common sense should prevail. Children cannot be permitted to bring in stray squirrels, raccoons, and similar animals. However, an occasional ladybug or cricket can teach valuable lessons. When live animals are brought into the classroom, follow the 24-hour rule recommended by the American Humane Society. The students can then study the animal during the course of the day. Encourage the students to use resource books to determine the animal's food, shelter, and space needs and to make as many observations about the animal's behavior as possible. After a day of being in the classroom, return the animal to the place where it was found or a similar habitat.

If you know that students will need access to certain materials, arrange materials so that they are on shelves or in cabinets within easy reach. If there are certain materials, such as chemicals or cleaners, that need to be out of the students' reach, a locked cabinet or cupboard is a necessity. Plans should be made to make shelves or cabinets if these do not exist in your classroom. Rather than looking at your classroom negatively and simply deciding that there is no place to put anything, think creatively. Could an unused corner make an ideal storage area? Could you get a local business to donate some unused bookshelves or storage cabinets? Could the school's maintenance personnel make some shorter shelf units for student access? Try to have these problems solved before the materials arrive.

Not all items will be stored. For instance, if you have a learning center that constantly requires the use of a balance, leave the balance out. Other activity areas may be set up where materials are always left out. The students should know that they are free to move items from one center to another. For example, going back to the first scenario, if Celeste and Sarah were working on their volcano at school in the science activity center and realized that they needed red food coloring, which was always out at the food center, they could go over and get the food coloring without having to ask for permission to move it from one center to the next.

Freedom to move materials creates a learning environment that is adaptable to the students' needs. To avoid creating an inventory nightmare, establish some simple task assignments. Most children like to be useful and help the teacher. In the primary grades, the teacher can create a poster for each center with a picture of the necessary items. Older students can have a written supply list for each center. Students can be assigned to the different centers on a rotating basis and be responsible for making sure that at the end of the school day the items for their assigned center are in place. When consumable items are needed, the students should write them on a master list for the teacher, indicating which items are needed at each learning center. The teacher can then use this list to obtain the materials, then give the items to the student responsible for that center to put in their proper place. Gentle reminders to students about returning items to the place where they found them will facilitate the task of taking inventory.

Storing and Dispensing Materials

No matter where materials are stored, you will need to decide how to store them. Will they be arranged according to units, such as electricity, weather, and simple machines, or will the items be stored separately? Once you make this decision, choose from among numerous ways to arrange the items, from shelves to shoeboxes to plastic storage bins. Table 6.1 identifies the advantages and disadvantages of several storage possibilities.

Whether items are kept in a central storage area (see Figure 6.9) or in the classroom, you still need to think about how the students will collect them for a particular activity. When items are stored in a central location, you may want to collect the materials at least a day ahead of time to make sure everything needed for a given activity is still available. Decide how many of what item you will need. Once the items are in the classroom, appoint students to arrange the materials for the various working groups.

In a safe and efficient activity-based science classroom, the teacher does not have to do all of the advance work for a particular science activity. The teacher can appoint responsible students to collect the science materials. A simple way to disseminate the materials is to have a materials list posted for the activity, assign particular students to gather materials, and provide those students with buckets or plastic bins to put the collected materials in for that activity. Each materials manager for the day should be responsible for collecting the correct number of items for his or her group to do the activity and be responsible for counting the materials at the end of the lesson, collecting them in the bucket, and returning them to their proper place.

The teacher could appoint one or two students to count the items in the buckets, making sure everything is returned after use. The teacher can put the used materials back in their proper storage areas in the classroom or assign students to help with that task. If the materials go back to a central storage area, the teacher should make sure they are returned to their proper place as soon as possible. Other teachers may be counting on the use of those materials.

Keep safety concerns in mind when returning used materials. Were hazardous materials used during the activity? (Any material labeled toxic, ignitable, corrosive, or reactive should be considered hazardous.) Many common household items used at the elementary level in science activities could fall into these categories—such items as bleach or ammonia, carpet shampoos, win-

◆ **TABLE 6.1   Materials Storage**

Materials Stored	Advantages	Disadvantages
As units	All material together Can present lesson at any time without rummaging through shelves for necessary materials	Question of who is responsible for replacing consumable items Scarce resources cause unit to be picked apart and used for other activities
Individually	Ideal storage in schools where resources are scarce Works well when materials are centrally stored, easier to collect	Time needed to pull several items together for each teaching unit Additional storage space necessary to store individual items in classroom
On shelves	Items can be shelved alphabetically for quick and easy retrieval Efficient method for storing glassware and large items	Difficult to determine where one letter ends and the next begins Difficult to store items in multiple quantities With multiple users, need to rearrange shelves frequently
In plastic bags	Sealable bags are ideal for small items Can be labeled with permanent markers Available in a variety of sizes to accommodate various sized materials	If seal not made, items fall out and get lost With extended use, labeling wears off Tear with frequent use
In shoeboxes or cardboard boxes	Inexpensive way to store multiple items like thermometers, magnets, and marbles Easily labeled and can be covered with an adhesive plastic for prolonged use An ideal size for storing on shelves	Since opaque, necessary to open to determine contents Even covered, eventually wear out
In plastic storage bins	Available in a variety of shapes and sizes Clear so items stored are visible Can be labeled with permanent markers Many guaranteed to last at least five years	Better-made containers are costly Lids crack on less expensive containers if heavy things are stacked on top
Using color coding	Ideal for identifying hazardous materials by using orange safety stickers Identify quickly consumed items with one color, facilitates reordering needs	Advantages lost if all teachers do not understand or remember color codes If color code key not posted, difficult to locate material

FIGURE 6.9 Central Storage Area Design

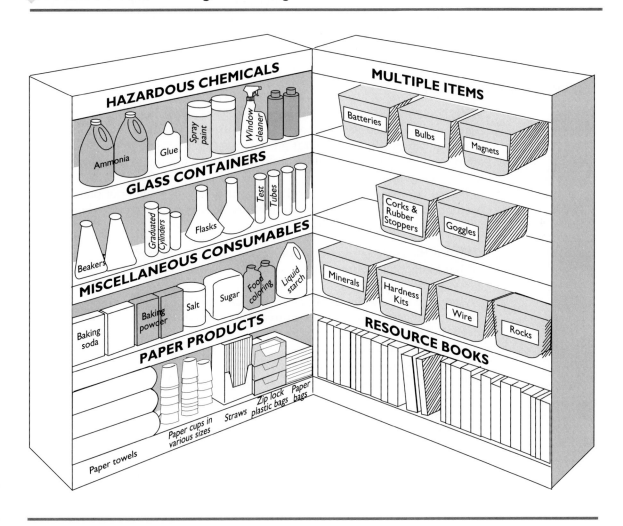

dow cleaner, paints, and glues. Does your school have an appropriate system to handle disposal of these wastes? Which materials could be recycled? What procedures should be followed to dispose of used materials? Remember that hazardous waste improperly handled can pollute drinking supplies, poison humans, or contaminate soil and air. The teacher should be responsible for disposing of used hazardous materials. If you are uncertain about disposing of a particular item, check with the local fire marshal or local office of the

Environmental Protection Agency. These agencies will be able to instruct you on proper disposal. Many local fire departments are equipped to handle low-level toxic waste. All high schools should have a plan in place for handling waste from the chemistry classes. Check to see if your district has one. If it does not, work with local agencies to develop a safe and reliable disposal system.

ROOM ARRANGEMENT

Carefully planned lessons and ample supplies are not enough to carry off a successful inquiry-based science activity. The physical arrangement of the classroom is an important consideration. Barriers such as classroom size, traffic patterns, blind spots, poles, and walls will require a teacher to be creative about utilizing the available space.

Before you begin moving furniture around, draw a scale floor plan of your classroom (see Figure 6.10). Ask yourself the following questions when deciding how to arrange the classroom:

- What is the best way to utilize the space I have available?
- What kinds of activities will my students be involved in?
- What kinds of materials will be used?
- What type of furniture do I have in my classroom?
- Will I need any additional furniture, or should I eliminate some of the furniture that is already in there?
- What kind of flooring does the classroom have? Is it appropriate for the activities my students will be engaged in?
- Where are the entrances and exits in this classroom?
- Where are the electrical outlets?
- What kind of traffic patterns do I wish to develop?
- What are the potential hazards with the arrangement I have in mind?

The suggestions that follow are designed to help you arrange your classroom to maximize your students' science experiences while allowing you to maintain flexibility to accommodate the teaching of other subject areas.

Large-Group Science Activities

Flat surfaces offer the best means of engaging in science activities when working with an entire class. If you are in a classroom with tilted desk tops, you will need to be creative; child-sized tables are one alternative. Another is to designate space on the floor for children to participate in science activities.

Divide the class into small working groups of three or four students each. Current recommendations are that elementary school classrooms should provide at least 30 square feet of space for each student and have no more than twenty-four students for labs and activities. Although elementary science classes are not laboratory based, if all students are to have sufficient feedback

FIGURE 6.10   Classroom Floor Plan

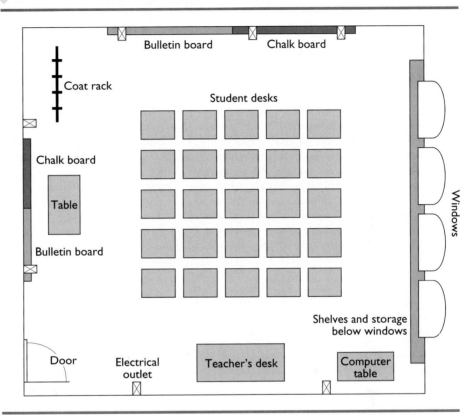

and guidance in science projects, twenty-four students is a manageable number. While the physical constraints of your classroom may not allow you this much area or your class size puts you beyond the twenty-four-student limit, whenever possible optimum space should be allocated and ideal class size should be maintained.

Whether the students are working at small tables, several flat-topped desks pushed together to make a larger working area, or on the floor, consider the type of flooring in the classroom. A nonslip tile floor is best but not a necessity. Carefully taping down an inexpensive vinyl floor remnant in the designated science area will save a carpet from messy spills and facilitate clean-up.

Create an area where you can collect materials for science activities before the class uses them. This place should also function as an area where science demonstrations occur. Preferably, this area should be close to the science storage area if supplies are stored within the classroom. Storage space for student

WHAT RESEARCH SAYS ◆◆◆

Class Size and Science Achievement

First, small classes are supported in primary grades. Kindergarten, first, second, and third grade classes should be as small as economically feasible. If cost were not an issue, the limiting factor to reducing class size . . . seems to be the social value of cooperation among very young children.

Second, . . . it seems evident that these changes should be accompanied by research-based changes in teaching methods that take advantage of these changes. One prominent study concludes that reducing class size and proportionally increasing educational expenses by as much as 50 percent might be necessary to increase the student's achievement by a mere 10 percentile points. It may be that reducing class size in itself is not an efficient use of public funds.

Third, the research on teaching and learning (rather than the research on achievement) supports the idea that very large class sizes cannot provide students with reasonable instructional and motivational systems. Safety problems also increase with class size. Small groups make it easier for teachers to monitor problem solving, attempt to improve understanding, and create an atmosphere of scientific inquiry. These factors are among the many that are not measured by most achievement tests.

Fourth, teachers must couple their arguments for smaller classes with requests for other improvements that would help their students achieve. . . . Most science classrooms . . . lack adequate supplies and equipment. . . . Such tools, along with reasonable inservice, might make science truly exciting and academically productive.

. . . Teachers need small classes [to] conduct hands-on laboratory activities and intense follow-up discussions. . . . In large classes, it is unlikely they can prepare and inspire students for tomorrow's world of science.

Source: W. Holliday, "Should We Reduce Class Size?" *Science Teacher* (January 1992): 14–17.

projects should also be planned near this area. If possible, choose an area near the sink.

The physical arrangement of the desks and tables should be dictated by the type of activity going on in the classroom on any particular day. If space and furniture availability permit, a permanent science area can be maintained within the classroom. If space is a problem, desks and tables that can be moved into configurations like those shown in Figure 6.11 will facilitate learning in an activity-based science classroom. Whenever possible, this area should be near windows to allow the use of natural light. Space should be arranged to eliminate traffic congestion and to provide a clear path to all classroom exits.

Science Learning Centers

When working with the entire class for science lessons, a teacher committed to learning cycle–constructivist approaches will find that science learning centers satisfactorily accommodate additional expansion activities for each lesson. You can design the learning center so that it focuses on a particular concept brought out in a class lesson and provides additional experiences for the students, who will come to a greater understanding of the concept. The center should not sim-

FIGURE 6.11   Arranging an Activity-Based Classroom

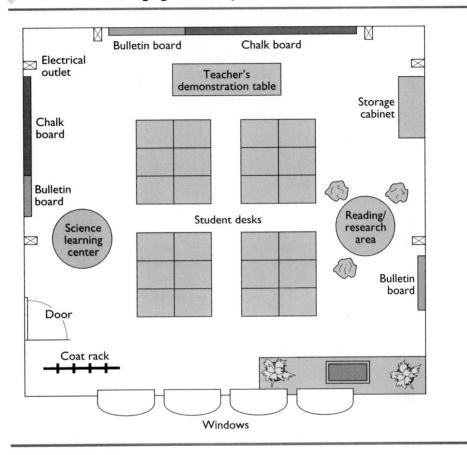

ply be a place where the brighter students or those who finished their assignments first get to go. All students should be encouraged to use the learning
center at their convenience, to engage in activities that provide additional experiences with a particular science concept. Once all of the students have had
sufficient time to use that expansion activity, change the activity at the center to
address a new concept you are teaching.

Another approach to science learning centers is to design them so that students gain greater experience in the processes of science. When you present science lessons to a large group of students, the chances that each student has
adequate time to make observations, predictions, measurements, and so on are
slim if a more-skilled peer blurts out the answer first. The learning center can
be designed so each child has a chance to work in the area, gaining experience

Arranging and Managing the Classroom

by Johanna Ramsey
Grade 6 science teacher, Marion Elementary School, Palmyra, NY

That teaching sixth-grade science by using the hands-on method has many challenges I learned when I began teaching science seven years ago. One of the challenges is to arrange the classroom to promote student activity and student learning. The classroom should be laid out in such a way that the students can move freely around the room. At various times the students need to work in the lab, get equipment, gather into small discussion groups, or meet for large-class discussion and directions. Since there is movement in class, there should be a good flow pattern to the room.

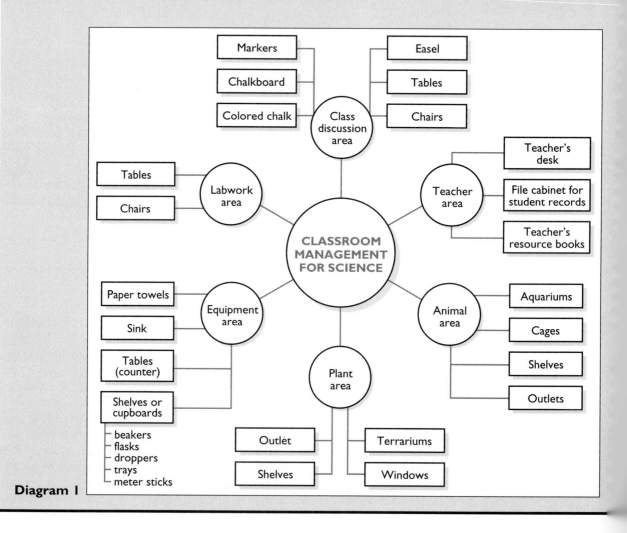

Diagram 1

After all directions have been given to the students in the class discussion area, they are dismissed to go to lab to run their experiments. At this point they move freely around the room to pick up the equipment they need. All materials should be clearly labeled so the students know exactly what they need, and each work area should be clearly posted so there is no confusion as to where in the room the students belong.

The plant and animal areas are in the room for the students to enjoy throughout the year. Much on-the-spot learning takes place about plant and animal life this way—sometimes more so than by a prepared lesson. They learn the parts of a plant, the changes a flowering plant goes through, animal behavior, animal reproduction, and plant and animal care.

Besides having a set display of plants and animals, the students have the opportunity to bring in other small animals and insects. (Make sure that they are not harmful before having them in the classroom.) Students are very curious about their surroundings, so tap into their interests. This makes learning fun, and the students don't realize they're learning when they're having fun!

When I began teaching science, I brainstormed on areas I wanted in my classroom. Diagram 1 shows the ideas I planned out. Diagram 2 shows what my classroom looks like today. The students come into my room and meet in the class discussion area for directions and questions. From here they are dismissed to go to their lab areas. They move to the equipment area as they need pieces of equipment for their experiment. During lab time the students conduct their experiments and discuss their procedures and results in groups of four. Once experiments are complete, the class gets back together in the discussion area to discuss the results they found in their small groups. Much learning takes place through this cooperative sharing of ideas and results.

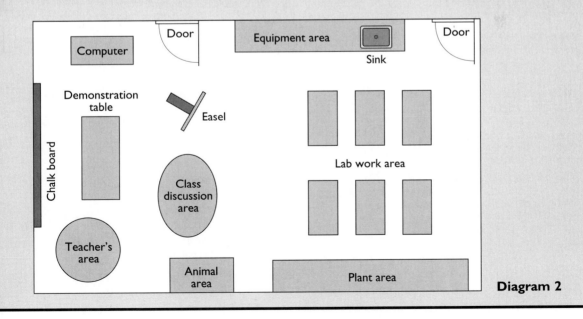

Diagram 2

in solving problems, measuring, predicting, using scientific instruments, and so on. You can change the learning center weekly, with different process skills as the focus (see Figure 6.12).

FIGURE 6.12   Process-Oriented Science Learning Center Lesson

1. Obtain light bulb record books

Process Skill: Recording data

Each student will receive a light bulb record book. The outer covers are made from yellow cardboard. Several sheets of white paper for students to record their data are stapled between the covers.

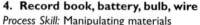

2. Page 1 of record book

Process Skill: Observing

On the table is a box with a bulb sticking out of the top. A switch protrudes from one side. A card near the box states:

> Make as many observations as possible. Write the word OBSERVA-TIONS on the top of page 1 in the light bulb record book. Record your observation on that page.

3. Record Book

Process Skill: Predicting

A card that is numbered with a 3 and has a drawing of the box with the bulb will be at the center with the following directions:

> Label the next blank page in your record book PREDICTIONS. Predict what is inside the box causing the bulb to light. List and/or draw your predictions on that page.

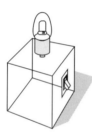

4. Record book, battery, bulb, wire

Process Skill: Manipulating materials

Card numbered 4 near a battery, bulb, and wire, asks the students to do the following:

> Label the next blank page of your record book MANIPULATING MATERIALS. Take the battery, bulb, and wire from the table. Using only those three pieces of material, get the bulb to light. Record in the record book draw-ings of ways you manipulated the materials—whether the bulb lit or not.

5. Record book, battery, bulb, wire, bulb holder, switch

Process Skill: Manipulating materials

At the next station the above materials will be laying near card number 5. The students will be asked to do the fol-lowing:

> Label the next blank page of your record book MANIPULAT-ING MATERIALS. Take the battery, bulb, wire, bulb holder, and switch from the table. Get the bulb to light as you did at sta-tion 4. This time wire it so that the switch will turn the bulb on and off. Record in the record book drawings of ways you manipulated the materials—whether the bulb lit or not.

6. Record book, box, battery, bulb, bulb holder, wire, switch

Process Skill: Interpreting data, inferring, formulating models

The above materials will be found at station 6. The students will be asked to do the following:

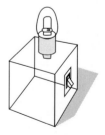

> Label the next blank page of your record book INTERPRETING DATA, INFERRING, FORMULATING MODELS. Using the materials given and your results from activi-ties 4 and 5, try to create a box like the one you observed at sta-tion 2 and 3. When finished go back to your prediction page in the record book. Was your prediction correct?

A science learning center can also be designed as a *discovery area*—a place where children create inventions from a variety of provided materials. They can be considered challenge areas, where the teacher creates a problem for the week, and using the materials provided, the students work to solve the problem. Science learning centers can be the place where students can play teacher-prepared or commercially prepared science games.

Whatever you decide the focus of your science learning center should be, a few simple rules must be upheld to ensure its success. The guidelines for a science learning center are set out in Table 6.2.

Figures 6.13 and 6.14 provide examples of some typical science learning centers. Centers should be found in an area of the classroom where they are least likely to interfere with normal classroom operations. The information provided on classroom safety should guide you in the placement of the science learning center.

A pegboard or a felt board can be designed so that it will stand on its own atop a table or desk and can easily be stored when necessary. Pockets made from cloth or heavy cardboard serve as areas to hold activity cards, instructions, or small materials needed for the activity. Any material sturdy enough to withstand student wear, without being so heavy that it topples over, will serve as the backdrop for your science learning center. Appropriate pictures or diagrams should be displayed on this board. If the activity requires a more formal means of record keeping, place record sheets or assessment sheets in a pocket on the board. Figure 6.15 provides an example of a typical science learning center backdrop.

TABLE 6.2   Science Learning Center Guidelines

1. The purpose and objectives for the activity are made clear; the students understand what they are supposed to do at each center. The activity is designed so that it enhances the students' understanding of a concept rather than serving to frustrate and confuse.

2. *All* students have an opportunity to work at the center before the activity is changed.

3. Activities at the center do not interfere with other lessons going on in the classroom. Activities that require darkness, loud noises, or excessive amounts of physical activity are not appropriate for a learning center. The center is in an area where the teacher can readily observe the children in action.

4. At least one 2-feet-by-4-feet table or work area of equivalent size is dedicated to this center. If the activity requires additional space, adequate floor space will be allocated. If audiovisual materials are to be used, electrical outlets are close by.

5. Consumable materials at the centers are replenished frequently.

6. When water is required for an activity, the center is located close to a water source. If this is not possible, care is taken so that children running to sinks or water fountains are not interfering with students engaged in other classroom tasks.

FIGURE 6.13   Science Learning Center

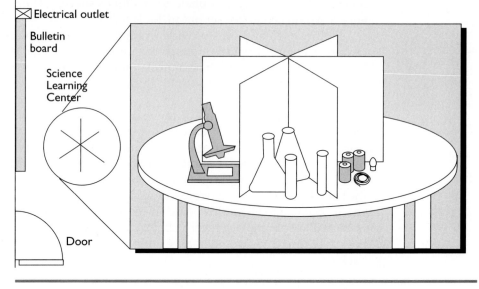

- Outlets should be available when needed
- Bulletin board contains pertinent science information
- Center is located near door to gain access to water from fountain in hall since no water is available in this classroom

⊠ Electrical outlet

Bulletin board

Science Learning Center

Door

Bulletin Boards and Other Displays

An activity-based science classroom should include a science bulletin board and a science display area. Lettering used for the bulletin board should be no smaller than 4 inches high. Plan the topic to be addressed, and focus on one concept. Don't use too many words. Try to find visuals that will enhance the students' understanding of the concept, but avoid using too much material. If display colors, sizes, and shapes change too frequently, the intended message may get lost.

Science displays should be designed to appeal to the students' natural curiosity. They can be theme oriented and designed by the teacher or a collection of unrelated items provided by the students. For a theme highlighting mammals, the display table could contain pelts of various mammals for the students to touch and to compare and antlers or horns for the students to determine the animal it came from and its age. There may be footprints of various mammals with a challenge to the students to determine which animal left the print. Books or picture of various mammals would be left at the table.

FIGURE 6.14   Science Learning Center

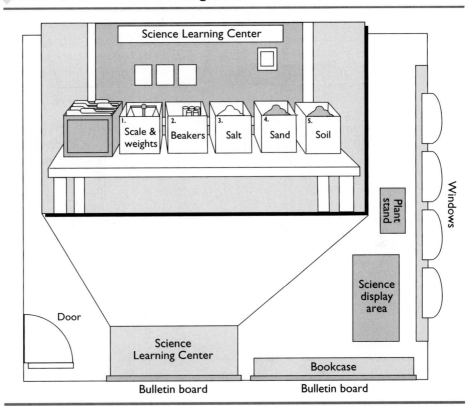

In a hodge-podge approach, the display area may be a catch-all for the various science-related items children come across that they would like to share. Items on the display table should be ones the students are allowed to touch: household items, like an old radio or clock that can be taken apart to examine the inner works, for example, or unusual rocks or plant parts that may serve to pique a student's curiosity. An item that requires special care, like a geode or a parent's rock collection, that a student brings in may be better suited for teacher-supervised display.

Large-group instruction or small science learning centers? No matter what the mode of instruction is, science learning will be facilitated when careful thought is given to the physical arrangement of the classroom. Allowing the students to travel freely to learning centers implies that certain behaviors are expected of the students. Using instruction time to teach cooperative roles will faciliate class exploration.

◆FIGURE 6.15   **Science Learning Center Backdrop**

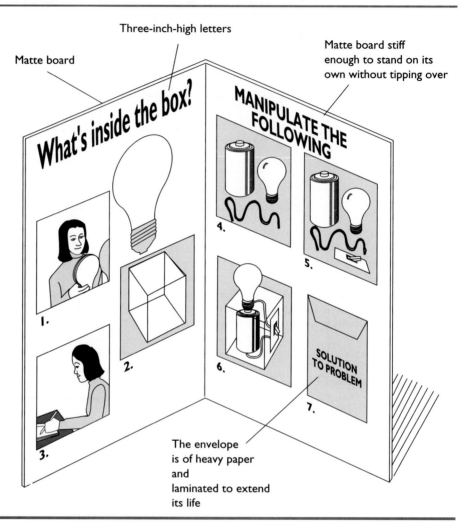

CHAPTER SUMMARY

By asking, "What are the foreseeable hazards associated with valued educational activities?" and "What materials are necessary for the activities?" teachers can be successful in creating an efficient, safe environment for activity-based science. Once the concepts to be taught are clearly identified and grade-level-appropriate activities are chosen, decisions about materials needed to teach those concepts, storage of the materials, and safe practices while handling them must be decided upon. Generally storage decisions depend on school building space restrictions and the safety philosophy embraced by the teaching faculty.

Teachers must attempt to foresee problems posed by activities and address them; teach appropriately for the emotional, physical, and intellectual levels of their students; and provide adequate supervision applicable for the environment and the degree of hazards anticipated, in addition to ensuring that the environment and equipment items are properly maintained. Teachers who are sure that they have addressed all of these concerns can proceed with confidence.

If they cannot, adjustments should be made—adding more safety features, limiting the activity to a teacher demonstration only, or eliminating the activity.

The physical arrangement of the classroom directly affects the success of the activity-oriented science lesson. When physical barriers impede the completion of an activity, the students can become frustrated. If materials are not readily available to bring a child from a state of disequilibrium to equilibrium, a teachable moment may be lost. A flexible learning environment, carefully planned and designed to promote student exploration, will greatly facilitate science learning.

DISCUSSION QUESTIONS AND PROJECTS

1. You are planning a field trip with your first-grade class to the local prairie ecosystem (or other special local ecosystem) to study plants. All parent and guardian release forms have been returned with the exception of one. Would you allow the student to attend the activity anyway? Give three reasons for your answer.

2. A student in your third-grade class asks you if he can bring his pet northern banded water snake to class to show during your reptile unit. What would be your response? What information would you want to support your decision? Where would you secure such information?

3. You are preparing to do a simple chemistry experiment with your sixth-grade class. A student says that she has new safety glasses provided by her optometrist and would rather wear them than your safety goggles. What would be your response? Why?

4. Develop a written plan for conducting a safety assessment of a school science classroom in your area. Include all necessary forms and checklists, as well as a time line for its completion.

5. Ask representatives from the local fire department to visit your classroom and demonstrate the proper procedure for dealing with a personal-clothing fire and the proper use of fire extinguishers. If possible, ask that the fire personnel set small demonstration fires outside in containers and show how the

various extinguisher types put out paper, electrical, and grease fires.

6. Select an elementary school in your area, and develop a written checklist for performing a safety assessment of its grounds. Be sure to address items that are indigenous to your area, including hazardous plants and animals, automobile traffic, difficult-to-supervise areas, natural hazards (streams, lakes, and so on), and human problems (construction areas, glass).

7. Interview an elementary science teacher responsible for ordering science equipment. Find answers to the following questions:

- What vendors does he or she use to purchase science equipment and why?
- How good is the service provided by that vendor?
- How quick is the vendor to process orders?
- What type of return policy does the vendor have?
- Does the vendor take purchase orders or require payment up-front?
- What procedures does the school follow in placing and paying for orders?
- If you had to set up an ordering system, would you recommend the one used by the teacher you interviewed? If not, how would you design it differently?
- What safety features are followed for classroom storage of materials?

8. Visit an elementary school that has a central storage area for science materials. Does this area appear well maintained? Is someone responsible for checking materials in and out? Who keeps inventory of supplies? How well managed do you think the storage area is? What recommendations would you make for it?

9. Design a science learning center for sixth-grade students with outer space as the theme (or select you own theme), and draw a diagram of what it will look like. What kinds of items, activities, and experiments would you place there? How would you change this design if it were for a second-grade class? Explain, and provide another diagram.

10. During a unit on insect behavior, several children bring to school both live and dead insects. What should be done with the dead insects? the live ones? Should the students be encouraged to bring insects into the classroom? Why or why not? What do you believe your responsibility is to the insects and to the students' attitudes toward insects?

ADDITIONAL READINGS

If you are interested in learning more about the topics raised in this chapter, consider reading the following:

Christine Chaille and Lory Britain, *The Young Child As Scientist: A Constructivist Approach to Early Childhood Science Education* (New York: HarperCollins, 1991). This short book details the constructivist learning theory and provides models for classrooms where this approach is utilized. In addition, an entire section is devoted to constructivist science with examples of science activities using the constructivist approach in the areas of physics, chemistry, biology, and ecology.

Curry College, Chemistry Department, *Speaking of Safety: The Laboratory Safety Workshop Newsletter* (Milton, MA). An excellent reference for case study reviews and safety tips.

G. Downs, et al., *Science Safety for Elementary Teachers* (Ames, IA: Iowa State University Press, 1984). This book provides educators with accident statistics, liability information, and safety considerations for physical science, life science, and chemicals. In addition, first aid and outdoor activities are addressed.

Flinn Scientific Co., *Flinn Chemical Catalogue Reference Manual* (Batavia, IL: Flinn Scientific, 1992). This annual publication provides science educators with a listing of chemicals sold by Flinn Scientific, as well as quick reference items regarding their storage, handling, and disposal.

Florida Department of Education, *Science Safety: No Game of Chance!* (Tallahassee, FL: Division of Public Schools, Bureau of Elementary and Secondary Education). This guide assists school personnel in developing a personal safety plan for their district or school.

Forum for Scientific Excellence, *Handbook of Chemical and Environmental Safety in Schools and Colleges* (Philadelphia, 1990). This brief monograph provides practical suggestions on chemical use to schools and colleges.

J. Gerlovich, "Safety First in the Elimination of Hazardous Chemicals from School Science Settings," in D. A. Pipitone, *Safe Storage of Laboratory Chemicals,* 2d ed. (New York: Wiley, 1991). This chapter outlines safe and cost-effective means for eliminating unwanted chemicals from schools on a statewide basis.

J. A. Gerlovich, et al., *School Science Safety: Elementary* (Batavia, IL: Flinn Scientific, 1984). This paperback is a rich reference for elementary teachers of science.

J. A. Gerlovich and T. Gerard, "Don't Let Your Hands-on Science Program Blow Up in Your Face," *American School Board Journal* (May 1984): 40–41. This article, written by a science safety consultant and an attorney, emphasizes the team approach to safety in school science settings.

J. Gerlovich and K. Hartman, *The Total Science Safety System: Elementary,* 2d ed. (Waukee, IA: JaKel, 1993). This is the most complete science safety system available for teachers of science. The set encompasses K–12 and includes laws, codes, and standards; case studies; forms and checklists for safety assessments; and chemical management information.

David C. Kramer, *Animals in the Classroom* (Menlo Park, CA: Addison-Wesley, 1989). This book serves as a reminder of teacher responsibilities when animals are brought into the classroom. Whether it is an invertebrate or a vertebrate, this book tells how to care for those visitors. Resource books for children and adults are listed, as well as addresses for state wildlife agencies.

Lab Safety Supply Co., *Safety and Compliance Directory* (Janesville, WI, 1992). An excellent handbook for information from safety hot lines, government agencies, professional societies, and private agencies.

National Science Teachers Association, *Science Scope: A Journal for Middle/Junior High School Science Teachers—Safety Supplement* 13, no. 3 (November–December 1989). An excellent safety monograph addressing chemicals, overcrowding, living materials in the program, and more.

New York State, "Elementary Science Program Evaluation Test (ESPET)" (Albany: New York State Department of Education, 1989). This test, which appeared on PSInet (People Sharing Information Network) on October 16, 1989, assesses student mastery of science process skills.

D. B. Phillips, "Chemistry for the Elementary School," *Science and Children* (October 1981). Excellent overview of chemicals commonly used in elementary school science programs.

L. Phillips and J. Gerlovich, *50 Safe Physical Science Activities for Teachers* (Skokie, IL: Sargent Welch Scientific Co., 1988). This booklet contains eighty-five activities for students in grades 7 through 10. Topics addressed include chemistry and physics.

Shlomo Sharan, ed., *Cooperative Learning: Theory and Research* (New York: Praeger Publishers, 1990). Many essays and articles have been written on the theory behind cooperative learning and examples of its implementation. This book collects much of that work into one volume.

Victor M. Showalter, *Conditions for Good Science Teaching* (Washington, DC: National Science Teachers Association, 1984). This booklet provides information on classroom organization recommended by the National Science Teachers Association (NSTA). In addition to resources, current NSTA recommendations for science instruction and professional growth are itemized.

CHAPTER OUTLINE

7 What Are the Characteristics of Effective Science Materials and Programs?

Marjorie Becker had divided the science methods class into research teams. Their purpose was to pick a science topic and locate all the materials available on that topic in the lab, library, and college curriculum collection. The team members were to examine and compare the materials, classify them by intended purposes, and then use their findings to speculate about what makes an effective science lesson. They were told to be prepared to generalize beyond single lessons because the class would attempt to identify the characteristics of an effective science program. The groans that were prompted by the need to include text and nontext publications of the last thirty years subsided when Professor Becker demonstrated the speed and ease of *Science Helper*, the CD-ROM system containing hundreds of government-sponsored lessons from experimental science programs.

Professor Becker reconvened the class and asked the groups to report. She listed the features the students found most often among the materials: objectives, suggested teaching methods, materials needed, background information, illustrations, assessment devices, and ideas for extending the activities. Some older materials and many newer lessons contained references to themes, conceptual frameworks, skills to be developed, ideal group sizes, key vocabulary, lesson rationales, competencies, and subjects with which the lessons could be integrated. When she asked for the groups' ideas about effective programs, she received such replies as: "They emphasize subject matter most and produce higher test scores," "Effective programs are those that children like," and "You can tell the program is effective if more children take science in high school and if more want to enter scientific careers." These replies fell short of Dr. Becker's hopes, so she guided the class into a discussion of the assignment, pressed them to give specific examples of what they found, and repeated the assignment's central question: What makes an effective science program?

The students' thinking expanded a bit with the observation that some materials prepared in the past decade have features that resemble those of the experimental programs of the 1960s but that the newer science textbooks seem to contain several features not found in science textbooks of the earlier era. Still, Professor Becker sensed frustration. Her suspicion was confirmed when one brave soul, Donald, asked, "I don't understand why you had us look at out-of-date materials. Why did you have us do this assignment? Don't the developers and publishers agree on what's best, and shouldn't we always just try to use the most recent materials?" ◆

INTRODUCTION

We are likely to repeat mistakes of the past if we are ignorant of history. In fact, the National Science Education Standards' history of science content standard encourages a historical development perspective of science. Looking back, we see considerable similarity among the recommendations that arose from several science education reports during the mid-1940s, again during the late 1950s and early 1960s, and still again during the late 1980s and mid-1990s. Calls for more intellectual rigor, increased standards, elevated expectations, improved student discipline, increased classroom time on task, improved test scores, and enhanced teacher subject expertise often make up the substance of these reports, but different approaches were used in attempts to fulfill the recommendations. Indeed, devoting more time to intellectual subject matter in science is a common and worthwhile goal, but when it is the only expectation, it falls short of fulfilling the larger goal of more effective science programs. The key to effective science instruction is selecting and using hands-on activities effectively with the proper mix of science content and processes.

Calls or mandates for improved pupil achievement and recommendations for producing these improvements may be naively based on uninformed right-wrong perspectives resting on faulty assumptions about what should be taught and learned and about how youngsters learn and should be taught. But what role are you expected to play? You will be involved, at some point in your career, with science program development. More immediately, your concern is probably for selecting the best materials available to plan and teach effective lessons. Can you afford to ignore the lessons of the past? This chapter provides a foundation that can help define what is best and help you form a rationale for what you choose to do.

This chapter:

1. describes dominant beliefs about science education in the past,
2. describes several model elementary science programs that have been influential in shaping modern elementary science curricula and research on effective teaching practices,
3. reviews the effects these model programs had on children's science achievement, skills, and attitudes,
4. exposes false assumptions about learning and teaching science and reveals assumptions that shape new science curricula,
5. offers recommendations for an effective elementary science program.

DOMINANT BELIEFS IN SCIENCE EDUCATION

Quality and *excellence* are two widely held goals for education in general. The elementary science program must have high quality and demonstrate excellence in its curriculum and teaching. Critics and supporters agree on these goals, but they by no means agree on the direction the program ought to take, the science subject matter that is most worth knowing, or the conditions that best foster that knowing (Hurd, 1986). As an example, consider these conflicting beliefs about science education:

- Science is structured and consists of a body of well-known facts, concepts, principles, and theories that are useful to all and that should be learned by everyone.
- Science is a way of doing and constructing meaning from what is done.
- Science is important for its own sake; everyone needs to learn about science.
- Everyone is affected by science; therefore, everyone needs to learn science.
- To be most useful, science must be relevant; therefore it must be taught so that it can be understood and useful to those who learn it.

Which of these beliefs appear compatible to you, and which appear to conflict? Why is it that experts' beliefs openly conflict?

Let us take a brief look back in time to understand the importance of the issues surrounding these beliefs as well as how they affect the answer to the main question that guides this chapter: What are the characteristics of science materials and programs?

CHANGES OVER TIME: LEGACY OF THE PAST

Biology, Chemistry, Physics, and *Earth Science* are common school science curriculum labels. Even within general science and elementary science courses these labels persist as topics or units of study. They arose from their parent scientific research disciplines, which were popular during the 1800s. However, since about 1900 these disciplines of study have not accurately represented the

Past programs prepared children to become scientists.

important areas of science. Thousands of diverse scientific journals now report experimental findings from a countless number of new fields of science and technology. Distinctions among the different fields of science are now made more by the type of problem being researched than by the discipline being served. Today there is simply too much—too many facts of science to be learned in a school science program. The amount of scientific information continues to double about every five years. So what should be taught? At times this question has been answered with an issues-and-problems approach.

A specific problem in science education has always been to resolve the issue of how the schools could best prepare "citizens to live in a culture most often described in terms of achievements in science and technology" (Hurd, 1986, p. 355). In the 1930s and 1940s, elementary schools tried to resolve this issue by teaching in a "prescribed authoritative manner almost exclusively through single-author textbooks" (Sabar, 1979, pp. 257–269). Basically, science was a reading program that covered a large body of information and used the subtle but powerful force of conformity and consensus to control the direction of American society and to aid citizens as they tried to adjust to society's new directions. The important facts, concepts, and theories of science that were taught were based on the consensus of specialists. Specialists told previous generations of teachers what was important to know and teach.

Teacher emphasis on pupil conformity and learning science by reading is still highly visible today. Another emphasis from the past that is still widely supported is the cry to get back to basics, with emphasis on reading, writing, and arithmetic. This chant began after World War II for the same reasons that it can be heard today: the perceived overall low quality of high school graduates as shown by their falling achievement scores and poor job skills and the need for citizens to keep pace with scientific and technological breakthroughs of other advanced countries (Sabar, 1979, p. 258). Ironically, this last need makes the study of science a basic need for all, a basic literacy subject in the school curriculum, as described in Chapter 4.

MAJOR ELEMENTARY SCIENCE PROGRAM MODELS: LOOKING BACK FOR THE SOURCE OF WISDOM

Efforts began earlier, but it was the launching of the Soviet satellite *Sputnik* in 1957 that caused the most serious attempts at science curriculum reform. During the twenty-five years after *Sputnik,* $2 billion was spent to support mathematics and science education in elementary and secondary schools. The main goal then, as many believe it should be now, was to prepare future scientists and engineers, mostly out of a concern for national defense. As important as this goal is, we now know that defense issues rise and fall in urgency and that "this is a goal that is appropriate for only 3 percent of high school graduates, and a goal where we have traditionally spent 95 percent of our time, efforts, resources and attention" (Yager, 1984, p. 196).

The Alphabet Soup

The decade after *Sputnik* is known for its alphabet soup elementary science programs (see Table 7.1). Three programs developed during that decade are worth mentioning now because of their goals, their effects on children's learning, and the eventually improved quality of modern textbooks and other curriculum materials. Several of the assumptions the programs were based on have been supported over time by a growing body of research, while other assumptions have fallen from favor. The programs we refer to here are known as SAPA, SCIS, and ESS.

Science—A Process Approach (SAPA), Science Curriculum Improvement Study (SCIS), and the Elementary Science Study (ESS) were regarded as innovative programs in their day. Designed and field-tested during the 1960s and then revised during the 1970s, these experimental programs had several features in common:

- They were developed by teams of scientists, psychologists, educators, and professional curriculum specialists rather than written by single authors or single expert specialists.

TABLE 7.1   Examples of Alphabet Soup Elementary Science Programs

SAPA (Science—A Process Approach), American Association for the Advancement of Science Commission on Science Education, 1963

COPES (Conceptually Oriented Program in Elementary Science), 1967

ESSP (Elementary School Science Project), University of California, Berkeley, 1962

E-SSP (Elementary-School Science Project), University of Illinois, 1963

ESSP (Elementary School Science Project), Utah State University, 1964

ESS (Elementary Science Study), 1964

IDP (Inquiry Development Program), 1962

MinneMAST (Minnesota Mathematics and Science Teaching Project), 1966

SSCP (School Science Curriculum Project), 1964

SCIS (Science Curriculum Improvement Study), 1961

SQAIESS (Study of a Quantitative Approach in Elementary School Science), 1964

USMES (Unified Sciences and Mathematics for Elementary Schools), 1973

WIMSA (The Webster Institute for Mathematics, Science and the Arts), 1965

Source: Information excerpted from Paul DeHart Hurd (ed.), *New Directions in Elementary Science Teaching* (Belmont, CA: Wadsworth Publishing 1968). Note that dates given are approximate beginning dates for each program.

- Federal funds were widely available for development, research, field testing, dissemination, and teacher inservice training.
- Each project was developed from particular assumptions about learning drawn from prominent theories and used to form a specific framework for each project. Behavioral and cognitive-development psychology had major influences.
- Each project was developed from what were assumed to be the ways children learned best. Specific teaching approaches were emphasized and were used to help children learn the ways and knowledge of science and to develop the attitudes of scientists.
- Active pupil learning was assumed to be very important. Each project provided hands-on learning experiences for all children because it was assumed that manipulatives help children learn best.
- The projects did not provide a standard textbook for each child. In fact, a workbook for recording observations was as close as some children came to anything that resembled a textbook.
- There was no attempt to teach all that should be known about science. Specific science processes or content areas were selected for each project, thus narrowing the field of topics to a specialized few.
- Attention was given to the basic ideas of science, the concepts and theories, with the intention of increasing the number of citizens who would seek careers in science and engineering.

- The programs were conveniently packaged. Equipment was included with curriculum materials. This made the programs easier to use and reduced teacher preparation time by eliminating the need to gather diverse equipment.
- Mathematical skills were emphasized. The programs were more quantitative than qualitative. Emphasis was placed on student observation, careful measurement, and the use of appropriate calculations to form ideas or reach conclusions.
- Science was taught as a subject by itself and was not associated with social studies, health, or reading. At times, science was treated as a pure subject that was believed to have inherent value for all children.
- The teacher's role changed. Teachers used such less direct methods of teaching as inquiry and functioned as questioners and guides for students. They avoided lecturing or more didactic forms of direct instruction. The teacher was *not* to be an expert who spoke what children should memorize.

SAPA, SCIS, and ESS are landmark elementary science programs, still available today. As shown in Figure 7.1, they differ essentially on two factors: the amount of structure or flexibility each contains in its design for classroom use and the emphasis each gives to science content, attitudes, or thinking processes. Let us explore each program briefly to understand better the legacy that has brought positive influences to the options available in elementary science education today.

Science—A Process Approach (SAPA)

SAPA's Prime Assumptions.

Children need to learn how to *do* science, and this means acquiring the skills essential to learning and understanding science information. These knowledge-

FIGURE 7.1 Structure and Emphasis Comparisons of Landmark Elementary Science Programs

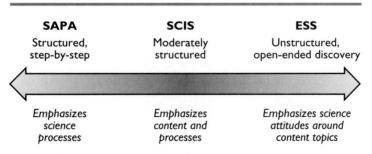

SAPA	SCIS	ESS
Structured, step-by-step	Moderately structured	Unstructured, open-ended discovery

| *Emphasizes science processes* | *Emphasizes content and processes* | *Emphasizes science attitudes around content topics* |

Note: Each program is available from Delta Education, P.O. Box 3000, Nashua, NH 03061-3000. Phone: 1-800-442-5444.

Effective programs promote scientific inquiry.

acquiring skills are called cognitive [thinking] skills or process skills and are similar to the procedures used by scientists to acquire new knowledge. Process skills may be compared to the program [of] a computer. Computers are incapable of handling information without a program to provide directions; the human mind does not cope effectively with incoming information in the absence of learning strategies (a program). (Hurd, 1968, pp. 11–12)

The American Association for the Advancement of Science's Commission on Science Education assumed that a sequential program was necessary for developing a child's intellect. In 1963, a team of scientists, psychologists, elementary teachers, and curriculum specialists developed plans and materials for trial versions of what became Science—A Process Approach. The program is based on two assumptions: first, that prepared materials must consider the intellectual development of the child, and second, that a total program must use a sequential approach for the long-range development of the child's intellectual skills. The first assumption worked well. Materials that were developed on the child's ability level were appropriate. Incremental advances in the complexity of the materials seemed to help children develop intellectually. However, the long-term sequential approach proved too rigid to use without difficulty in schools where children attend school irregularly or transfer in mid-year.

Description of SAPA.   SAPA is the most structured of the three programs we explore here. Its structure arises from behavioral psychology. The underlying psychological assumptions were that any skill can be broken down into smaller steps and that children need to learn lower-level skills before they can learn more advanced skills. Predictably, the original version of SAPA developed into a set of skills to be mastered through a complex, highly structured hierarchy (see Figure 7.2) and step-by-step teaching.

Skill development takes precedence over science subject matter in SAPA. Even after revision and the development of SAPA II, the content of science is important only as it serves as a vehicle for developing thinking processes. The complex task of inquiry, therefore, is broken into a series of smaller, easier-to-acquire skills. All skill development is expected to arise from a child's direct experiences performing prescribed learning tasks, usually with concrete manipulable objects. Hands-on learning involves children in doing science the way many scientists say they do it themselves—carefully planned step-by-step procedures.

SAPA science process skills are divided into two types: *basic* and *integrated* skills. In the primary grades (K–3) children develop these basic process skills: observing, using space/time relationships, classifying, using numbers, measuring, communicating, predicting, and inferring. In the intermediate grades (4–6) children use the basic process skills as a foundation for developing more complex skills: controlling variables, interpreting data, formulating hypotheses, defining operationally, and experimenting.

The knowledge explosion in the sciences helps SAPA justify its approach; it is a unique program that emphasizes science skills over content. Creators of SAPA believe that it is impossible for individuals, including scientists, to keep up to date in all the sciences and that it is also unrealistic to expect children to learn everything about science. SAPA's intention is to equip each child with the thinking skills that can be used to solve problems they find in the future.

SAPA is a complete K–6 program. The learning activities in the revised SAPA II are packaged in a series of 105 ungraded learning modules, with approximately 15 modules per traditional grade level. Each module is devoted to a specific skill. SAPA II arose in 1975 from extensive field testing, program evaluation, and materials revisions, and it is an improvement over the original design. Clusters of modules help teachers overcome the rigid sequence of skills used in the original flowchart approach (Figure 7.2). SAPA II strives to reflect important changes in science education, is more flexible than the original design, reflects a greater emphasis on environmental topics, and attempts more pupil individualization. Students have no books, yet copy masters are available; modular teacher guides are used in place of a teacher's textbook guide.

Each learning module has the same features and structure (Figure 7.3). The cover of each module presents the specific process skill that is emphasized within. The module title identifies the science content selected, and behavioral objectives specify what each child should be able to do at the end of the module. The sequence chart inside the cover shows the relationship and fit of the module's objectives with those of related modules (refer to Figure 7.2). A

FIGURE 7.2   SAPA Then and Now

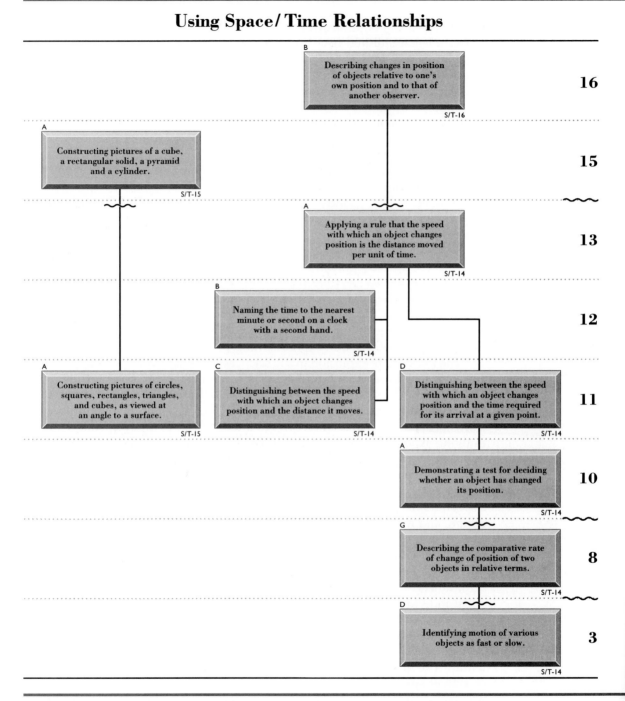

Using Space/Time Relationships

Describing changes in position of objects relative to one's own position and to that of another observer.   S/T-16   **16**

Constructing pictures of a cube, a rectangular solid, a pyramid and a cylinder.   S/T-15   **15**

Applying a rule that the speed with which an object changes position is the distance moved per unit of time.   S/T-14   **13**

Naming the time to the nearest minute or second on a clock with a second hand.   S/T-14   **12**

Constructing pictures of circles, squares, rectangles, triangles, and cubes, as viewed at an angle to a surface.   S/T-15   **11**

Distinguishing between the speed with which an object changes position and the distance it moves.   S/T-14

Distinguishing between the speed with which an object changes position and the time required for its arrival at a given point.   S/T-14

Demonstrating a test for deciding whether an object has changed its position.   S/T-14   **10**

Describing the comparative rate of change of position of two objects in relative terms.   S/T-14   **8**

Identifying motion of various objects as fast or slow.   S/T-14   **3**

Source: Delta Education, Inc., Nashua, NH 03061-3000. Reprinted by permission of copyright holder.

Science... A Process Approach
Planning Chart

IX	X	XI	XII

Module 32
Classifying/d
Terrarium

Separating living organisms into categories. Constructing a simple classification system and demonstrating its use. Placing new organisms in the appropriate categories of an established classification system.

PREMOD: 16

Module 39
Measuring/g
Solids, Liquids, and Gases

Measuring the volume of liquids using metric units. Naming a substance as being a solid, a liquid, or a gas. Describing a substance as a solid, a liquid, or a gas by using various physical characteristics, such as shape and appearance.

PREMODS: 17, 23, 32

Module 42
Classifying/e
Sorting Mixtures

Demonstrating a specified method for classifying the components of a mixture by size. Ordering the components of a mixture by size. Ordering the components of a mixture by volume or weight.

PREMODS: 26, 39

Module 41
Measuring/h
Temperature and Thermometers

Demonstrating how to use a thermometer to measure the temperature of a gas or liquid, and naming temperature in degrees Celsius. Using a thermometer to measure temperature change, and naming initial and final temperatures in degrees Celsius.

PREMODS: 21, 27, 30

Module 31
Communicating/d
Life Cycles

Describing an animal according to several of its characteristics. Describing the changing characteristics of a young animal as it grows from one stage to another.

PREMOD: 16, 28

Module 36
Observing/l
Animal Responses

Describing the kinds of locomotion characteristic of animals having various shapes and appendages. Identifying an animal's response to an identified stimulus.

PREMOD: 31

Module 43
Communicating/e
A Plant Part That Grows

Distinguishing between a developing new plant and the original plant it is growing from. Describing vegetative growth qualitatively. Describing the techniques used to produce growth from plant parts other than seeds.

PREMOD: 36

Module 33
Inferring/a
What's inside?

Distinguishing between statements that are observations and those that are explanations of observations, and identifying the explanations as inferences. Constructing inferences in terms of likelihood rather than certainty.

PREMOD: 18

Module 40
Inferring/b
How certain can you be?
Shake and Peek

Describing new observations that are needed to test an inference. Identifying observations that support an inference. Distinguishing between an inference that accounts for all of the observations and one that does not.

PREMODS: 29, 33

Module 35
Using Space/Time/f
Symmetry

Identifying objects that have line or plane symmetry. Demonstrating that some objects can be folded or cut in one or more ways to produce matching halves. Identifying and describing bilateral symmetry.

PREMOD: 12

Module 45
Using Space/Time/g
Lines, Curves, and Surfaces

Identifying, naming, and constructing straight and curved paths on plane and curved surfaces. Determining whether a surface is a plane surface. Identifying linear and circular motion.

PREMODS: 27, 35

Determining Sequences Within the Program

One convenient order for using the modules is the *numerical sequence* with which they are coded. If that order is followed, children will have the opportunity to develop skills in a sequence in which success is highly probable. Frequently it is necessary or desirable to alter the sequence when several teachers share materials, weather conditions interfere, or other scheduling problems arise. It is not necessary to use the modules in numerical sequence so long as the children have mastered the prerequisites before a module is begun.

◆ **FIGURE 7.3   Excerpts from a SAPA II Module**

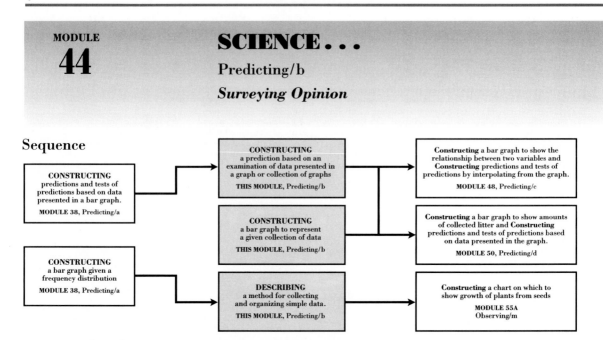

MODULE

44

SCIENCE...

Predicting/b

Surveying Opinion

Sequence

CONSTRUCTING
predictions and tests of
predictions based on data
presented in a bar graph.
MODULE 38, Predicting/a

CONSTRUCTING
a bar graph given a
frequency distribution
MODULE 38, Predicting/a

CONSTRUCTING
a prediction based on an
examination of data presented in
a graph or collection of graphs
THIS MODULE, Predicting/b

CONSTRUCTING
a bar graph to represent
a given collection of data
THIS MODULE, Predicting/b

DESCRIBING
a method for collecting
and organizing simple data.
THIS MODULE, Predicting/b

Constructing a bar graph to show the
relationship between two variables and
Constructing predictions and tests of
predictions by interpolating from the graph.
MODULE 48, Predicting/c

Constructing a bar graph to show amounts
of collected litter and Constructing
predictions and tests of predictions based
on data presented in the graph.
MODULE 50, Predicting/d

Constructing a chart on which to
show growth of plants from seeds
MODULE 55A
Observing/m

Rationale

It is essential that contributing evidence upon which a prediction is based be collected, organized, and recorded in a clear and usable way. The activities in this module provide children with experience in making predictions based on data recorded in a survey of children in the school, thus using the children's natural interest in collecting, interviewing, and surveying.

You must be sure to point out carefully the limitations on the dependability of predictions based on an opinion survey. Emphasize that accurate predictions are difficult in the early phases of the survey, and are impossible if they are based on only small bits of information. As more data are added, trends or patterns are often noticeable. These trends can be used to make more reliable predictions...

Because favorite kinds of snacks are the subject matter of this module, the results of the surveys are unpredictable and may vary considerably with locale, time of year, the children's previous experience, and other factors. Remember that although the children will be very much interested in the results of the survey, these results are merely a means to an end. The objective is to provide experience in making predictions based on available evidence...

In *Activity 3*, the children survey other groups in the school. Take advantage of the excitement that such surveys create and the opportunity they provide for improvement of communication skills, but be sure to plan the surveying procedures carefully with the other teachers involved...

Vocabulary: predict, prediction, survey, opinion, tally, poll, polling

Instructional Procedure

Ask the children what the word *predict* means to them. They may have several suggestions. For example, they may recall that when they studied *Shadows, Using Space/Time Relationships e, Module 29*, they were asked to predict the two-dimensional shapes of the shadows of a three-dimensional object...

The children should also recall the predictions they made from the bar graphs they constructed in *Using Graphs, Predicting a, Module 38*.

Perhaps some child will mention that the weather man predicts the weather. Another may recall a time of national elections when there were predictions about which candidate would win. Remind them that predicting is telling what you think is going to happen based on experience.

If possible, bring periodical or newspaper examples of polls that have been taken. A copy of a survey made within the school would be useful too. Discuss the value of surveys. Use questions as these: What is an opinion? What is a survey? How is the information obtained when we survey opinion? Suggest that the class make its own survey...

Materials: Surveys, several examples from periodicals or newspapers.

Activity 1

Give each child a piece of paper and a pencil. With no preliminary discussion ask the children to write down the names of three of their favorite kinds of snacks. Be sure that they do this independently. Then collect their papers.

Tell the children that you have just taken a *poll* of their favorite snacks. Ask which snack the children think was named the most times. After several children have expressed their ideas, ask why they think a particular snack was the most popular. Suggest that their ideas are largely guesses because, at this point, they have little or no evidence to use as a basis for making predictions...

Materials: Writing paper, 1 sheet for each child, Pencils, 1 for each child

Source: Delta Education, Inc., Nashua, NH 03061-3000. Reprinted by permission of copyright holder.

A Process Approach II

Objectives   At the end of this module the child should be able to:

1. **Describe** a method for collecting and organizing simple data.
2. **Construct** a bar graph to represent a given collection of data.
3. **Construct** a prediction based on an examination for the data presented in a graph or collection of graphs.

Activity 2

Ask the children for their ideas about organizing the data so that each child can have a copy of the results. There should be a number of suggestions. Try to accept one of them.

If the children do not suggest a feasible plan, use the following procedure. Give each child one paper marked during the previous activity, a clean sheet of paper, and a pencil. Call on the children to read from their marked papers. When a snack is first mentioned, tell everyone to write it down and put a tally mark next to it; each time it is mentioned again, have everyone put another mark next to the snack. Several children will probably have listed specific candy bars, flavors of ice cream, and so forth. Have the children tally all such listings under general headings, such as "candy" and "ice cream." Some children may list two items such as "cookies and milk." In this case put one tally next to "cookies" and another next to "milk…"

For the purpose of discussion, ask the children to imagine that milk was named more often than any other kind of snack, and that it was listed 20 times. Also ask them to imagine that candy was named 6 times and ice cream was mentioned 4 times. Figure 1 shows how these data may be graphed…

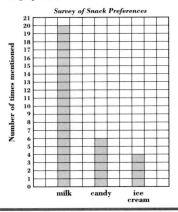

Survey of Snack Preferences

Generalizing Experience

Some children may be much more interested in this series of activities than are others. You should provide opportunities for the most interested children to continue with the surveys and to report the tallies to the others in the room…

Ask the children to make additional surveys about snack preferences. For example, have them ask a teenager, their mother or father, or some other friend to list three favorite kinds of snacks. You will get greater cooperation from the parents if you send a note with the child describing the project and the importance of the information. The children should get data from the same number of adults as there are members in their room. Tell the children that they should make their predictions beforehand and discuss the reasons for them. Then have them make the tabulation and discuss the results. If you find that more practice in graphing is desirable, you could have the children graph these data before they discuss the results…

Appraisal

Divide the children into two groups, each containing about the same number of boys and girls. Ask everyone to write on a piece of paper the names of their three favorite flavors of ice cream. Have the children in one group tabulate their own data, and ask the other group to do the same. Be sure the groups do not overhear each other's results…

Competency Measure

Task 1 (Objective 1): Say to the child, *In planning for the school picnic, the P.T.A. members want to get an idea of how many hamburgers, hot dogs, and cold-meat sandwiches to make. Tell me how they could get the information they need.* The child should describe a method of surveying some of the children in the school.

Task 2 (Objective 2): Say, *A poll in Miss Brown's room of 30 children gave the following data abut preferences: hamburgers, 15 children; hot dogs, 10 children; cold-meat sandwiches, 5 children.* Give the child the data on a piece of paper or write the information on the chalkboard. Then give him a piece of graph paper and say, *Make a graph showing the number of times each kind of food was chosen.* The child should include the following entries on the graph: a proper title that identifies the subject of the graph, a scale of numerals on the vertical number line, the name of the teacher whose children were surveyed—perhaps included in the title, the proper labeling of the horizontal base line and vertical number line, bars drawn to the correct height to show the number of choices. If the child makes any errors in constructing the graph, correct them before continuing.

Task 3 (Objective 3): Ask the child, *Could you use your graph to predict exactly how many times hamburgers would be chosen by the children in another room?* The child should indicate that an exact prediction probably cannot be made.

Task 4 (Objective 3): Show the child the two picture cards of graphs—one showing a graph that represents the choices made by the children in Mr. Smith's room, the other showing a graph that represents the choices made by the children in Miss Jones' room. Read the labels below the horizontal base line of each graph. Say, *Look at the three graphs—the one you made and the two I have just given you. Make a prediction about which kind of food the children in Mrs. White's class will select most often.* The child should say, "Hamburgers."

Task 5 (Objective 3): Ask, *Why did you make that selection?* The child should identify a pattern that supports his or her answer.

complete rationale justifies the purpose and describes the benefits of the module's activities for children and their intellectual development. The instructional procedure gives an overall introduction and describes each specific learning activity. Materials needed are listed with each activity, and modules contain about three to six activities. Each module contains a section, generalizing the experience, for extension of the learning activities. Evaluation is emphasized strongly in SAPA. An appraisal section describes class performance options for evaluation, and the competency measure section fully describes evaluation tasks that can be used with individual children. Specific questions and suggested answers are given. Competency measure tasks are keyed to the specific module objectives.

SAPA Program Effects.   Did SAPA make a difference? James Shymansky et al. (1982) and Ted Bredderman (1982) say "yes." Shymansky et al. specifically report that students learning science in the SAPA program outperformed children who learned from traditional science programs by seven statistically significant percentile points on measures of achievement. (Traditional programs were defined as those whose development followed pre-1955 models, emphasized the information of science, and used laboratory activities to verify or to supplement lessons.) This difference may not seem great, but take a closer look. Let us suppose that two classes of elementary students take the same standardized achievement test in science and all differences are controlled except the program that they learn science from. One class learns from the traditional textbook approach that is designed to teach science facts through reading and memorization; the other class learns from a program—SAPA—that does not stress facts or science information but instead focuses on doing science and developing thinking skills. The result? Let us say that the average student score from the traditional science program class is at the fiftieth percentile on a test designed to measure knowledge of science facts. Then by comparison, the average student in the SAPA class achieves at the fifty-seventh percentile on the same test—a distinct and significant achievement gain. The SAPA students knew more facts.

SAPA has several other factors going for it even more important than the performance of the average children from our example. In each case, these findings arose from research and careful study the findings are real, not imagined. SAPA students scored fifteen percentile points higher than non-SAPA students on measures of attitude toward science. On tests of process skills, SAPA students scored thirty-six percentile points higher than children from traditional programs. In such other areas as related study skills (reading and mathematics), creativity, and Piagetian tasks, SAPA children scored higher by 4, 7, and 12 percentile points, respectively. Many of the assumptions that undergird SAPA appear to produce differences, just as its developers envisioned.

Science Curriculum Improvement Study (SCIS)
SCIS's Prime Assumptions.

> In a world where there is so much to learn and know, concepts provide an intellectual economy in helping to organize large amounts of information. [T]his is the way concepts serve scientists and it is also the way concepts can improve children's learning. There is too much to be known, even by children, to expect it can be learned by rote and as isolated facts. But a large amount of information can be organized into a few concepts. Systems of related concepts can then be built to form principles or rules whereby children are able to interpret and explain new observations and experiences. . . . One advantage of having children form concepts is that new information can be more easily related to that already known. The result is the likelihood that both the new information and related concept will have greater meaning, and understanding will be increased. If on the other hand, new information cannot be brought into an organized form, there is a likelihood that the new information will confuse rather than aid understanding. . . . [E]ach new relevant observation acquires meaning because it becomes associated with many previous experiences. (Hurd, 1968, pp. 9–10)

The Science Curriculum Improvement Study (SCIS) was developed to help elementary school children form a broad conceptual framework for understanding science. Teams of scientists, educators, and psychologists began work in 1961 to produce the first of what eventually became three SCIS versions: SCIS and SCIIS were developed by the same team and SCIS II by another. The most recent version is called SCIS III. The related versions are described here and are generically called SCIS.

The conceptual curriculum is organized around the structure of science as scientists see it. Specific concepts are chosen for their wide application and potential usefulness in each child's future. The unique challenge of SCIS is to provide a program that will help children explore science, guide children's thinking, and help children to form concepts and link them together within SCIS's conceptual structure.

Description of SCIS.
SCIS is a sequential program that emphasizes both process and content, making SCIS rather middle of the road according to Figure 7.1. The instruction is less structured than in SAPA. Specific teaching approaches complement the program's intention: to reach pupils at their current level of development as they form the intended science concepts.

The original version of SCIS introduced concepts that were new to elementary science. These concepts were linked together to form such units of study as properties, relativity, systems, interactions, variation and measurement, and ecosystems. Understanding these concepts yielded the primary goal of SCIS: scientific literacy. The program is divided into two parts: a physical/earth science sequence and a life/earth science sequence. Each grade level's program contains concepts and essential processes prerequisite for study at the next grade level (see Figure 7.4).

The SCIS concepts represent different levels of abstraction. For example, the first level pertains to matter, living things, variation, and conservation of matter. The second level includes concepts of interaction, causal relations, relativity, and geometric relations. The third level concepts pertain to energy, equilibrium, steady state, and the behavior, reproduction, and speciation of living things. These concepts are somewhat complex when compared to simpler collections of facts; therefore, in SCIS instruction receives special attention.

SCIS gives children direct, concrete experiences. The teacher's role is to help children acquire and use their observations to form the broad conceptual ideas of science—to guide, not to tell. The instructional method has three distinct phases and is known as the *learning cycle* (Karplus, 1964):

- Phase 1, *exploration* in an activity-oriented setting, permits the children to explore the learning materials or phenomena.
- Phase 2, *invention,* does not leave children to their own devices but guides them toward the concepts by gathering their observations and using them to invent ideas that help the children organize and understand their experiences.
- Phase 3, *application,* helps the children discover relationships and broaden their experiences by giving them opportunities to use the newly formed concepts in new contexts.

FIGURE 7.4   SCIS Structure and Sequence of Units

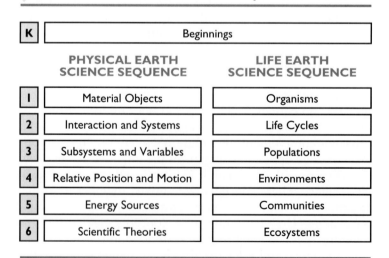

K	Beginnings	
	PHYSICAL EARTH SCIENCE SEQUENCE	**LIFE EARTH SCIENCE SEQUENCE**
1	Material Objects	Organisms
2	Interaction and Systems	Life Cycles
3	Subsystems and Variables	Populations
4	Relative Position and Motion	Environments
5	Energy Sources	Communities
6	Scientific Theories	Ecosystems

Source: Delta Education, Inc., Nashua, NH 03061-3000. Reprinted by permission of copyright holder.

How Can You Create an Effective Science Program?

by Earnestine Blakely
Grade 3 Teacher, Bessie Ellison Elementary School, St. Joseph, MO

My science classes are all about hands-on, minds-on, and problem-solving experiences. In all situations I challenge my students to think and to interact with the physical world around them. They realize that science is discovery; it's excitement, it's magic, and it's fun!

An effective science program should offer youngsters the opportunity to experiment with the natural world around them. Students should be permitted to discover facts rather than having mounds of isolated data thrust upon them. Science teaching and learning should be a time of movement and interaction.

Science in my classroom is a high-energy period of thinking, manipulating, and problem solving. When I was teaching a unit on gas, the students created carbon dioxide by mixing baking soda and vinegar. The trapped gas they created was used to blow up a balloon. First I gave the students a 1-liter plastic beverage bottle (remember to use safety goggles in case the bottle breaks). They placed 4 tablespoons of vinegar inside the bottle. Next, they funneled 2 tablespoons of baking soda into a balloon. Then they carefully placed the mouth of the balloon over the opening of the bottle so that the baking soda would not escape.

Finally, they raised the balloon to an upright position so that the baking soda could flow into the vinegar in the bottle. Their eyes widened with amazement as they watched the balloon expand. I then began to ask cause-and-effect questions: What happened and why?

After the discussion and questions, I posed another problem: What would happen if we used a 2-liter bottle and added the same amount of vinegar? We would use the same amount of baking soda and the same size balloon. The only change would be the size of the bottle. The students made their predictions, and I recorded their responses on the chalk board. We then proceeded with the experiment. Afterward, we used a tape measure to measure the size of each balloon. From the comparison, we concluded that the balloon attached to the 2-liter bottle was somewhat smaller. We discussed possible reasons for the difference in size.

Learning science will never be dull as long as youngsters can predict, observe, measure, compare, manipulate, and interact with the world around them. With such experiences, the students will treasure fond memories of science throughout their lives.

Although most of the attention is given to academic skills through concept formation, SCIS also gives attention to student attitudes and thinking skills. The skills developed in the program are similar to those developed in SAPA: Students carefully observe, record their observations, make comparisons, recognize similarities, use measurements, and develop vocabulary as they discuss their experiences and form meaningful concepts.

Each grade level of SCIS is packaged conveniently, and most grades have two modular kits: one for physical science and one for life science. Each kit contains all the equipment and materials needed for teaching the specific unit and accommodates classes of up to thirty-two children. Materials are carefully selected to provide the specific experiences each child needs to form the selected concepts; some materials are consumable and need regular replacement. Print materials include wall charts, game boards, card decks, and visual transparencies. Student manuals (record books) are provided for each grade level except kindergarten. Children use the manuals to record their observations and complete investigations that help to evaluate their progress. An evaluation packet provided for each unit helps the teacher determine each child's concept formation, skill, and attitude development. Living materials are needed for approximately half of the school year; these materials are provided for a fee at the time specified by the teacher. Extending Your Experiences (EYE) cards for concept expansion, review, remediation, and special projects can be used with individual children, small groups, or an entire class.

The teacher's guide is exceptionally well organized. Guides contain a concise lesson plan, the synopsis, lists of materials, background information, tips for advance preparation, specific teaching suggestions, helpful illustrations, descriptions of optional activities, and descriptions of ways to do concept and process evaluation. All of these materials are packaged with a complete kit for every unit (see Figure 7.5).

SCIS Program Effects. What kinds of effects did SCIS have on children? Again, we can look to James Shymansky and his fellow researchers (1982) for some answers. In achievement tests, students in SCIS programs scored 34 percentile points above children from traditional science programs. Of the three programs we describe in this chapter, SCIS had the greatest effect on pupil achievement, outdistancing SAPA and ESS by 30 and 27 percentile points, respectively.

Concurrently, SCIS produced gains of 21 percentile points in science process skills and 34 percentile points in children's creativity when compared to traditional programs. Smaller improvements were measured in pupil attitudes, related study skills such as reading and mathematics, and Piagetian tasks. An unexpected benefit of SCIS is reported by Renner and Marek (1988). The first-grade unit, material objects, was compared to a commercial first-grade reading readiness program. Children in the experimental group studied material objects without reading readiness, and children in the control group studied traditional reading readiness materials without material objects. Both groups were equivalent and were pretested with the Metropolitan Reading Readiness Test and then posttested six weeks later. The SCIS experimental group outscored the control group in all areas—word meaning, listening, matching, alphabet, numbers, and total score—except copying (Renner & Marek 1988, pp. 193–196). Apparently the thinking skill development in the SCIS program was much more potent than direct reading readiness instruction. The assumptions that SCIS developers made about children's learning appear to be valid, given the extent of gains in achievement, process skills, and other important aspects of learning.

FIGURE 7.5 SCIS Teacher's Guide Kit

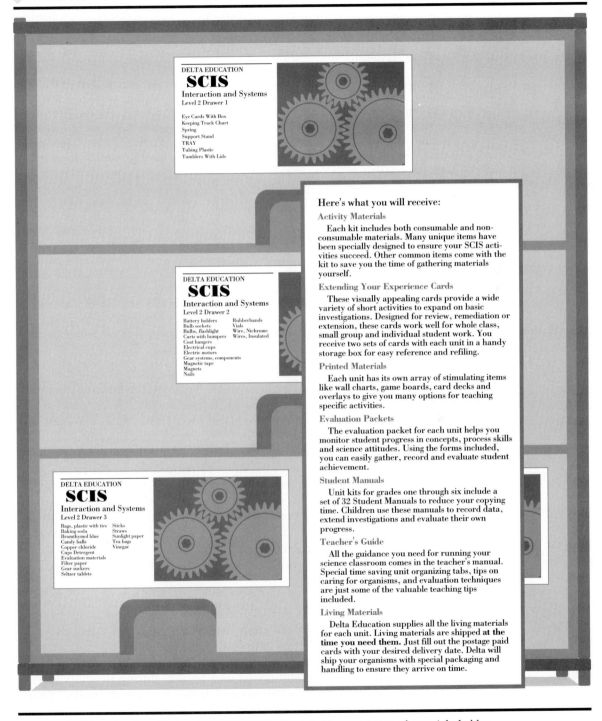

DELTA EDUCATION
SCIS
Interaction and Systems
Level 2 Drawer 1

Eye Cards With Box
Keeping Track Chart
Spring
Support Stand
TRAY
Tubing Plastic
Tumblers With Lids

DELTA EDUCATION
SCIS
Interaction and Systems
Level 2 Drawer 2

Battery holders	Rubberbands
Bulb sockets	Vials
Bulbs, flashlight	Wire, Nichrome
Carts with bumpers	Wires, Insulated
Coat hangers	
Electrical cups	
Electric motors	
Gear systems, components	
Magnetic tape	
Magnets	
Nails	

DELTA EDUCATION
SCIS
Interaction and Systems
Level 2 Drawer 3

Bags, plastic with ties	Sticks
Baking soda	Straws
Bromthymol blue	Sunlight paper
Candy balls	Tea bags
Copper chloride	Vinegar
Cups Detergent	
Evaluation materials	
Filter paper	
Gear suckers	
Seltzer tablets	

Here's what you will receive:

Activity Materials
Each kit includes both consumable and non-consumable materials. Many unique items have been specially designed to ensure your SCIS activities succeed. Other common items come with the kit to save you the time of gathering materials yourself.

Extending Your Experience Cards
These visually appealing cards provide a wide variety of short activities to expand on basic investigations. Designed for review, remediation or extension, these cards work well for whole class, small group and individual student work. You receive two sets of cards with each unit in a handy storage box for easy reference and refiling.

Printed Materials
Each unit has its own array of stimulating items like wall charts, game boards, card decks and overlays to give you many options for teaching specific activities.

Evaluation Packets
The evaluation packet for each unit helps you monitor student progress in concepts, process skills and science attitudes. Using the forms included, you can easily gather, record and evaluate student achievement.

Student Manuals
Unit kits for grades one through six include a set of 32 Student Manuals to reduce your copying time. Children use these manuals to record data, extend investigations and evaluate their own progress.

Teacher's Guide
All the guidance you need for running your science classroom comes in the teacher's manual. Special time saving unit organizing tabs, tips on caring for organisms, and evaluation techniques are just some of the valuable teaching tips included.

Living Materials
Delta Education supplies all the living materials for each unit. Living materials are shipped **at the time you need them.** Just fill out the postage paid cards with your desired delivery date. Delta will ship your organisms with special packaging and handling to ensure they arrive on time.

Source: Delta Education, Inc., Nashua, NH 03061-3000. Reprinted by permission of copyright holder.

The Elementary Science Study (ESS)

ESS's Prime Assumptions.

> The central question is whether whatever a child learns is more meaningful and is retained longer if he works his own way through a topic [discovery] or if it is taught him by assertion. Proponents of the discovery approach cite the following values in its favor: (1) Children are motivated by the satisfaction they receive from finding out things for themselves, and satisfaction is recognized as an important attitude in stimulating learning; (2) since children are more personally involved with information and ideas in a discovery approach, deeper understanding of subject matter results and forgetting is reduced; (3) discovery procedures help children develop strategies of inquiry, or process skills . . .; and (4) transfer of learning is improved.
>
> [Discovery in ESS means that] children explore freely with the materials of a topic until they begin to ask questions of their own. These questions form the basis for further investigation. Teacher direction is at a minimum and the pupils are permitted to pursue their own lines of inquiry in a capitalization on the natural curiosity and ability of children to profit from self-directed experiences. Given this freedom, each child can delve into features of a problem that are interesting and important to him. Discovery learning in this approach is seen as increasing motivation and improving the intuitive meaning of observations. (Hurd, 1968, pp. 18–19)

The developers of ESS believed that the elementary school should provide children with abundant time to explore and to examine relationships between humans and the physical and living world. Terms like *free discovery* and *guided discovery* arose from the teaching methods used with ESS. David Hawkins, developer of ESS, used the term *messing about* to describe the class time students should spend in unguided exploration activities—the initial learning phase of ESS. Developers believed that learning must provide children with interesting and enriching experiences and that abundant, varied activities must be available. A number of psychologists supported the ESS goals by stressing the importance of free, unstructured periods of exploration during the initial phases of learning. Also, psychologists affirmed that children learn at different rates, have different interests, and learn different things from the same learning activity. These views support the notion that learning must be individualized—a feature of ESS.

Description of ESS.   The main goal of ESS for teachers is to provide students with a wide variety of learning materials, which are packaged into unit booklets. Some topics stress experiences with skills fundamental to learning, such as weighing, graphing, and using instruments, while other topics emphasize science concepts. All have been field-tested and revised during development so that they continue to motivate children and foster positive attitudes toward science.

ESS originally contained fifty-six different units with a suggested range of grade levels. Now about thirty-eight different units are in print (see Figure 7.6 for some examples). Each unit takes several weeks to complete and contains material useful for a K–9 science program. Although no prepackaged course of study exists, the units can be easily adapted to fit most existing curricula. Each unit stretches across a range of grade levels and can be used in any sequence, unlike SAPA and SCIS. Each unit strives to develop science concepts and thinking skills simultaneously. The rationale is that children acquire mental strategies for organizing their observations as they form science concepts based on those same experiences. This belief is consistent with Piagetian developmental psychology and the learning theory of Jerome Bruner (1962).

The questions children ask are highly valued in ESS. In fact, this is the main intent of the ESS materials: that children will raise all kinds of questions about their experiences and try ways to work with the materials that have not been pre-planned by the teacher. As a consequence, teachers have to expect that children will talk with other children as they compare observations and form explanations about what they experience.

ESS has a flexible structure and emphasizes attitudes as the discovery method is used by children to learn science content. The kits consist of low-cost materials and provide the kinds of direct experiences favored by program developers. As the units vary, so do the kits. Some kits are meant for entire classes of thirty students, but most are for smaller numbers: groups of about six, or individual students for certain activities (see Figure 7.6). Each kit and teacher's guide can be purchased separately, giving more freedom and flexibility when selecting curriculum materials for the science program than either SAPA or SCIS. Some ESS units may be used by purchasing only the teacher's guide without the expense of a commercial kit.

A teacher's guide accompanies the pupil kit. The guide contains background information and teaching tips that are suggestions rather than specific directions. Notes on classroom management share examples of the kinds of questions that teachers could ask children and examples of the kinds of answers children may give or the types of questions children may ask. Other suggestions help the teacher become a guide or adviser of inquiry rather than a provider of information. This teacher role ensures that the responsibility for learning is shifted to the child, as each is stimulated to devise her or his own way of acquiring and making meaning out of information from the exploration (see Figure 7.7 on pp. 262–263).

ESS has no student textbooks. Worksheets, pictures, and supplementary brief booklets, called readers, accompany some of the units, while brief film loops provide learning experiences not easily acquired otherwise. There is considerable variation among the many ESS units, but this variation serves a fundamental purpose: to promote unguided exploration that motivates children to pursue topics of interest. ESS assumes that this kind of experience will help

FIGURE 7.6   ESS Scope and Sequence Chart

Elementary Science Study Scope (ESS)

UNIT	K	1	2	3	4	5	6	7	8	9

1 Growing Seeds
Children learn what seeds are, how seeds grow and change, and how seeds differ from other small objects. Activities, including observing and recording growth, may be done as a class or in small groups.

2 Match and Measure
This practical unit is an introduction to measurement. Children determine length, area, and volume with a variety of tools and materials.

3 Mobiles
Construction of mobiles introduces students to principles of balancing, develops a feel for symmetry of shape and motion, and shows effect of weight on a balanced system.

4 Primary Balancing
After the initial challenge of balancing the beam, children learn the importance of weight and its position on the beam in relation to the fulcrum point. Further explorations reveal that weight is not a function of volume. Other activities include sorting, counting, and balancing odd-shaped boards on a half-ball fulcrum.

5 Pattern Blocks
With 250 blocks in six colors and shapes, children progress from casual play to creating elaborate mosaic designs, they also use mirrors to create new patterns. Math content includes measurement, symmetry, counting, shape, and proportion.

6 Geo Blocks
With the set of 330 unpainted, hardwood blocks the children move from free play activity to concepts of size, shape, one-to-one correspondence, and conservation of volume.

7 Eggs and Tadpoles
Observation of the changes from egg to tadpole to frog gives students direct experience with the concept of a life cycle.

8 Tangrams
Children assemble the 7 piece puzzle into various configurations, including the basic 4-inch square. They soon discover basic geometric relationships between the pieces and through visual experience learn to deal with problems analytically.

9 Attributes Games and Problems
Manipulation of the blocks, cubes, and people pieces provides experience in classification, class and relationship, and logical thinking processes.

10 Spinning Tables
Children explore the effects of circular motion by making designs and observing liquids and solid objects placed on revolving discs. Predictions and error stimulate discussion and further experimentation.

Source: Delta Education, Inc., Nashua, NH 03061-3000. Reprinted by permission of copyright holder.

Scope and Sequence Chart

UNIT	K	1	2	3	4	5	6	7	8	9

11 Brine Shrimp
This durable organism provides children with concrete evidence of a life cycle and effects of environmental conditions on living things.

12 Printing
Through the handling of individual letters and formulation of words in the type holders, children learn the basics of printing. They also develop an appreciation of the printed word as a means of communication.

13 Structures
Students build structures with materials chosen to create structural problems. They learn to deal with properties such as size, strength of materials, and design configuration.

14 Sink or Float
Students discover that buoyancy of an object is a property of both the object and the liquid. Investigations involve different materials and shapes placed in liquids of varying densities.

15 Clay Boats
Children discover how to make clay float, and develop predicting, weighing, and measuring skills while learning about volume displacement and buoyancy.

16 Drops, Streams & Containers
Children observe characteristics of common liquids when these liquids are poured into one another or dropped on different surfaces. New ways to transfer liquids are developed.

17 Mystery Powders
Through use of scientific method, students progress from identification of harmless, common white powders to more advanced analysis of properties.

18 Ice Cubes
Activities with ice introduce the students to the effects that heat, insulation, shape, and conductivity have on melting rates. Thermometers are used to measure freezing and melting points.

19 Rocks and Charts
Children discover the many individual characteristics of a mineral which make it different from others. Rock sorting and chart making develop useful classification skills.

Physical Science	Life Science	General Skills	Earth Science	Math

(continued)

FIGURE 7.6   *(continued)*

GROWING SEEDS: Exploration of Simple Plants ▶

Students determine which samples are seeds. This is accomplished through external and internal observation, and planning. Growth rate is recorded on graphs.
Grades K–3 (6–8 week program)

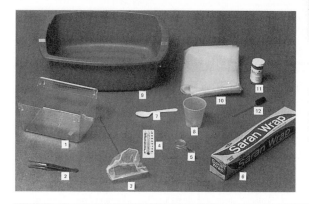

◀ **BALLOONS AND GASES: Introduction to Common Gases**

An introduction to common gases. The generation of common gases allows students to discover some properties of gases and to differentiate between one gas and another. Students work with simple acids, bases, and bromothymol blue, or color indicator. "Mystery" gases are introduced by the teacher and the students attempt to identify them using their previous experiences.
Grades 5–8 (1–22 class sessions)

◀ **EGGS & TADPOLES: Observing a Frog's Life Cycle**

Students observe a frog develop from egg through various tadpole states and, with great care, even to a young frog. The students will answer many of their questions through observation and group discussions.
Grades K–6 (3 week to 6 month program)

each child develop useful learning skills and that knowledge gained from this approach is meaningful and long lasting.

ESS Program Effects.   ESS strives to help children learn science and thinking skills through positive attitudes. Does this work? Again we can refer to the report of James Shymansky and his fellow researchers (1982) (see Table 7.2). Yes, to an extent ESS is successful. Achievement gains were less than with SCIS and SAPA, yet children who learned science by ESS did outperform their age-mates in traditional science programs by an average of 4 percentile points. Attitude improvements were impressive: average ESS scores were 20 percentile points above the averages of children from traditional programs, by far the largest advance of the three programs we compare in this chapter. Substantial increases in creativity and process skill development were shown by 26 and 18 percentile point gains, while completion of Piagetian tasks was 2 percentile points above those of traditional programs. Achievement gains were not as great as the theoretical assumptions of ESS might suggest, yet these assumptions were not completely wrong given the other substantial gains children made from the ESS program.

SAPA, SCIS, and ESS have shown some superior characteristics and effects when compared with traditional science programs. Yet each program is based on a different design and a different teaching approach, and for different reasons. Developers of the programs made different assumptions but shared some in common as well. What are the characteristics of effective science teaching that should be included in a science program?

WHAT WORKS?

Take a look in a large number of elementary classrooms where science is taught and what do you see? Perhaps you observe what Donald Wright reports: "Fifty to 80 percent of all science classes use a single text or multiple texts as *the* basis for instruction. . . . For students, knowing is more a function of reading,

TABLE 7.2 Performance Improvement for Students in Classrooms Using ESS, SCIS, or SAPA as Compared to Students in Traditional Classrooms

Performance Area	Percentage Points Gained		
	ESS	SCIS	SAPA
Achievement	4	34	7
Attitudes	20	3	15
Process skills	18	21	36
Related skills	*	8	4
Creativity	26	34	7
Piagetian tasks	2	5	12

*No studies reported

Source: James A. Shymansky, William C. Kyle, Jr., and Jennifer M. Alport, "How Effective Were the Hands-On Science Programs of Yesterday?" *Science and Children* (November–December 1982): 15.

FIGURE 7.7   Excerpts from an ESS Teacher's Guide

Part 1: Simple Circuits

Beginning Circuits

Before Starting to Teach

Materials you will need:

2 8-inch pieces of #20 bare copper wire
2 8-inch pieces of #22 plastic-covered copper wire
3 #48 (PB) bulbs
3 D batteries
1 wire stripper

The following suggestions will guide your initial exploration. If you take enough time to try your own ideas as well, you will be ready for the variety of ideas your students are sure to propose.

Try to light one of the bulbs, using a piece of bare wire and a battery. Some people have taken 20 minutes to light the bulb the first time, so do not worry if yours does not light right away. See how many different ways you can devise to make the bulb light. It is helpful to make sketches of your various attempts, including those that do not work.

Using the plastic-covered wire, light a bulb. You will have to remove the covering from the ends. The wire stripper is designed to remove the plastic cover without cutting the wire. You can adjust the knob so that the wire opening will cut only the plastic.

Stripper

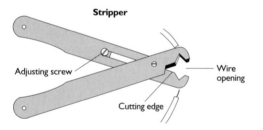

Place the wire in the opening and close the handles; then pull the stripper toward the end of the wire, so that it strips off a piece of the covering.

Now try some connections using a battery, a bulb, and two wires. You may find some surprises. For example, you know that the bulb in *A* below will light, but what will happen when you add another wire, as in *B* or *C*?

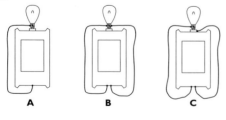

In the Classroom

Materials you will need for each child:

1 8-inch piece of #22 plastic-covered copper wire
1 #48 (PB) bulb
1 D battery

For each group:
1 wire stripper

To have available:
extra supplies of the above materials

It is suggested that the students work in groups of two to four. Although they don't need to share equipment for the initial activity, they will soon need to do so.

Each student should have a box or paper bag in which to keep his materials at the end of each class period. It has worked well for children to keep the materials originally passed out to them for the duration of the unit. They use these materials, as well as others to be distributed later, continually. Whether or not the children take equipment home to work with is up to you.

LEAD-OFF QUESTION
Can you make the bulb light with one battery and one wire?

Some children will take 20 minutes to light the bulb, while others will take only five. Once one child in a class manages to make the bulb light, his method catches on quickly. Probably only five or six will light the bulb on their own. The rest will follow a neighbor's lead.

As the bulbs are lighted, assure the children that there are different ways to light bulbs, and have them look for more. Invite them up to the chalkboard to draw the various ways they have tried. Ways in which the bulb does not light are just as important and should be drawn on the board, too.

It is extremely important to give children this time for free investigation with the equipment, so that they can pursue whatever questions occur to them. Their questions at this early stage will provide good leads for later work. After doing these first experiments, some children may bring household bulbs into the class. One such class connected seven batteries to a 50-watt bulb and still saw no light. Then a girl felt that the bulb was warm; they added another battery or two and were rewarded by a slight glow. One battery was removed, and the bulb dimmed. The class then went on to compare the number of batteries required to light bulbs of various sizes.

FOLLOW-UP QUESTION
How many different ways can you light the bulb?

ACTIVITIES CHILDREN MAY TRY
• Using two or more batteries, light the PB.
• Find out how many bulbs can be lit with one battery.
• Find out how brightly a bulb will shine when three, four, or eight batteries are used.
• Find out how many batteries it takes to burn out a bulb.
• Use plastic-covered wire, light a PB.
• Use more wire to see if a PB will still light.

Source: Delta Education, Inc., Nashua, NH 03061-3000. Reprinted by permission of copyright holder.

- Find out which will wear out first, if contact between a battery and a PB is maintained for a long time. How long does it take?
- Attach a wire from one end of the battery to the other. See how the battery feels after five minutes in this situation and after an hour.
- See if the battery will light a bulb after an hour.

Note: When investigating the different ways that will light the bulb, children often discuss the question, "Does turning the battery around make another way?" The fact that a battery works both ways is an exciting discovery to many.

POSSIBLE DISCUSSION QUESTIONS

After three or four sessions with these materials, the children will be ready to come together as a class to share their experiences. One way to begin such a discussion is to draw some circuits on the board and ask if the class can predict whether the bulbs in the arrangements will light. Below are examples of some circuits you may want to discuss.

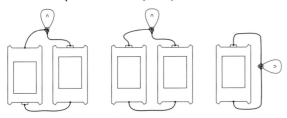

Will these bulbs light? Why?

Let the children discuss all their ideas. Have them try out each new circuit with the equipment to verify their predictions. Perhaps some students will want to make generalizations about the features of those circuits in which the bulb lights and those in which the bulb does not light.

What did you find out in the last few lessons?

You'll find that many children will have forgotten some of their work because they did not keep a record of it. They should now see the need for simple notes and diagrams.

How many ways did you find to make the bulb light?
Does the bulb have to be touching the battery?
Does the wire have to be wrapped around the bulb?
What special places must be touched on the bulb for it to light?
Can you make a "rule" about lighting the bulb?"

Be prepared for a variety. Give each child who has something to say a chance to be heard.

Teaching Background

Since this is the initial section of the unit, it has been designed to open the way to many later areas of investigation. The general background presented here is, therefore, intended to suggest ways in which you can help children both to go further and to understand where they are going.

A bulb can be lit essentially in four ways, using one wire and one battery. (Actually, turning the wire around could be considered to be creating new ways, too.)

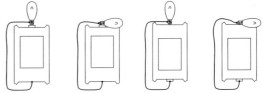

In each case, the bulb lights with the same brightness. Asking a child about the brightness of different arrangements helps him to see that brightness is a way to tell something about a circuit.

Since the battery lights the bulb with equal brightness, regardless of which way it is facing in the circuit, children may wonder why some batteries are marked with a "+" (positive) and a "–" (negative) at the top and the flat end respectively. If the bulb can't tell one end from the other, why do we bother about designating the poles positive and negative? This question will be answered when the children start working with more than one battery. At that time, the students will see that with two or more batteries in a circuit, the direction of each is important.

The "flow" of electricity usually comes up sooner or later. Does the electricity "flow" in circuits from the positive to the negative end of the battery or vice versa? This is a very difficult question to answer experimentally. It is further complicated by the fact that when different materials are used in circuits, different things happen. Students who are quick to explain simple circuits in terms of a particular direction of flow might profit from a question such as: "Are you sure? What difference would you notice if the flow were actually the reverse?" Since the students have noticed that the bulb works equally well on both ends of the battery, they should begin to realize that the particular direction of electricity flow doesn't matter in this situation.

When students start lighting more than one bulb with one battery, or one bulb with more than one battery, a great many possibilities for further investigation emerge.

The changes in brightness of the bulb can be accounted for, if you recognize that the bulb is acting like a meter, giving a measure of how much or how little of "something" is in the wire. If children can group the results of their experiments in such a way that they see relationships between, and common elements in, activities that dim and activities that brighten a bulb, they are on the way to understanding what is happening.

Predicting Sheet 1

Prediction Sheet 1 illustrates twelve situations closely related to many of the activities your children may have investigated in the first section.

After a child has thought about each circuit and marked the sheet accordingly, discuss some of his predictions with him. What reasons are given for a particular answer? When a child predicts incorrectly or cannot describe a convincing basis for his prediction, recommend that he test his prediction by making the circuit. He may then be able to give a clearer explanation for some results.

digesting, and regurgitating information from the textbook or lab manual than it is of analyzing, synthesizing, and evaluating" (Wright, 1980, p. 144).

Furthermore, you may have an impression that a direct, authoritative, prescriptive approach with the same pace for everyone and where the 3 Rs are emphasized is actually the best way to teach science. As added support for this view you could refer to the fact that the three NSF-sponsored programs we have just mentioned have never been used by more than 30 percent of the school districts in the United States; also, only 7 percent of K–6 teachers have ever attended an NSF-sponsored meeting (Weiss, 1978). Certainly if the government spent millions to develop these programs, they would be used if they actually worked, right? Wrong.

What the three programs we compare all have in common is a hands-on curriculum and teaching approach. Despite what is widely believed and practiced, the hands-on, minds-on learning approach is superior to the traditional approach. James Shymansky and his colleagues (1982) tell us that synthesis of the abundant research shows conclusively that children in a hands-on science program achieve more, like science more, and improve their problem-solving skills more than children who learn from traditional textbook-based programs. The hands help the minds grow by constructing meaning. These conclusions endured resynthesis even though original statistics have been revised to yield results of greater precision (Shymansky, et al., 1990).

Hands-on, minds-on learning makes the difference.

Ted Bredderman (1982) adds support to this view. Bredderman's research is provided as a part of *Project Synthesis,* a massive research effort funded by the National Science Foundation to determine the effects of past experimental programs so that present and future science education goals could be revised. Bredderman's research collected the results from sixty studies that involved 13,000 students in 1,000 elementary classrooms over fifteen years. He analyzed the results of these studies carefully through meta-analysis procedures to sort out conflicting findings reported in the literature. His conclusion clearly shows what works:

> With the use of activity-based science programs, teachers can expect substantially improved performance in science process and creativity; modestly increased performance on tests of perception, logic, language development, science content, and math; modestly improved attitudes toward science and science class; and pronounced benefits for disadvantaged students. (Bredderman, 1982, pp. 39–41)

Hands-on, minds-on learning makes the difference. Exploring, investigating, and discovering are essential to meaningful learning and effective science teaching. When children solve problems and make discoveries, they are learning how to learn and constructing meaning for themselves. Jerome Bruner (1961) points out the benefits for children as they make discoveries through active learning:

- Children's intellectual potency is increased; their powers of thinking improve.
- Children's rewards for learning shift from those that come from the teacher or someone else to those that are found inside themselves from the satisfaction they feel.
- Children learn the procedures and important steps for making discoveries and find ways to transfer these to other learning opportunities.
- What children learn takes on more meaning, and they remember it longer.

While all three programs surveyed here report successes, they also have limitations. From the research that has been synthesized, it seems prudent to mix emphases on science content and process skills for the most potent teaching and learning combination. Yet researchers like Ted Bredderman and James Shymansky and his colleagues warn against abandoning the traditional textbook-based programs in complete favor of SAPA, SCIS, ESS, or the like. Instead, they recommend incorporating the useful methods and materials into existing science programs as a step toward improvement.

What are we to do? First, realize that some of the effective science programs remain. Several schools still use SAPA, SCIS, and ESS. Parts of these can be added to existing school programs to provide children with more hands-on learning opportunities. Next, be aware that there have been substantial improvements in recent editions of textbooks and that new generations of curriculum supplements have been developed. These supplements may be available

WHAT RESEARCH SAYS

Criteria for Excellence in K–6 Science Programs

All citizens need science competence to make the most of their individual potential, and to cope with an increasingly technical world. And as participants in a democratic society, individuals must be prepared to make informed, responsible decisions about science-related social issues. Moreover, as the pace of change accelerates, new careers are being created almost daily, as diverse as the interests and aptitudes of students themselves. Alerting students to the ever-widening range of opportunities in careers related to science and technology, teaching science for life, and teaching science for citizenship: these are the three challenges the Project [Search for Excellence in Science Education, SESE] poses to the science programs of today and tomorrow.

SESE consists of a network of fifty-two state committees that meet each year to nominate the best science programs for national award. A national panel of judges screens the states' nominations and then selects six to thirteen programs that most closely achieve the ideal. In reality, no program ever meets all the criteria for excellence. Just the same, the criteria set the direction for the future of science education. An effective and exemplary elementary science program meets the following criteria:

Students
- Demonstrate effective consumer behavior.
- Acquire good health habits.
- Understand the relationship between people and their environments.
- Use scientific resources to solve problems.
- Realize that science is hard work and that the resolution of one problem can cause other problems.

Curriculum
- Emphasizes hands-on learning for all students through a planned, sequential program.
- Uses well-defined objectives that are demonstrated through effective teaching.
- Uses evaluation for periodic review and ongoing assessment of science content, teaching, and learning.
- Provides information and experiences that students can use in their everyday lives.
- Provides useful guidelines for teacher planning and science activities.

through your university or state department of education. Both of these types of resources have capitalized on several features that made the alphabet soup programs successful. For example, we find more frequent use of student learning activities with a focus on specific conceptual outcomes, better organization of teaching materials, and convenient packaging of curriculum materials; we can attribute these improvements to the effects of the hands-on, minds-on programs.

What science should be taught largely remains an unresolved issue. Several initiatives, such as the National Science Foundation's Project Synthesis, the American Association for the Advancement of Science's Project 2061, the National Science Teachers Association scope and sequence project, and the National Research Council's National Science Education Standards have produced useful materials to help resolve this issue; many state curricula pursue it as well. We now know that if the elementary science program is to serve *all* children well, specific assumptions must guide program development and science teaching. Science must be taught so that children construct meaning from direct

Instruction
- Has an adequate budget and administrative guidance.
- Offers realistic problem-solving activities for students.
- Provides enough materials for every student to benefit from direct experiences and experiments.
- Exceeds state and national minimum class time expectations (number of minutes in science per week).
- Integrates the subject matter of science into other subject areas regularly.

Teachers
- Understand and use he goals of the school science program.
- Seek new ideas and experiment with new teaching methods.
- Provide varied experiences for children within the subject matter, science processes, and other aspects of science.
- Provide learning experiences from various fields of science (life, physical, and environmental), as well as from technology, the community, and larger social problems.
- Encourages students to think and solve problems by using their science experiences.

The criteria are predictions of the future. How these criteria may be articulated can be found in the many classrooms of people who are committed to excellence. These teachers are talented, dedicated, and generous individuals who have developed and who guide programs that really work. The Search for Excellence in Science Education Programs selects new recipients of the prestigious award each year. Check with the National Science Teachers Association, you state NSTA-affiliated organization, or your state department of education to see which elementary programs in your area have received the award.

Source: Portions excerpted from *Criteria for Excellence* (Washington, DC: National Science Teachers Association, 1987) pp. 4–7.

science experiences and expand their problem-solving and thinking skills. Furthermore, the subject matter must provide opportunities for children to develop personally; to learn about the many interrelationships among science, technology, and our society; to grow intellectually through inquiry; and to be exposed to the history and nature of science.

Each science program can evolve from its present condition to a level where relevant learning opportunities are provided for all children. The following list of assumptions and supported research is associated with effective science programs. The list is gleaned from research supported by the National Science Foundation and the National Science Teachers Association's recommendations for exemplary elementary science programs. These assumptions reveal some of the impact of historically significant science programs and predict the future trends science programs will face. We suggest that you keep these assumptions handy and let them help you plan more effective science instruction as well as advise your school principal or curriculum committee.

Supported Assumptions About Effective Elementary Science Programs

1. National Science Foundation experimental elementary science programs and sponsored new approaches to teacher preparation have been successful, even though a low percentage of schools (30 percent) have used the programs and an even smaller percentage of teachers (7 percent) have received direct training.

2. Effective elementary science programs keep pace with changes in science, society, knowledge, and trends in schooling.

3. Most current elementary school science programs do not serve all children well. Effective programs have meaning for diverse audiences.

4. Effective science programs strive to promote children's personal development; to help children explore the interrelationships among science, technology, and society; to continue academic preparation through inquiry; and to build awareness of the history and nature of science.

5. Effective programs have no single author but are developed by teams with teacher involvement. Extensive classroom testing and program revision are necessary and must be done frequently.

6. Students learn successfully in different ways; multiple views on learning add diversity and help to balance the effective science program.

7. Programs that emphasize conceptual learning appear to be most effective overall and produce the greatest and most enduring gains in achievement when conception is a learner's construct.

8. Multiple teaching methods are useful, and hands-on learning opportunities are necessary for all children. Overall, inquiry methods and learning cycles are useful methods for helping children learn science concepts.

9. What is taught—the substance of science—must be useful and relevant for each child. Publications such as the National Science Education Standards help guide content selection.

10. Packaging the program is helpful and reduces teachers' preparation time. New generation science curriculum supplements have several common features that add impact to the materials. They identify relevant themes, define purposes or objectives, give background information, list materials needed, state procedures for teaching, identify essential vocabulary, offer ideas for evaluation or lesson expansion, and so on.

11. The history and nature of science makes it possible to integrate topics into other subject lessons. Science's diversity enriches other parts of the school curriculum and adds to its power as a literacy subject.

12. A less direct, teacher-as-guide instructional role is effective because students are encouraged to assume greater responsibility for their own learning.

13. Conceptual learning takes time and should not be rushed; effectiveness rather than time efficiency should be the driving force of the curriculum.

14. Learners in constructivist science programs achieve more, like science more, and improve their problem-solving skills more than children who learn from traditional textbook-based programs. Innovative newer generations of science textbooks incorporate many of the features of the effective experimental programs.

15. Effective science programs promote children's intellectual development by improving their thinking through inquiry and problem-solving processes.

16. Materials and learning activities must match the child's level of development to have the greatest impact.

17. Students receive intrinsic rewards from the personal discoveries they make through firsthand learning experiences with manipulatives.

18. The science students learn from effective programs helps them transfer their learning to other circumstances better, get more meaning, and remember what they learn longer.

THE NEXT GENERATION OF SCIENCE PROGRAMS

Lessons from the past have helped to improve the wonderful new resources available to teachers. This exciting era of curriculum and program development has helped to renew interest in science. Science programs are attempting to keep pace with changes in the fields of science and technology and to investigate the impact of each on our society through the eyes and experiences of children.

The new generation of science programs strives to serve the needs and interests of all learners, not an intellectual elite. New programs often emphasize conceptual development through constructivist techniques, use multiple teaching methods to fill multiple student interests, and incorporate multiple views on human diversity. Many programs promote such additional science outcomes as students skilled at science inquiry and problem solving; investigations of interrelationships among and between science, technology, and society; awareness of the history and tentative nature of science; and an expanded awareness of career opportunities in science.

The direct and sustained involvement of classroom teachers is one of the greatest factors shaping new science programs. Attempts are made to match the students' levels of development to appropriate learning experiences and help strengthen the conceptual constructions of learners by connecting learning experiences and central concepts to science themes. Table 7.3 illustrates the thematic similarities and differences among several new science programs. Continual classroom testing of materials and lessons and frequent revision through formative evaluation assist these programs through rapid stages of evolution. Hence, conceptual flaws are reduced, and supported assumptions about learning are expanded.

Although there are numerous small-scale efforts to produce the next generation of science programs, space permits us to share only a sample of the larger efforts that have endured rigorous evaluation and received national (often international) attention.

◢ **TABLE 7.3   Common Science Themes**

Earth Systems	Benchmarks	California Framework	Biological Sciences Curriculum Study (BSCS)	National Assessment of Educational Progress (NAEP)	National Science Education Standards (NSES)	Project Learning Tree (PLT)
					Order and organization	
Aesthetics	Constancy	Stability	Cause and effect		Constancy	
Interaction	Patterns of change	Patterns of change	Change and conservation	Patterns of change	Measure-ment and change	Patterns of change
		Energy	Energy and matter			
	Scale	Scale and structure	Time and scale			Structure and scale
Evolution	Evolution	Evolution	Evolution and equilibrium		Evolution and equilibrium	
Scale & Systems	Systems	Systems and interactions	Systems and interactions	Systems		Systems
Nature of Science			Probability and prediction			
			Structure and function		Form and function	
Careers						
			Diversity and variation			Diversity
	Models		Models and theories	Models	Models	
Human impact						Inter-relationships

AIMS.   *Activities to Integrate Mathematics and Science* publishes elementary and middle school curriculum materials that integrate mathematics and science for grades K–9. These materials are provided in easy-to-use teacher manuals that have been produced and classroom tested by teachers. Workshops and semi-

New science programs provide a variety of experiences to help children understand their complex worlds.

nars are available through the AIMS organization, P.O. Box 7766, Fresno, CA 93747, (209) 291-1766. Titles include *Floaters and Sinkers, Jawbreakers and Heart Thumpers, Glide into Winter with Math and Science, Pieces and Patterns,* and *The Sky's the Limit!* Some are available in Spanish.

Delta Science Modules. This series of forty paperback modules ranges from *Air* to *Observing an Aquarium* to *You and Your Body.* Lessons are suitable for intermediate and middle school grades, provide easy-to-follow instructions that help teachers guide students through constructivist learning opportunities, and offer reasonably authentic assessment devices. Modules may be purchased separately or as a set. Kits of hands-on materials are available at additional cost. Available from Delta Education, P.O. Box 3000, Nashua, NH 03061-3000.

Earth Systems Education. This middle school science resource guide is a joint product of the Ohio State University and the University of Northern Colorado.

Through a K–12 scope and sequence, teachers are urged to use the classroom-tested materials to develop among learners the values of aesthetics and stewardship through practical local learning experiences that help students to explore state, national, and global earth issues within the context of various science disciplines. Six principles unify the learning experiences. Contact the Earth Systems Education Program at the Ohio State University, (614) 292-9826.

ECO-NET.   Downloadable resource files, e-mail, and conferencing support are available through this Internet access resource. The resources cover an array of environmental issues and provide real-time support. A computer and modem are necessary, and a monthly fee plus connect time charges apply. Contact the Institute for Global Communications, 18 DeBoom Street, San Francisco, CA, 94107.

FOSS.   *Full Option Science System,* of the Lawrence Hall of Science in Berkeley, California 94720, is distributed by the Encyclopaedia Britannica Educational Corporation. For grades 3 through 6, student equipment kits and print materials are accompanied by some of the most innovative assessment alternatives we have seen. Children do science, construct concepts, and perform direct evaluation exercises in the areas of life, physical, and earth science and scientific reasoning and technology.

GEMS.   *Great Exploration in Math and Science* is designed for students in grades K through 12. Science and mathematics are integrated in twenty-four different teacher activity publications and student project booklets. Available through the Lawrence Hall of Science in Berkeley, California 94720, topics include *Animals in Action, Bubble-ology, Buzzing a Hive, Crime Lab Chemistry, Fingerprinting, Mapping Fish Habitats, Oobleck,* and *Vitamin C Testing.*

INSIGHTS: Hands-on Inquiry Science Curriculum   Seventeen multigrade-level modules are available and represent a balance of life, earth, and physical science. Module topics are organized around such themes as diversity, cause and effect, structure and function, systems, change, and energy. Modules are closely linked with children's common experiences and basic science phenomena. Concepts are selected for developmental appropriateness. Many ESS science ideas have evolved into the INSIGHTS modules. Available from Improving Urban Elementary Science, Project Education Development Center, 55 Chapel Street, Newton, MA 02160.

Kids-Net.   *National Geographic Kids Network* of Education Services, Dept. 5389, Washington, D.C. 20036 involves children in a nationwide computer network; learners collect data in their home environments and send the information to the national server. Sharing information helps children to make comparisons and discover concepts about water quality and rain, for example, on a national and global scale. Learners are linked with practicing scientists.

Projects WILD and Aquatic.   Two different versions of a great idea, these projects emphasize wildlife and aquatic life, respectively. Interdisciplinary and for grades K through 12, the materials accommodate major school subjects and skills areas by involving children in direct and simulated wildlife experiences. The purpose is to increase awareness first, then to build toward making personal decisions and taking responsible human actions. The teacher-designed materials make it easy to bring outdoor wildlife concepts into the classroom. Students love the outdoor action sections. The activity guides are available only through training sessions. Information can be obtained by contacting Project WILD, 5430 Grosvenor Lane, Bethesda, MD 20814.

Project Learning Tree.   This new generation of a classic is designed to help learners better understand the forest community and its relationship to the day-to-day lives of people and animals. Each lesson is classroom-tested, linked to a specific science theme, and supported by conceptual story lines. Themes include diversity, interrelationships, systems, structure and scale, and patterns of change. The materials are available by attending special workshops. Contact the American Forest Foundation, 1111 19th Street, N.W., Suite 780, Washington, D.C. 20036.

Project WET (Water Education for Teachers).   This program helps teachers explore water issues with learners. One hundred multidisciplinary activities support this resource, which are also supported by such supplements as special topic modules, models, children's literature books, and living history materials. Write to Project WET, 201 Culbertson Hall, Montana State University, Bozeman, MT 59717.

Science for Kids.   This collection of multimedia programs developed for ages 5–14 years is growing rapidly. Scientists, engineers, educators, artists, programmers, and psychologists have collaborated to develop CD-ROM experiences. Teacher's edition and support materials for learners are available. Individual topics may be purchased. Titles include *"Cell"ebration, Forces and Motion, Simple Machines,* and *Home Connections.* The address is P.O. Box 519, Lewisville, NC 27023.

SEPUP.   *Science Education for Public Understanding Program* is developed and provided by the Lawrence Hall of Science in Berkeley, California 94720-5200. The materials are arranged in modules. The original program, CEPUP, emphasized chemical education; new modules address physical, earth, and life sciences as well as science processes. SEPUP emphasizes an integrated approach to teaching issues-oriented science. SEPUP kits are designed for children in grades 6 through 8 and address topics like pollution, household chemicals, waste, and chemicals in foods. Yearlong SEPUP courses for grades 7 through 10 strive to make science concepts relevant to the real world.

Zero Population Growth.   Scientific concepts are constructed through applied basic mathematics using population issues. Various resources support ZPG, including newsletters, fact sheet, curriculum materials, and videotapes. The address is 1400 16th Street, N.W., Suite 320, Washington, D.C. 20036.

CHAPTER SUMMARY

This chapter explores many assumptions that are made while forming an answer to the principal guiding question: What are the characteristics of effective elementary science instruction? A broad view is taken by examining assumptions that undergird landmark experimental programs tested extensively in elementary schools. The characteristics of these effective older programs provide a foundation for learning and practicing techniques of effective instruction.

The historical sense of this foundation can help you separate the gimmicks from genuine improvements. At times the assumptions are explicit; at other times we find subtle hidden assumptions that tend to reveal themselves as we probe into past events and future recommendations for science education.

The primary concept of this chapter is that effective elementary science programs are built on dominant beliefs that arise from the past and effectiveness research. Assumptions change as some fall from favor or are proven wrong; new ones are added to reflect changes in the knowledge base and different priorities. Assumptions help guide changes in science programming and affect your teaching by stimulating changes in science materials as well as by setting new expectations and identifying future trends.

The chapter concludes with a brief answer to the question "What works?" The answer is drawn from recent program evaluation research and the National Science Teachers Association's criteria for program excellence. The planning techniques, sample lessons, and teaching strategies of subsequent chapters arise from supported assumptions about effective elementary science programs.

DISCUSSION QUESTIONS AND PROJECTS

1. What do you think an effective elementary science program should contain? How would you defend your position to a teacher or school administrator who holds an opposing view?

2. Examine copies of several different science textbooks for the same grade level. What evidence do you find that shows inclusion of the criteria for effective programs?

3. Refer to the assumptions about elementary school science summarized at the end of this chapter. How could you use these assumptions to form a philosophy of science teaching? What is your philosophy?

4. Which would you believe, the research findings and criteria for effective programs such as those from sources cited in this chapter, the opinions of several teachers, or a report made by a presidential advisory committee? Why?

5. Examine a school's course of study or curriculum guide for elementary or middle school science. Identify the assumptions about effective science programs and compare them to those stated at the end of this chapter. Report your comparison.

6. Use the assumptions about elementary science programs to develop a survey, and then use the survey to interview several elementary teachers, principals, scientists, parents, and so on. What do you conclude about the accuracy of different people's assumptions?

7. Examine samples of SAPA, SCIS, and ESS materials and compare them with current elementary science textbooks and supplementary curriculum materials such as Project WILD, Project Learning Tree, FOSS, SEPUP, AIMS, and others. How do the older experimental elementary science programs compare with the newer generation of textbooks and teaching materials? What features are similar? Why?

ADDITIONAL READINGS

If you are interested in learning more about some of the topics raised in this chapter, consider the following sources:

Patricia E. Blosser, "What Research Says: Improving Science Education," *School Science and Mathematics* 86, No. 7 (November 1986): 597–612. Dr. Blosser draws on her access to extensive information from the ERIC Clearinghouse for Science, Mathematics, and Environmental Education to identify past and present trends and issues for reform of science education. She provides a succinct historical account of the evolution of science education, lists the barriers to improvement, and reports the researched effects of various programs. Blosser confirms the need to teach science interactively.

Ronald J. Bonnstetter, John E. Penick, and Robert E. Yager, *Teachers in Exemplary Programs: How Do They Compare?* (Washington, DC: National Science Teachers Association, 1983). This is one of a series of monographs devoted to excellence in science teaching. It is peppered with profiles and statistics about effective science teachers. The conclusion is that "teachers in programs which stand out as different are themselves different from teachers in general" (p. 30).

Criteria for Excellence (Washington, DC: National Science Teachers Association, 1987). Among other program areas, this compact book provides specific criteria for exemplary programs in K–6 science, middle/junior high science, science-technology-society, environmental education, inquiry science, science teaching, and career awareness. The writing is straightforward, and descriptions are complemented with lists of school programs that have received national recognition for excellence in science programs and teaching.

Norris C. Harms and Robert E. Yager, *What Research Says to the Science Teacher*, vol. 3 (Washington, DC: National Science Teachers Association, 1981). Used extensively for portions of this chapter, this book provides the source recommendations attributed to Project Synthesis. We highly recommend that you read parts I, II, V, VI, VII, and VIII.

Kenneth R. Mechling and Donna L. Oliver, *What Research Says about Elementary School Science* (Washington, DC: National Science Teachers Association, 1983). This is Handbook IV from the Project for Promoting Science Among Elementary School Principals, which was funded by the National Science Foundation. Although written for school principals, this particular handbook is also valuable for teachers who want to get the facts from research and avoid the myths that surround the purposes and practices of elementary science. Oliver is a former elementary school teacher who brings practical experience to the "Recipe for Success" section.

CHAPTER OUTLINE

How Can You Improve Your Science Instruction Through Human, Print, and Multimedia Resources?

"I wish I knew more about environmental education. I don't remember learning much about it during my undergraduate work," admitted Rosita Martinez, a third-grade teacher, while she was eating lunch with fellow teachers.

Another third-grade teacher, Kara Larson, agreed. "I don't either. I know it's important for students to be concerned about the land and its resources. An appreciation of conservation is something they have to learn. It's scary to think what our land will be like in thirty years. Resource management and education are both critical, and education is our job."

Overhearing the discussion, Cade Beaver, a fifth-grade teacher, described a good session on environmental education presented by a state naturalist that he had attended at the last state inservice meeting. He thought he could find her name and suggested putting a message on the state telecommunication network for science teachers. He often got help with activities from other teachers and staff at state and national agencies.

Kara suggested, "You might want to look in the school resource file in the principal's office for information on volunteers and field trips within the community. This information can be very helpful."

Later that afternoon, Cade used the school computer to connect to a science education network and requested information or assistance for Rosita. After the school day, he found his program from the state meeting and identified the naturalist, copied her name and agency, and left them in Rosita's school mailbox. When Rosita found the note from Cade, it reminded her to stop at the principal's office to review the school resource file that Kara had mentioned. Instead of one file, she found a drawer packed with information on many community resource persons, volunteers, and field trip locations.

Within two days, the network had provided several suggestions from teachers across the state. Many cited examples of activities, lesson plans, and resources. Three messages from teachers suggested that Rosita obtain some supplementary curriculum programs such as Project WILD, Project WILD—Aquatic, Project Learning Tree, and Project WET. One teacher even provided the names and telephone numbers of the state contacts for these programs.

Rosita called the state contacts of the programs and learned about the supplemental programs and their activities designed to provide information to help students evaluate choices and make decisions about the environment. Rosita also learned about the inservice workshops funded through the state's Dwight D. Eisenhower Mathematics and Science Education Program (Appendix C) inservice funds. Rosita promptly enrolled in an upcoming Project WILD workshop.

The two-day workshop provided Rosita with a book of hands-on elementary activities that closely matched the goals and objectives of the unit she would be teaching. During the workshop she also met a local naturalist who had made the presentation at the state conference. Rosita asked the naturalist to visit her class, to bring some animals, and to arrange for the class to visit the park where she worked.

Rosita's class received enriched educational experiences because she used resources to enrich her teaching. For example, her students became bears searching for food during one lesson and artists during another. Rosita's students became active participants in their own learning experiences. ◆

INTRODUCTION

What can you recall about your school experiences that excited you about a topic? The learning experiences and opportunities people most often recall are those of active participation. "I remember when we held the snake,. . . when we went to the zoo,. . . when I stood inside the 6-foot-tall bubble at the science museum." Students learn best when actively involved with their learning and when the topics are of interest to them. Today's students have grown up in front of TV screens as both inactive and active participants in videos, video games, and cartoons. They interact constantly with software that offers instant motion and movement, and they become involved to excess. These experiences raise student expectations for active and innovative classroom instruction.

Think comprehensively about the educational experiences you offer your students. Consider their interests, learning styles, and educational needs. Are the learning experiences and opportunities that you provide students varied and multifaceted? Do you use the read-write-review-test approach to textbook material? Do your students pursue activities that will help them to develop the skills necessary for scientifically literate citizens or even scientists, explore their surroundings, or construct connections between themselves and their world?

Rosita's program is just one example of a teacher's attempt to extend the classroom beyond its walls. Let us examine the resources she utilized:

- colleagues
- state professional organization
- state telecommunications network
- state naturalist
- supplementary curriculum materials
- volunteer
- inservice provided through federally funded program
- school-level resource file.

Each resource provided an additional facet to her instruction.

If science is a way of doing and learning from doing, then it is necessary for you to identify and use the resources that will enable students to do the work of science. Using multiple resources is an effective way to provide educational experiences that address the goals of a balanced, comprehensive science education program.

To assist you in identifying and using science resources, this chapter will help you to:

1. examine why supplemental resources are necessary,
2. review human and print resources,
3. explore the different levels of microcomputer usage and applicable software,
4. review telecommunications networks.

WHY USE SUPPLEMENTAL RESOURCES?

Resources are things that can be turned to for support or help. We encourage you to be resourceful—to be readily able to act effectively—as you arrange science experiences for your students. A teacher who uses the textbook as the entire teaching guide limits the variety and quality of instruction. Adding community resources increases learning opportunities, allows experiences that address the goals of a comprehensive science education program, provides the link between the students' present and future experiences, and makes the teaching process personal for both students and the teacher. Including additional resources requires time and planning, but teachers discover through experience that the addition of information and hands-on activities goes beyond the walls of the

Community resources stimulate children's interests in science and its practical value.

classroom and the world of academia and often creates the most memorable learning experiences of all. For example, the Thomas Jefferson Magnet School in Euclid, Ohio, uses animals in its curriculum. Each room has permanent animal residents: chinchillas, hamsters, a pot-belly pig, iguanas, finches, a turtle, a python, a snake, a parakeet, a parrot, and a rabbit. An English springer spaniel resides in the office and greets all arriving guests. This novel use of resources within the classroom provides an exciting learning experience.

You may never fully know the effect any learning activity has on your students, but many class reunions are spent discussing the memorable events of the school years. You should hope that the experiences you provide students are ones they will remember and value. The classroom may be the typical location for learning, but the walls may be extended to the community where students will spend their lives.

The link between the community and the classroom is not a new concept. John Dewey (1916) made the following statement, still appropriate, in his *Democracy and Education* more than seventy years ago:

The development within the young of the attitudes and dispositions necessary to the continuous and progressive life of society cannot take place by direct conveyance of beliefs, emotions, and knowledge. It takes place through the intermediary of the environment, the environment consists of the sum total of conditions which are concerned with the execution of the activity characteristic of the living being. The social environment consists of all activities of fellow beings that are bound up in carrying on the activities of any of its members. It is truly educative in its effect, in its efforts, in the degree in which an individual appropriates the purpose which actuates it, becomes familiar with its methods and subject matters, acquires needed skills, and is saturated with its emotional spirit. (quoted in Decker, 1981, p. 39)

The need for relevance in education is paramount as the country finds its educational system questioned in relation to a new technological and global society. This society's ability to respond to profound and rapid changes is dependent on an adequate and educated human resource base. Therefore, our mission as educators is to prepare an educated and scientifically literate citizenry capable of responding to technological advances. Demographic studies predict that fewer students will be prepared for and interested in pursuing science in the 1990s. The characteristics of the future workforce likely will mirror these changing demographics, with more minorities and women prepared to enter employment than at the present. Programs within schools must respond to these changes, promote a comprehensive understanding of the role of science in human affairs, and stress the importance of a scientifically literate workforce.

Areas of emphasis within the classroom should attempt to:

- encourage student interest in science by broadening K–12 initiatives that emphasize the interrelatedness of science and society,
- strengthen the curricula so that they better address societal and ethical concerns, internationalize course content, and focus on communication and analytical skills,
- utilize innovative instructional delivery systems that reach wider audiences more economically with more effective learning experiences,
- promote education that relates to emerging technologies and careers and includes the development and dissemination of career information and networking with science professionals and stressing scientific literacy in grades K–12.

Gladys Dillion (1977), inservice director of the Flint (Michigan) Community Schools, contends that using community resources has the following effects:

- Gives learning in school closer relations with actual life situations, needs, and problems.
- Develops interest in school work that impels (rather than compels) children to come to school.
- Clarifies teaching and learning by making use of concrete, firsthand illustrations and demonstrations.

- Provides experience in planning, problem solving, and critical thinking.
- Develops skills of observing, asking questions, searching for information, and seeking relationships.
- Places knowledge and skill in the context of functional learning: learning to use by doing.
- Brings related content areas and skills together and uses them to meet problems and situations.
- Provides common learning and common adjustment to problems and differences in needs, abilities, and interests.
- Emphasizes achieving good human relations and practicing them.
- Increases opportunities for understanding and practicing the responsibilities of community citizenship.

School communities can become laboratories that assist with effective and relevant teaching. Our community resources can also help us to involve parents. Safran (1974) gives examples that directly relate to teachers. Community involvement:

- enables teachers to draw on supplemental and often unique adult resources,
- provides teachers with additional information about the children they teach,
- encourages teachers to recognize other perceptions of what they do,
- permits teachers to understand more about the community their school serves,
- makes possible political alliances between teachers as workers and parents as consumers to contend with school bureaucracies.

WHAT RESOURCES ARE AVAILABLE?

Human Resources

A readily available and often overlooked resource is your colleagues. Using colleagues as resource persons for instructional guidance and assistance enables us to broaden educational activities and to foster cooperation.

Your colleagues—other classroom teachers, the principal, the school nurse, the resource teacher, the librarian—are all potential sources of assistance. The experienced teacher who is willing to share activities, materials, and support is a natural aide. Teachers in another school or grade level may be able to suggest teaching activities and loan equipment or share materials. Upper-grade-level students are also sources of help because they may be available to provide a demonstration or to serve as a teaching assistant or tutor.

Community volunteers can provide enriching services. Communities may contain engineers, professors, sewage treatment personnel, medical professionals, computer specialists, and mechanics who are interested in education. In addition, parents may offer suggestions. Corporations and institutions may have an educational officer who can assist by providing names of employees who are willing to volunteer their time and talent to assist within the schools. Consider

Volunteers can enrich your science teaching and help children learn to appreciate the community.

contacting retirement groups, chambers of commerce, local women's clubs, local, state, or national agencies, or even the Yellow Pages. Their members are experienced and may have time to volunteer.

A volunteer can enable you to devote more time to planning, diagnosing the individual needs of students, and prescribing learning activities for these needs. Volunteers may offer other benefits. They extend the number of people available to help the teacher and often bring skills that professional educators do not have, so the educational process maximizes opportunities for all students. Perhaps most important are the positive effects that volunteering can have on the volunteers themselves, and the public relations value is certainly important (Hager-Shoeny & Galbreath, 1982).

Table 8.1 lists vocations that volunteers might have. Look to individuals such as these to help with your school program.

Not all volunteers feel confident to make a presentation to a classroom on their particular area of interest. They may prefer instead to be involved in one or more of the following ways:

- demonstrating scientific concepts
- serving as a mentor
- tutoring
- providing science fair project assistance

⬥ **TABLE 8.1   Science Classroom Volunteers**

Area of Science	*Volunteer*
Animals	Zoologist, entomologist, microbiologist, zookeeper, veterinarian, beekeeper, marine biologist, paleontologist, cytologist, animal trainer, physician, forest ranger, physiologist, chemist, ecologist, neurobiologist, wildlife manager, farmer, rancher, geneticist, anatomist, mammalogist, limnologist, nurse, dietitian, x-ray technician, pharmacologist, forensic specialist, pharmacist
Plants	Botanist, paleobotanist, agronomist, horticulturist, farmer, forest manager, chemist, ecologist, geneticist, paleontologist, nutritionist, landscape architect, soil pathologist, soil scientist conservation officer, park ranger, agricultural extension agent
Weather	Meteorologist, ecologist, agronomist, TV weather forecaster, airport flight controller, geologist, oceanographer, climatologist, fisherman, boat captain, farmer, pilot, environmentalist, soil and water conservation agent
Physical and chemical properties	Chemist, biochemist, pharmacologist, architect, inventor, mechanic, carpenter, molecular biologist, physicist, ecologist, musical instrument maker, musician, toxicologist, metallurgist, geologist, photographer, builder, police lab forensic criminologist, materials scientist, technician, water company technician, engineers: chemical, textile, industrial, cosmetics developer, gemologist, acoustical engineer, optical engineer, mechanical engineer, civil engineer, building inspector, potter, nuclear engineer, agricultural engineer, ceramic engineer
Electricity	Physicist, geologist, computer hardware/software designer, electrician, radar technician, amateur radio operator, designer, industrial engineer, electrical engineer, telephone system technician, thermal engineer, mechanical engineer, electronic engineer, electrical inspector, inventor, radio/TV engineer
Earth and space science	Astronomer, geologist, paleontologist, pilot, astronaut, geographer, cartographer, ecologist, physicist, biologist, chemist, surveyor, geotechnical tester, aerial photographer, volcanologist, seismologist, oceanographer, soil scientist, aeronautical engineer, aviation engineer, construction engineer, civil engineer
Behavioral and social science	Animal psychologist, clinical psychologist, marketing professional, business manager, psychiatrist, sociologist, anthropologist, city planner, applied economist, school psychologist, historian, archaeologist, geographer, pollster, market research analyst, demographer, statistician

Source: North Carolina Museum of Life and Science, *Science in the Classroom,* as cited by Triangle Coalition for Science and Technology Education, *A Guide for Planning a Volunteer Program for Science, Mathematics, and Technology Education* (College Park, MD: Triangle Coalition, 1992), p. 59.

- providing career choice assistance
- reviewing school safety equipment
- assisting in science competition instruction
- demonstrating societal and technological applications of content
- furnishing specialized equipment
- assisting in speakers' bureaus

- spearheading public awareness campaigns
- encouraging projects for girls and minorities
- arranging field trips
- maintaining equipment
- assisting with special demonstrations

The tips in Table 8.2 may help volunteers feel comfortable in their roles. Volunteers may not always be aware of the relevance of their knowledge and skills to elementary students; explain the benefits the students will receive from his or her assistance. The following advice was adapted from list of suggestions for volunteers prepared by the Lane County Juvenile Department in Eugene, Oregon (Hager-Schoeny & Galbreath, 1982):

- Invite volunteers to serve as partners.
- Clearly define the differences in the tasks and roles of employees and volunteers.

TABLE 8.2   Tips for Teachers Working with Volunteers

1. Take time to talk with the volunteer outside the classroom, explaining class procedures, schedules, expectations, and objectives.
2. Prepare the volunteer with specifics about the assignment, where materials can be found, and what the learning objectives are.
3. Make the volunteer comfortable by explaining the obvious support facilities: where to place personal items, find a rest room, and get a cup of coffee.
4. Keep channels of communication open with the volunteer. Exchange a home number if appropriate and convenient. Plan and follow the schedule developed for the volunteer. Inform the volunteer of a schedule change as soon as possible. Keep in mind that volunteers have additional responsibilities and cannot be expected to wait for an assignment or materials preparation and that their responsibilities may prevent them from fulfilling their commitment. You will need to be understanding if this occurs.
5. Keep a special folder for regular volunteers with current assignments.
6. Inform volunteers about the students' level of ability, special problems, and students who need assistance.
7. Encourage your volunteer to sign in and to wear a name tag. Other faculty members and administrators will want to acknowledge a volunteer in the building.
8. Let every volunteer know how much you and the class appreciate the help. A thank-you note goes a long way toward making the experience a rewarding one for a volunteer.
9. Evaluate the volunteer encounter. Consider the specific request, the background of the volunteer, and the constraints of the situation.

Source: Project Technology Engineering Applications of Mathematics and Science, Yakima Valley/Tri-Cities MESA, *Tips for Teachers Working with Volunteers,* as cited by Triangle Coalition for Science and Technology Education, *A Guide for Planning a Volunteer Program for Science, Mathematics, and Technology Education* (College Park, MD: Triangle Coalition, 1992), p. 54.

Give volunteers tips that will help them be successful with your students.

- Screen volunteers and accept only the ones who can contribute. Check references and interview each candidate as you would a prospective employee.
- Require a specific commitment of time and resources from volunteers.
- Provide an orientation program to acquaint volunteers with their functions.
- Provide supervision.
- Make assignments based on the volunteer's skills, knowledge, interests, capacity to learn, time available, and resources.

For additional information on using volunteers in the classroom, contact the Triangle Coalition for Science and Technology Education (Appendix D). This organization's *A Guide for Planning a Volunteer Program for Science, Mathematics and Technology Education* (1992) includes tips for volunteers, volunteer applications, a community organizational needs assessment, tips on making presentations for volunteers, and other related topics. Another source of information on orientation, recruitment, recruitment techniques, volunteer recognition, and volunteer evaluation is *Community Involvement for Classroom Teachers* by Donna L. Hager-Schoeny et al. (1982).

Print Resources

Professional organizations can provide a richly varied form of support. The leading national organization in K–college science education is the National

Science Teachers Association (NSTA). With headquarters in Washington, D.C., it provides services to nearly 50,000 members in the United States and Canada. NSTA activities include professional conventions, publications and journals, and science education position statements.

NSTA holds three regional conventions each fall and an annual national convention in early spring. NSTA's national conferences reach more than 18,000 science educators, perhaps the largest gathering of science educators in the world. The organization also produces journals appropriate for different grade levels: *Science and Children* for the elementary grades, *Science Scope* for middle schools, and *The Science Teacher* for secondary schools. NSTA has developed the following policy papers that might be useful resources:

- *Science and Technology Education for the 21st Century*
- *Science Competitions*
- *Environmental Education and the Use of Natural Resources in Science Teaching*
- *Liability of Teachers for Laboratory Safety and Field Trips*
- *Use of the Metric System*
- *Women in Science Education*
- *Energy Education*
- *Code of Practice of Animals in Schools*
- *Substance Use/Abuse Information*
- *Science for the Handicapped*
- *Preschool and Elementary Level Science Education*

Membership applications, samples of publications, copies of the policy position statements, and an annual catalog of resources and materials can be obtained through the NSTA national headquarters located at 1840 Wilson Boulevard, Arlington, Virginia 22201-3000; (703) 243-7100; S&C@NSTA.org.

NSTA has chapters and affiliated groups in most states. The activities of the state organizations, which vary by state, are an excellent resource. Membership costs are usually very low, and state groups provide a mechanism for building professional contacts and learning from colleagues.

For other organizations that provide services to teachers, see Appendixes D and E.

In addition to professional organizations, state and federal agencies provide educational services. County agricultural extension services give information on soils, insects, and related information. These services are directly connected with universities and will be of assistance in locating additional information. The U.S. Department of Agriculture has many initiatives directed at improving K–12 science education through both nontraditional areas such as 4-H and traditional resource curriculum offerings. State land management or natural resources departments usually have education directors who provide assistance and training to teachers and recommend such classroom volunteers as geologists, conservationists, and agronomists. To contact personnel in these agencies, consult the telephone book for your county seat or state capital.

The National Aeronautics and Space Administration (NASA) has an extensive education infrastructure throughout the country, with regional centers offering educational resources that include lesson plans and extensive slide, photo, and video libraries. Teacher workshops are provided through the agency. NASA also provides a mobile display bus for hands-on activities for both students and teachers. A listing of the centers can be found in Appendix F.

State departments of education are also a source for information or print resources. States organize their agencies differently, but most have at least one science consultant. Many states are organized around regional centers that provide inservice, equipment, and assistance to classroom teachers. Write to your state science consultant for specific information. Addresses for all state and territorial education agencies can be found in Appendix C.

Microcomputer Applications

Modern technology can strengthen the understanding of concepts if we recognize the experiences the students bring to us and use the technology to clarify any misconceptions and stimulate proper concept formation (Nickerson, 1995). Simply sitting students in front of a computer will not bring about conceptual understanding. Choosing software that promotes active mental processing and student discoveries is vital and must ensure for students a state of mindfulness while they interact with the technology and motivate and engage the students to enable them to form appropriate conceptualizations. Computer software, however, is no substitute for active teaching and learning.

It is important to select software that promotes thinking.

There is software that simply *tells* that objects are different, and there is software that assists the student in understanding *how* objects are different (Wiser, 1995). Some software may stimulate science perceptions; however, truly engaging software extends student senses so that explanatory conceptions may be formed. Technology can be used to create dynamic and interactive representations for phenomena that extend far beyond what is possible in the typical science laboratory environment.

Utilizing a microcomputer in a science classroom may appear to be in direct conflict with a constructivist approach to science teaching. When appropriately applied, however, it can be used to construct an understanding of complex concepts. There are three levels to computer-based instruction and several types of software that can be used at the different levels (see Figure 8.1).

Level I. In the first level, microcomputer software applications can be used to observe scientific phenomena directly. The software can provide a concrete example of an object, provide facts, or recall basic information. Typical drill and practice software falls within the simplest use of a microcomputer. Rarely is there a mindfulness associated with this type of computer-assisted instruction (Berger et. al., 1994).

Computer-managed instruction may also fall within the first level of computer use. This occurs when the computer is used to evaluate student performance, keep records, or guide students to resources. Multiple software applications exist that are designed to provide scientific information. Typical kinds of information accessed in this way include information on oceans, rain forests, space, and plant and animal life. The information may come on a computer disk, a CD-ROM disk, or even laser disk. Encyclopedias and atlases—items that use a large amount of computer memory to run—are typically available on a CD-ROM or laser disc.

Level II. The second level of microcomputer use in the classroom takes the facts found through Level I uses, assists in conceptualization, and provides concept expansion. Hypermedia software helps teachers to fit any concept being explored to the needs of the classroom. *Hypercard* or *HyperStudio* authoring software has text and graphic capabilities and can be used by a teacher to create stacks of cards. Students can access these cards as a part of a learning cycle's exploration. *Toolbook* is another program that teachers can use to organize still and animated images into an interactive program for student use.

Some software can simulate an experiment. These virtual experiences can lead to conceptual understanding as suggested in Level II. A simulation may be a pictorial, verbal, numerical, or graphical representation of reality. Simulations that integrate all four forms of representation appear to offer the best opportunity to stimulate conceptual change. *The Voyages of Mimi I and II* (Bank Street College of Education, 1994, 1995) are popular programs that effectively integrate all four representations. This interactive program, designed primarily for

FIGURE 8.1   Computer-Based-Education Levels and Software Types

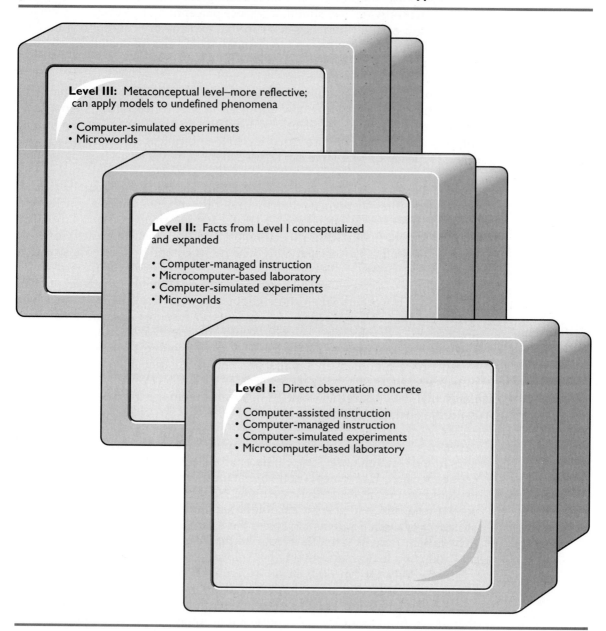

Level III: Metaconceptual level–more reflective; can apply models to undefined phenomena

• Computer-simulated experiments
• Microworlds

Level II: Facts from Level I conceptualized and expanded

• Computer-managed instruction
• Microcomputer-based laboratory
• Computer-simulated experiments
• Microworlds

Level I: Direct observation concrete

• Computer-assisted instruction
• Computer-managed instruction
• Computer-simulated experiments
• Microcomputer-based laboratory

middle school students, makes use of video, print, and computer software to engage students in an interdisciplinary unit centered around the real adventures of the explorer ship *Mimi*.

Microcomputer-based laboratories can effectively integrate numerical and graphical data as quickly as a probe attached to the computer can record it. Using sensors and timing devices attached to a microcomputer, students can do such things as monitor heart rate, detect strength and direction of external forces, determine the strength of magnetic fields, record temperature, record pH of liquids, measure amplitudes of audio sources, sense and record humidity changes, imitate the spectral response of the human eye, sense and record changes in pressure, and use an ultrasonic motion detector to measure distance, velocity, and acceleration (Arbor Scientific, 1996).

Operation: Frog (Goldhammer & Isenberg, 1984) is a simulation that offers students the opportunity to dissect a frog without having one in the classroom. However, since all the screens are predetermined, it can never model an unexpected situation. This type of simulation is attribute mapped. While it may lead to student integration of concepts from isolated facts, it will not allow the student to create models of unidentified phenomena (Snir, Smith, & Grosslight, 1995). Hence, such a computer simulation may be an insufficient substitute for a certain level of dissection.

Level III.   Level III uses software designed to simulate experiments in which variables may be manipulated and extended beyond ordinary phenomena. At this level, computer models can be created that lead to explorations of unidentified phenomena. This metaconceptual level is one whereby a student uses models to explain reality, reflects on those models, and then suggests the manipulation of variables that project far beyond what can be created in the laboratory. This type of software is *structure mapped*. This means that a code is built into the software that allows it to search for laws that govern the behavior of objects (Snir, Smith, & Grosslight, 1995). One such computer application is *Sir Isaac Newton's Games* (Schwartz, 1985, 1995). This software has the capability of removing the abstraction of friction so that a student can perceive the motion of an object in a friction-free environment. Removing friction helps a student to arrive at a more complete understanding of Newton's laws of motion, phenomena that cannot be accurately observed or understood in the friction-filled environment of a typical school laboratory.

Microworlds are microcomputer-based laboratory experiences that simulate real-world phenomena. Students can explore undefined phenomena when given proper guidance and intervention by the teacher. Students can be given "what-if" predictive situations in order to evaluate and reflect on scientific theories, pose problems that can be solved only through computer-enhanced simulations, and construct the meaning of concepts based on computer-simulated evidence. A truly constructivist science educator can bring the use of microcomputers to their highest level of application by using microworld environments to give students opportunities to explore and discover scientific theories by using problem-solving strategies to ask: "What is the real problem?" "How do we know it's a problem?" "How can we go about solving the problem?" Microworlds are a fairly new software application; many are still in the prototype stage. We recommend that you seek out software of this nature; it truly embodies the spirit of constructivism in its application.

Computer-based education has been found to increase learning efficiency (expressed as the ratio of amount of learning to the time taken to learn); produce significant positive effects on student science achievement; help students acquire cognitive skills, which can be transferred to other subject areas; and encourage positive student attitudes toward computers and the subject matter taught (Berger et al., 1994; Gorodetsky, Fisher, & Wyman, 1994). The success of any computer application is dependent on the skills of the teacher. When carefully integrated into the science learning cycle (Chapter 9), computers can be used to promote conceptual change and to enhance concept attainment.

Accessing and Sharing Information Through Telecommunications Networks

Microworld software applications can engage students at the highest level of microcomputer use although they are only a simulation. Telecommunications networks enable us to expand the boundaries of the classroom walls and to create a virtual classroom with schools across the globe. A network provides increased opportunities for teachers to collaborate with other educators over matters of daily instruction or educational reform. Teachers have greater access to additional information, knowledge, and points of view by eliminating barriers of time and place. Networkers may discuss issues and access varied resources, including other teachers and resource agencies. A network encourages the development of professional skills: deliberation, collegial consensus building, and development and sharing of ideas related to the profession of teaching.

There are numerous computer-linked projects open to teachers with real-world applications. The national *Pill Bug Project* encouraged students to collect data about the common pill bug, experiment using known activities and those created by the students, and share the data nationwide. The *Antarctica Project* used videotapes to observe research scientists in the Antarctic and provided computer access for students to send questions to the scientists about their research. The scientists replied and posed questions to the students as well.

Parks as Classrooms, a more recent interactive computer-based project funded primarily by the National Park Service, is designed to promote greater understanding and appreciation of the natural and cultural heritage of the United States and to develop sustainable partnerships among parks, schools, and communities. Through computer links, data are collected to monitor air,

Networks help you and your students to have greater access to ideas.

water, and land resources on park lands. The computers are also used to simulate landform changes and cycles in populations within the parks (CPB, 1995).

The National Geographic Society offers *Kids Network,* a combination of software designed to meet curricular needs, telecommunications access to classrooms around the world, teacher guides and lesson plans, hot-line support, and access to unit scientists (NGS, 1995). There are various problem-based links to join. The introductory link introduces students to scientific research methods; another deals with what is in water; others allow students to explore phenomena such as solar energy, food, acid rain, trash, and weather.

While national projects can be accessed and joined, having an Internet address readily accessible within the classroom can permit educators to start their own science research projects and to invite schools throughout the nation to join the research effort. Collaborative projects can be designed to explore bodies of water, landfills, groundwater movement, seasonal changes per latitude, or any local problem or issue that may have global impact. The impact of projects like these is best stated by one teacher who responded to the question, "What are your most compelling reasons for integrating technology into the curriculum?" as posed by Randy Knuth over the Internet in September 1995:

> I think we should go beyond integration into the classroom and create a new context for learning that maximizes the learning potential of technology and

telecommunications. From my perspective . . . the reason is relevancy. We can extend learning beyond the walls of the classroom . . . to do real stuff with real people for compelling reasons . . . with real results that have real significance. Students are not dumb . . . they know when it matters and when it is simply an exercise. . . . Connect them to their communities through technology! And give them economic viability! (Knuth, 1995)

Telecommunication networks can be used as a means to access resources as described in this chapter's opening scenario. Networks remove teacher isolation. Local and statewide networks may supply a site where teachers can share lessons they created to teach science more effectively. The Eisenhower National Clearinghouse for Mathematics and Science Education is a national database that provides lessons and lists of resources and identifies which print, video, or computer software is available to teach science or mathematics. You may log onto this database by using a toll-free number (1-800-362-4448) and enter as a guest. Once into the database, you will receive prompts on how to register and access information.

Two other national databases provide science-related resources. *Inter-Disciplinary Education Access (IDEA)* is a menu-driven telecommunication network designed to increase communication between teachers and National Park rangers, to share educational resources, and to find out about National Park Service programs. IDEA is available free of charge and can be reached through the Internet (telnet idea.uml.edu). *EE Toolbox* is a collection of publications for K–12 educators who conduct environmental education inservice programs. This network is designed to help teachers help students become stewards of the land. Teachers are trained in the use of *EE Toolbox* by the National Consortium for Environmental Education and Training (NCEET). Information on NCEET materials and EE resources is available through the Internet via gopher and World Wide Web (WWW) sites. The EE-link address is: eelink@nceet.snre.umich.edu. To access WWW site, use: http://www.nceet.snre.umich.edu.

No matter what network is used to acquire science resources, teachers should critically review electronically accessed lesson plans. Just because it was found electronically does not necessarily mean it is a worthwhile task. Table 8.3 suggests evaluation criteria for judging the worthiness of electronically accessed lessons.

Telecommunication networks are transporting more than graphics and text information. Fiber optic communication networks have facilitated the transportation of voice, video, and data. Schools throughout the nation are linking together to share in scientific explorations with full motion video and voice interface. Linkages like these promote greater student interaction and discussion of concepts. Providing students with as many opportunities as possible to articulate their understanding of concepts will promote greater conceptual construction and retention. Advancing technologies offer students opportunities on an ever-increasing basis.

⯅ **TABLE 8.3   Is This a Worthy Task?**

Is the task based on sound and significant content?

- Identify the concepts and/or skills.
- Is the content accurate?

Is the task based on knowledge of students' understandings, interests, experiences, and the range of ways that diverse students learn?

- Identify why the task might appeal to your students.

In your opinion to what extent would the task:

• engage students' intellect?	4 a lot	3	2	1	0 not at all
• actively involve students?	4 a lot	3	2	1	0 not at all
• develop students' understandings and skills?	4 a lot	3	2	1	0 not at all
• stimulate students to make connections to other disciplines?	4 a lot	3	2	1	0 not at all
• stimulate students to make connections to the real world?	4 a lot	3	2	1	0 not at all
• call for problem formation, problem solving, and reasoning?	4 a lot	3	2	1	0 not at all
• promote communication/interaction among students?	4 a lot	3	2	1	0 not at all

CHAPTER SUMMARY

Sometime in the future, you and your students may pick up a newspaper and read a headline like "Genetic Engineering Unravels the Aging Process" or "Ozone Hole Increases." The stories following these headlines will be important to both you and your students. They will deal with important quality-of-life issues that you, as citizens, may need to form an opinion or make a decision concerning your future. Being able to understand the consequences of your choices is important to you and to your students.

As a teacher, you will need to ask yourself if you have done your best to provide your students with the skills they need to make these same future decisions. Scientific and technological knowledge is changing so rapidly that it is becoming more difficult to prepare students for this complicated task. Textbooks cannot keep pace with the new discoveries in science; however, you as a classroom teacher can supplement your textbook and your program with experiences and opportunities that are not available through regular textbook and media materials.

Stimulate learning by serving as the bridge between the resources that are relevant and available to you and the students in your classroom. The effective use of a volunteer or a network-based project may bring the world beyond the classroom inside to your students. An alliance with a business may provide the expertise and equipment needed for laboratory studies in a science learning center, and a telecommunications network may yield current and timely reform information. Appropriate choices of microcomputer software will enrich your students' experiences and stimulate further conceptualization.

Your use of resources is limited only by your imagination and energy. They can provide learning opportunities that stimulate your students and provide an atmosphere of scientific interest and inquiry in your students. Science can be fun, and resources can be the toys.

DISCUSSION QUESTIONS AND PROJECTS

1. Brainstorm resources not mentioned in this chapter that are useful in elementary science instruction. How can you enhance your instructional methods by including resources in your teaching plans?

2. Brainstorm ideas related to the development of a school resource file and ways to ensure it is useful and current.

3. Compose a list of supplemental resource curricula that you would like to include in your lesson plans on three different topics. Compare your list with that of two or more classmates; combine the three lists to keep for future reference.

4. Locate three hands-on resources not mentioned in this chapter that have the potential to be used within an elementary classroom for science instruction. Define the planned use, and identify specific goals and objectives that would be met by the use of these resources.

5. Identify one resource each that will enhance a lesson in environmental education, electricity, digestion, or plate tectonics, and show how the resources correlate with your goals and outcomes.

6. Identify an activity from one resource curriculum that will enhance a lesson by providing experiences that will increase your students' skills in observing, questioning, classifying, measuring, and using numbers.

7. Identify three resources that are especially useful in the instruction of students with special needs. Share these resources with teachers, and ask them for a critique of the materials.

8. Research the purposes, fee structure, and service of the National Science Teachers Association, and identify publications that will be useful as you plan science lessons. Locate membership information, meeting schedules, and publications from your state or local science education organization.

9. Use the Internet to access science resource information on a topic such as weather. Identify the network used and the various forms of information available on that topic. Share the electronic address with other students in your class or a teacher.

10. Identify resources that will assist in making your classroom instruction non–gender biased. Where did you find these materials?

11. Design a microcomputer-based project that can be shared through a computer network across schools throughout your state that expects the students to integrate understandings of science concepts in real-world applications.

12. Choose a science concept. Identify at least three pieces of science software that will promote greater concept attainment. Identify if the software is considered drill and practice, a tutorial, a simulation, or a microworld application.

ADDITIONAL READINGS

If you are interested in learning more about the use or source of resources raised in this chapter, consider the following sources.

Ellen Doris, *Doing What Scientists Do: Children Learn to Investigate Their World* (Portsmouth, NH: Heinemann, 1991). This easy-to-read and informative book provides insights into creating an environment for science in the classroom in addition to discussing and interpreting children's work.

David L. Drotar, *Learn and Discover: Fun Science* (New York: Creative Child Press, 1988). An inexpensive coloring book–like publication that serves as an excellent source of easy, inexpensive demonstrations for teacher use in the classroom.

Beau Fly Jones, Gilbert Valdez, Jeri Nowakowski, and Claudette Rasmussen, *Plugging In: Choosing and Using Educational Technology* (Oak Brook, IL: North Central Regional Laboratory, 1995). This publication provides educators with the tools they need to make decisions about choosing effective technology resources that will fit in with school district goals for technology.

T. K. Leim, *Invitation to Science Inquiry* (Lexington, MA: Science Inquiry Enterprises, 1990). This book provides hands-on activities for use in the classroom.

Resources Center of the Smithsonian Institution and the National Academy of Science, *Science for Children: Resources for Teachers* (Washington, DC: National Academy Press, 1988). This document contains a comprehensive listing of curriculum materials, supplementary resources, and sources of information and assistance.

Science and Children (Washington, DC: National Science Teachers Association). This periodical provides information on content, teaching practices, educational research, and professional activities of elementary school science.

Science Scope (Washington, DC: National Science Teachers Association). This periodical provides information on content, teaching practices, educational research, and professional activities related to middle school science.

Barbara S. Spector, *Community Resources for Meaningful Learning* (Dubuque, IA: Kendall Hunt Publishing Company, 1988). This is one of many fine resource books available that delves into the use of community resources for classroom practices. It examines both traditional and nontraditional uses of community resources.

Sara Stein, *The Science Book* (New York: Workman Publishing, 1980). Provides knowledge in the areas of Outsides (animals in the home), Insides (observations on the inside of plants and animals), and Invisibles (things too small to be seen).

Marvin N. Tolman, *Earth Science Activities for Grades K–8* (West Nyack, NY: Parker Publishing Company, 1996). A collection of 160 stimulating hands-on experiences to develop students' thinking and reasoning skills along with important earth science concepts and facts.

———. *Life Science Activities for Grades K–8* (West Nyack, NY: Parker Publishing Company, 1996). A collection of 140 stimulating hands-on experiences to develop students' thinking and reasoning skills along with important science concepts and facts.

———. *Physical Science Activities for Grades K–8* (West Nyack, NY: Parker Publishing Company, 1996). A collection of 160 stimulating hands-on experiences to develop students' thinking and reasoning skills along with important physical science concepts and facts.

CHAPTER OUTLINE

CHAPTER 9

What Teaching Methods Help Learners to Construct Meaning?

Mrs. McDonald has loved science since she was very young. She communicates this love to her students through her enthusiasm for teaching science. Her third-grade classroom is an active place to learn. A visitor walking into her room sees no neat rows of student desks; rather, the desks face each other in groups of four. The walls are covered with brightly colored posters of the Young Astronauts Program. The aquariums are located along the back wall, and a gerbil's cage sits near the window.

Today the students are actively involved in making observations. It takes a moment to determine what it is that they are observing, since their heads are pressed closely together in a tight group.

"One, two, three, four, five. There are five crickets."

"No. I counted six. There's one hiding behind the stick."

"Six," says Johnny as he records the number on his worksheet.

"For the past few days we've been observing our terrarium," Mrs. McDonald says. "Can anyone tell me what the plants and animals in our terrarium need to grow?"

"Light."

"Water."

"Air."

"Very good," replies Mrs. McDonald. "Then we added some crickets to the terrariums. You have had a chance to watch the crickets for a couple of days. Today I have something new to add to your terrariums." The children murmur excitedly as Mrs. McDonald reaches into a paper bag and removes a clear plastic bag containing a chameleon.

"What's that?"

"It looks like a lizard."

"We have those in our backyard."

"Does anyone know what I have in this bag?" asks Mrs. McDonald. Several hands are raised. "Brenda."

"It's a chameleon."

"That's right. What do you know about chameleons?"

"They can change colors."

"They eat insects."

"Those are good ideas. I want each group to add a chameleon to your terrarium and observe the chameleon carefully." Mrs. McDonald moves to each group to distribute a plastic bag containing a chameleon.

"How do we get it out?" Mary asks her group.

"Just reach in and grab it."

"Don't squeeze too hard. You'll hurt it!"

After some hesitancy, Peter puts a chameleon into his group's terrarium. At first the chameleon stands still, moving its head from side to side to survey the area. Slowly it begins to move about the terrarium as the children watch, spellbound. Suddenly the chameleon lurches forward and grabs one of the crickets in its jaws.

"Mrs. McDonald! Mrs. McDonald! The chameleon ate one of the crickets."

"Oh, yech!"

"Now there are only five crickets," says Johnny, erasing his previous answer and recording the new number.

After giving the students time to observe the chameleons and the crickets, Mrs. McDonald tells them to return the terrariums to the shelf and requests their attention.

"I would like to teach you two new words," she says, writing the words *predator* and *prey* on the chalkboard. "This word is *predator*. Can you all say that with me?"

"Predator," the class echoes.

"And this word is *prey*. Can you all say that with me?"

"Prey," they respond.

"A predator is an animal that eats another animal. Can you think of any examples of predators?"

"The chameleon."

"A lion."

"A hawk."

"Yes, those are all good examples. Prey is an animal that is eaten by a predator. Can you think of any examples of prey?"

"A cricket."

"A mouse."

"A small fish."

"Yes, those are all good examples of prey. Today at recess, we are going to play a game where some of you will be field mice and some of you will be hawks. It's called the Predator-Prey Game." ◆

INTRODUCTION

Mrs. McDonald's method of teaching supports the new expectations for middle and elementary science (Rakow, 1986, pp. 8–11). She shares control, responsibility, and decision making in her classroom, and she uses the science textbook as a guide. Students learn by inquiring and by constructing meaning from those experiences called discoveries. Students read the textbook after they have acquired direct experiences with the science topics as one type of reinforcement for constructed understanding. Mrs. McDonald's approach involves the students in doing science; her classroom encourages cooperation.

What is the best way to teach science in the elementary school? As is often the case, the answer is not so simple as selecting a single method for all occasions. Yet effective teachers do have a repertoire of methods they can draw on for maximum effect and to fit their preferred teaching styles and student learning styles. To help you expand your repertoire, the purposes of this chapter are to

1. encourage you to explore several constructivist teaching methods that use inquiry to promote student discovery and concept constructions,
2. describe and provide examples of teaching methods that promote student cooperation,
3. recommend effective constructivist techniques.

WHAT ARE INQUIRY AND DISCOVERY?

An understanding of inquiry and discovery is essential to promoting student discovery and concept construction.

Inquiry

Those who *inquire* exert "an effort to discover something new to the inquirer— though not necessarily new to the world" (Birnie & Ryan, 1984, p. 31). Children are able to inquire when they are given hands-on learning opportunities, appropriate materials to manipulate, puzzling circumstances or problems for motivation, enough structure to help them focus or maintain a productive direction, and enough freedom to compare ideas and make personal learning discoveries. Other definitions may include:

- the process of investigating a problem,
- a search for truth or knowledge that requires thinking critically,

Inquiry is a means to an end—the discovery.

- making observations, asking questions, performing experiments, and stating conclusions,
- thinking creatively and using intuition (Birnie & Ryan, 1984).

Discovery

Thinking to obtain new knowledge or to solve a problem is the single element that unites the different inquiry methods. If a child is able to "acquire a new fact, concept, principle, or solution through the inquiry, the student is making a discovery" (Birnie & Ryan, 1984, p. 31). Therefore, the cognitive, affective, and psychomotor processes the child uses become the inquiry. The end result of those processes becomes the *discovery*—the substance of what is learned, what the learner constructs in the mind.

What procedures or approaches can teachers use to help children follow constructivist learning processes? Effective methods include inquiry principles, such as: the science learning cycle, Suchman's inquiry, a scientific inquiry method, playful discovery, and inquiry with children's questions. All of these methods recognize the importance of direct experience and promote it for children.

The Importance of Experience

Traditional textbook-based science programs use an inform-verify-practice approach to learning. The teacher informs or tells the students what they are to learn, the students verify that what they have been told is true, and then they practice what they have been given. This teaching and learning approach is called *teacher-centered exposition*. Experimental studies have shown that this type of learning approach in science is usually less effective than experiential learning methods, in which the instruction is more student centered and oriented toward making discoveries. Inquiry as a learning process promotes higher levels of science achievement and develops process skills and attitudes (Shymansky, Kyle, & Allport, 1982; Bredderman, 1982). Inquiry science teaching methods pay useful dividends. For example, the methods have been found to help Spanish-speaking children learn English and develop oral communication skills (Rodriguez & Bethel, 1983). They also help children who have learning disabilities that affect their reading to learn to become better readers (Windram, 1988).

CONSTRUCTIVIST SCIENCE TEACHING METHODS

Constructivist science teaching methods include science learning cycle, scientific experimental methods, Suchman's Inquiry, and playful science.

The Science Learning Cycle

A learning cycle is a method for planning lessons, teaching, learning, and developing curricula. This teaching method was originally designed for the SCIS curriculum and has produced the largest achievement gains of the experimental elementary science programs of the 1960s (see Chapter 7). These increases are largely a result of the learning cycle as an inquiry teaching and learning method.

In science, a learning cycle is a way of thinking and acting that is consistent with how pupils learn. It provides an excellent approach for planning effective science instruction. The science learning cycle originally consisted of three phases: exploration, concept invention, and application. With today's goals emphasizing new dimensions of science and accountability, we recommend a 4-E learning cycle: exploration, explanation, expansion, and evaluation. Each phase, when followed in sequence (see Figure 9.1), has sound theoretical support from the cognitive development theory of Jean Piaget (Renner & Marek, 1988) and applies constructivist learning procedures (see Chapter 2).

Phase One: Exploration.   The exploration phase is student centered, stimulates learner mental disequilibrium, and fosters mental assimilation. (You might review the section in Chapter 2 devoted to Jean Piaget if these ideas are unclear.) The teacher is responsible for giving students sufficient directions and materials that interact in ways that are related to the concept. The teacher's directions *must not tell* students what they should learn and *must not explain* the concept. The teacher's role is to:

◆ FIGURE 9.1   The 4-E Science Learning Cycle

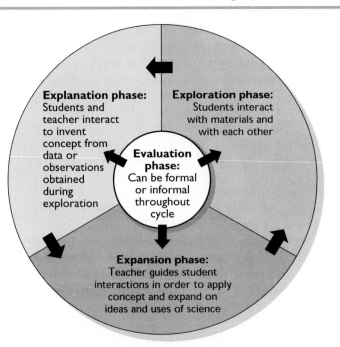

Explanation phase: Students and teacher interact to invent concept from data or observations obtained during exploration

Exploration phase: Students interact with materials and with each other

Evaluation phase: Can be formal or informal throughout cycle

Expansion phase: Teacher guides student interactions in order to apply concept and expand on ideas and uses of science

Source: Adapted from a figure by Charles Barman, "The Learning Cycle: Making It Work," *Science Scope* (February 1989) 28–31.

- answer students' questions,
- ask questions to guide student observations and to cause students to engage in science processes or thinking skills (see Figure 9.2),
- give hints and cues to keep the exploration going.

Students are responsible for exploring the materials and for gathering and recording their own information. Teachers rely on questioning skills such as those shown in Figure 9.2 to guide learning.

Children must have concrete materials and experiences too if they are to construct science concepts for themselves. Use these guiding questions to help you begin your planning process:

- What is the precise concept the students will explore?
- What activities must the children do to become familiar with the concept?
- What kinds of observations or records should the children keep?
- What kinds of instructions will the children need? How can I give the instructions without telling the concept?

FIGURE 9.2   Using Questions During a Learning Cycle

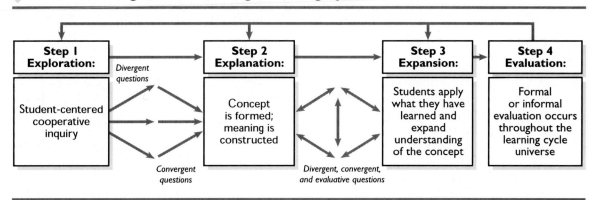

This last question directly transforms into verbal or written instructions you will give the children. Instructions need to direct the children's activities, suggest what kinds of records they should keep, and *not tell or explain the concept.* Instructions may be stated succinctly, perhaps in the form of an objective. What questions will you ask to encourage student exploration?

Phase Two: Explanation.   The explanation phase is less student centered and provides for learner mental accommodation. The purpose of this phase is for teachers to guide student thinking so the concept of the lesson is constructed cooperatively, not merely given by the teacher. To accomplish this, the teacher selects and sets the desired class environment. The teacher asks students to give the information they have collected and helps students to process and mentally organize the information. Once the information is organized, the teacher introduces the specific language needed for the concept, much as Mrs. McDonald did *after* her students had observed and explored what happened when a new organism was introduced into their terrariums. Teachers help students to construct and attach meaning to these new science words—the concepts.

This phase helps to lead to mental accommodation, as described by Piaget's theory. Here students must focus on their primary findings from their firsthand explorations. The teacher must introduce language or concept labels to assist mental accommodation. These questions can help teachers guide students so they construct their own explanations of the concept:

• What kinds of information or findings should the students talk about?
• How can I help students summarize their findings?
• How can I guide the students and refrain from telling them what they should have found, even if their understanding is incomplete? How can I help them use their information to construct the concept correctly?

- What labels or descriptions should the students attach to the concept?
- What reasons can I give the students if they ask me why the concept is important? This question automatically leads to the next phase, expansion.

Phase Three: Expansion.   The expansion phase should be student centered as much as possible and organized to encourage group cooperation. The purpose of this phase is to help learners mentally organize the experiences they have acquired by forming connections with similar previous experiences and by discovering new applications for what they have learned. Constructed concepts must be linked to other related ideas or experiences. The purpose is to take the students' thinking beyond where it is presently. You must require students to use the language or labels of the new concept so that they add depth to their understanding. This is a proper place to help students apply what they learned by expanding examples or by providing additional exploratory experiences for stimulating students' science inquiry skills, encouraging them to investigate science-technology-society interrelationships, and for understanding the history and nature of science. (See goals in Chapter 4.) The expansion phase can automatically lead to the exploration phase of the next lesson; hence a continuing cycle for teaching and learning is established. Exhibit 9.1 shows how to do this in a sample lesson plan.

Teachers help students organize their thinking by relating what they have learned to other ideas or experiences that relate to the constructed concept. It is very important to use the language of the concept during this phase to add depth to the concept's meaning and to expand the range of the children's vocabulary. Consider these questions:

- What previous experiences have the students had that relate to the concept? How can I connect the concept to those experiences?
- What are some examples of how the concept encourages the students to see science's benefits to themselves? to help them understand the relationships among science, technology, and society? to help them develop science inquiry skills? to help them be informed about the history and nature of science?
- What questions can I ask to encourage students to discover the concept's importance? to apply the concept? to appreciate the problems it solves? to understand the problems it causes? to identify the careers influenced by it? to understand how the concept has been viewed or used throughout history?
- What new experiences are needed to apply or expand the concept?
- What is the next concept related to the present one? How can I encourage exploration of the next concept?

Phase Four: Evaluation.   The purpose of this phase is to overcome the limits of standard types of testing. Learning often occurs in small increments before larger mental leaps of insight are possible. Therefore, evaluation should be continuous, not a typical end-of-chapter or -unit approach. Several types of measures are necessary to form a wholistic evaluation of the students' learning and

Make a Sinker Float: Clay Boats

**GRADE
4–6
DISCIPLINE
Physical
Science**

Concept/statement

Buoyancy: If the upward force of the liquid is greater than the downward force of the object, the object will float because it is buoyed (lifted up or supported) by the water. This concept is called *buoyancy,* and it explains why some heavy objects, such as steel ships, will float in water.

Additional concepts that are important to expansion

Displacement, flotation, Archimedes' principle, specific gravity

Materials needed

Small tubs or buckets to hold water, small objects that will sink or float in water, modeling clay (plasticene), small uniform objects to use as cargo (weights, such as ceramic tiles or marbles) in the clay boats, a container modified like the illustration shown in phase 3 (expansion), a small container to catch the water that spills from the modified container, and a scale or balance to measure the weight of the spilled water.

➡ **Safety precautions:** Have students notify you in case of spills. Use a room with a nonslip floor surface if possible.

1. EXPLORATION

Instructions: Have the students examine the variety of objects given to them and predict whether each object will sink or float in the water. Have the students write their predictions on an organized data sheet that you provide. Use as one of the objects a lump of clay about the size of a tennis ball. Provide time for the students to test their predictions and then gather the students together to explore what their predictions reveal.

2. EXPLANATION

Concept: Buoyancy. If objects of different sizes and weights are used in the exploration phase, students will discover that heaviness is not the factor that determines whether an object will sink or float. For example, a large piece of 2-by-4-inch wood will be heavier than a glass marble or a metal washer, but it will float while the marble and washer will sink. Explain that Archimedes, a Greek philosopher, is credited with discovering that an object immersed in a liquid (water) will appear to lose some of its weight. Ask students to speculate why this seems to be. A suitable explanation may be: "If the upward force of

(continued)

EXHIBIT 9.1 A Sample Lesson Plan Based on the 4-E Science Learning Cycle

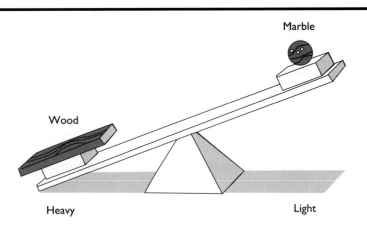

the liquid is greater than the downward force of the object, it will float because the object is buoyed (lifted up or supported) by the water." This factor is called *buoyancy*, and it explains why some heavy objects, such as steel ships, will float in water when it can be easily illustrated that steel sinks. Steel has been given a special shape (the ship) that gives it a greater volume, which helps to spread its weight across a larger amount (volume) of the water, making it possible for the buoyant upward force of the water to be greater than the downward force of the ship's weight. How might buoyancy be affected by the amount of cargo a ship carries? Why is it important to keep a ship from taking on water?

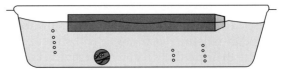

3. EXPANSION

Weigh the lump of dry clay and the smaller container to be used to catch the water spill; record the measures. Take the lump of clay and use the device as illustrated. Carefully lower the clay into the container of water and measure its weight while it is submerged. Catch the water that spills out of the container and weigh the container again; subtract the dry container weight to determine the weight of the water displaced by the sinking clay. The weight of the submerged clay should be less than the dry weight because of the upward (buoyant) force of the water. Challenge the students to find a way to change the shape of the clay so that it will float in water. Challenge them to see who can make the clay boat that will carry the largest amount of cargo before it sinks. Have students draw pictures of their boats' shapes and/or measure the size of the boats'

EXHIBIT 9.1   *(continued)*

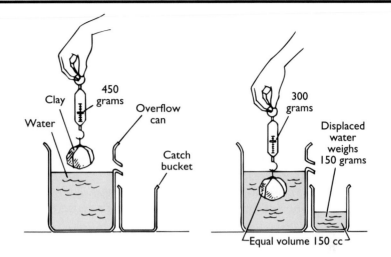

Clay
Water
450 grams
Overflow can
Catch bucket

300 grams
Displaced water weighs 150 grams
Equal volume 150 cc

bottoms. Capable students could calculate the surface area of the boats' bottoms and graph the amount of cargo carried (before sinking) as a function of area. Ask them to observe carefully what happens to make their clay boats sink and to describe later what they observe.

Science in personal and social perspectives

Ask the students why the Coast Guard requires flotation devices on boats and why these devices make it possible for a person who otherwise might sink to float. Why does the Coast Guard set passenger limits on pleasure craft?

Science and technology

Ask the students to search for other inventions that apply the buoyancy principle. Ask how these uses have had an impact on people. Examples might include floats connected to switches or valves that control pumps or appliances, seat cushions on airliners that are removable and can be used as flotation devices, channel buoys for navigation or to mark danger zones.

Science as inquiry

Ask the students to identify other examples of buoyancy in liquids and to describe differences. As examples, ask the students to redo their sink-or-float tests in denatured or isopropyl alcohol, or a mixture of alcohol and water, or water with different amounts of salt added. (This can lead to another concept and another lesson: specific gravity.)

Ask the students to explain why a submarine can sink and float, and how it is possible for a submarine or a SCUBA diver to remain at a particular depth.

Construct a Cartesian diver using a 2-liter soft drink container filled with water. Place a glass medicine dropper in the container, and put the cap on tightly. Squeeze the sides of the container, release, and watch what happens to

(*continued*)

the dropper. Why does the dropper sink and rise? What is necessary to keep the submarine dropper at a constant depth in the container?

Ask students to explain why it is easier to swim and float in salt water than in fresh water.

History and nature of science

As an expansion assignment, have the students search for pictures and examples of careers that require some knowledge of the buoyancy concept. Examples may include ship builders, navy and marine personnel, fishermen, marine salvage crews, plumbers, SCUBA divers. How have the inventions used by these changed over time?

Read Pamela Allen's *Archimedes' Bath* (1980) to the class and discuss what the author needed to know about science to write this children's book.

4. EVALUATION

- Using the ball of clay and/or Cartesian diver, the students will demonstrate and explain the concept of buoyancy.
- The students will draw a picture of what happens when their clay ball is placed in water and when its shape is changed. They will write a paragraph in their own words that explains why and how the clay floats.
- The students will demonstrate proper use of the balance when weighing the clay dry and submerged.
- The advanced students will measure and calculate the area of the clay boats and graph the maximum cargo carried as a function of the surface area of the boats.
- Students will research the buoyancy inventions used by a single career over a period of time (perhaps fifty years) and explain how different understandings of buoyancy and technical advancement influenced persons in those careers.

EXHIBIT 9.1   *(continued)*

to encourage mental construction of concepts and process skills. Evaluation can be included in each phase of the learning cycle, not just held for the end. Ask yourself:

- What appropriate learning outcomes should I expect?
- What types of hands-on evaluation techniques can the students do to demonstrate the basic skills of observation, classification, communication, measurement, prediction, and inference?
- What techniques are appropriate for students to demonstrate the integrated science process skills of identifying and controlling variables, defining oper-

ationally, forming hypotheses, experimenting, interpreting data, and forming models?

- How can I use pictures to help students demonstrate how well they can think through problems that require understanding fundamental concepts and the integration of ideas?
- What types of questions can I ask students to help them reflect and to indicate how well they recall and understand what has been learned?

Planning and Teaching Science Learning Cycle Lessons

The four phases of the learning cycle provide most of the structure for planning an effective science lesson. Once the concept that is to be learned has been identified, the learning activity can be structured to take advantage of the learning cycle. Descriptions of ways to evaluate what the children learn also can be added. For your convenience, a sample science learning cycle lesson plan is shown in Exhibit 9.1.

HOW CAN YOU USE PRINCIPLES OF SCIENTIFIC EXPERIMENTATION WHILE TEACHING?

> Scientific method is defined as the systematic pursuit of knowledge involving the recognition and formulation of a problem, the collection of data through observation and experimentation (the experiential element), the formulation of a hypothesis, and the testing and confirmation (or rejection) of that hypothesis. (Fields, 1989, p. 15)

What went through your mind as you read the definition? When and if a scientific method was taught to you, it was probably taught in a high school science class separately from actually doing science. Some scientists and educators object to the notion of a scientific method and, justifiably, cite that all scientists do not think or investigate in such a linear way. Often a method is memorized as a series of steps like these:

Step 1: Define the problem.

Step 2: Find out what is already known about the problem.

Step 3: Form a hypothesis or educated guess.

Step 4: Conduct an experiment to test the hypothesis.

Step 5: Use the results to reach a conclusion.

Unfortunately, many textbooks and teachers have treated these steps as a recipe for doing and learning science. The new vision presented by the National Science Education Standards (NSES) encourages inquiry beyond the "science as a process" approach. The principles of scientific experimentation encourage learners to combine science skills (such as observing, classifying, predicting, and experimenting) and scientific knowledge by reasoning and thinking to develop their understanding of science. According to the NSES, students who inquire through scientific experimentation:

- construct understanding of science concepts
- "know how we know" in science
- develop an understanding of the nature of science
- develop many skills necessary to become independent inquirers about their natural world
- develop mental habits of using their skills and abilities (NRC, 1996)

The principles of scientific inquiry and experimentation offer ways to form cooperative problem-solving groups, particularly when the principles are used flexibly to help learners design a procedure they wish to follow. Most children need structure and considerable guidance until they develop the mental habits of thinking like a scientist. Begin simply, perhaps by saying that science deals with answering questions or solving mysteries, or as Fields (1989), says, "Science invents stories and then sees if they are true" (p. 15). Use thoughtful questions to guide classroom discussions and pursue answers to those questions, and soon you will find students asking their own questions, inventing their own stories, and pursuing those stories to see if they are true. These questions usually serve to define the problem and point out what needs to be known and implies how the inquiry ought to occur.

The Principles of Scientific Inquiry as a Teaching Method

The teaching strategy can have five steps that parallel those listed above. Steven Fields's fine article in *Science and Children* (Fields, 1989) provides many practical examples of how the steps you have memorized can be turned into a motivating, interactive, and effective teaching method. We paraphrase his ideas below.

Step 1. Have students conclude that experimenting will provide the best answer to the science question.

If a child shows interest in a topic by asking a question, or if children become curious about a topic after you ask a question, look for a way to discover the answer by acting on it. For example, how can you discover the answer to a question like, "If rudders (and flaps) steer an airplane in flight, which rudders steer it in which direction?" (See Figure 9.3.) Problem questions such as this can make good challenges for cooperative group investigations in which each learner has a specific duty to fulfill.

Step 2. Focus the science question to seek a specific answer.

Try a brainstorming session. Accept all ideas related to the question, then limit the question to the kernel of the problem it poses. Identify a hypothesis from the ideas offered. Help the student groups find out all they can about the prob-

FIGURE 9.3   Paper Airplane Illustration On this paper airplane, the wing rudders and vertical stabilizer rudder are located as shown. Of course, creating various models of airplanes is a scientific endeavor in its own right. Let students experiment with making planes and rudders themselves.

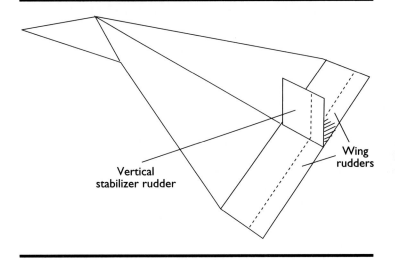

Vertical stabilizer rudder

Wing rudders

Source: Steve Fields, "The Scientific *Teaching* Method," *Science and Children* (April 1989): 15. Reprinted with permission from NSTA publications, 1840 Wilson Boulevard, Arlington, Virginia 22201-3000.

lem; then encourage them to make and test predictions. Continuing with Steve Fields's airplane example, some predictions could include:

- Wing rudders control up-and-down movement.
- Tail rudders control movement to the left and right.
- When rudders are set in any given way, the plane will fly up and down or side to side.

Step 3. Guess the answer to the science question, and use references to try to find out if the answer is already known.

Individual students and groups can brainstorm and decide the best way to find out the answer. Guiding questions can steer their thinking. Examples include:

- "Can you find the answer in a book?" If "yes," what kind of book?
- "Whom do you know who might already know the answer?" (Other children, teachers, outside resources, experts, and so on.)
- If these questions do not help, try: "How can you (we) design a test to find out the answer?" For older children, this a good place to discuss variables that can affect the outcome and reliability of an experiment.

WHAT RESEARCH SAYS

The Science Learning Cycle

The learning cycle is an approach to teaching and learning that ensures that students are involved in the types of thinking (inquiry) that constructivists argue is necessary for production learning. Jean Piaget's research on cognitive development helped to establish the first two phases of the learning cycle: exploration and explanation (concept invention). Mental activities in these phases promote what Piaget called *assimilation* and *accommodation*. Imagine the mind as a file cabinet: faced with information, the mind seeks a place to put it. Placing new information in an existing file with similar information would be an example of assimilation, as the mind adds to what already exists. However, when it does not find a file with information similar to that to be stored away, the mind must create a new file.

Robert Karplus, director of the Science Curriculum Improvement Study (SCIS), is credited with adding a third phase to the learning cycle. He named this phase *discovery* and then later changed the name to concept *implementation*. Some science educators prefer to call this the *application phase.* John Renner and Edmund Marek have made improvements and call the third phase *expansion of the idea.* There is considerable research to support uses of the learning cycle for improving children's science achievement and process skill development.

Renner and Marek note that the SCIS program relies on the learning cycle to organize its materials and to guide its teaching methods. Consequently, they have used the SCIS materials to conduct their own research, and they report conclusions that build on the effects of SCIS reported in Chapter 7.

Renner and Marek have used Piagetian mental conservation tasks to design experimental studies that indicate what effect the learning cycle may have on the intellectual development of young children. They found that when the learning cycle was used, children in an experimental group significantly outperformed other children who learned within a traditional textbook control group. Number, weight, liquid amount, solid amount, length, and area were the measures of conservation. The researchers believe "the data support the conclusion that the rate of attainment of conservation reasoning is significantly enhanced by the experiences made possible by [the first graders who learned through a learning cycle]." They also claim that the learning cycle enhances the intellectual development of young learners.

Step 4. Follow the procedures suggested by the guiding questions in Step 3 to find the answer to the science question raised in Step 2.

Help children during this stage by limiting their temptation to overgeneralize. For example, if the wing rudders are set up and the plane flies up, guide the students to the conclusion that these settings *probably* affect all planes the same way. One could not know for certain that larger planes are affected the same way unless they also are tested.

Step 5. After experimenting, interpreting, and concluding, have the students use what they have learned.

Focus on everyday experiences and have the children apply the main ideas they have learned—the concepts—to things they can understand. The rudder

The learning cycle has also been used to test the ability of children to use science processes. In a study that investigated fifth graders who were controlled (via a matched-pairs design) for intellectual development, chronological age, gender, and socioeconomic level, Renner and Marek found that all differences in the performance of science process skills favored the group that used the learning cycle. They concluded that the learning cycle helped children learn to use the processes of science much better than did a traditional program using a conventional science textbook.

In still another study, Renner and Marek investigated the influence of the learning cycle in a science program on student achievement in mathematics, reading, and social studies. They discovered that children learned *just as much and just as well* from the learning cycle as those who learned from a traditional program on understanding mathematics concepts, learning mathematics skills, learning social studies content, and understanding word meaning. However, they conclude that the *learning cycle was superior* for helping children apply mathematics; master social studies skills that involve interpreting graphs, tables, and posters and assimilation of data for problem solving; and determine paragraph meaning. In yet another study, Renner and Marek discovered that the learning cycle used in the SCIS first-grade program helped children outperform other children in a reading program on reading readiness skills.

The researchers maintain that the learning cycle is a natural way to learn and that it fulfills the major purpose of education: helping children learn how to think. Furthermore, Renner and Marek state that their research provides a rebuttal to school people who say, "We just don't have time or cannot afford to invest in the resources to teach science." They conclude: "The truth of the matter is that any school that teaches science using the learning cycle model is teaching much more than good science; it is also teaching reading, mathematics, and social science. In fact, schools cannot afford *not* to teach science using [the learning cycle model]."

Source: Adapted and quoted from J. W. Renner and E. Marek, *The Learning Cycle and Elementary Science Teaching* (Portsmouth, NH: Heinemann, 1988), pp. 185–199.

example applies to paper airplanes as well as kites, model rockets and planes, spoilers on racing cars, and rudder steering on conventional boats and swamp or airboats.

Limitations and Benefits

Like most other inquiry approaches, this method requires more time and planning to cover concepts. Equipment is needed, although often simple and inexpensive materials will do. Certain concepts lend themselves to experimentation more easily than others. The emphasis on concepts, however, is precisely what makes student comprehension greater and retention last longer. The cooperative group problem investigation approach helps to leverage the students' ideas by stimulating new approaches to the problem.

Suchman's Inquiry: How Can You Get Students to Think and Question?

Science Magic?   Dressed in cape and top hat, Mr. Martinez was ready to deliver his promised special treat to the fourth-grade class. With the theatrical flair of an amateur magician, he proposed to take his very sharp magic wand (the straight steel shank cut out of a coat hanger and filed to a pin-sharp point on one end) and pass it through a balloon without bursting it. Mr. Martinez played the crowd. He blew up a balloon, tied it off, and enlisted the aid of the audience by having them chant, "I believe! I believe!" and then on his signal say the magic words. As the magic wand of a super-sharp pin was about to touch the stretched side of the balloon, several children furrowed their brows and covered their ears. And with good reason: Pop!

The giggles were meant to tell Mr. Martinez "I told you so," but he persisted with jabs about not all of them believing or not selecting the right magic words. "Let's try again," he said as he began working the crowd again. Martinez blew up another balloon, tied it, and then remembered that he should add a drop of elixir from an oil can to his magic wand. Through the routine they all went, again, and this time, to the amazement of the children, the wand pierced one end of the balloon and slowly came out the other—a perfect axis through the top of the balloon and at the bottom near the knot (Figure 9.4). The children clapped and immediately wanted to know how he did it.

Mr. Martinez explained that he was not aware of any magic that really worked and that part was only an act. He emphasized that there are usually scientific explanations for the discrepancies we observe. But he assured the children that the balloon trick was no illusion. To convince them, he passed the balloon around for the children to inspect and then said: "You usually expect for me to ask *you* questions, but today is a special opportunity for *you* to ask the questions. Let's pretend you are super sleuths who are going to find out the explanation for this balloon trick. You can ask me all the questions you want, but there are some special rules you must follow. First, you can only ask me questions I can answer with a 'Yes' or 'No.' Second, begin by asking questions to establish the facts of what you have just seen. Don't take anything for granted: Verify that it was done as you *think* you saw it. Finally, after you think you have all the facts you need, tell me the reason you think this trick was possible. Let's begin. Lucinda?"

"Did you do anything special to the second balloon, like make it stronger?"
"No."
Then other children asked:
"Were they the same kind of balloons?"
"Yes."
"Were they the same size? I mean when you blew them up?"
"Yes—I *tried* to have them the same."
"Did you let a little air out of each one?"
"Yes."

FIGURE 9.4   Balloon Discrepant Event

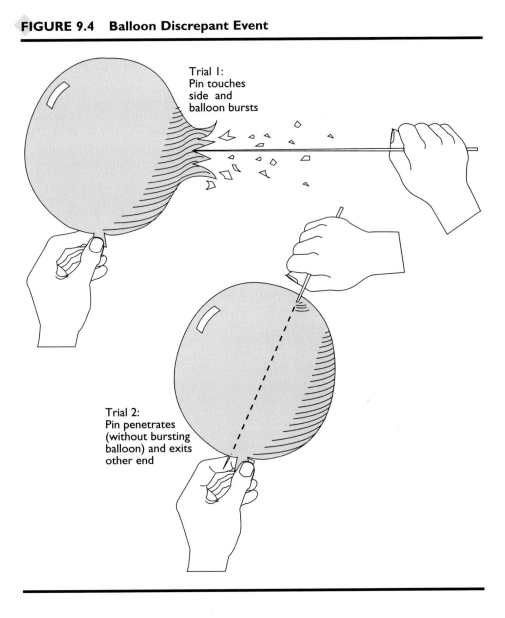

Trial 1:
Pin touches
side and
balloon bursts

Trial 2:
Pin penetrates
(without bursting
balloon) and exits
other end

"Does the oil make it work?"

"That sounds like an explanation type of question to me. Let's hold that one a while until after we uncover some more facts," said Mr. Martinez. Then the lesson continued until eventually the children discovered the *real* answer, and it wasn't because of the oil. The answer was related to the position, thickness, and strength of the balloon's fabric.

Discrepant Events.   This inquiry technique, developed by J. Richard Suchman (1962), relies on the use of discrepant events. *Discrepancies* are differences from what we normally expect, like the sharp pin's penetrating the balloon without bursting it. Theory has it that the human mind is intolerant of discrepancies and needs to maintain consistency (Petty & Cacioppa, 1981). The theory refers to an inconsistency between two cognitions—cognitive dissonance—between what one observes and what one believes. The balloon is a good example: Everyone knows sharp objects cause them to pop, but that one didn't!

The Method.   Your students' needs for cerebral consistency can motivate even those who are less alert and attentive. Why not use it to your advantage and teach science concepts with it? Suchman's method uses inquiry to help children construct theories (best explanations) for the discrepancies they observe. The approach is student centered and requires children to ask the questions—possibly a difficult task, because it requires considerable thought to ask useful questions and to build the answers into some order that will explain the discrepancy. The approach can be cooperative if the class is divided into detective teams to organize questions, conduct research, and form scientific explanations. The questions to use are convergent and must be answered with either a *yes* or a *no*. (See Figure 9.5 for a visual map of how the inquiry is structured.) These are the phases of Suchman's method:

1. Present the discrepant event.
2. Students ask yes-no questions to verify the events and collect information.
3. Students discuss ideas and do library research or further investigations to gather additional information to help them form explanations or theories.
4. The teacher reconvenes the class and leads a discussion to help students give and test their explanations or theories.

Suchman's approach is successful with intermediate and middle school children, but younger children need more teacher guidance. With K–2 children we have successfully used versions of the game Twenty Questions to accomplish the same outcome. The Additional Readings section at the end of this chapter provides sources for discrepant teaching events you can try.

The need to know is the powerful force of motivation with this type of method. However, this power can lead to student frustration and unproductive activity. Robert Shrigley suggests bringing closure or resolution to the discrepant event at least by the end of the class period; otherwise, the discrepancy can lead to an overload of frustration.

> At an inservice meeting . . . teachers had sat through a lengthy inference demonstration using a mystery box with objects sealed inside. Announcing that they should learn to live with the unknown, the science educator refused to open the box for inspection or tell the participants what its contents were. During the break, one teacher, who until that point had been poised and cooperative, bolted

FIGURE 9.5   Discrepant Event Map

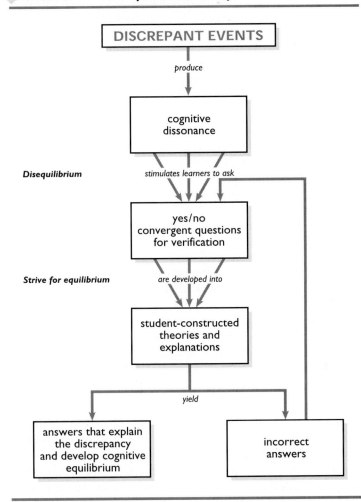

to the table on which the box had been left, and ripped off the lid to see what was inside. (Shrigley, 1987, p. 25)

Can Children Learn Science Through Play?

Playful discovery is a method based on the innate curiosity of very young children, in which play becomes the method for learning science. The method uses some of the elements of inquiry, but it is much more open ended. Children are natural investigators. Combine a child's interest with some adult encouragement and opportunities to play around with interesting materials, and playful discovery becomes a method that is useful for helping very young children begin to form fundamental science concepts they can build on for the rest of their lives (McIntyre, 1984). The method also encourages cooperation among very young learners.

Playful discovery is based on the theories of John Dewey and Jean Piaget, who stated that young children learn best through active involvement with interesting and meaningful materials. Dewey and Piaget, however, reminded us that we as teachers must go beyond simply passing out interesting materials and letting children play with them. Both believed that teachers should direct the hands-on learning through encouragement and guiding questions. Dewey was most concerned about the quality of this hands-on experience, about which he wrote: "Everything depends upon the quality of the experience which is had. The quality of the experience has two aspects. There is an immediate aspect of agreeableness or disagreeableness, and there is an influence upon later experiences (Dewey, 1937, p. 27).

Versions of playful discovery strive to provide young children with a variety of rich and immediately agreeable experiences. The method is used in child care centers and preschools with three- to five-year-old children and in progressive kindergarten classrooms. Playful discovery is stimulated initially by teacher-planned experiments that are based on phenomena, substances, and/or materials that are interesting and familiar to the children. For science, the learning activities can promote positive attitudes, lay the foundation for learning simple science concepts, and stimulate development of such process skills as observation, comparison, classification, prediction, and interpretation. The following scenario (Rogers, Martin, & Kousaleos, 1988, p. 21) helps to illustrate the method. Figure 9.6 briefly describes its six stages.

Christopher: A Blossoming Scientist.   Mrs. Kousaleos invited her group of four- and five-year-olds to gather by her and experiment with ice cubes in hot and cold water. Five small bodies were arched over the two containers of water observing and comparing the effects. Christopher suddenly announced with obvious excitement, "Look! The ones in hot water are really getting small." At Mrs. K's suggestion to check the water with their fingers, the children were surprised to discover how very cold the formerly hot water had become.

A week later, after repeating the ice activity, Mrs. K suggested another experiment to find out how to melt an ice cube quickly. Eager children generated ideas, then tested them by several methods. Putting ice cubes into mouths and breaking ice cubes into smaller pieces were by far the most popular methods. Midway through the experiment, however, Christopher, eyes wide open and a "Eureka" tone in his voice, proclaimed, "Let's try hot water!"

After duplicating the ice experiments with slight variations (such as exploring effects of amounts of water, numbers of ice cubes, and sizes of contain-

◆ FIGURE 9.6   Six Stages of Playful Discovery

Stage 1: Self-selected teacher-proposed experiment.
Encourage children to discover if ice cubes melt at the same rate in hot and cold water.

Stage 2: Repeat experiment with slight variation.
Encourage children to
• Vary amount of water used.
• Vary size of containers used.
• Determine if stirring the water makes a difference.
• Vary number of ice cubes placed in water.

Stage 3: Elaborate further on completed experiment.
Encourage children to discover how many ways you
can break up ice cubes (with hands, feet, teeth,
hammer, and so on).

Stage 4: Provide opportunities for and actively
encourage children's self-initiated experiments.
Make a variety of materials accessible, read books,
use teacher questioning. For example:
• Child makes ice cubes in a variety of containers (egg carton, muffin tin, plastic
  bottle, small bucket).
• Child also explores ways to remove ice from container and uses knowledge from
  Stage 1 to solve problems.
• Child discovers whether or not magic markers melt in hot water.

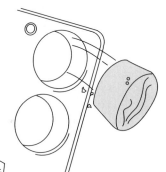

Stage 5: Communicate with parents and inform them of
child's interest.
• Parent encourages child to experiment at home and
  while on vacation (exploring ice cubes in bath water, mixing
  sand and water, discovering effect of jumping in water).
• Parent provides materials as child expresses interest.

Stage 6: Conduct a new experiment.
Encourage
• Children to explore the effect of pressure or force on water.
• Children to explore the effects of adding sand to container of
  water (e.g., displacement).

Source: D. L. Rogers, R. E. Martin, Jr., and S. Kousaleos. "Encouraging Science Through Playful Discovery," *Day Care and Early Education* 16 (1988): 1, 23. Reprinted with permission.

ers), the children began to ask permission to conduct their own experiments, Christopher in particular. These requests usually meant making ice in some uniquely shaped container, mixing various ingredients together, or adding a variety of materials to water.

During one of Christopher's self-initiated experiments, he noted that pouring salt into a container of water made the water "lift out." Since Christopher seemed intrigued with this phenomenon, Mrs. K planned some activities on displacement.

Later, when Christopher took a vacation, his parents sent a postcard that said, "Christopher is spending much time on the beach experimenting with water, observing changes as he adds shells and sand." Christopher had become fascinated by how the water "came out" when he and his dad jumped into their vacation swimming pool.

When Christopher returned, his class did a displacement experiment using different sizes of containers and different amounts of water with marbles, to assess and extend some of his vacation learning. After exploring the effect of adding marbles to water in narrow and wide containers, Christopher observed, "When the water's up high, the marbles lift the water out." He later concluded in response to a question about the difference between the narrow and wide containers, "In a fat one the water spreads out. In a thin one it goes up to the top."

The Playful Science Classroom.   Christopher's response is an example of what can happen when sensitive teacher guidance and well-planned experiences are combined to set the stage for the high-quality "later experiences" John Dewey wrote about. Numerous and different ongoing experiments will be evident in the playful discovery classroom. Many experiences will be based on common activities that use ordinary materials such as sand, water, and blocks.

Playful discovery gives young children opportunities to explore freely and to begin to understand the nature of materials before more structured lessons try to teach them concepts. Figure 9.6 outlines the stages Mrs. K followed to guide the children and improve the quality of their experiences. First she stimulated interest by proposing class experiments; later she stimulated sustained learning and experiential elaboration by permitting children to self-select experiments. Children will function at different stages at different times. For example,

> Some children may not go beyond Stage 1 because of lack of interest or understanding, and the teacher must proceed to Stage 6 for them. Others may spend a great deal of time on Stages 1 and 2, but not be able to make the leap to Stages 3 and 4. In this case it may help to skip these stages and go to Stage 5, so as to promote elaboration and self-initiation [by] suggesting that parents provide experiences in "science experiments" at home. (Rogers, Martin, & Kousaleos, 1988, p. 23)

Is this approach worth the effort? How long do the experiences endure? Perhaps you will find the answer here:

> Even months after the [first ice] experiment, a mother of one of the children [said] that when she was trying to figure out how to get ice cubes in a small-necked thermos, her four-year-old daughter suggested she could melt them a little in hot water first so they would fit. (Rogers, Martin, & Kousaleos, 1988, p. 23)

Playful discovery works best when the experiments chosen deal with phenomena and substances that the children encounter every day. The everyday environment adds a practical aspect to science by showing its usefulness, and it helps the children to construct a better understanding of their own world.

HOW CAN YOU TURN STUDENTS' QUESTIONS INTO AN INQUIRY TEACHING METHOD?

Fred Biddulph and Roger Osborne (1984) provide an inquiry approach to teaching that involves children in science investigations that are based on *their* own questions. They believe children's questions ought to be central to the process of inquiry because they show the extent of the ideas children have about a science topic, and they can be used to generate interest. Basing inquiry on student's questions:

- helps them gain understanding,
- provides them a powerful incentive to improve their own information-processing skills,
- helps them learn to interact with ideas and construct meanings for themselves from an interesting situation or topic,
- gives them occasional opportunities to learn from their own mistakes.

The teacher's role in this approach is to

- encourage students to ask questions about their encounters,
- encourage students to seek more information and rely less on teachers and others,
- help students find ways to test their ideas,
- help students construct well-reasoned explanations for their questions (Biddulph & Osborne, 1984, p. 2).

Table 9.1 provides a quick visual outline of the method. We paraphrase Biddulph and Osborne's work in the following steps.

Step 1. Elicit and record the students' questions.

Time required is perhaps one lesson. It is easier for students to ask questions if they already know something about the topic from prior experience. If experience is lacking, provide a demonstration, perhaps a discrepant event; show a film, poster, photograph, or slides; give descriptions of situations, encounters, or examples of the topic; read them a relevant story; or give them time for free exploration with materials.

324

Chapter 9   What Teaching Methods Help Learners to Construct Meaning?

TABLE 9.1   Students' Questions as an Inquiry Approach

Step 1: Provision of initiating activities.   Provide your students with experiences that will enable them to ask questions. Record their questions.

Step 2: Decision about questions.   Decide which questions are to be investigated.

Step 3: Guidance with planning.   Assist the students to plan their investigations.

Step 4: Assistance with investigations.   Provide assistance to the students during their investigations.

Step 5: Help with findings.   Help the students to record, interpret, and report their findings.

Source: Fred Biddulph and Roger Osborne, "Children's Questions and Science Teaching: An Alternative Approach," *Learning in Science Project* (Primary), working paper 117 (Hamilton, New Zealand: Waikato University, 1984). (ERIC Reproduction Document no. ED 252400), p. 4.

These opportunities may spark a wide range of questions; it may be necessary to help the children focus the points of their questions. Students may be reluctant or uncertain about how to form good questions if they have not had practice. Teacher modeling of proper question-asking behavior can help; so can using divergent questions to stimulate thoughtfulness and multiple possibilities. After a while, eliciting questions is not a great matter of concern; deciding *when* to stop is.

Step 2. Decide which questions to investigate.

The time needed may be as much as one lesson. Once you have obtained genuine questions to which students do not know the answers, selection must occur. These are some possible ways to proceed:

- Have individual students select questions for independent projects, or have groups choose a question of interest and work on it collectively.
- When separate questions may be related, let the students group them in ways that make sense to them.
- Refine the selection process by classifying the questions according to which ones may be investigated by practical activities or by consultation with books or people. Eliminate or defer questions that are outside the range of the science topic or that may be too difficult conceptually for the students.

Step 3. Help students plan their investigations.

Time required may be one or more class periods. Encourage practical hands-on investigations as well as consultations with resources. Guide the students so that they learn to:

- identify and use appropriate materials,
- carry out fair an accurate tests of their ideas,
- select and consult suitable print, media, and human resources,

A child's question can become the source of an important experiment.

- collect useful information,
- have realistic expectations for how long they will need to test their ideas,
- show concern for the environment and treatment of people.

Intermediate and middle grade students may benefit from a written framework to help organize their investigation, such as the one in Table 9.2.

Step 4. Monitor the students' investigations and provide assistance.

Several class periods will be needed. Young or inexperienced older students will need considerable help as they concurrently develop research and thinking skills while they pursue science learning. You can encourage students by showing empathy for their frustrations and providing sympathetic challenges to strengthening their ideas. You can support students' inquiry by directing their attention to factors they may have overlooked or by suggesting alternatives.

TABLE 9.2   Organization Framework

1. Name
2. Science topic
3. My question
4. My investigation
   (a) What do I want to ask someone?
   (b) Whom can I ask?
   (c) What should I read about?
   (d) What could I do to find out?

TEACHERS ON SCIENCE TEACHING

What Is a Question Box?

by Mary Ann Sloan
Grade 1 Teacher, Paumanok Elementary School, Dix Hills, New York

My first-grade classroom can best be described as a whole science classroom, where cooperative learning takes place throughout the day. I have found that cooperative learning is a powerful tool. In my classroom, science provides the platform for an interdisciplinary approach. The children raise questions; make predictions; devise plans; obtain, organize, and analyze data; and make many decisions while they gain experiences in using science inquiry skills. All of this is the result of the introduction of a very simple device—a question box!

The question box has helped me to begin the process of transforming the class into groups of cooperative learners. This strategy takes full advantage of the children's natural curiosity and allows them to become active participants in the learning process.

To make the question box, cover a cardboard box about the size of a mailbox with dazzling foil paper. Then cut out five-inch question marks from bright construction paper. Be sure to have one for each child and one for you too. To introduce the question box to your class and to provide a model for the first questions, select an exciting book to read to the whole class. One of the books that I have used with great success is *Papa Please Get the Moon for Me*, by Eric Carle. After reading the story, I ask the children what questions they would ask Monica, the main character, if she could come to our classroom and visit them. I record the questions they ask. Now I take out the question box. I explain that the question box is the place where they can put any questions they would like to have answered, that they can write their questions on their own or have someone help them, and that I will set aside time each day to work with the question box. I invite each child whose questions I recorded to put his or her question into the box. While we decorate our paper question marks, I move from table to table, modeling the kind of on-task behavior I expect. As I decorate my question mark, I think aloud of questions I might put into the question box and ask them about the questions they may be considering.

After a few days of working with the box—reading the questions aloud and adding more of their questions to it—I randomly select a question to be answered. Our first question was: Are elephants afraid of mice? The children made a list of what they already knew about elephants. When we reread the list, they decided that they needed to know more. They wanted to know: How big are elephants and their trunks? Why does an elephant

Step 5. Help the students record and report their findings.

Several class periods may be necessary. Consider that children probably will need help with:

- knowing what to record and learning that several tests (repeated measures) will provide more accuracy than a single measure;
- organizing information to record it in chart, table, graph, or narrative form (this is a good place to integrate mathematics and language arts skills);
- knowing what meaning is or is not possible to take from certain information; meaning can be enhanced if children are encouraged to use analogies;

have a trunk? Had anyone ever seen a mouse attack an elephant? We made predictions and developed a plan of action. The children began to meet in their cooperative learning groups. Each group worked to answer one of the questions. Now science became what we do to find answers, and the children loved it!

One product that developed from their explorations was a full-size painting of an African and an Indian elephant, with attention to the length and width of the trunk, which demanded measuring with many different devices. Three charts showing objects bigger, smaller, and the same size as an elephant were completed, requiring lots of comparisons. Two world maps showing where elephants and mice are found were drawn using the overhead projector. A diorama, using clay and construction paper, was created to depict an elephant habitat. Marker drawings of the kinds of foods elephants eat were labeled. Clocks were made to show when elephants sleep, eat, and travel. One group found that elephants don't breathe through their trunks and that it takes lots of food to keep an elephant healthy. This news helped the group that was working to determine how elephants actually use their trunks. They made paper bag elephant costumes and put on a play. The last group wrote letters to the Big Apple Circus, the Bronx Zoo, the Washington Zoo, and the San Diego Zoo. None of the zoo personnel had ever seen a mouse attack an elephant. In fact, they wrote to say that in their experiences mice seemed to be afraid of elephants. We made elephant T-shirts that the letter-writing group designed. This group was also responsible for keeping a record of money collected. They enlisted a mom to help them buy the shirts. She also helped with the stenciling.

This was just the beginning of the question center. Throughout the year, many questions are answered, and the children have many opportunities to classify, create models, generalize, form hypotheses, identify variables, infer, interpret data, make decisions, manipulate materials, measure, observe, predict, record data, replicate, and use number and language skills. You will know when your class is a community of cooperative learners. I promise this center will never be empty. The children will not want to leave for recess or lunch, and three o'clock will come too soon. They will miss school on weekends and won't be able to wait until Monday mornings, when they can put more questions into or take another question out of the question box.

- reporting the results in an organized format such as posters, charts, models, film, video, and so on.

WILL YOU SURVIVE?

Science inquiry encourages learners to construct their understanding from direct physical experiences and guided thinking. The methods have risks and potential difficulties. If all teachers were responsible for only one student at a time, this constructivist approach to science education would be rather simple to manage. Problems arise when two or more learners independently attempt to inquire. That students or a group may pursue several different questions and work on various projects at the same time presents management and organization difficulties for most teachers. Sufficient resources may also be in short supply. Postponing or even canceling lessons are options if the initial difficulties become too much to risk. With encouragement and time to develop the needed skills, students can grow into the role of posing questions and need less help researching their answers. With practice, you too will become more skilled at managing the busy class activity and will know what questions and needs to anticipate. You will also learn many fascinating things about science that you probably never had a chance to investigate. One procedure that can help you manage the inquiry from children's questions is associated with learning teams or cooperative groups.

Cooperative Learning in Science

Science teachers frequently group students during science activities to manage crowded classes and stretch precious materials that always seem to be in short supply. Cooperative learning, even if used mostly for science management, is more than asking students to group their desks together, however. F. James Rutherford and Andrew Ahlgren, writing in *Science for All Americans,* tell us:

> The collaborative nature of scientific and technological work should be strongly reinforced by frequent group activity in the classroom. Scientists and engineers work mostly in groups and less often as isolated investigators. Similarly, students should gain experience in sharing responsibility for learning with each other. In the process of coming to common understandings, students in a group must frequently inform each other about procedures and meaning, argue over findings, and assess how the task is progressing. In the context of team responsibility, feedback and communication become more realistic and of a character very different from the usual individualistic textbook-homework-recitation approach. (Rutherford & Alhgren, 1990, p. 189).

Scientists and engineers work in an environment that is more cooperative than competitive. Roger Johnson and David Johnson (1991) and Robert Slavin (1995), well-known promoters of cooperative learning methods, maintain that the research base for cooperative learning (in its many forms) indicates that students would learn more science, like it more, and feel more positive about their performance if more of their science experiences were obtained through cooperative learning. In their extensive review of the research on instructional strategies for teaching science, Tobin, Tippins, and Gallard (1994) remind us that cooperative learning should not be viewed as a panacea. Rather, it is valuable because of the potential for students to clarify, defend, elaborate, evaluate, and argue their constructed thoughts with one another. Table 9.3 compares the advantages of cooperative learning teaching and management techniques over those of customary small groups. This comparison illustrates that clear learning outcomes and systematic management procedures are keys to success.

TABLE 9.3   Benefits of Cooperative Science Groups

Cooperative Groups	Small Groups
Positive interdependence; students sink or swim together; face-to-face verbal communication	No interdependence; students work on their own, often or occasionally checking their answers with other students
Individual accountability; each pupil must master the material	Hitchhiking; some students let others do most or all of the work, then copy
Teachers teach social skills needed for successful group work	Social skills are not systematically taught
Teacher monitors students' behavior	Teacher does not directly observe student behavior; often works with a few students or works on other tasks
Feedback and discussion of students' behavior are integral parts of ending the activity before moving on	No discussion of how well students worked together, other than general comments such as "Nice job," or "Next time, try to work more quietly."

Source: P. E. Blosser, "Using Cooperative Learning in Science Education" (Columbus, OH: ERIC Clearinghouse for Science, Mathematics, and Environmental Education, 1993) (ERIC Reproduction Document No. ED 351 207), p. 4.

Cooperative Inquiry Groups

Three to five is a functional number for inquiry groups or cooperative learning groups. When each group member has a special job, the group inquiry process can be both effective and functional. The research on this management approach shows that "students who work in groups learn concepts just as well as those who work individually, with the added bonus that students who work together can develop both interpersonal skills and a sense of group responsibility" (Jones, 1985, p. 21).

Form groups, assign roles, and give each child a job description. The *principal investigator* (PI) is in charge of managing the group. Duties are to check the assignment and ask the teacher any clarifying questions, then lead the group by conducting the activity for the rest of the group or by assigning duties to the other group members. The PI is also in charge of safety.

The *materials manager* is in charge of picking up and passing out all equipment and materials that are necessary. Inside the classroom, the materials manager is usually the only student who has a reason to be moving around.

The *recorder* is in charge of collecting the necessary information and recording it in the proper form: graph, table, tape recorder, and so on. The recorder works with the principal investigator and the materials manager to verify the accuracy of the data.

The *reporter* is in charge of reporting the results, orally or in writing, back to the teacher or the entire class.

Children learn responsibility by sharing tasks in cooperative groups.

The *maintenance director* is in charge of cleanup and has the power to involve others in this group responsibility. Equipment must be returned and consumables must be cleaned up.

Recorder and reporter can be combined, as can materials manager and maintenance director for groups as small as three. Badges, sashes, headbands, photo IDs, or other role-identifying management devices can be used to limit confusion. Rotate the roles and form different groups often to promote fairness and group responsibility. This group technique can be used with any inquiry method in which groups are used. Robert Jones provides further tricks of the trade in Table 9.4.

TABLE 9.4   Tricks of the Trade for Cooperative Group Inquiry Activities

- Let each group choose a name for itself. It is a good social activity, and the names will help you identify the different groups.
- Change group members from time to time. Try out introvert-extrovert or boy-girl teams; experiment with cultural and racial mixes; form academically heterogeneous groups.
- Talk only to the principal investigators about the activity. This will set up a chain of command and prevent a repetition of questions. The students should discuss questions and problems among themselves so that it will only be necessary for you to clarify points with the principal investigator.
- Employ both indoor and outdoor activities. Badges work well indoors; armbands and headbands are more visible on school grounds. Hand-held walkie-talkies (inexpensive children's type) are also useful and (if they are available) should be used by the principal investigators.
- Use groups of three when working outdoors or on a field trip. This size group is better for safety.
- To ensure clear communication, post class rules, group names, job descriptions, and any other important information on a bulletin board in the classroom.
- Develop a system for rotating roles.
- Use job descriptions for classroom management and discipline. Most of the time you will simply need to ask which person has which role to resolve problems.
- Develop a worksheet, data recording sheet, or some other instrument for each activity.
- Make yourself a badge and join in the fun.

Source: R. M. Jones, "Teaming Up," *Science and Children* (May 1985): 23.

Successful, problem-free science lessons can occur if each member of the group understands the importance of his or her role. In a cooperative learning environment, the groups purposely comprise boys and girls of different ability levels. Each student realizes that on any given day, he or she could serve in any capacity as a member of the cooperative group. Therefore, each member is responsible for learning the material. The grade earned by participating in the lesson is a reflection of the group effort, not an individual. The group is interdependent; they will sink or swim together. The students within a group need to communicate to one another problems, observations, and successes before they go to the teacher with them. Courtesy, respect, and encouragement are interpersonal skills needed by each member of the cooperative group.

One useful cooperative method is known as a *jigsaw approach* (Watson, 1992). Use it, for example, when you are teaching third-grade students about the state tree, flower, and bird. Within each cooperative group, a different member will be assigned one of the following tasks:

- to determine the criteria for becoming the official state tree,
- to determine the criteria for becoming the official state flower,
- to determine the criteria for becoming the official state bird,
- to find out who suggested the state tree, bird, or flower, and where these are found in the state,
- to learn what the state tree, bird, and flower are in one bordering state.

The students in the cooperative groups should decide which student will take on each of the five tasks. Once these students are determined, then all of the students in the class assigned to task 1 should get together to find answers to that task, those assigned to task 2 should do the same, and so on. After a sufficient amount of time has passed (for this topic with third graders, two or three 35- to 40-minute class periods should be enough time) the students should have found answers for their task. They must now return to their original cooperative groups to share their information. The success of the cooperative group will depend on how well the expert gets his or her information across to the members of the group. After two class periods of sharing information from the five tasks, it is time for the quiz. This can be done by student experts for task 1, moving to different cooperative groups. Those experts will then quiz each member of a different cooperative group individually on task 1 information. After task 1 experts quiz the students and record their results, then task 2 experts will do the same, and so on. The success of each student will be reflected by how well his or her cooperative group expert prepared the group for the quiz.

RECOMMENDATIONS FOR SUCCESSFUL COOPERATIVE CONSTRUCTIVIST SCIENCE TEACHING

All of the inquiry methods we have presented are student centered to various degrees. They engage children in active thinking and learning and differ only in approach, but despite these procedural differences, each method guides children toward making discoveries. What elements unite these different procedures, which lead to a common outcome (Rakow, 1986)?

1. Successful constructivist teachers model scientific attitudes. The scientific attitudes we most wish to develop in children must be evident in the people who teach them. Successful inquiry teachers must be curious, open minded, tolerant of different viewpoints, skeptical at times, willing to admit it when they do not know answers to all questions, and able to view those occasions as opportunities to expand their learning.

2. Successful constructivist teachers are creative. Effective teachers find ways to make deficient materials effective. They are masters at adapting others' ideas, and they become comfortable taking risks with the unknown. They encourage creativity in students by being creative themselves.

3. Successful constructivist teachers are flexible. Inquiry takes time. Students need time to explore, think, and ask questions. Successful constructivist teachers are patient and use time flexibly to afford children the time they need for effective inquiry learning.

4. Successful constructivist teachers use effective questioning strategies. Types of questions used, wait-time, and proper uses of praise, reinforcement, and encouragement are the fodder of inquiry learning.

5. Successful constructivist teachers focus their efforts on preparing students to think in order to construct meaning. The constructivist teacher most wants students to develop an ability to solve problems. Successful problem solving depends on numerous thinking skills that arise from the processes of science that guide all phases of the inquiry. The end result of the inquiry process is the construction of scientific concepts. The end justifies the means, but exclusive focus on the end product does not provide the means for future problem solving.

Take the first step by beginning small. Trying to adapt all lessons into a constructivist approach is an overwhelming task and can be frustrating. If yours is a conventional textbook science program, focus on only one or two chapters at first by mapping the concepts. Then develop the material into good inquiry activities or find other supplementing resources. Each year add more, and soon you will develop an effective collection of material. Combine your efforts with those of other teachers (particularly those who teach the same grade level), pool your materials, improve them, and help your program become more effective. Read such journals as *Science and Children* for elementary teachers and *Science Scope* for middle and junior high teachers. These journals, available from the National Science Teachers Association, contain activities reported by experienced teachers and describe new materials available through government-sponsored programs and commercial publishers.

CHAPTER SUMMARY

Constructivist science teaching methods are interactive: Students and teachers investigate together and share many responsibilities that are carried only by the teacher in conventional classrooms. Constructivism is encouraged by a family of science teaching methods that promote student inquiry in a hands-on, minds-on way. Inquiry is a process, a way of pursuing learning. The outcomes of its methods are students' discoveries. Discoveries are mental constuctions. All constructivist methods are based on a belief about the power of experience. The methods rely on effective questioning to promote concept development.

Five constructivist science teaching methods are described in this chapter. The science learning cycle is appropriate for concept development in all grades and is particularly well suited for implementing the new goals in science education described in Chapter 4. A sample plan is included in this chapter.

Principles of scientific inquiry help us develop an approach for turning what once were memory exercises into a powerful teaching and learning method. This approach is most suitable for the intermediate through middle school grades and lends itself to cooperative inquiry groups.

Suchman's inquiry makes use of puzzling phenomena—discrepant events—that permit teachers to build on intrinsic motivation and turn children into questioners and pursuers of explanations. Playful discovery is a little-known inquiry method that was developed for very young children. Preschool and kindergarten children benefit from its playful atmosphere, accumulating agreeable and valuable experiences that help them build concept structures for later study. Inquiry with children's questions is another approach for turning children's questions into a teaching and learning method. With so many possible different questions children may wish to pursue, classroom management can become a nightmare; therefore, we offer practical recommendations for using cooperative learning groups.

Effective teachers who use constructivist methods demonstrate several common attributes: They model science attitudes, are creative in their approaches to science material and flexible in classroom management, and tend to focus more on developing children's abilities to think than on mere acquisition of subject matter. Research verifies the superior effects of student-centered constructivist approaches over traditional text-based teaching methods for science achievement, and the attitudes and skills of scientific inquiry.

DISCUSSION QUESTIONS AND PROJECTS

1. What arguments support using constructivist science teaching methods? What barriers seem to limit constructivism's acceptance and use in elementary classrooms? Will you use some of the methods described in this chapter? Why?

2. What are the similarities and differences in the approaches described in this chapter? Under what circumstances would you favor any one approach over the others?

3. Why is it that as children get older and presumably more capable of thinking independently, they appear to rely more on an authority figure for information than on their own experiences for discovering it?

4. Constructivist methods tend to promote greater independence among learners. What are several things you can do to help students become more independent learners?

5. Constructivist teaching strives to accommodate individual student differences. Individual differences do, however, tend to complicate teaching. What are some things you could do to manage the diversity of individuality without losing your cooperative focus?

6. How do constructivist methods help slow and fast learners?

7. Select a method described in this chapter and prepare a lesson for it. Teach the lesson and evaluate the effects of the method. How could you modify the method to make it more effective?

8. Try teaching lessons the conventional way and then with a suitable constructivist approach. Determine the extent to which learners obtain and retain the points of the lesson. What does your analysis reveal?

9. Investigate the ways you use questioning during constructivist lessons. Report the frequency and your use of different types of questions, the frequency and different types of children's questions, and uses of wait time. What skills can you use to make the inquiry more effective?

10. Develop original lessons for each of the methods described in this chapter. How do these lessons vary? What aspects of planning are emphasized more and less as the instruction becomes more cooperative?

ADDITIONAL READINGS

If you are interested in learning more about some of the topics raised in this chapter consider the following sources.

Steve Fields, "Introducing Science Research to Elementary School Children," *Science and Children* (September 1987): 18–20. Fields's practical approach gives more insight into using a form of the scientific method as an approach for science teaching. He focuses on helping children become classroom researchers.

Maeve Zamarchi Foley, "What? Me Teach?" *Science and Children* (January 1988): 10–13. Foley describes another approach to using student groups. Her technique motivates students to become teachers of fellow sixth-grade science students.

Tik L. Liem, *Invitations to Science Inquiry* (Lexington, MA: Ginn Press, 1987). This is the largest collection of discrepant events we have seen assembled. Liem's 411 activities span seventeen chapters representing science areas such as the environment, energy, forces and motion on earth and in space, and living things. Detailed drawings by the author and explanations for the phenomena make this an easy-to-use book.

Thomas R. Lord, "Right-Handed and Left-Footed? How Andrea Learned to Question the Facts," *Science and Children* (October 1986): 22–25. Using the left-brain, right-brain dominance theory as a backdrop, this scientist describes how he worked with his daughter to pursue her questions and discover that the teacher's textbook was *wrong!* This article is a good example of how children's questions can be used for inquiry and science discoveries.

James T. Scarnati and Craig J. Tice, "Lighting That One Little Candle," *Science and Children* (March 1988): 31–33. Fifth graders become patient and observant enough to list fifty things they discover by observing a candle. This article is good for reminding us about how often we overlook that which is under our very noses—and how much we can learn if we follow the suggestions of inquiry.

Robert E. Slavin, *Cooperative Learning* (Boston: Allyn & Bacon, 1995). This brief but definitive handbook establishes the theory and research base of cooperative learning and provides practical classroom uses for different purposes.

Wayne W. Welch, "Inquiry in School Science," in Norris C. Harms and Robert E. Yager (eds.), *What Research Says to the Science Teacher*, vol. 3 (Washington, DC: National Science Teachers Association, 1981), pp. 53–74. Welch reviews the desired and actual state of teaching science as inquiry. Discrepancies between these two states are further explored as dilemmas; alternatives are provided.

Emmett L. Wright, "Fifteen Simple Discrepant Events That Teach Science Principles and Concepts," *School Science and Mathematics* (November 1981): 575–580. Wright describes fifteen discrepant events, many of them in disciplines other than physical science. Materials, procedures, and explanations are given.

CHAPTER OUTLINE

What Do You Need to Know About Using Questions as a Science Teaching Tool?

Mrs. Barcikowski extended warm greetings to each as the children came running into the lab. A table in the middle of the room was piled with rocks of many different types, colors, shapes, and sizes. Each child was encouraged to pick up several samples and look at them carefully. The children rubbed the samples, held them up to the light, and used magnifying glasses to make closer inspections. The room was buzzing with activity, including the predictable horseplay of a few, and the buzz was punctuated with the exclamations of scientific discoveries. All the while, Mrs. B expressed her interest by asking many different questions that helped the children sharpen their observations.

Then she had the children gather around her on the piece of old carpet. When all were seated, Mrs. B began making conversation with such casual questions as, "How many of you have a hobby? How 'bout your parents or brothers or sisters? What are some of your hobbies?"

After a moment of listening and encouraging, Mrs. B said, "It seems that many of you collect different things for a hobby. Right?" Smiles and nodding heads gave her an entry. "I do too. In fact one of my favorite things to do on vacation is to look for unusual rocks to add to the collection I've been sharing with you today. Would you like to see one of my favorites?" Holding up a smoothly polished quarter-sized sample for all to see and passing around others for them to hold, Mrs. B said, "We've been studying the concept of *properties* for many of our lessons. Let's use properties to help us study rocks. What kinds of properties do you observe in this rock?" The children's observations were accepted with encouragement and occasional praise. Another key question Mrs. B asked was, "What other rocks from our pile seem like this one?" After noticing variety in the color, size, and shape of the other samples, a child pointed out that some of them were more different than alike. "True," Mrs. B confirmed. "I guess we need to focus a bit. What property appears to be the same in each of the samples?"

"Crystals?" offered a child.

"That's right! This type of rock is known especially for its crystals. What kind of rock do you think this is?" Mrs. B reminded the children to refer back to their observations while they tossed ideas around among themselves. She watched them closely and then invited Elizabeth, who seemed unsure, to venture a guess.

"Well, it looks kinda milky so I guess it's called . . . a 'milk rock?'" asked Elizabeth as she groped for an answer. The other children laughed, but Mrs. B reminded them to be polite; then she smiled as she saw how a connection could be made.

"I know you go to the grocery with your parents. What sizes of containers does milk come in?"

Elizabeth thought to herself: gallon? half gallon? Somehow those didn't seem right. Then an idea came to her. "A quart rock?" Elizabeth hesitantly asked.

"Good try. Almost, Elizabeth, just one more letter," encouraged Mrs. B as she wrote the word *quart* on the lap chalk board and held it up for all to see. "Let's add a zzz sound to this and see what we have. Q-u-a-r-t-z. What does that spell, Elizabeth?"

"Quartz!" exclaimed Elizabeth, with emphasis on the z.

"Now everyone," encouraged Mrs. B.

For the next several seconds, the class spelled and pronounced the new word like cheerleaders. Then Mrs. B referred them back to the samples and continued her questions, always waiting patiently, encouraging, and building on the children's ideas. She paused periodically to add a point or two of her own. By the lesson's end the children had learned that quartz is a common mineral found in rocks and comes in many different colors. When polished smooth, quartz may be used in jewelry as a semiprecious stone, and quartz crystals are used to manufacture prisms, lenses, watches, computer chips, and other electronic gadgets. They even learned that the scientific name is silicon dioxide, SiO_2. ◆

INTRODUCTION

Questions are tools for planning, teaching, thinking, and learning. What do you know about classroom uses of questions and your own questioning skills? It is typical for teachers to use questions intuitively or even out of habit. Some may even achieve satisfactory results. Yet considerable research suggests that many teachers do not realize that modest improvements in their questions can result in substantial gains for their students. In science, the students' questions play an important role in their learning; they need to be encouraged. The mission of this chapter is to:

1. raise questions about questions and report the effects that questions have on students' achievement, attitudes, and thinking skills,
2. explore the different types and uses of questions,
3. investigate how questions can be used,
4. offer some suggestions you can use to monitor and improve your own questions,
5. provide a rationale for using students' questions as an important part of your teaching.

QUESTIONS ON QUESTIONS

What is a question? We use questions often, but do you know much about their proper uses and effects? This part of the chapter raises seven important questions about questions. Try answering them from what you already know. Then read on to check your answers (see Figure 10.1). How well informed are you about this most potent teaching tool?

- What kinds of questions do teachers ask, and what kinds of answers do they require?
- Why do teachers use questions?
- How do questions affect students?
- How are teacher questions and student answers related?
- How do teachers use questions to involve all students?
- What is wait-time, and why is it important?
- What types of questions are used most in elementary science books and tests?

What Kinds of Questions Do Teachers Ask and What Kinds of Answers Do They Require?

Research verifies that elementary teachers use questions more than any other teaching tool. For example, one study reports that third-grade teachers asked reading groups a question every 43 seconds (Gambrell, 1983), while another study found that teachers ask as many as 300 to 400 questions each day; the average is 348 (Levin & Long, 1981). Most of these questions seem to be asked in a rapid-fire question-answer pattern. The pattern and extent of question use appears to have changed little for more than fifty years, with teachers asking about 93 percent of all questions and giving children little time to respond or opportunity to ask their own questions (Martin, Wood, & Stevens, 1988). The questions' effectiveness is limited by this type of use.

Abundant use of questions would suggest considerable room for variety, but, in fact, the questions teachers usually ask require factual answers and low levels of thinking. Knowledge and comprehension levels make up at least 70

FIGURE 10.1   What Is a Question?

A question is an interrogative sentence that asks for a response. A question is expressed in simple, clear, straight-forward language that students can understand. A good question stimulates thinking and should be adapted to the age, abilities, and interests of the students.

A good question is one that is appropriate and is used for a specific purpose. Questions are used:

- to find out what is not known or to find out whether some-one knows
- to motivate
- to provide drill and practice
- to help students organize thinking
- to develop an ability to think
- to interpret meaning
- to emphasize a point
- to show relationships

- to establish cause and effect
- to discover interests
- to help develop appreciation
- to provide review
- to reveal thinking processes
- to diagnose learning difficulties
- to evaluate
- to give practice
- to permit expression

Four types of questions:
1. Memory questions establish or review the facts.
2. Convergent questions have one correct answer and require reasoning.
3. Divergent questions have several answers and help to promote possibility thinking and creativity.
4. Evaluative questions promote decision making and defensible judgments.

How do you use questions?

How do you use children's questions?

percent of the questions, while questions that require application, analysis, synthesis, or evaluation thinking are used much less often (Martin, Wood, & Stevens, 1988).

Why Do Teachers Use Questions?

According to Mary Budd Rowe (1973), a science educator, teachers use questions for three main purposes:

1. To evaluate or to find out what the pupils already know.
2. To control the functions of the classroom: inquisition used as a classroom management strategy or to reduce off-task behavior.
3. To instruct children by suggesting resources and procedures, focusing observation, pointing out differences and discrepancies, and so on.

Questions have other uses as the stock in trade of teachers, and the potential far exceeds the three fundamental uses Rowe details. (See Table 10.1.)

How Do Questions Affect Students?

The questions teachers choose and use can influence students in three areas: attitudes, thinking, and achievement.

How Do Questions Influence Students' Attitudes? Attitudes influence how students participate, think, and achieve. Students with positive attitudes tend to look more favorably on a subject, teacher, or method of teaching. Students with negative attitudes often link them to a subject, school experience, or teacher and tend to resist and perform poorly. From his research, William Wilen (1986) concludes that teachers' uses of questions play an important part in shaping children's attitudes, thinking, and achievement. "Students must develop positive attitudes toward higher-level questioning if instructional approaches such as inquiry are to be effective," Wilen (1986, p. 21) writes.

How Do Questions Influence Students' Thinking? Hilda Taba (Taba, Levine, & Elsey, 1964) discovered that the questions teachers used influenced the stu-

TABLE 10.1 How Can Teachers Use Questions?

- To arouse students' interest and motivate participation
- To determine students' prior knowledge before a lesson begins
- To determine students' thoughts and other information essential to a problem before it is explored
- To guide students' thinking toward higher levels
- To discipline disruptive students by asking them to explain their behavior
- To provide listening cues for students with difficulties and to focus inattentive students' attention
- To diagnose students' strengths and weaknesses
- To help students develop concepts or see relationships between objects or phenomena
- To review or summarize lessons
- To informally check students' comprehension
- To evaluate planned learning outcomes, such as performance objectives

What other uses can you add to this list?

Appropriate questions can improve children's attitudes, thinking, and achievement.

dents' levels of thinking. Teachers expected students to think at a certain level (according to Bloom's taxonomy of the cognitive domain), composed and used questions for the expected level, and then received responses from students that matched their expectations. Teachers can and do control the thought levels of students (Arnold, Atwood, & Rogers, 1973). In fact, Gallagher and Aschner (1963) reported that a mere 5 percent increase in divergent questioning can encourage up to a 40 percent increase in divergent responses from students. Divergent thinking is important for problem-solving tasks and for learning that requires creativity. Also, high-level questions help students to evaluate information better and improve their understanding of lower-level facts (Hunkins, 1970).

How pupils think must match the requirements of teachers' methods if students are to become confident learners. The questions learners ask are indicators of the thinking they are doing and of the impact of your questions. Dorothy Alfke gives us this recommendation to help children improve their thinking through questioning:

> Inquiry learning must involve questions **asked by, meaningful to, and potentially productive for** the learners. . . . Young people must ask the kinds of questions which lead them back to doing something with the materials in order to derive answers. They need to ask the kinds of questions they can get answers to. . . . [If] learning how to learn, inquiry learning, and conceptual learning are high in your value system, develop the skill of asking operational questions in your classes. Listen to the kinds of questions your children are asking as they interact with new observations of science phenomena. Listen also to the questions

you, as a teacher, are asking your students, because your questions have a heavy influence on the kinds of question patterns your students are developing. (Alfke, 1974, pp. 18–19)

Even young children can learn to change their thinking behavior. For example, second-grade nonnative speakers of English learn to modify their own thinking and question-asking strategies when they are exposed to proper questioning and reinforcement (Zimmerman & Pike, 1972). Iva Brown (1986) sums up best the importance of questioning on pupil thinking:

> The key to successful classroom experiences with hands-on science activities is clearly the use of questioning in the instructional process. Without well-thought-out questions in the lesson, manipulative activities may soon deteriorate into rather meaningless messing around. (p. 152)

Questions can make the difference between learning from *meaningful* manipulation of materials and *meaningless* messing around. This belief is based on a process-product model of classroom learning, in which specific teaching behaviors provide useful pupil learning experiences. The product of this process is pupil achievement. This model suggests that "increases in the quantity and quality of pupil behaviors should result in concomitant increases in pupil achievement" (Tobin & Capie, 1982, p. 3). The assumed increases are attributed to the quality of verbal interaction. For example, teachers and students are reported to talk about 71 percent of the time in activity-based classrooms, compared to 80 percent of the time spent talking in nonactivity-based classrooms. In average activity-based elementary science classrooms, 29 percent of the questions are at a high level, while only 13 percent of teachers' questions are high level in average nonactivity-based classrooms (Bredderman, 1982).

How Do Questions Influence Students' Achievement? Do the changes in verbal interaction make a difference? Apparently, yes. The studies here are limited, but the results show that a teacher's questions can produce pupil achievement superior to levels attributed to written questions found in textbooks and on worksheets (Rothkopf, 1972; Hargie, 1978). Some earlier studies appear to conflict with this conclusion (Rosenshine, 1976, 1979). However, more recent studies suggest that key ingredients of effective verbal interaction may have been missing in the earlier research. For example, Kenneth Tobin (1984) describes increased achievement for middle school students in science when teachers redirected questions, used probing strategies, and used wait-time to increase student discourse and reaction. Higher-level questions seem to stimulate greater science achievement when combined with a longer wait-time (Riley, 1986).

How Are Teacher Questions and Student Answers Related?

Raising the level of questions is all well and good, but it makes a difference only if students actually think and respond on the same level as that required by the questions used. Is this what happens?

Greater use of higher-level questions may be a significant difference between hands-on science learning and traditional teaching, according to Ted Bredderman (1984). He reports a direct relationship between the level of questioning and the level of response in elementary science lessons. Bredderman observed specially trained teachers (such as reading teachers trained in the SCIS program) raising the level of questioning in reading lessons. His research suggests that questioning levels "can be raised through activity-based science training, which could have the effect of raising the cognitive level of classroom discourse and could result in increased achievement" (Bredderman, 1984, p. 289–303). Other researchers found that higher-level questions had a positive influence on the language development of young children and on skills such as analytical thinking (Kroot, 1976; Koran & Koran, 1973). What is the general conclusion? There is a positive relationship between higher-level questions and higher-level student answers (Barnes, 1978). We recommend using more advanced questions to obtain more thoughtful answers from children.

How Do Teachers Use Questions to Involve *All* Students?

Exemplary teachers treat different pupils equitably and are capable of adapting instruction according to student needs, including the levels of questions they use. How equitable is the questioning treatment that is found in typical elementary classrooms?

Studies done in urban classrooms show that teachers call on students whom they perceive as high achievers more frequently than on students they perceive as low achievers. Also, teachers are less likely to react to the responses received from low achievers: 3 percent fail to react to high achievers and 18 percent fail to provide feedback to low achievers. When high achievers hesitate to answer, they are given more time to think. Low achievers receive less and often no time, perhaps out of regard for the students' feelings. High achievers also receive more opportunities to exchange ideas with teachers at higher thought levels. Similar data show questioning differences between Caucasian and African-American students, with African-American males most deprived of opportunity (Los Angeles Unified School District [LAUSD], 1977).

What is the relationship between where a student sits in a classroom and the number of opportunities the student receives to answer questions? In a study of first-, sixth-, and eleventh-grade classrooms with traditional seating arrangements of rows facing the teacher's desk, the students most likely to be asked questions were seated in a T shape, with the top of the T across the front of the room and the stem of the T down the middle (see Figure 10.2). Certainly the shape was not always perfect, yet there were distinct areas in the back of the classrooms along the sides where students were seldom involved in questioning and instructive verbal interaction (LAUSD, 1977). Who sits in these areas most often? Who needs more opportunities, feedback, and encouragement? Answer: lower-achieving students.

FIGURE 10.2 Where a Child Sits Can Make a Difference

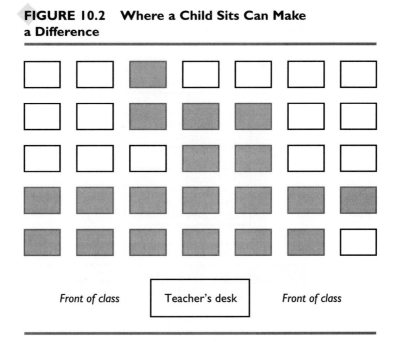

Front of class   Teacher's desk   Front of class

What Is Wait-Time and Why Is It Important?

Pause for a few seconds and think about what happens when you are the student and a teacher asks you a question. Unless you have memorized the answer, you must decode the meaning of the question (no small task if it is unclear or if multiple questions are used); think, "What do I know?" about the question's possible answer; ask, "How can I say the answer without sounding foolish?"; actually form the answer; and then give the response to the teacher. All of these steps take time, as suggested by Figure 10.3.

Wait-time is defined in different ways, but usually two types of wait-time are recognized. *Wait-time 1* refers to the length of time a teacher waits for a student to respond. *Wait-time 2* is the length of time a teacher waits after a student has responded before the teacher reacts to what was said.

How long do teachers typically wait? Rowe (1974) first researched this topic and reported an average for wait-time 1 of about one second. Wait-time 2 was equally short, with teachers often only parroting the students' answers or providing very low-value feedback, such as, "Okay," "Uh-huh," or "Good." Many teachers wait about 1 second for students to respond without any adjustment for the difficulty of the question and then almost immediately react to what the students have said without giving the response much thought. "Evidently students are expected to respond as quickly to comprehension questions as they

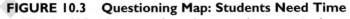

FIGURE 10.3   Questioning Map: Students Need Time to Think   What happens after a learner asks a question?

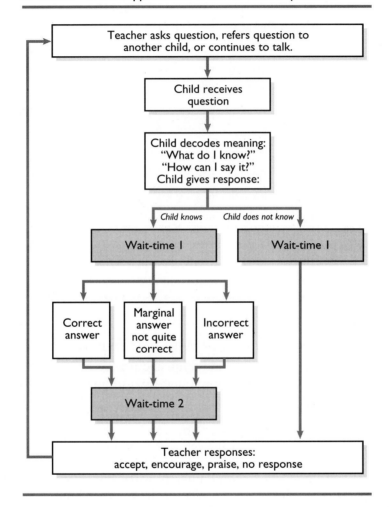

are to knowledge-level questions," and teachers believe they can accurately predict what students will say (Riley, 1986). Under what conditions do you think wait-times of 1 second or less *are* appropriate?

There is a growing list of advantages we can expect from increasing the length of wait-times. Kenneth Tobin (1984) reports increases in the length of student responses, increases in student achievement, and changes in teacher discourse. Teachers tend to "probe and obtain further student input rather than mimicking pupil responses" (p. 779). Yet there is a possible threshold effect; a certain optimal length of wait-time exists depending on the type of question, advises Joseph Riley II (1986). Tobin and Capie (1982) recommend an overall wait-time of about 3 seconds with an approximate mix of 50 percent lower-level questions and 50 percent higher-level questions to produce optimal pupil responses. They advise us to establish the facts first in order to give the students something worthwhile to think about before building on the base of knowledge by using higher-level questions. Tobin (1984) even suggests that an effective strategy is to ask the question, wait, call on a student to answer, wait, then redirect the question or react accordingly (see Figure 10.4).

FIGURE 10.4   A Whole Class Questioning Strategy   There are times when questions should be used with the whole class. This questioning strategy can maximize student involvement.

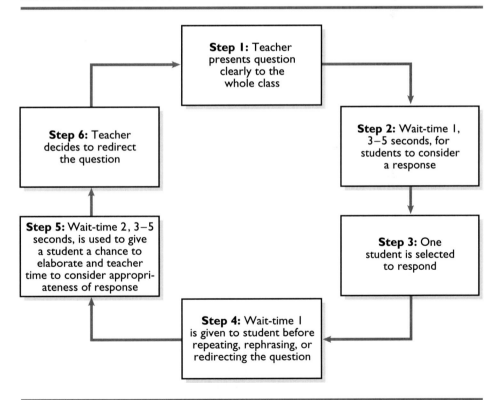

Source: This strategy is based on the research of Kenneth Tobin (1984) as reported in "Effects of Extended Wait-Time on Discourse Characteristics and Achievement in Middle School Grades," *Journal of Research in Science Teaching,* vol. 21, no. 8, pp. 779-791.

Some teachers encourage cooperative types of learning by using the think-pair-share approach. A teacher asks the question and waits; students think about possible answers for 10 to 20 seconds; students then pair up and compare answers. A student pair is then asked to share its answer with the class.

Students might find the waiting time awkward at first and misinterpret your intentions. We have had considerable success with learners by telling them about wait-time and why we are going to use it, then cueing them to think before responding. Try waiting at least 3 seconds before you respond, and you may discover the benefits reported by Rowe (1970):

- Student responses can become 400 to 800 percent longer.
- The number of appropriate but unsolicited student responses increases.
- Failure of students to respond decreases.
- Pupils' confidence levels increase.
- Students ask more questions.
- Low achievers may contribute up to 37 percent more.
- Speculative and predictive thinking can increase as much as 700 percent.
- Students respond and react more to each other.
- Discipline problems decrease.

What Types of Questions Are Used Most in Elementary Science Books and Tests?

Textbooks have a profound impact on curriculum, teachers, and instruction because student texts and teacher guides often determine the level of questions used. Questions, as we have learned, influence the extent of thinking and learning that takes place. Low-level questions have been consistently used in textbooks for several school subjects, but high-level questions have seldom been found. For example, of more than 61,000 questions from history textbooks, teacher guides, and student workbooks, more than 95 percent were devoted to recalling facts (Bennett, 1986). Another researcher found that only 9 out of 144 lesson plans in the teacher guides from the basal readers of four major publishers contained questions distributed over Bloom's various cognitive levels (Habecker, 1976). Overall, series of elementary science textbooks are no better, but recent improvements are encouraging. Excellent resource experiment books are also available; they pose questions based on the science processes (see Exercise 10.1).

These findings also raise concern for tests and the printed materials they represent. What types of test items are provided? Tests supplied by text publishers appear to be devoted to low levels of thought as well. Gregory Risner (1987) studied the cognitive levels of questions demonstrated by test items that accompanied fifth-grade science textbooks. Rated on Bloom's taxonomy, Risner found about 95 percent of the test questions devoted to knowledge or comprehension, about 5 percent used for application, and 0.2 percent used for evaluation; analysis and synthesis questions were neglected completely. All types of

EXERCISE 10.1

Science Process Questions[*]

The questions below are representative of those found in books for children. Use these science processes to label the questions: observing, communicating, hy-pothesizing/experimenting, measuring, comparing/contrasting, and generalizing/predicting.

Process	Question
_____	1. Which plants seem to be sturdier: ones left in sun or ones left in shade?
_____	2. Most rain in clouds comes from the ocean; why doesn't it rain over the ocean and nowhere else?
_____	3. Which plant do you think will grow better?
_____	4. Do the creatures react to such things as light or shadows or an object in their path?
_____	5. What was the temperature?
_____	6. Which length works best?
_____	7. What can you move with the air you blow through a straw?
_____	8. Which seeds stick to your clothes as you walk through a weedy field?
_____	9. What happens to the number of breathing movements as the temperature drops?
_____	10. How long does the solution bubble?

[*]For a complete discussion, see Sandra Styer, "Books That Ask the Right Questions," *Science and Children* (March 1984): 40–42, or W. Harlen, *Teaching and Learning Primary Science* London: Paul Chapman Publishing, 1993), pp. 83–86.

questions are important, but consistent overuse of any one type can limit learning. You must be able to identify questions necessary for stimulating desired levels of thought and then build those questions into your teaching.

WHAT ARE THE DIFFERENT TYPES OF QUESTIONS?

Many innovative scientists would never have made their most important discoveries had they been unable to think divergently in their pursuit of the new. Through thinking nontraditionally and divergently, scientists like Copernicus, Galileo, Pasteur, and Salk discovered solutions, formulated theories, and made discoveries that revolutionized the modern world. The need for divergent thinking did not die with their achievements (Pucket-Cliatt & Show, 1985, pp. 14–16).

These scientists learned to think divergently—broadly, creatively, and deeply about many possibilities. They learned how to ask the right questions at the right time. "Wrong questions tend to begin with such innocent interroga-

WHAT RESEARCH SAYS ◆◆◆

Using Questions in Science Classrooms

One function of teaching science is to help learners develop higher levels of thinking. To do this you must facilitate better communication with and among your students. One way to encourage communication is by asking questions. "Teacher questions can serve a variety of purposes," such as:

- Managing the classroom ("How many of you have finished the activity?")
- Reinforcing a fact or concept ("What name is given to the process plants use to make food?")
- Stimulating thinking ("What do you think would happen if . . .?")
- Arousing interest ("Have you ever seen such a sight?")
- Helping students develop a particular mind-set ("A steel bar does not float on water; I wonder why a steel ship floats?")

Science teachers are concerned about helping students to become critical thinkers, problem solvers, and scientifically literate citizens. If we want students to function as independent thinkers, we need to provide opportunities in science classes that allow for greater student involvement and initiative and less teacher domination of the learning process. This means a shift in teacher role from that of information giver to that of a facilitator and guide of the learning process.

Central to this shift in teacher role are the types of questions that teachers ask. Questions that require students to recall data or facts have a different impact on pupils than questions that encourage pupils to process and interpret data in a variety of ways.

The differential effects of various types of teacher questions seem obvious, but what goes on in classrooms? In one review of observational studies of teacher questioning, spanning 1963–1983, it was reported that the central focus of all teacher question-

ing activity appeared to be the textbook. Teachers appeared to consider their job to be [seeing] that students have studied the text. Similar findings have been reported from observational studies of teachers' questioning styles in science classrooms. Science teachers appear to function primarily at the recall level in the questions they ask, whether the science lessons are being taught to elementary students or secondary school pupils.

Why doesn't questioning behavior match educational objectives? One hypothesis is that teachers are not aware of the customary questioning patterns. One way to test this hypothesis is to use a question analysis system.

You can do several things if you want to improve you questioning behavior by using a wider variety of questions. First,

> locate a question category system [you] can use comfortably and then apply it, during lesson planning and in post-lesson analysis. Because of the variety of things that go on during a lesson, a post-lesson analysis is best accomplished by tape-recording the lesson or at least those parts of the lesson containing the most teacher questions.

Are the kinds of questions you ask different? What kinds of teacher-student interaction patterns seem to exist? Are some patterns of interaction more effective than others? Compare your written and oral questions. Do they accomplish what you intend? If you use a variety of oral questions to promote different levels of thinking, quiz and test questions should do the same. Students quickly figure out what you value and then strive for it.

Source: Excerpted from Patricia Blosser, "Using Questions in Science Classrooms," in Doran, R. (ed.), *Research Matters . . . to the Science Teacher,* vol. 2 (1985) (ERIC document no. 273490).

Questions can encourage children to develop science process skills.

tives as why, how, or what" (Elstgeest, 1985, p. 37). Jos Elstgeest (1985) provides an excellent example in this brief story:

> I once witnessed a marvelous science lesson virtually go to ruins. It was a class of young secondary school girls who, for the first time, were let free to handle batteries, bulbs, and wires. They were busy incessantly, and there were cries of surprise and delight. Arguments were settled by "You see?" and problems were solved with "Let's try!" Hardly a thinkable combination of batteries, bulbs, and wires was left untried. Then in the midst of the hubbub, the teacher clapped her hands and, chalk poised at the blackboard, announced: "Now, girls, let us summarize what we have learned today. Emmy, what is a battery?" "Joyce, what is a positive terminal?" "Lucy, what is the correct way to close a circuit?" And the "correct" diagram was deftly sketched and labeled, the "correct" symbols were added, and the "correct" definitions were scribbled down. And Emmy, Joyce, and Lucy and the others deflated audibly into silence and submission, obediently copying the diagram and the summary. What they had done seemed of no importance. The questions were in no way related to their work. The rich experience with the batteries and other equipment, which would have given them plenty to talk and

think about and to question, was in no way used to bring order and system into the information they actually did gather. (pp. 36–37)

Elstgeest defines *good questions* as those taking a first step toward an answer, like a problem that actually has a solution. The good question stimulates, invites the child to take a closer look, or leads to where the answer can be found. The good question refers to the child's experience, real objects, or events under study. The good question invites children to show rather than say an answer. Good questions may be modeled after the science process skills in which learners are asked to take a closer look and describe what they find. Try matching the questions and skills in Exercise 10.1.

There are several additional ways to classify questions. When presenting information from the research on questions, we have often referred to Bloom's taxonomy of the cognitive domain. It is possible to write questions for each level of the taxonomy. See Figure 10.5 for examples.

- *Knowledge-level* questions request the memorized facts.
- *Comprehension-level* questions stimulate responses of memorized information in the students' own words.
- *Application-level* questions cause students to use information while thinking about how to put what they have learned to use in a new context.
- *Analysis-level* questions require that students break down what they know into smaller parts to look for differences, patterns, and so on.
- *Synthesis-level* questions stimulate children to consider variety, new ideas, or original possibilities.
- *Evaluation-level* questions require children to make choices and provide reasons.

Educators often disagree about the level at which a question is written. This can make Bloom's taxonomy difficult to use, but it is worth learning. Spreading your questions across the taxonomy's range can make you a more effective teacher.

Gallagher and Aschner (1963) offer a simple and useful method for classifying questions. This method has four types of questions that address all of Bloom's levels and incorporate the science processes. The simplicity of this method makes it useful for all subject areas. Table 10.2 provides a level-of-thinking context, and Figure 10.6 provides examples of the following kinds of questions:

- *Cognitive memory questions* require students to recall facts, formulas, procedures, and other essential information. This is similar to Bloom's knowledge and comprehension levels and helps students establish the facts before moving toward higher levels. Memory questions also assist observations and communication. *Example:* "Do you see the bubbles rising from the liquid? What is the common name for H_2O?"
- *Convergent thinking questions* cause students to apply and analyze information. To do this successfully, children must have a command of cognitive memory types of information. Convergent questions assist in problem solv-

FIGURE 10.5   Bloom's Taxonomy of Cognitive Domain

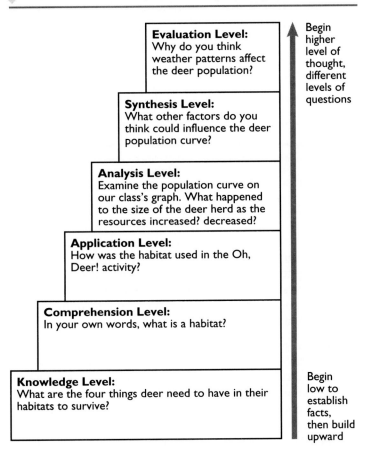

Evaluation Level:
Why do you think
weather patterns affect
the deer population?

Begin
higher
level of
thought,
different
levels of
questions

Synthesis Level:
What other factors do you
think could influence the deer
population curve?

Analysis Level:
Examine the population curve on
our class's graph. What happened
to the size of the deer herd as the
resources increased? decreased?

Application Level:
How was the habitat used in the Oh,
Deer! activity?

Comprehension Level:
In your own words, what is a habitat?

Knowledge Level:
What are the four things deer need to have in their
habitats to survive?

Begin
low to
establish
facts,
then build
upward

Source: B. S. Bloom, *Taxonomy of Educational Objectives, the Classification of Educational Goals, Handbook I: Cognitive Domain* (New York: Longman, 1956).

ing and are useful for the basic science processes: measuring, communicating, comparing, and contrasting. *Example:* "What kind of chart, graph, or drawing would be the best way to show your results?"

- *Divergent thinking questions* stimulate children to think independently. Students are given little teacher structure or prior information; they are encouraged to do possibility thinking by combining original and known ideas into new ideas or explanations. Questions of this type require synthesis thinking and promote creative problem solving and the integrated science processes (hypothesizing and experimenting). *Example:* "Why do you think these seedlings are taller than those?"

TABLE 10.2   Levels of Thinking Questions Require

Question Type	Level	Type of Thinking Expected
Closed questions	Low	Cognitive memory operations; convergent operations
Open questions	High	Divergent thinking operations; evaluative thinking operations

Source: A comparison of Gallagher and Aschner's questions as adapted from P. Blosser, *How to Ask the Right Questions* (Washington, DC: National Science Teachers Association, 1991), p. 4.

- *Evaluative thinking questions* cause students to choose, judge, value, criticize, defend, or justify. Often the simple question "Why?" or "How?" propels thinking to this level after students are asked simple choice or yes-no types of questions. Processes stimulated by evaluation questions include making predictions, reaching conclusions, and forming generalizations. *Example:* "What things make a difference to how fast the seeds began to grow?"

Science for many children, unfortunately, may be an exercise in closed thinking, in which memory and convergent questions are emphasized. Children are prodded to seek the so-called right answer or verify the correct results. Teachers should use both open and closed types of questions. *Open questions* are those that encourage divergent and evaluative thinking processes. Because they are traditional and expedient, *closed questions* have been used most often by teachers. Yet there is a danger associated with overuse of closed questions. "Convergent questions sacrifice the potential for many students to be rewarded for good answers, since their focus is a search for one right or best answer" (Schlichter, 1983, p. 10). Because science is a creative process, much more divergent thinking must be encouraged. Try your hand at classifying convergent and divergent questions in Exercise 10.2, and experiment with both while you teach. Be advised that there are risks for teachers who use divergent or open-ended questions:

> The risks for the teachers who practice divergent question-asking should not be underestimated: an open-ended question can alter the day's schedule, spark discussion on topics the teacher may not be prepared for, and shift the teacher's role from guardian of known answers to stimulator of productive (and often surprising) thinking. But they are risks well worth taking. (Schlichter, 1983, p. 10)

There are risks associated with using *any* type of question. What can you do to limit the risks? How can you learn to use questions more effectively?

FIGURE 10.6 **Composing the Correct Level of Questioning: Higher Levels of Thought**

QUESTION CATEGORY			SAMPLE QUESTION PHASES
Evaluative Thinking	**Bloom's Evaluation Level:** • Make choices • Form values • Overlap critiques, judgments, defenses	**How and Why Reasonings:** • Choose, appraise, select, evaluate, judge, assess, defend, justify • Form conclusions and generalizations	• *What do you favor...?* • *What is your feeling about...?* • *What is your reason for...?*
Divergent Thinking	**Bloom's Synthesis Level:** • Develop own ideas and information • Integrate own ideas • Plan, construct, or reconstruct	**Open-ended Questions for Problem Posing and Action:** • Infer, predict, design, invent • Hypothesize and experiment • Communicate ideas	• *What do you think...?* • *What could you do...?* • *How could you design...?* • *What do you think will happen if...?*
Convergent Thinking	**Bloom's Application and Analysis Level:** • Uses of logic • Deductive and inductive reasoning • Construct or reconstruct	**Closed Questions to:** • Focus attention, guide, encourage measurement and counting, make comparisons, take action • Use logic, state relationships • Apply solutions • Solve problems • Hypothesize and experiment • Communicate ideas	• *If "A", then what will happen to "B"...?* • *Which are facts, opinions and inferences...?* • *What is the author's purpose...?* • *What is the relationship of "x" to "y"...?*
Cognitive Memory	**Bloom's Knowledge and Comprehension Level:** • Rote memorization • Selective recall of facts, formulas, instructions, rules, or procedures • Recognition	**Managerial and Rhetorical Questions:** • Simple attention focusing, yes-no responses **Information:** • Repeat, name, describe, identify, observe, simple explanation, compare	• *What is the definition of...?* • *What are the three steps in...?* • *Who discovered...?* • *In your own words, what is the meaning of...?*
Intended mental activity			Key function or science processes

EXERCISE 10.2

Identifying Convergent and Divergent Questions

Convergent questions mean to elicit the single best answer, while divergent questions encourage a wide range of answers without concern for a single correct answer. Use the letters C and D to classify the following questions:

_____ 1. What kinds of food make your mouth water?

_____ 2. What name do we call the spit in your mouth?

_____ 3. What is another name for your esophagus?

_____ 4. How many intestines does your body have?

_____ 5. How many weights do you think you can add to your structure before it falls down?

_____ 6. Are you kept warm by radiation, conduction, convection, or all three?

_____ 7. Why does sound travel faster through solids and liquids than it does through air?

_____ 8. What kinds of uses does a balloon have?

_____ 9. How does electricity work?

_____ 10. How do you use electricity?

Check your answers with those at the end of the chapter. How well do we agree? What makes it difficult for you to classify questions?

WHAT ARE THE KEYS TO EFFECTIVE QUESTIONING?

Plan specific questions. Take the time to write specific questions before you teach. List six to eight key questions that cover the levels of thinking you wish to promote, and then use the questions as a guide for what you teach. The questions should help establish the knowledge base of information and then help build toward higher levels. Avoid yes-no questions unless that is your specific purpose; instead, focus the questions on the lesson topic by building toward the objectives. Open-ended questions can stimulate exploration, and convergent questions can focus concept invention. Both, along with evaluation questions, can contribute to expansion of the lesson's main idea. Pay attention to the types of questions used in children's books; then select books and materials with many different types, and supplement them with your own questions for special purposes.

Ask your questions as simply, concisely, and directly as possible. Make your purpose clear, and use single questions. Build upon previous questions once they have been answered, and avoid multiple, piggy-backed questions. These confuse students and indicate that the question is not well defined in the teacher's mind.

Ask your question before selecting who should answer. This helps keep all learners listening and thinking. Pause briefly after asking the question so everyone can think about it. Then select an individual to respond. Give both high and low achievers a chance to answer, and try to provide equal and genuine feedback. Involve as many different types of students as possible, volunteers and nonvolunteers. A total class shouting out answers could create discipline problems.

Limit rapid-fire, drill-and-practice questions to times when specific facts need to be gathered or reviewed. Avoid parroting the students' answers, but do try to use the students' ideas as much as possible.

Practice using wait-time. Wait-time 1 is often 1 second or less. Practice waiting at least 3 seconds for students to respond to most questions, especially if students are exploring or trying to expand on the lesson's main idea. Wait-time gives the children opportunities to think, create, and demonstrate more fully what they understand. Higher-level questions may require a wait-time longer than 3 seconds.

Wait-time 2 may need to be longer than wait-time 1. Rowe (1974) believes this wait-time is more important, especially when the occasion calls for critical or creative thinking. Quality and quantity of student responses increase, low achievers respond more, and the teacher has more time to think carefully about the questioning sequence.

Listen carefully to your students' responses. Encourage students nonverbally and verbally without overkilling with praise. Make any praise or encouraging remarks genuine. Check to make certain the children's responses match the level intended by your questions, and prompt them if the level is not appropriate. Do not always stop with the right answer. Probing benefits students who are partially correct and helps them construct a more acceptable answer. As a general rule, do not move on to another student before giving the first student a chance to form a better answer. This is a great opportunity to gather clues about students' misconceptions, incomplete information, or limited experiences. A brief questioning sequence may be all that is needed to overcome important learning problems.

Try using more questions to produce conceptual conflict. Piaget's research (Wadsworth, 1996) suggests that learners should be in a state of mental disequilibrium to help them adapt or add new mental constructions to their thinking:

What do you think will happen if we add more weight to the boat?

If we add a drop of soap *then* what could happen to the surface tension?

How would you design a test to determine the effects of fertilizer on plant growth?

What evidence do you have to support your identification of the limiting factors?

What other ways are possible to explain the effects of sunlight on plant growth?

How can you explain to the others what you did and what you discovered?

What do you think causes newsprint to look larger when viewed through a water droplet?

Talk less and ask more, but make your questions count. Ask, don't tell. Use questions to guide and invite your students to tell you. Work with students by exchanging ideas instead of conducting an inquisition. Try to make discussions

Listen carefully, ask concise, direct questions, practice wait time, and match the level of the questions to the level of the child.

more conversational by asking students to share thoughts and react to each other.

Try to use questions that yield more complete and more complex responses. Given consistently adequate wait-time, students should give longer and more thoughtful answers. The effectiveness of any specific question you use is never any greater than the answer you are willing to accept. Establish a base of information first; then build on it by asking questions that require more complex answers. Ask students who give short, incomplete answers to contribute more.

Ask different types of questions to encourage all children. Some learners seem unprepared for or incapable of answering high-level questions. If this is the case, try beginning your questions at a low level before attempting a higher level; build upward. Recalling information with frequent low-level questions for review, recitation, and drill helps children experience success, develop confidence, and establish a reliable foundation to build higher thinking upon. But do not let your questioning stagnate. Begin with closed questions to establish a firm footing, and then move on to more open-ended questions. Use divergent and evaluative questions less often initially, and increase their use over time if your students have difficulty responding as you desire.

Learners who have already had more successful and satisfying school experiences are eager and appear more capable of responding to higher levels of questions sooner. Reflective discussions that mix convergent, divergent, and evaluative questions can form a strategy for critical and original thinking. Yet despite the type of student, several studies show that lower-level questions promote greater achievement gains for all primary children when learning basic skills.

Several learning theorists and researchers remind us about differences in how primary and upper elementary children think. Each group processes information differently because of differences in mental development. Yet appropriate experiences can help mental development reach its full potential in each group. Questions related to the processes of science provide the momentum for this development.

For younger children in primary grades (ages 5 to 10), use questions to stimulate:

- observation of basic properties. *Example:* "What do you see happening to the Silly Putty?"
- classification based on similarities and differences. *Example:* "Which of these animals is an insect?"
- communication to show thoughts and increase the value of the experience as well as to develop cooperation and interpersonal relations. *Example:* "What are you observing? How do you feel about what you see?"
- measurement, using numbers and time. *Example:* "What is the final temperature? How much time did it take to reach that temperature?"
- prediction to form guesses based on what is known. *Example:* "What do you think will happen to the brightness of the bulb if we use a longer wire?"

For older children in upper elementary and middle grades (ages beyond 11), use questions that will help them to:

- identify variables. *Example:* "What variables did we keep the same?"
- control variables. *Example:* "What variables seemed to affect the size of your soap bubbles?"
- form operational definitions based on verified information. *Example:* "From what we did in this experiment, how should we define 'force?' "
- form and test hypotheses to reach conclusions. *Example:* "Why did the electrical resistance increase in this experiment?"
- interpret data from experiments. *Example:* "What do the green and pink color changes of the purple cabbage juice indicate?"
- form models to explain occurrences or represent theories. *Example:* "What kind of relationship between the species is suggested by their population graphs over the same length of time?"

Finally, determine whether the children are providing answers equal to the level of your questions. To do this you will need to monitor your questions and your students' responses.

HOW CAN YOU IMPROVE YOUR QUESTIONING?

You can improve your questioning with training and practice. One way to improve is to videotape or tape-record a lesson in which you use questions, play back the recording, identify the questions, and analyze them. Observation instruments or checklists such as those in Table 10.3 can be used. A more infor-

▲TABLE 10.3   Effective Questioning Checklist

Do you:

____   1. use broad or narrow questions to accomplish your objectives?

____   2. avoid yes-no questions unless that is your intention?

____   3. avoid repeating student answers?

____   4. encourage students to ask questions?

____   5. expand on students' ideas?

____   6. not stop the discussion after receiving the right answer?

____   7. use wait-time of at least 3 seconds?

____   8. avoid asking multiple questions?

____   9. avoid answering your own questions?

____ 10. ask students to clarify, summarize, and review material?

____ 11. avoid repeating your questions?

____ 12. rephrase misunderstood or unclear questions?

____ 13. call on volunteers and nonvolunteers?

____ 14. ask questions at different levels?

____ 15. talk less and ask more?

____ 16. use good grammar on a level understood by the children?

____ 17. encourage student-to-student discussion?

____ 18. not use questions to punish or embarrass students?

Source: Adapted from Iva D. Brown, "Topic 4: Teacher Questioning Techniques," *Staff Development Project—Science Grades K–6* (Jackson, MS: Mississippi Association for Teacher Education, 1986) (ERIC Document no. ED 285726), p. 159.

mative approach is to structure your observation and analysis around your questions. For example:

- How often did you use cognitive memory questions?
- How does this amount compare to your uses of convergent, divergent, and evaluative questions?
- How are your questions phrased? Do you avoid yes-no questions as much as possible?
- How do you know your questions are on the appropriate level for your students?
- What evidence did you find indicating that you adjust questions to the language and ability levels of the students?
- Are your questions distributed among all learners regardless of ability, gender, socioeconomic status, and where they are seated?

- How often do you call on nonvolunteers? How do you decide which non-volunteer to call upon?
- How often do you use probing to encourage students to complete responses, clarify, expand, or support a decision?
- How long do you wait? How do you use wait-time? What benefits do you receive from using wait-time? How does your use of wait-time 1 compare with wait-time 2?
- How well do the written questions on your plan match the verbal questions you use in class? Do your test questions represent the same levels as questions used in class?
- How often do children ask questions? What types of questions do they ask? Under what circumstances do they ask questions?

WHY USE STUDENTS' QUESTIONS?

> The children's questions worry me. I can deal with the child who just wants attention, but because I've had no science background I take other questions at face value and get bothered when I don't know the answer. I don't mind saying I don't know, though I don't want to do it too often. I've tried the let's-find-out-together approach, but it's not easy and can be very frustrating. (Jelly, 1985, p. 54)

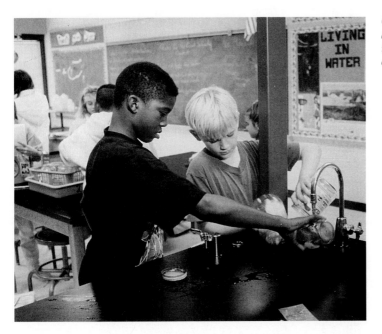

Children's questions can be used to develop interesting problems for science inquiry and to encourage the useful habit of reflection.

> **TEACHERS ON SCIENCE TEACHING**

How Do Questions Create Independent Thinkers?

by Ursula M. Sexton
Grades 1–5, Green Valley Elementary School, Danville, CA

I moved away from pouring information, most of which students forgot, to facilitating discussions, providing opportunities for explorations and ways to assess our progress and goals. I guess you could say I've gone from being an informational witness to becoming a thinking coach.

I am now defining my teacher role as one who provides the means for my students to make connections of big ideas; to guide them through process-oriented activities; to demonstrate circumstances that would otherwise be dangerous, foreign, or inaccessible to them; and to be the listener and facilitator. It works best when they are given situations, open-ended explorations, dynamic roles, and the tools or options to build, to research, to communicate, and to share their thinking. I tell my students our most used questions are, "Why do you think so?" "How can you support it?" "What do you mean by that?" "How does it work and why?" and "What do you think would happen if . . . ?"

Some ideas foster a climate not only for higher thinking questions and answers but for inclusion of all students:

• Set the stage like a mystery scene, in which students are given the clues, and they need to prove that these clues are valid to solve the mystery, or they need to use them to find further clues (process skills). They share with the class their approaches and solutions, back them up, and record them on graphs, videotape, illustrations, journals, or portfolios.

• Provide scenarios to visualize, make mental images, or think of characteristics by which they could describe an object, animal, plant, place, person, or situation. We make and write brainstorm umbrellas of big ideas for categorization, such as color, weight, time, location, traits, extinct or not, parts, functions, habitats, means of survival, and so on, and hang them around the room for reference.

• Give plenty of opportunities and different materials and means to classify and label their sorting. This one is especially dear to me, because it was my wake-up call to learn to encourage and understand the children's thinking. One day my little first-grade scientists were reviewing the process of classification by sorting ourselves into three groups. Silently I would point to a child and direct him or her to an assigned area in the classroom, within clear sight of the rest of the class. To play, they could not call out the answer to the rule or pattern being sorted, but had to point to the team they thought they belonged to, once they studied it and recognized the rule. If they were correct, they would stand with the team. If not, they would remain seated for a later turn. At the end, everyone was standing in one of the teams. As I inquired what their team characteristic or pattern was, most children called out what I, as the chooser, had thought for the rule. "We all have turtlenecks," called one. "We all have collars," said the others. Finally, in the

Why Bother with Students' Questions?

"Can one black hole swallow another?"
"Why do fireflies light up?"
"How does a steel ship float when it weighs so much?"

third team, the speaker said, "We all have jackets." At that moment, one of the girls in the middle team said, "I thought I was here because we all have red and none of the other teams do." Indeed, she was right! So I decided to capitalize on the thought and asked the rest of the class, "Can you think of any other ways by which we all might be sorted while in the teams we are now?" Oh! it was just wonderful to hear their reasoning! They were very proud of themselves. These are the circumstances that teachers need to act upon repeatedly throughout the day and not in isolated instances. Becoming aware of them takes a little self-training and practice.

- "What ifs . . .?" are just wonderful, open-ended questions that can be connected to real-life circumstances.
- Have a discovery corner with manipulatives and questions promoting scientific processes.
- Have the children design new questions to go along with the discovery corner boards for another class to try out.

One of the most important elements of science instruction is the teacher's attitude toward science. You own attitude toward learning will be the underlying gift you pass on to your kids. If and when you need to be the guide, do it with enthusiasm. Facilitate in a motivating, nonthreatening, and enthusiastic manner. If you were asked to write a newspaper advertisement for a science classroom guide and facilitator, what would you write? Check how this description matches the way you teach in the classroom. Take notes on your style if you need to focus more in this direction. You'll probably be pleasantly surprised to see how much you really do to foster the childrens' previous knowledge and their questions. When you introduce new concepts, ask yourself, "New to whom? to a few? How new? new to me? What questions might they have that will definitely show growth when we are done learning about it? What am I learning from this process?" Listen to their discussions and their questions; take notes. Make comments, bring out to the light awesome and small achievements, discoveries, questions that foster further questioning. With ownership of their thinking processes, they'll become independent thinkers. For assessment, remember that tests are merely a reflection and a tool to tell how well you've conveyed a message and how well they have received it. That is why assessments should be ongoing, by observation, cooperation, participation, and communication.

I have learned so much from my students' attitudes about learning, their question, their inquisitiveness or lack of it, and their experiences. The gifts they bring on their own are assets to all. It is because of them that I enjoy teaching. They challenge me on a daily basis. I grow with them on a daily basis.

"Why are soda cans shaped like a cylinder and not a rectangle?" (Perlman & Pericak-Spector, 1992, pp. 36–37)

Children's questions give precious insight into their world and illustrate topics of interest. Their questions can surprise teachers who might underestimate the ability of particular children and may suggest that certain learners have more ability than is evident from their reading and written work. The questions students ask also give a guide to what they know and do not know, and when they want to know it. These questions give clues about what science content is understood and the level of concept development—if we are willing to listen closely. Questions could also indicate an anxious child, or simply reveal a habit formed by one who has been reinforced to ask questions (Biddulph, Symington, & Osborn, 1986).

Questions help students focus and gain knowledge that interests them. Incessant "Why?" questions can be a method of gaining attention, but unlike the 2-year-old, the school age child who asks, "Why?" reveals an area where understanding is lacking and is desired. Questions help young children resolve unexpected outcomes or work through problem situations; they can also be a way of confirming a belief. Children's questions also help them learn more quickly. "When they are following their own noses, learning what they are curious about, children go faster, cover more territory than we would ever think of trying to mark out for them, or make them cover" (Holt, 1971, p. 152).

Encouraging students to ask questions develops a useful habit: reflection. Habits take time to form, and question asking is a habit that can enrich a school's curriculum. Time spent in contemplation helps form this habit. Asking oneself questions and hazarding guesses about their answers stimulate creative thinking, provide a means for solving critical problems, and can help a child learn "to find interest and enjoyment in situations that others would see as dull or boring" (Biddulph, Symington, & Osborn, 1986, p. 78).

How Can You Stimulate Students' Questions?

Four factors stimulate children to ask questions. If you want children to ask more questions, you should provide adequate stimulation, model appropriate question asking, develop a classroom atmosphere that values questions, and include question asking in your evaluations of children.

Stimulation.   Direct contact with materials is a first step. What kinds of materials stimulate curiosity in children and provide them opportunities to explore? The best indicator is the materials children bring in spontaneously. The sharing has a built-in curiosity factor and requires little effort to conduct discussion; simply invite them to share and ask questions. The mind will be on what the hands are doing.

Modeling.   Teacher question asking is modeling. Learners must be shown how to ask good, productive questions. Showing genuine enthusiasm and consideration for what interests others can show children how to do the same. Consider some of the following ways to bring this modeling into the routine of your classroom (Jelly, 1985).

Share collections and develop classroom displays, much as Mrs. B did in our opening scenario. Link these activities to regular classwork and organize them around key chapter questions. Use one of the question classification systems described earlier in this chapter to help you ask questions at many different levels. Invite children to share their own collections and create class displays while building questions into the discussion the children share with classmates.

Establish a problem corner in your classroom or use a "Question of the Week" approach to stimulate children's thought and questions. These approaches can be part of regular class activity or used for enrichment. Catherine Valentino's (1985) Question of the Week materials could be a good place to start until you acquire enough ideas of your own. Consider one of her examples, "I Lava Volcano," a photo of an erupting volcano, which asks these questions: "Do volcanic eruptions serve any useful purpose? Over millions of years, what changes would occur on the earth if all volcanic activity suddenly stopped?" Valentino's full-color weekly posters and questions stimulate curiosity and inquiry.

Prepare lists of questions to investigate with popular children's books. Encourage students to add their own questions to the list.

Use questions to organize any teacher-made activity cards that learners may use independently. Encourage children to think of their work as an investigative mission and to see themselves as clue seekers.

John Langrehr (1993) recommends two additional tools that teachers can use to model effective questioning and help learners improve their thinking and question-asking skills. Figure 10.7 provides sixteen question starters that

FIGURE 10.7   Question-Formation Matrix

	Object/Event	*Situation*	*Reason*	*Means*
Present	What is . . .?	Where is . . .?	Why is . . .?	How is . . .?
Possibility	What can . . .?	Where can . . .?	Why can . . .?	How can . . .?
Probability	What would . . .?	Where would . . .?	Why would . . .?	How would . . .?
Imagination	What might . . .?	Where might . . .?	Why might . . .?	How might . . .?

Source: S. Langrehr, "Getting Thinking into Science Questions," *Australian Science Teachers Journal* 39 (4), (1993): 36.

should help any student to design focused, thoughtful questions. Consider the topic of insects. Using the question starters shown in the matrix, students should be able to expand their inquiry by asking questions such as: *What is* an insect? *How is* an insect different from a spider? *What can* insects do that humans cannot? *Where would* you expect to find insects? *Why might* insects be better able to survive a forest fire than mammals? and so on.

Langrehr also recommends that we show students how to use a *connection map* (Figure 10.8) in order to improve their questioning and construction of mental connections among and between the various ideas that may be illustrated by the map. Less able thinkers tend to think more generally, while more capable thinkers tend to think more abstractly. As a tool, the connection map encourages each student to record several key words in boxes that surround a central idea. Encourage students to write connecting words between the boxes that form simple sentences that make sense. This student-designed map can help you peer inside the thinking of the student. Simple questions such as "Why?" or "How?" can encourage students to construct more thought-provoking questions that stimulate productive experimentation.

FIGURE 10.8   Question Connection Map

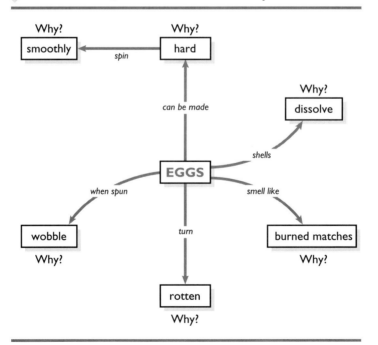

Source: Adapted from J. Langrehr, "Getting Thinking into Science Questions," *Australian Science Teachers Journal* 39 (4), (1993): 36.

Classroom Atmosphere.   Suchman (1971) believes students inquire only when they feel free to share their ideas without fear of being censored, criticized, or ridiculed. Successful teachers listen to children and do not belittle their curious questions. Establish an atmosphere that fosters curiosity by praising those who invent good questions; reinforce their reflective habits. You can provide opportunities for questions by:

* using class time regularly for sharing ideas and asking questions as learners talk about something that interests them,
* having children supply questions of the week and rewarding them for improvements in their question asking,
* helping children write lists (or record lists for nonreaders) of questions they have about something they have studied. These questions can be excellent

FIGURE 10.9   How Should You Respond to Children's Questions?

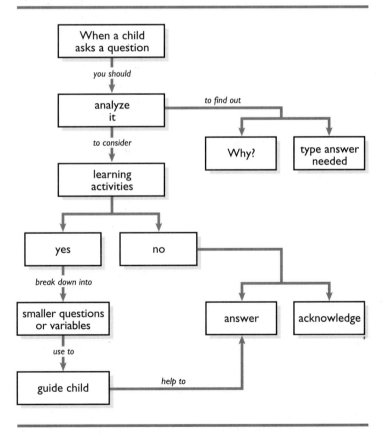

means for review, for showing further interest, and for providing an informal evaluation of how clearly you have taught a topic.

Question Asking and Evaluation.   Have students form questions as another way of evaluating their learning. This factor can stimulate habits of question asking and is different than if you, as teacher, ask questions children must answer. Include a picture or description of a situation in a test occasionally, and call for children to write productive questions about it. In another approach, the students list questions they believe are important for a more complete understanding of the material they have just studied. Lists of their questions can be evaluated for the number and the quality of the questions; quality should refer to the relevance of the question to the topic as well as the thought required to answer it.

How Can You Use Students' Questions Productively?

When children ask, focus your listening on the ideas represented by their questions. You will need to help them clarify their questions until they learn to ask better ones by themselves. Sheila Jelly (1985) offers a strategy you can use to turn children's questions into productive learning opportunities. Figure 10.9 is based on Jelly's recommendations.

CHAPTER SUMMARY

If there is a universal teaching tool, the question is it. Questions provide unique opportunities for teachers and students to become involved in productive dialogue; questions invite both teachers and learners to think and respond in many different ways.

We know that the potential of questioning is underused and that many teacher questions are closed and stimulate low-level thinking. Questions may be misused if the wrong types of questions are used before children are capable or ready to respond at the level demanded. Appropriate questions stimulate productive thinking and curiosity. Effective questions contribute to students' improved attitudes, expanded capability for thinking, and increased achievement.

As teachers, we need to afford all learners equal opportunities to learn through our questioning techniques. Old habits may have to be changed. We must strive to give children adequate time to think by expanding wait-time; screen textbooks, tests, and other print materials for evidence of good questions; and help children develop the habit of reflecting by encouraging them to ask their own questions.

All questions are not equal; they come in such different types as Bloom's taxonomy, open and closed, science processes, memory, and evaluation. Questions should be selected or composed for specific purposes.

You can question well by using the keys for good questioning described in this chapter. Periodically analyze how you use questions, and form a plan for self-improvement. Check your skills against your plan and revise as necessary.

Students' questions provide benefits for teachers, children, and the science program.

Teachers can encourage learners' questions if they use materials and activities that simulate questions, model good questioning skills, provide a supportive classroom atmosphere, and include children's question asking in evaluation techniques.

DISCUSSION QUESTIONS AND PROJECTS

1. Based on your school experiences, what differences have you noticed about how your teachers used questions? How do your elementary, secondary, and college teachers compare on using questions?

2. What types of questions do your teachers usually ask? How well do the questions match with the teachers' intentions? Justify your answer.

3. How do the elementary teachers you have observed use questions to begin a lesson? to focus children's observations? to lead children toward conclusions? to bring closure to a lesson?

4. What priority do you believe teachers should give to children's questions? What strategy should they use?

5. How important is it for teachers to monitor their own uses of questions?

6. How well do you use questions? What evidence do you have to support your answer? What do you think you can do to improve your questioning skills? Audio- or videotape yourself using questions when you practice teaching. Use the recommendations of this chapter to focus an evaluation of your questioning skills, and begin by comparing the numbers of closed and open questions you use.

7. Using any of the methods for classifying questions described in this chapter, write and label samples of two questions for each level. Work within class groups to evaluate the quality of the questions. How well do you avoid yes-no questions, require more than rote memory, and avoid unproductive questions?

8. Use several of the questions you have written to speculate about pupil replies and appropriate teacher responses. List the questions and the replies for the pupil and teacher.

9. Observe a science lesson. Record the number and types of questions asked by the teacher, and try to measure the average wait-time. How do your observations correspond to the average uses of questions and wait-time described in this chapter?

10. Tape-record a class session in which children ask questions. Transcribe these questions, and describe how you could respond to them if you were the teacher. How does your response method compare with Sheila Jelly's suggestion?

ADDITIONAL READINGS

If you are interested in learning more about some of the topics raised in this chapter, consider the following sources.

Patricia Blosser, *How to Ask the Right Questions* (Washington, DC: National Science Teachers Association, 1991). This booklet includes questions for science, discusses the value of science, describes important factors relevant to questioning, and provides descriptions of techniques you can use to analyze your questioning style.

Arthur Carin and Robert B. Sund, *Creative Questioning and Sensitive Listening Techniques—A Self-Concept Approach* (Columbus, OH: Merrill Publishing, 1978). This is an authoritative text for increasing your questioning skills in a unique way. The end product of effect questioning, according to the authors, is improving children's self-concepts. Many practical examples are given.

J. T. Dillon, *Questioning and Teaching: A Manual of Practice* (New York: Teachers College Press, 1988). Dillon's manual focuses on skill development.

Chapters are devoted to student questions and teacher questions, with particular emphasis given to questions used with recitation and discussion. A lengthy appendix provides classroom transcripts, which are useful for seeing concrete relationships between the pedagogy and effects of questioning.

Susan Pearlman and Kathleen Pericak-Spector, "Expect the Unexpected Question," *Science and Children* (October 1992). This article provides a brief list of children's amazing questions. Sources they recommend for finding the answers include B. Ardley, *The Random House Book of 1001 Questions and Answers* (New York: Random House, 1989); D. McCaulay, *The Way Things Work* (New York: Houghton Mifflin, 1988); J. Makower, *The Air and Space Catalog* (New York: Tilden, 1987); S. Parker,

McGraw-Hill Encyclopedia of Science and Technology (vols. 1–20), (New York: McGraw-Hill, 1987); and R. H. Wynne, *Lizards in Captivity* (Neptune, NJ: T. F. H. Publications, 1981).

William W. Wilen (ed.), *Questions, Questioning Techniques, and Effective Teaching* (Washington, DC: National Education Association, 1987). This source provides some of the most extensive coverage on questioning we have seen in one book. This collection provides a rationale for using questions, a review of the years of research on questioning, and information on the multiple uses of questions. Question classification, wait-time, effective question uses, and students as question askers are covered. A chapter is also devoted to improving teachers' questions.

ANSWERS TO EXERCISE 10.1

1. Observing
2. Hypothesizing/experimenting
3. Generalizing/predicting
4. Observing
5. Communicating
6. Measuring
7. Hypothesizing/experimenting
8. Comparing/contrasting
9. Generalizing/predicting
10. Measuring

Questions come from the following sources:

1. Seymour, S. (1978). *Exploring fields and lots: Easy science projects.* Champaign, IL: Garrard Publishing.
2. Bendick, J. (1971). *How to make a cloud.* New York: Parents' Magazine Press.
3. Seymour, S. (1970). *Science in a vacant lot.* New York: Viking Press.

4. Zubrowski, B. (1979). *Bubbles: A children's museum activity book.* Boston: Little, Brown.
5. Seymour, S. (1978). *Exploring fields and lots: Easy science projects.* Champaign, IL: Gerrard Publishing.
6. Renner, A. G. (1979). *Experimental fun with the yo-yo and other scientific projects.* New York: Dodd, Mead.
7. Milgrem, H. (1976). *Adventures with a straw: First experiments.* New York: E. P. Dutton.
8. Selsam, M. E. (1957). *Play with seeds.* New York: William Morrow.
9. Seymour, S. (1969). *Discovering what frogs do.* New York: McGraw-Hill.
10. Zubrowski, B. (1981). *Messing around with baking chemistry: A Children's Museum activity book.* Boston: Little, Brown.

ANSWERS TO EXERCISE 10.2

1. Divergent, because *how* many different kinds of food make *your* mouth water?
2. Convergent, saliva.
3. Convergent, gullet.
4. Convergent, small and large intestines.

5. Divergent, because this question asks for a prediction that depends on several factors that stimulate many different answers.
6. Convergent, because you are asked to select an answer from those given.

7. Convergent, because a specific concept is used to answer the question.

8. Divergent, because who knows the answer to this one? Only your imagination limits the possibilities.

9. Convergent, because descriptions about electron flow rely on a specific concept.

10. Divergent. Think about it: How many *different* ways do you use or depend on electricity?

CHAPTER OUTLINE

CHAPTER 11

How Can You Use Science Demonstrations and Textbooks Effectively?

Doris Smith's classroom is next door to Mrs. McDonald's (of the Chapter 9 scenario) (Rakow, 1986, pp. 8–11). Mrs. Smith is also conducting a lesson on predator-prey relationships in animals. Her approach to the lesson differs dramatically from Mrs. McDonald's. Mrs. Smith's style reflects, in part, her lack of confidence in teaching science. She does enjoy teaching, however, especially teaching reading.

Her classroom is arranged much more conventionally—five rows across and six seats deep. There are posters on the walls featuring Newbery Award books and travel posters of interesting places to visit. In front of the classroom is a student duty chart: class monitor, pledge leader, and so on.

"In our science reading today, we will learn two new words," begins Mrs. Smith as she writes the words *predator* and *prey* on the chalkboard. "This word is *predator*. A predator is an animal that eats other animals. A hawk is a predator because it hunts field mice. The other word is *prey*. Prey is an animal that is eaten by other animals. The field mouse is an example of prey. Please open your science text to page 48. Who would like to begin reading? Adam."

"Many animals live together in the forest. Some of these animals hunt other animals for food. These hunters are called pred . . ., pred . . ."

"Pred-a-tors," says Mrs. Smith, pronouncing each syllable.

"Predators."

"Who would like to continue? Rebecca."

"The animals that are eaten for food are called prey. Predators and prey are part of the life cycle of all living things."

The children continue reading until they have finished the section on predators and prey. "Please take out a pencil," says Mrs. Smith. "I would now like you to complete this worksheet on predators and prey."   ◆

INTRODUCTION

Avoiding Authoritarianism and the Exclusive Use of Textbooks

Mrs. Smith's approach is typical of about 90 percent of traditional science teachers. They use a textbook about 95 percent of the time and rely on teacher-centered methods consisting of lectures, reading, and questions and answers (Holdzkum & Lutz, 1984). Their approaches are often limited to the information provided by the adopted textbook and assume that

> students should mainly pay attention to teacher presentations, read textbook passages, participate in teacher-led discussions, answer questions from the textbook and teaching plans, complete worksheets, and carry out hands-on activities as directed. Both the student textbooks and teacher lesson plans give students a mainly passive role as receivers and memorizers of information rather than as active seekers of answers to important scientific questions, although some [textbook science programs do] offer follow-up suggestions for keeping records of observation, writing reports, taking field trips, and caring for living things. (Elliott & Carter, 1986, p. 11)

Texts are *not* all bad. They do present important science information that is useful in addressing some of the National Science Education Standards content. Complete reliance upon textbooks, however, usually means students will be deprived of other worthy science education goals relevant to understanding the nature of science, developing science inquiry skills, and understanding personal, technological, and societal issues.

Reliance on a single science textbook can promote an authoritarian approach to teaching and learning. The text or the teacher becomes *the* authority, with the textbook becoming the principal determiner of what is taught. The science topic usually is selected because it is "in the book" (Staver & Bay, 1987). Furthermore, textbooks by themselves, without teacher modification, usually do not promote or encourage the development of scientific thinking or attitudes; nor do they engage students in applying the cognitive processes that are basic to understanding the content covered. If teachers use these programs to teach science without drawing on supplementary resources, students will understand science mainly as a collection of conclusions to be memorized: They will not be brought to an adequate understanding of the nature and methods of science nor will they be afforded sufficient opportunities to explore the relationship of science to technology and to the problems of living in the modern world (Elliott & Carter, 1986, p. 11).

Driver (1994) reinforces the message we have delivered throughout this book: Constructing science knowledge in the classroom depends on the interplay of various factors such as personal experience, language, and socialization and the involvement of learners in the problematic relationships of compilations of scientific information (a.k.a. textbooks), learning processes, and teaching methods. As von Glaserfeld (1993) reminds us,

> Knowledge is always the result of a constructive activity and, therefore it cannot be transferred to a passive receiver. [Knowledge] has to be actively built up by each individual knower. A teacher, however, can orient a learner in a general direction, and constraints can be arranged that prevent the learner from constructing in directions that seem unsuitable to the teacher. (p. 26)

There are no simple rules or recipes to follow for foolproof teaching and learning, and "teacher-proof" curricula simply do not work. Instead, there are many guiding principles that a well-informed, reflective teacher can use to create effective learning conditions. According to Driver and associates (1994), "If students are to adopt scientific ways of knowing, then intervention and negotiation with an authority figure, usually the teacher, is essential" (p. 11). The National Science Education Standards make a compelling case for helping learners develop scientific ways of knowing.

As science teacher authority figures, we have important functions: to introduce new ideas or cultural tools where they are necessary; provide support and guidance to students so that they can make sense for themselves; listen to learners' responses so that we can interpret the ways that our learning activities are being interpreted; and form diagnoses that inform the further actions we choose to take (Driver, 1994). Classrooms require successful interaction between and among teachers and students if the new vision of science learning is to occur. The overall intent of this chapter is to offer adjustments and alternatives to the tools that teacher authority figures typically use so that they can become more supportive of and successful with constructivism in science education.

Why Is an Interactive Classroom Important?

An authoritative method, such as the lecture, is not recommended for extensive use in elementary science teaching. What is recommended are *interactive* teaching approaches. Mary Iatridis (1981) tells us that the young child's "capacity to think and reason is limited by extreme dependence on experience" (p. 26). Mary Willert and Constance Kamii also remind us that authoritative teacher-centered forms of direct instruction are "based on the erroneous assumption that children are like empty glasses who learn by having bits of knowledge poured into them, and that the sooner we start to fill the glasses, the sooner this process will be completed" (Willert & Kamii, 1985, p. 3).

Interaction is an important tool that helps learners to construct meaning from materials and experiences.

Interactive classrooms are places where teachers and students exchange ideas and observations. Classrooms of this type develop learners who are intrinsically motivated and who will go much further than those who wait to be told what to learn (Willert & Kamii, 1985). The purpose of this chapter is to help you to

1. explore ways of making a teacher-centered classroom more interactive,
2. develop skills in using effective teacher demonstrations that encourage constructed learning,
3. teach more effectively those lessons when you may choose to use exposition as a method to support other constructivist efforts,
4. become informed about how to select and use science textbooks that support constructive learning.

HOW CAN YOU USE TEACHER DEMONSTRATIONS TO FOSTER CONSTRUCTED LEARNING?

With most demonstrations, a central figure stands before a class and shows something and then tells what happened. The central authority figure, often a teacher, usually is the only individual actually involved with the demonstration. Students' reactions to demonstrations may range from wide-eyed excitement to sleepy apathy (Wolfinger, 1984). How can you conduct a demonstration that stimulates curiosity and motivates the children so they actually *want* to hear an explanation? Clara Guerra (1988) succeeds nicely, combining a bit of showmanship with the magic of science. She describes an exciting demonstration that can be done safely with sufficient planning and safety protection. We recommend that the demonstrator wear approved safety goggles, have a fire blanket on hand, and seat the front row of students at least 10 feet from the demonstration table; the observers should wear goggles as required by state law. We recommend that you review the safety and management recommendations found in Chapter 6 before trying the demonstartion. Let's watch Guerra's (1988, pp. 23–24) approach and learn about her techniques.

> "A Bit of Science—A Bit of Magic" is a presentation I do for the elementary schools. It is nothing more than simple science dressed up as magic. I am the magician and the children are my dutifully amazed audience. I explode cans based on the rapid oxidation principle, I turn liquids blue with chemical reactions,

Creative demonstrations help to increase interaction with pupils.

and I pull the tablecloth out from under dishes, thanks to Newton's law of inertia. While many in the audience may remember only the razzle-dazzle, the pops and bangs of the show, every so often one of their parents will tell me later that their son or daughter wants to be a scientist. That's when I know that a spark has been ignited. Someone has taken the first step toward discovering the real magic of science.

"Ladies and gentlemen, boys and girls, I am a scientist!" I begin, standing in front of the students in a sorcerer's hat. "I am someone who sees things a little differently." As I talk, the house lights go out and black lights come on. My hat, decorated with stars and crayoned with fluorescent colors, catches the light and seems to stand alone on the stage. Without a drum roll or a more formal fanfare, the show begins.

Nothing quite catches the attention of a young audience like a big bang does. And a big bang is what they get with the exploding dust can trick.

To perform this, I use a candle and candle holder, lycopodium powder (flour will also work) and a small metal doll's cup, a paint can with the cup inside, and an air hose leading into the cup.

First, I fill the cup half full of the lycopodium powder and place it in the paint can. Then, I place a lit candle in its holder inside the paint can and put the lid back on. The air hose has been inserted through a hole in the side of the paint can and sits in the cup. I take a deep breath, blow deeply into the air hose, and stand back quickly. (See Figure 11.1.)

Within seconds, the top explodes off the can. Then I explain. When I blew into the can, I made the dust spread throughout it. The candle then ignited the mixture, causing the gases in the air to expand. When the gases expanded, they needed more space than the inside of the can had. There was only one place

FIGURE 11.1   The Exploding Can Demonstration

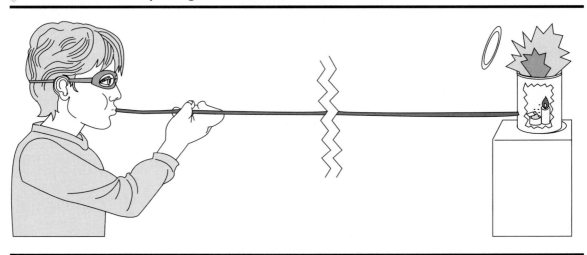

for the gases to go—out of that can. I tell the children this sometimes happens in grain dust elevators or flour mills or even in the family woodworking shop.

After the explosion, I set the lit candle on the table. I sprinkle a small amount of lycopodium dust onto the lid of the paint can. Holding the lid, I sprinkle some of the dust directly into the candle's flame. This shows the children what happened inside the can. A word of caution, if you try this: Move away from the candle quickly, and don't wear flowing sleeves.

Tips for Effective Demonstrations

Guerra's (1988) technique provides a vivid illustration of several effective tips for planning and delivering classroom demonstrations. We do not suggest that you must always be an entertainer. However, a little panache does enliven the class. Demonstrations can be effective teaching tools if you follow these suggestions:

1. The demonstration should have a *specific purpose,* and this purpose must *be clear* to all learners. Focus on the point to be learned, and make it evident in the demonstration. Also discuss how it relates to past or future lessons. If it is intended only to entertain and not teach a concept, the demonstration has little value.

2. *Plan carefully.* Collect all the necessary materials and practice the demonstration in advance. Follow the instructions and inspect them for inaccuracies. Modify the demonstration, if necessary, for safety. Remember, we recommend that you use goggles, distance, and fire protection if you try Guerra's demonstration. Sometimes a substitution may be useful; a safer but still exciting alternative to explosion is implosion. For example, try a clean, empty metal can with a top (like a rinsed Ditto fluid can). Add 70 mL water (about a quarter cup) and heat it to a boil on a hotplate (without the cap). Wearing oven mitts, remove the can from the heat, replace the cap, cool it under a faucet or in a bucket of cold water, and watch what happens. (The can is crushed by a greater air pressure outside the can than inside.)

3. *Involve the students when possible.* Let the students participate in the demonstrations, or permit them to conduct the demonstration. Interactive teaching techniques such as questions and guess-making stimulate thinking, enthusiasm, and participation.

4. *Stimulate thinking and discussion.* "What do you think will happen if . . .?" questions help stimulate original thinking and bring forth children's ideas for productive discussion. This technique also releases you from giving away too much information before the demonstration and running the risk of destroying interest. Refer to Chapter 10 for additional questioning ideas.

5. *Repeat the demonstration.* A rapid flash, a loud bang, or an imploding can is sure to get attention and will demand a repeat performance. During the repeat, students will pay closer attention, and their powers of observation will be keener. Also, they will be given chances to acquire ideas or form mental connections that seem simple for us but are difficult for them because of their limited experiences.

6. *Use simple materials.* Unfamiliar equipment may distract the students' attention. Familiar objects and equipment will help them focus on the cause of the action or the purpose of the demonstration rather than on the gadgets being used. Students may also choose to try the demonstrations for themselves. Importation of high school equipment for elementary classroom use should be selective and always screened for safety (see Chapter 6).

7. *Keep the demonstration easily visible.* A cluttered demonstration table will distract children from seeing what you intend. Similarly, objects that are too small to be seen by those sitting beyond the first row will frustrate viewers and cause them to lose interest. Use a tall table or counter, gather the students around when feasible (and when safe), or consider using such projection devices as the overhead projector or microcomputer.

8. *Connect* with the students' environment. Interact in order to connect the point of the demonstration with the children's personal interests, community, or social issues to expand the benefits of the demonstration and the scientific concepts or principles. Guerra did this when referring to the grain elevator, flour mill, or family wood shop.

9. *Rely on quality, not quantity.* Avoid a large number of demonstrations hoping the students learn *something.* A single well-designed, timely demonstration can communicate powerful ideas more effectively than an overwhelming number of entertaining shows. Focus on a central concept.

When Should You Use a Demonstration?

"To keep the room neat" and "to prevent the kids from tearing things up" are not good reasons for doing demonstrations. These reasons only prevent learners from gaining necessary experience with the materials and also prevent them from learning how to interact appropriately with learning aids. Nevertheless, there are some reasons for teachers to do demonstrations:

- to avoid putting students in danger by using a demonstration as a safer alternative;
- to help students learn such skills as the proper ways to use equipment or the proper way to handle and care for plants and animals,
- to stop the class action so it can be focused on an important event for concept development,
- to overcome equipment shortages when there is not enough equipment for all children to benefit firsthand from the exercise,
- to arouse student interest, raise important questions, or pose learning problems that require critical and creative thinking,
- to help solve academic problems,
- to apply what has been studied to new situations by expanding experiences,
- to encourage slow learners and challenge rapid learners.

When Should the Students Do a Demonstration?

Student demonstrations may also be helpful. Proper times for children to demonstrate for their peers include:

- when the child has designed an original activity and should receive recognition for the effort,
- when a child's demonstration and explanation will help other students understand better,
- when a child cannot otherwise tell in words what has been done,
- to help children build self-confidence by speaking before others, to help build verbal communication skills, to help the rapid learner gain new insights.

Demonstrations inevitably open the door for questions. Along with questions come children who are intrinsically motivated and who want more information. These interaction-rich moments provide opportunities to guide students' knowledge construction.

HOW CAN YOU USE EXPOSITION EFFECTIVELY?

Exposition, or lecture, is an efficient way to convey information. While it may be time efficient, exposition is not necessarily effective unless certain steps are taken that enable students to form conceptual constructions and connections. Exposition consists of verbal teaching by an authority such as a teacher, textbook, speaker, film, or video. Information is presented, usually without planned interaction between the authority and the student. Teacher lecture and textbook reading are the most common forms of exposition. The way to use exposition most effectively is rather simple: Plan for interaction to occur often between the authority and the student, and relate the interaction to student science experiences.

Problems and Uses

Exposition carries several problems when used in elementary classrooms. Young children need concrete experiences during most of the elementary grades: verbal presentations of information are difficult for them to follow, and their attention span is limited. The logic of the adult mind may not match well with that of the younger mind, and textbook-ordered information has this same problem. Two other problems are related to exposition: Under the best circumstances the most capable learners only retain about half or less of what they hear, and what is said is not always what is heard or remembered.

Expository teaching does have several appropriate uses: to provide necessary background information before the lesson, to provide important instructions for an activity, to summarize, to bring a lesson to a close, and, most important, to make mental connections.

What can you do before the lesson to help the children understand the concept?

Before the Lesson.   The *advance organizer* is an effective verbal device to use before an expository method. According to David Ausubel (1963), its purpose is to provide a mental structure or framework for thinking before the lesson begins and the actual material is taught. Advance organizers "are broadly defined as bridges from the [learner's] previous knowledge to whatever is to be learned; they are supposed to be more abstract and inclusive than the more specific material to be learned, and to provide a means of organizing the new material" (Stone, 1982, p. 1). The lesson then may progress with a teacher presentation, reading, film, or video program; the students already know which important points they should attend to. Use of the advance organizer promotes more active mental participation during the presentation and has contributed to significantly greater pupil learning and retention because presentations are made more meaningful to learners through conceptual connections (Stone, 1982).

There are two types of advance organizers. *Expository* organizers are used with unfamiliar material, often at the beginning of a unit or lesson. For example, a teacher may begin a lesson by saying: "Today we are going to begin a study of animal habitats with an activity. At the end of the activity you should be able to define 'habitat' by describing its parts and how they are related. A habitat consists of five main parts: food, water, shelter, space, and arrangement. Look for examples of these as we do the activity and then read about habitats in our textbooks."

Comparative organizers work well when the children are going to learn new material but already are familiar with the topic in other ways. Comparative organizers help to link new information with what is already known. A lesson with a comparative organizer may begin this way: "Doors and gates open and close. A switch is like a door or a gate. It opens and closes a circuit. When the switch is open the circuit is open and will *not* permit the electrical device to operate. When the switch is closed, the electricity can pass through the circuit and the devices connected to it *will* work. Today we are going to make switches and construct different types of circuits to see how they operate."

To Provide Instructions or Give Directions. Exposition is always used when a teacher gives instructions to the class. Effective steps for giving directions include: read, review, and question. It is incorrect to assume that the children will read and follow the directions by themselves if given printed instructions. Instead, read the directions to them or invite a student to read to the class or for a cooperative group, and then review with the children what should be done first, second, and so on. Next, answer their questions. If the children have no questions, offer some of your own that they may think of later, and be prepared to review the answers again. All of this should be done *before* the children receive the materials to ensure safe, orderly completion of the learning activity.

For Summary or Closure. Exposition can be a useful tool for review at the end of the lesson or the activity if modified from a teacher-centered approach into one that is more student centered. The teacher can review for the pupils the important points by linking them with specific experiences and by redefining or reexplaining. Ask review questions to encourage the children to construct the summary for themselves. These techniques can help the important concepts to be developed in the same order of the lesson and to be linked with what the children have experienced.

These three uses of expository teaching complement parts of a deductive teaching method. They may be used within a larger framework of deductive teaching and thinking for effective exposition.

Using Deduction

Exposition often follows a deductive approach and is organized from the general idea of the lesson to the specific participation of the learners. Figure 11.2 shows a general deductive model, with four steps proceeding from the broad, general base to the specific learner experiences provided by the lesson. Simple enhancements can be added to make the teaching more interactive. In the case of our chapter scenario, Mrs. Smith's lesson could have proceeded along the following steps if she had chosen to use deduction.

Step 1. Give the generalization.

"Predators and prey are part of the life cycle of all living things. Our lesson today is about predators and prey."

FIGURE 11.2   Deductive Science Teaching   In deductive teaching, the lesson progresses from the general (a rule, concept, or formula) to the specific student experience (a learning activity, seat work, problem solving).

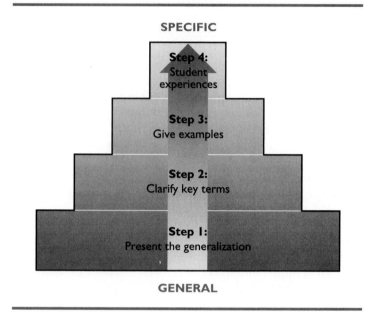

SPECIFIC

Step 4:
Student experiences

Step 3:
Give examples

Step 2:
Clarify key terms

Step 1:
Present the generalization

GENERAL

Step 2. Clarify key terms.

"Pred-a-tor [written on the chalkboard and carefully pronounced for the class, and then with class participation in its spelling and pronunciation] refers to animals that hunt other animals for food. Prey [written, spelled, and pronounced] is the name given to the animals that are hunted and eaten by other animals."

Step 3. Give examples.

"Some examples include hawks that catch and eat mice, spiders that catch other insects in their webs, foxes that prey on a farmer's young chickens, and big fish, like a largemouth bass, that eat smaller fish." Textbook reading can also help to give examples.

Step 4. Students gain experiences by working with and/or by giving specific examples.

"Here is a list of animal names. I'd like you to look at it and tell which are the predators and which are the prey: lion, skunk, insect, frog, human, cow, pig, deer, rabbit, fish, bear." After a while the children classify the animals into a predator and prey list, but with difficulty since some animals may be both predator and prey. The children also learn that a single predator may prey upon more than one type of animal and that humans are predators too, an idea that many students had not recognized but now think about as they eat and help parents shop.

"Now please add to our list of predators and prey." Ideas are obtained from the children until two long lists are constructed with a wide variety of animals represented. The teacher then groups the children, has them draw pictures of the animals, and adds them to a mural of an outdoor scene constructed during a previous lesson on habitat. Children then take string or yarn and use tape or thumbtacks to connect the predators with their prey, noting the multiple connections between several and the web of life that is a part of the life cycle of all living things. A discussion about what happens to predators when their preferred prey is not available could close the lesson, or the students could identify the relationships found in popular videos, such as Disney's *The Lion King*.

For expansion or for pupil evaluation, the children could write stories to describe or perform skits to demonstrate the relationship between predator and prey, including stalking and hiding habits. Students can also research what happens when predators hunt *not* to eat, such as poachers who prey on the rhino for its horn or on elephants for their ivory tusks. Their research can lead to position statements on ethics and any responsibility governments may have for regulation of commerce, export, or import. Research is also useful for comprehending the difference between preservation and conservation and possessing a better understanding of wildlife protection careers.

Teaching Explicit Material

Science textbooks introduce more new words or phrases than are introduced in foreign language textbooks (Yager, 1983). This type of treatment assumes explicit material must be learned and that it is the teacher's job to present it so learners can master it. Exclusively treating science material in this fashion does a disservice to the learners and misrepresents the nature of science. However, there are occasions when a body of information or well-defined skills must be taught. Science facts, some concepts, selected laboratory skills, and science vocabulary may be taught effectively with explicit teaching methods. Barak Rosenshine (1986) identifies the actions of effective teachers when they teach facts, concepts, or skills explicitly:

1. Begin a lesson with a brief statement of goals.
2. Begin teaching with a brief review of the previous lesson in order to lay a foundation for the connections.
3. Present new material in small steps with practice after each step to make connections.
4. Give clear and detailed instructions and explanations.
5. Provide active practice for all children to strengthen connections.

Explicit teaching requires teacher guidance.

6. Ask many questions to check for learner understanding; obtain responses from all children and correct misconceptions.
7. Guide children when they start to practice.
8. Provide systematic feedback for all children, and correct their mistakes.
9. Provide explicit instruction and practice for seatwork and monitor learner progress.
10. Continue practice until all children are independent and confident.

Rosenshine clusters the major parts of this method into several small steps, as shown in Table 11.1. He concedes that this approach does not apply to all students or for all teaching situations. Used with discretion, the method can support constructivist efforts.

The method is based on information processing research that recognizes the limits of human memory, the importance of practice, and the elements of task mastery. Learners can only attend to and process effectively small amounts of information at any one time. Abstract learners can process only seven unrelated items at a time without confusion; learners whose cognitive development has not reached that level (which includes most elementary children) can process even fewer than seven. Material must be processed (connected to what is understood) before it can be remembered and used. Active mental processing such as reviewing, summarizing, and rehearsing moves material into long-term

TABLE 11.1 Explicit Teaching Functions

1. Teach for review.
   - Review homework.
   - Review previous learning important to the present lesson.
   - Review prerequisite skills and information needed for the present lesson.

2. Present the lesson.
   - State the lesson goals and/or outline the lesson.
   - Teach in small steps.
   - Model the skills and procedures children are to follow.
   - Provide concrete positive and negative examples to assist comprehension and connection making.
   - Use clear language.
   - Check for student understanding.
   - Avoid digressions or tangents.

3. Guide the practice.
   - Use many questions to help guide practice, to clarify, and to overcome misconceptions.
   - Ensure that all students respond and receive feedback about their learning.
   - Strive for a high success rate; optimal is 75–80 percent correct answers during guided practice.
   - Continue guided practice until all students are competent.

4. Make corrections and give feedback.
   - Give process feedback when children are correct but hesitant.
   - When children are incorrect, give them clues or encouragement.
   - Reteach when necessary.

5. Provide for independent practice.
   - Actively supervise to give children help.
   - Continue practice until students can respond automatically (when this applies).
   - Use routines to help slower pupils; this may include peers helping peers.

6. Use weekly and monthly reviews to strengthen learning and to form multiple connections.
   - Select a special day to review the previous week's concepts.
   - Use a TV show format.
   - Involve children in constructing questions.
   - Develop a special monthly format and promote it like a coming big event on television.

Source: Adapted from B. V. Rosenshine, "Synthesis of Research on Explicit Teaching," *Educational Leadership* (April 1986): 65.

memory. Teacher questions, student summaries, and active supervision assist this processing. Finally, if learning is to appear automatic through effortless recall, extensive practice and frequent review are necessary.

Interaction is a constructivist tool that can unite the methods presented in this chapter. Interaction can be used to make teacher-centered methods less authoritarian, less reliant on a textbook, and more effective by:

- stimulating students' interests
- more actively involving children in the lesson
- promoting more thinking, information processing, and connection making
- providing relevant learning experiences

Teacher-centered methods work well with science textbooks. Aside from the teacher, the single most dominant factor in most elementary science programs may be a textbook. Selection of an appropriate textbook and effective use of it can improve your students' achievement, skills, attitudes, and help you encourage learners to make progress toward the national standards.

HOW CAN YOU USE SCIENCE TEXTBOOKS EFFECTIVELY?

Reams of research reports support the superiority of activity-based science programs and teaching methods (Meyer, Greer, & Crummey, 1986). Unfortunately, "what was intended to be joyful discovery for students too often turned out to be a lost sojourn into the abstract and difficult" (Mechling & Oliver, 1983, p. 43) because teachers returned to textbooks even though textbooks continue to be criticized for their shortcomings.

Be Aware of Shortcomings and Differences

Science textbooks vary considerably on such factors as readability, reading and study aids, treatment of gender, and emphasis given to vocabulary versus concepts. Readability studies show greater levels of difference mostly for the upper elementary and the middle grades. Students' science achievements decline when they use textbooks written above their reading ability levels. Reading and study aids, such as chapter headings, help pupils comprehend and recall, particularly when children are taught to use these features. Gender bias has been reduced recently, with more balance now seen toward male and female representation. However, the disabled and nonwhites often do not receive substantial recognition in textbooks. Science vocabulary is emphasized much more than science concepts, although researchers report that emphasis on concepts rather than vocabulary results in *increased* science achievement (Meyer, Greer, & Crummey, 1986). In contrast to this finding, Paul D. Hurd (1982) has found science texts often introduce "as many as 2,500 technical terms and unfamiliar words" (p. 12). He notes that a beginning foreign language course attempts to cover only half as many new words.

A comparison of eleven elementary science textbook series that have represented over 90 percent of the national science textbook market shows some improvements, but there are still tremendous shortcomings in quality. For example, Elliott and Nagel's analysis claims that elementary textbook series "do not promote or encourage the development of scientific thinking or attitudes, nor do they engage students in applying the cognitive processes that are basic to understanding the content covered" (Elliott & Carter, 1986, p. 1). In addition, Staver and Bay's (1987) analysis reports:

- Most textbook prose focuses on academic science.
- Most remaining textbook prose focuses on personal uses of science.
- The career and societal goal aspects of science receive only minor attention.
- Illustrations exhibit a pattern similar to prose.
- Activities and experiments are academic in orientation, almost to the exclusion of other goals.
- End-of-chapter sentences are largely academic.
- Science inquiry is absent or present only in limited forms in activities and experiments.
- Textbooks allocate only a minor portion of space to activities and experiments.

Staver and Bay (1987) also found some decreases in the amount of academic emphasis with accompanying increases in several topics now found in the national standards.

Who decides what material science textbooks will include and how they will be organized? Recommendations from credible sources such as the National Research Council, the National Science Teachers Association, or the American Association for the Advancement of Science do not always drive the development or revision of printed materials like school textbooks. Authors, teachers, editors, marketing staffs in publishing houses, boards of education, and textbook censors have less influence than you may imagine. A single large state, such as Texas, that adopts one or two science textbook series for use by all schools, carries a tremendous influence because of its large market. What one large state wants in a textbook, it usually receives, and therefore it can influence what the books contain for the rest of the country. Approaches and material that appear radical or unconventional stand little chance despite their academic merits, origin, or proven effects.

If it seems unlikely that textbooks will be dramatically improved, what options do you have? You *do* have a choice of programs. The choice you make will influence the amount of teacher direction you use to guide your students and the extent of the positive impact on their interactive learning experience. You can:

- enhance the textbook in use
- change the sequence of topics to reflect better the concepts to be learned
- select the textbook that most closely represents the needs of your students and fulfills the recommendations for effective science teaching and learning.

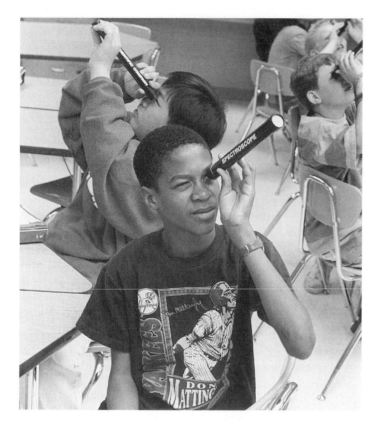

Student activities can enhance the use of a textbook.

Enhancing the Textbook

Each teacher can enhance the textbook to include more effective learning activities and interesting information, rather than wait for authors and publishers to do it. You can add enhancements that are timely and that match learner interests and abilities. There are some other ways you can use textbooks to foster constructivism. You can:

1. Combine the best elements from published programs. Use old editions or the most interesting materials from unadopted examination copies of textbooks. Cut out pictures, information, and activities to make mini-books or a resource file by topic.

2. Select relevant supplements from laboratory programs. Experimental programs like ESS, SCIS, and SAPA may have been used and then discarded by your school. Remnants can often be found stored away. Conduct an inventory of equipment and teaching materials from the past, and select useful materials relevant to the concepts you are teaching.

3. Identify local resources. School and community professionals, local businesses, parks and recreation facilities, libraries, and museums all provide rich

WHAT RESEARCH SAYS ◆◆◆

How Are Scientists Portrayed in Children's Literature?

Allen Evans, assistant professor and fifth-grade teacher at the Ackerman Lab School at Eastern Oregon State College in La Grande, investigated popular children's literature to uncover the ways scientists are portrayed to children. His research was stimulated by his students' stereotypical images of scientists. Children's literature is rapidly replacing a single text in classrooms where whole language approaches are favored. Therefore, it is important to expand our concerns about textbooks to the collection of literature used with children. We use many of Evans's words to report what he found.

Elementary classroom teachers have long been aware that books influence children's perceptions of the world. Characters found in children's books provide inspiration, consolation, and motivation. They entertain, inform, and encourage, and they can provide positive examples for overcoming adversity.

Sadly, however, not all characters in children's books present accurate depictions of their real-life counterparts, and teachers must be vigilant in looking out for stereotypes in order to make informed and appropriate choices of instructional materials.

With recent trends of "reading-across-the-curriculum," classroom teachers, and science teachers in particular, need to know how scientists are portrayed in children's books. Is the image of the scientist an accurate one? Or, do children's books reinforce the absentminded, bubbling-pot, blow-up-the-laboratory stereotype? Furthermore, as teachers encourage their students to consider careers in science, knowledge of the scientists in children's books becomes more important. If children's books do in fact depict scientists in stereotypical ways, children may be less likely to view science as a desirable career choice. To answer these questions, I decided to investigate the portrayal of scientists and science-oriented characters in seventeen selected children's fiction books.

The selection criteria resulted in books that had either a science-oriented plot or at least one science-oriented character, were written for upper elementary or middle school children, had been published within the last twenty years (the majority were published during the last ten), were realistic fiction or science-fiction books, and had been cited and reviewed in at least one major professional journal devoted to children's literature.

Twenty-five science-oriented characters were found, and 88 percent were male. Eleven of the seventeen books were written by females. Sixty percent of the science-oriented characters were adults, 20 percent were teenagers, and 20 percent were children. Science teachers, professors, and laboratory researchers represented 52 percent of the characters; 20 percent had a personal interest in science, perhaps as a hobby; 4 percent were involved in school science activities; the rest had an unclear orientation toward science. Evans's report sums up the portrait of a scientist in children's literature this way:

Scientists are adult males whose orientation is due to a professional relationship. They are generally ordinary in their actions and mannerisms, as well as ordinary in their physical appearance, and are of above-average intelligence. For concerned science teachers, the news is good—the image of the scientists appearing in these books is one that is reasonably free of the typical stereotypes.

There does, however, appear to be room for improvement. While it is true that the sciences are currently a white-male-dominated field, more and more women and minorities are pursuing science as a viable career option. Therefore, the inclusion of female and minority science-oriented characters in children's books must be encouraged.

Science teachers in particular should benefit from an increased awareness of how scientists and science-oriented characters are portrayed in children's books. With that understanding, teachers can work more closely with other nonscience professionals, such as reading teachers and librarians, in identifying and selecting children's books depicting scientists in positive, nonstereotypical roles.

Source: A. Evans, "A Look at the Scientists Portrayed in Children's Literature," *Science and Children* (March, 1992): 35–37.

resources for classroom speakers and field trips. These enhancement resources also help to demonstrate the relationship of science and everyday life as well as update or fill in gaps not covered by dated textbooks. (See Chapter 8 for more ideas.)

4. Check with your state's department of education. Some states compare commercial materials and keep on file survey-style coverage of important science findings and laboratory programs that make fine enhancements for standard textbook programs. An example is the California *Science Addendum.*

5. Screen supplementary materials for the appropriate reading level. Deemphasize use of a textbook written on a reading level too high by substituting suitable materials. Use accelerated material if the writing is too simple.

6. Select evaluation devices that reflect the preferred outcomes. If your desire is development of a particular process skill, select performance-based evaluation tasks that require the children to demonstrate the skill. Carefully screen all textbook questions and written exercises and select those that match the intended level of thinking and skills. Adapt project ideas and improve the types of questions used in the textbook or teacher's guide.

7. Work to organize building- or district-level committees in which teachers form supplement teams. More hands make lighter work, and more heads generate a greater number of effective ideas. Teams of teachers can share the research and swap ideas.

8. Attend professional conferences. States have affiliates of the National Science Teachers Association, and large cities have their own science education organizations. Attend their annual conferences and listen to other teachers to get ideas for your own classroom. Adapt these ideas to your science program. Remember, your ideas are just as important as those of others. Why not make your own presentation at a conference or provide a workshop for other teachers?

9. Relearn the concepts and processes of science. Take workshops or courses to learn about the most recent ideas in science and its teaching. This continues your education and professional development; both can help you enhance the science textbook. Request a staff development program for yourself and for helping the other school staff members relearn and elevate their own levels of scientific literacy. Other teachers will be more likely to enhance the textbook if they feel more confident and informed.

Changing the Sequence

The textbook's chapter order and the organization of the information within chapters may not be what is best for your students. Perhaps some simple resequencing will bring improvements in science achievement, attitudes, and interest and help you to help learners make clearer and stronger conceptual connections.

Cognitive scientists emphasize the importance of anchoring ideas to the learner's mental structure. New information becomes more meaningful when it can be attached to concepts already in the children's minds. Science material is better understood when it interrelates "in such a way as to make sense to the learner" (Hamrick & Harty, 1987, p. 16). Resequencing material so ideas relate in ways that make more sense to the children adds meaning. In a study of sixth graders,

> the findings revealed that students for whom content structure was clarified through resequencing general science chapters exhibited significantly higher science achievement, significantly more positive attitudes toward science, and significantly greater interest in science than students for whom general science content was not resequenced. (Hamrick & Harty, 1987, p. 15)

Concept mapping is a method of sequencing the ideas of a lesson, and a version of it can be used to sequence the text effectively. A concept map shows ideas graphically according to their relationships. (See Chapter 5 for more information.) The relationships communicate important connections that show an intended mental structure to be formed about the map's topic. Consider the following when resequencing:

1. Proceed from the smallest to the largest ideas, or from the simple to the complex, when resequencing a text. Researchers recommend that rearrangements first be made into an interrelated pattern based on the size of the ideas (Hamrick & Harty, 1987). A hierarchy of ideas is formed; perhaps physical science leads to life science topics, which progress to earth and space science concepts. See Figure 11.3 for an example of the hierarchy of ideas and Table 11.2 for an example of a typical textbook sequence of topics with a revised sequence. You can determine the children's hierarchical views of the material by doing a webbing exercise in which they refer to the table of contents or chapter titles of the text and connect them in a web that makes sense to them. Begin at the chalkboard with a single word such as *science* and have the children refer to the ideas in the chapter titles and sections within chapters to add the ideas of science to the chalkboard. Engage the children in a discussion of how they see these ideas of science connected; ask for their reasons. Your prompts can help them to order material from the simple to the more complex in a way that is more understandable. At the same time, you will be reinforcing higher levels of thinking.

2. Convey the interrelated structure to the students. An overview of the restructured material can be made on a student handout, placed in a notebook, and used for clarification, reinforcement, and review throughout the year. Children can check off the major concepts as they are studied. This serves as a structure of information for learners, gives you an opportunity to teach for concepts, and provides a ready guide for reinforcement. Figure 11.4 shows an example of a student handout with text overview.

3. Help learners to clarify the content structure. They will not absorb all the ideas of the resequencing overview at once. Take advantage of any opportunity to discuss the structure of the material you have chosen for your class. Help learners to paint the big picture and to see how the smaller ideas fit into a pattern with the larger ideas.

FIGURE 11.3   A Sample Hierarchical Structure of Science Content

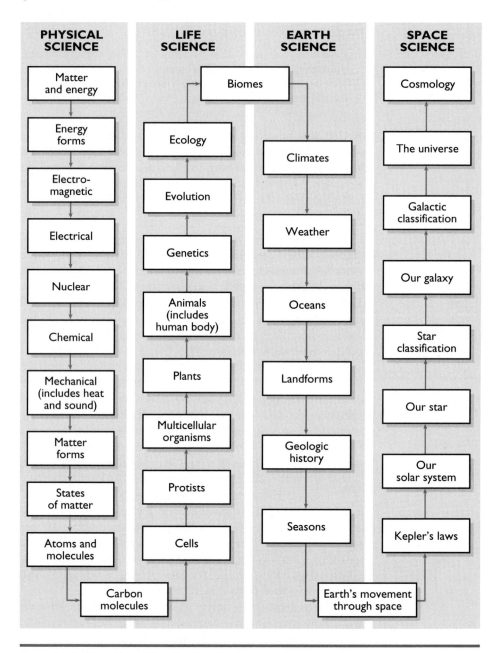

TABLE 11.2   A Sample Comparison of Unrevised and Revised Textbook Content Sequence

Textbook Sequence	Revised Content Sequence
Animals with backbones	Matter (elements and compounds)
Classifying animals without backbones	Sources of energy
Plants	Light
Life cycles	Electricity and magnetism
Matter (elements and compounds)	Communications
Electricity and magnetism	Energy outcomes and the future
Sources of energy	Energy for living things
Light	Plants
Communications	Life cycles
Climates of the world	Classifying animals without backbones
Energy for living things	Animal with backbones
Energy outcomes and the future	Climates of the world

Source: L. Hamrick and H. Harty, "Influence of Resequencing General Science Content on the Science Achievement, Attitudes Toward Science, and Interests in Science of Sixth Grade Students," *Journal of Research in Science Teaching* 24(1) (1987): 20.

Selecting the Best Textbook

No one of the recent bestselling textbooks was in the top thirteen in 1979 (Meyer, 1986). Teachers are becoming more selective, and it may be that their efforts to identify the best are having effects on textbook changes. Textbooks are often selected because they offer many activities, worksheets, tests, and programmed teacher's guides. They appear busy or glitzy and may require little more than reading and writing exercises. Such textbooks fall short of meeting recommendations for effective science instruction and do not support constructivism. What can you do to select a better textbook or to use the one you have in ways that improve the experience for students? As a starting point for screening textbooks, ask yourself:

- What does the textbook expect my students to do?
- What should they be able to do after they study the textbook that they could not do before?
- For every student activity, project, or question, ask, "What kind of thinking is required?" "How does this address the National Standards?"
- Examine the textbooks for inclusion of the science content standards (Chapter 4) and ask, "To what extent is each new dimension emphasized?" and "How is it included in the textbook?"
- Consider the goals of Project 2061 or the National Science Education Standards (Chapter 4), especially conceptual science content emphasis, and ask, "How well do the textbook's concepts represent those recommendations?"

FIGURE 11.4   A Sample Student Overview of Resequenced Material with Chapter Numbers

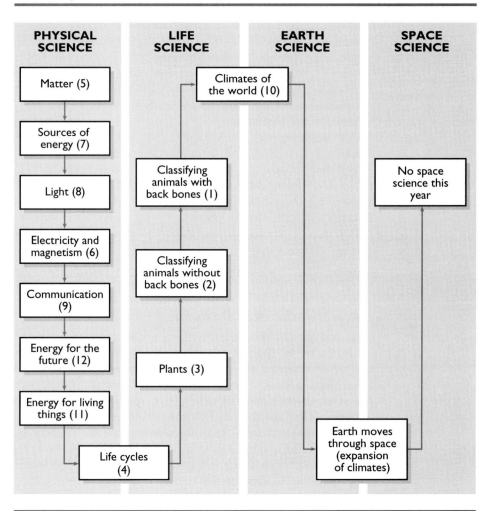

Source: Linda Hamrick and Harold Harty, "Influence of Resequencing General Science Content on the Science Achievement, Attitudes Toward Science, and Interest in Science of Sixth Grade Students," *Journal of Research in Science Teaching* 24, no. 1 (1987), p. 19.

- Summarize your initial screening by asking, "Will this textbook really help my students reach the goals I have set for them—or is it going to waste their time?"

Look again at those textbooks that pass your initial screening. Now is the time to be more critical. An effective textbook should involve children in the

The best science textbook will challenge children to improve their thinking.

processes of science by guiding them toward making discoveries. How does the textbook help students to experience the history and nature of science? The activities should not be cookbook recipes that encourage learners to follow the steps mindlessly. Focus on the student activities, sample several from each book, and ask these questions:

- Are students required to make careful observations?
- Are students encouraged to make inferences?
- Is classification a skill used in the experiments?
- How often are students asked to make a prediction based on observation or data?
- How often are students encouraged to display data in a systematic way that will enhance their ability to communicate?

These questions will help you select a textbook that delivers a strong blend of expository information and productive interaction through sound activity-based learning. Table 11.3 provides a list of factors to beware when selecting a textbook. Table 11.4 provides a brief instrument for screening textbooks and

<TEACHERS ON SCIENCE TEACHING>

How Can Toys Enhance Your Teaching

by Michael E. Cawthru
5th Grade Teacher, Kyffin Elementary School, Golden, Colorado

There are literally dozens of books out on the market to help teachers bring science demonstrations into the classroom. I know, I'm on the mailing list for all of them. But it is worth it to have an assortment of ideas at your fingertips. Don't let anyone tell you that you must teach the textbook and never vary from it. Textbooks are nice, but you have to be yourself. Go for it!

When you start to do classroom demos, make certain you have practiced and are prepared. Nothing can kill the demo faster than the teacher's leaning over the file cabinet or searching through the closet muttering, "Just a second kids, I'll have what I need. Just sit still." Yeah, right. Before you can turn around, Johnny is all over the room and into everything you had out for the demo. Likewise, nothing can get and hold their attention like all the equipment laid out on the table.

Speaking of equipment, it would be great to have thousands of dollars' worth of glassware, burners, chemicals, and such. But you can also use mason jars and propane torches and check out the chemicals that are sold over the grocery store counter. Ping-pong balls—I keep at least a dozen on hand for all sorts of demonstrations: atomic

structure (color them and give kids colored marshmallows for their set so they can eat them at the end), planets, physics—well, you get the idea. A globe and a ball, the diameter of which is the same as the distance from San Francisco to Cleveland on your globe, will be the perfect model for the earth and the moon. Also include a string that has been wrapped around the globe ten times; that's the distance from the earth to the moon. And never underestimate the toy department. Oh boy, my wife won't let me go in unescorted. Slinkies, cars, marbles, magnets, and models—models of space shuttles, human bodies, eyes, just about anything.

Yes, I must admit, my room looks like a toy store. But the bottom line is this: Are the kids learning? You bet your atom they are. Because I also don't just sit. When kids with Ping-pong balls are walking around the room imitating electrons moving about the nucleus, and another kid is trying to hit a ball with a marshmallow, they understand the reason electrons pass through matter without hitting anything, that atoms are mostly empty space. Yeah, they learn. And that is the whole point, the "ah-hah" moment we all live for, when Suzy says, "I get it, Mr. C!"

printed curriculum materials. All the information in this section of the chapter can be developed into your own customized form for rating and selecting textbooks or other printed curriculum materials.

We cannot force students to learn. We can help them make discoveries and form connections for themselves, and our guidance is an important factor. Go slowly and guide with purpose. Avoid merely covering information without ensuring student understanding. Strive for quality rather than quantity. Remember the maxim: Less is more. Listen to students more and talk less. Try to emphasize student cooperation instead of competition. Blend learning activities to include discovery opportunities, group work, and learning that requires different types of information processing—thinking. Try to concentrate on students doing right thinking rather than getting right answers. If you must use a

TABLE 11.3   Things to Beware When Choosing a Textbook

At least two issues must be considered when choosing a textbook: the pedagogical (teaching method) points and the content (subject matter) points.

Pedagogical Points

1. Beware a text that claims to cover all students need to know about a subject. Consider instead a text that is selective and attempts to cover the important ideas of a subject area, not one that looks like an encyclopedia and expects students to memorize a great deal of information.

2. Beware a text that emphasizes large amounts of science vocabulary and expects students to memorize it. Page after page of bold vocabulary words distract readers from the important ideas. Specialized vocabulary should not be overrepresented, but selected useful vocabulary can serve to broaden understanding.

3. Beware a text that does not read well. Avoid texts that use short, choppy sentences to focus on detail and offer many conclusions. The ideal text will maintain the narrative of inquiry and will not provide a passive reading experience.

4. Beware the dogmatic text. The information of science changes as new discoveries are made and new ideas replace the old. Avoid texts that show science as absolute and unchanging. Also avoid the other extreme. Texts that appear to show science as a body of untested hypotheses and guesses do not represent science properly.

5. Beware the text as the sole source of information. A good text should be adequately supplemented with learning activities, project ideas, and lists of resources that can be used to expand children's thinking and their experiences.

Content Points

1. Beware the text that does not represent the nature of science. One chapter or a paragraph about the scientific method is inadequate and a waste of time. Scientists do have methods, but they do not follow them in the single artificial step-by-step fashion portrayed. The processes of science should permeate the text and give children opportunities to investigate interesting topics and outcomes that are unknown to them, just as scientists do.

2. Beware the text that does not clearly show the role of controlled experiments, development of hypotheses, and uses of theory. These are the real tools of scientists, which are not easily mastered and certainly not turned into skills by reading about them. They must be practiced.

3. Beware the text that emphasizes only one aspect of a science discipline. No single text can cover all viewpoints about a subject, but each should include acceptable alternatives. As an example, biology topics often include only morphology and systems, but they should include topics like ecology, genetics, growth and development, evolution, and behavior. If these areas are included, a student's personal development and academic growth will be enhanced. Science texts should never be written in isolation from society and technology; the history of science should be liberally represented.

4. Beware the bland textbook. Texts written to avoid controversy will not accurately portray science or expose children to its value. Unresolved problems of science should be discussed. Children should be presented with accurate information and be given opportunities to process the information, make up their own minds, and defend their positions.

5. Beware the classical textbook. Science portrayed retrospectively will not deal with current areas of research and problems. This approach will not contribute to the preparation of children to face and function in the future.

Source: Adapted from William V. Mayer and James P. Barufaldi, *The Textbook Chooser's Guide* (Berkeley, CA: National Center for Science Education, 1985).

TABLE 11.4 Screening Textbooks and Other Printed Curriculum Materials

You can learn about the science program by examining the textbooks and other written curriculum materials available.

	Yes	No	Unsure
Science Content			
1. Is there a balanced emphasis among the life sciences, earth sciences, and physical sciences?	_____	_____	_____
2. Do the materials include study of problems that are important to us now and in the future? *Examples:* acid rain, air and water pollution, effects of spraying, energy production and availability, medical research, world hunger, population, deforestation, ozone depletion	_____	_____	_____
3. Do the materials require students to apply major science concepts to everyday life situations?	_____	_____	_____
4. Other	_____	_____	_____
Science Processes			
1. Do the materials include liberal amounts of hands-on investigations and activities the children can do in order to experience the nature of science?	_____	_____	_____
2. Is scientific inquiry an important part of the materials the children will read? *Examples:* observing, measuring, predicting, inferring, classifying, recording and analyzing data, and so on	_____	_____	_____
3. Do the materials encourage children to explore, discover, and find answers for themselves rather than tell them how things should turn out?	_____	_____	_____
4. Do the materials require children to apply science processes to problem-solving situations and to construct conclusions?	_____	_____	_____
5. Other	_____	_____	_____
Other Considerations			
1. Are the materials consistent with the science goals of your school (or in the absence of such goals, those of the National Standards or your state framework of science goals)?	_____	_____	_____
2. Are the materials clearly written, accurate, up to date?	_____	_____	_____
3. Do the materials proceed from the simple to the complex, and are they designed for the children's developmental levels?	_____	_____	_____
4. Is the information written at the proper grade level?	_____	_____	_____
5. Do the materials for children appear interesting and relevant?	_____	_____	_____
6. Are there opportunities for children to learn about the history of science and career opportunities?	_____	_____	_____
7. Are valid evaluation materials used or included? *Examples:* performance demonstrations, pictorial assessment	_____	_____	_____
8. Is a teacher's guide included, and is it helpful for using the materials?	_____	_____	_____
9. Do the materials include enough application of science content and processes to make science meaningful to students?	_____	_____	_____
10. Other	_____	_____	_____

Source: Adapted from Kenneth R. Mechling and Donna L. Oliver, *Characteristics of a Good Elementary Science Program* (Washington, DC: National Science Teachers Association, 1983).

textbook and teacher-centered approaches, incorporate several of the suggestions offered in this chapter to make your classroom more interactive. Chances for effective teaching will be greater through your efforts, and your reward will be improved student achievement, positive attitudes toward science, and greater interest in school through more student-centered, constructivist teaching practices.

CHAPTER SUMMARY

About 90 percent of science classrooms use a single textbook the majority of the time for instruction. The teaching methods used are often teacher centered and authoritarian, even though considerable evidence reveals the limits of these approaches and more effective methods are available. Teacher-centered methods can be made more effective by using interactive techniques that enhance the children's learning experiences and help meet the goals of an effective science education.

The interactive techniques described in this chapter include demonstrations, exposition, deductive teaching, explicit teaching, and uses of textbooks. Used with care, these techniques can support constructivist teaching. Exposition includes use of advance organizers, giving direc-

tions, and summary techniques for lessons. Deductive teaching organizes lessons from science generalizations to specific learner experiences. Explicit teaching is a technique of interactive lecture, student recitation, feedback, misconception correction, and practice. It is based on the effective teaching research.

The quality and features of textbooks vary considerably. The last section of this chapter acquaints readers with the shortcomings and differences of textbooks. Positive actions teachers can take to use textbooks more effectively include enhancing the text, changing the instructional sequence of textbook topics, mapping the chapter concepts, and exercising discretion when selecting a textbook.

DISCUSSION QUESTIONS AND PROJECTS

1. Why do most teachers revert to teacher-centered methods and authoritarian treatment of science through extensive use of the textbook even though they may know about more effective alternatives?

2. What can be done to motivate teachers to use more interactive teaching methods with young children?

3. How does the planning teachers must do to use the methods recommended in this chapter compare with the constructivist methods described in Chapter 9?

4. What characteristics do you think a science textbook must have in order to address *all* of the National Science Education Standards?

5. Why do you think something as simple as re-sequencing the topics of a textbook is related to increased student science achievement?

6. What signs indicate that a textbook should be considered or avoided?

7. How can teachers evaluate process skills and higher thinking? To what extent are these promoted by teacher-centered methods and textbooks?

8. How can reading enhancements (such as bold print for special words) found in textbooks interfere with the goals of science education? Do you believe the goals for scientific literacy run counter to the goals of general literacy? Why?

9. Plan a lesson (or a unit) using an advance organizer, demonstration, and techniques of deductive and/or explicit teaching with a textbook. Teach the lesson and have it recorded (video preferred). Compare your skills with the ideal requirements for each method described in this chapter. How do your skills compare? What can you do to become more effective? Which methods made it possible for you to be more interactive with the children?

10. Examine a school's science program for inclusion of the methods of effective teacher-centered teaching. To what extent is each method encouraged? Write a summary and offer recommendations for improving the program.

11. Analyze several science textbooks written for the same grade level. What are their advantages and shortcomings? Which textbook do you prefer? Why? What is needed to overcome the shortcomings of your choice?

12. Analyze your preferred science textbook (or textbooks from different publishers) across grade levels. Use the criteria for selecting the best textbook given in this chapter. Which textbook series do you prefer, and why? Which series comes closest to fulfilling the recommendations of Project 2061 or the National Standards?

13. Examine a school district's course of study, and compare it with the actual science program or textbook used. Which was done first, the writing of the course of study or the selection of the science program? To what extent does the course of study reflect the organization of the program or textbook? Compare your findings with those of your classmates. What do you conclude about the extent to which a program relates to a course of study?

14. Use the ideas provided in this chapter to develop your own form for science textbook and curriculum materials analysis. What are the main categories you feel must be included to yield a useful form? Try your form and ask others to try it. What revisions may be necessary and why?

15. Write to your state's department of education and ask what information it provides to help teachers and school districts improve science programs. Does your state have recommended programs or textbooks? If yes, determine how they were selected for recommedation. If no, determine why your state takes no position and what services it does provide to teachers and schools seeking assistance.

16. Select a textbook, read one of its chapters, and record the science words emphasized in the titles, headings, and bold or italicized print. Develop a strategy for mapping the concepts of these words and for helping students understand the connections between and among the concepts.

ADDITIONAL READINGS

If you are interested in learning more about some of the topics raised in this chapter, consider the following sources.

Candy Carlile, "Bag It for Science!" *Science and Children* (March 1992): 15–16. This article describes a book-bag approach in which interesting trade books, teaching materials, instructions, and student enthusiasm combine for hands-on learning in an easy-to-manage fashion.

Paul Eggen and Donald Kauchak, *Strategies for Teachers: Teaching Content and Thinking Skills* (Englewood Cliffs, NJ: Prentice-Hall, 1988). Traditional models of teaching are described, with an emphasis on developing skills. Each chapter includes brief concept maps and is easily organized for study about the methods; each method is de-scribed in terms of teaching phases to be accomplished. Most strategies promote teacher-pupil interaction.

H. Jerome Freiberg and Amy Driscoll, *Universal Teaching Strategies* (Boston: Allyn and Bacon, 1996). Seven chapters are devoted to instructional strategies that promote various forms of interaction. Teachers can use these strategies to support science constructivism by changing passive instruction into active learning. Additional information is devoted to assessment strategies.

Peter Geaga, "Convert Your Text Series into a District Science Program," *Science and Children* (November–December 1982): 28–30. This article provides practical examples for supplementing or supplanting the typical science textbook. Geaga offers a case against the packaged program and urges teachers to draw on many printed resources; he gives examples of practical approaches that any teacher can try.

Thomas Gee and Marly Olson, "Let's Talk Trade Books," *Science and Children* (March 1992): pp. 13–14. Suggestions for using science trade books for children effectively are offered in this article.

Kenneth Hoover, *The Professional Teacher's Handbook* (Boston: Allyn and Bacon, 1982). This book, designed for middle and secondary school teachers, is conveniently divided into several units: preinstructional activities, individual and small-group methods focus, large-group methods focus, methods for effective learning, assessment techniques, and working with special students.

How do reading ability and listening ability affect science test scores? To find out, review articles with similar titles in the September 1991 and October 1991 issues of Science and Children.

James Scarnati and Cyril Weller, "The Write Stuff," *Science and Children* (January 1992): pp. 28–29. The authors describe ways to use science inquiry skills to help students think positively about writing assignments.

Appendixes

National Science Education Standards: Content Standards for K–4 and 5–8

K–4 Physical Science Standards

Content Standard B—K–4:

All students should develop an understanding of:
- Properties of objects and materials
- Position and motion of objects
- Light, heat, electricity, and magnetism

Properties of objects and materials concepts
- Objects have many observable properties, including size, weight, shape, color, temperature, and the ability to react with other substances. These properties can be measured using tools such as rulers, balances, and thermometers.
- Objects are made of one or more materials, such as paper, wood, and metal. Objects can be described by the properties of the materials from which they are made, and these properties can be used to separate or sort a group of objects or materials.
- Materials have different states—solid, liquid, and gas. Some common materials such as water can be changed from one state to another by heating or cooling.

Position and motion of objects concepts
- The position of an object can be described by locating it relative to another object or the background.
- An object's motion can be described by indicating the change in its position over time.
- The position and motion of objects can be changed by pushing or pulling and the size of the change is related to the strength of the push or pull.

- Vibrating objects produce sound. The pitch of the sound can be varied by changing the rate of vibration.

Light, heat, electricity, and magnetism concepts
- Light travels in a straight line unless it strikes an object. Light can be reflected by a mirror, refracted by a lens, or absorbed by the object.
- Heat can be produced in many ways such as burning, rubbing, and mixing chemicals. The heat can move from one object to another by conduction.
- Electricity in circuits can produce light, heat, sound, and magnetic effects. Electrical circuits require a complete loop through which the electrical current can pass.
- Magnets attract and repel each other and certain kinds of metals.

K–4 Life Science Standards

Content Standard C—K–4:

All students should develop an understanding of:
- The characteristics of organisms
- Life cycles of organisms
- Organisms and environments

The characteristics of organisms concepts
- Organisms have basic needs, which for animals are air, water and food. Plants require air, water and light. Organisms can only survive in environments in which they can meet their needs. The world has many different en-

Source: NRC. (1996) Science content standards, *National Science Education Standards.* Washington, D.C.: National Academy of Sciences, pp. 123–160.

vironments, and distinct environments support the life of different types of organisms.

- Each plant or animal has different structures which serve different functions in growth, survival, and reproduction. For example, humans have distinct structures of the body for walking, holding, seeing, and talking.
- The behavior of individual organisms is influenced by internal cues such as hunger and by external cues such as an environmental change. Humans and other organisms have senses that help them detect internal and external cues.

Life cycles of organisms concepts

- Plants and animals have life cycles that include being born, developing into adults, reproducing, and eventually dying. The details of this life cycle are different for different organisms.
- Plants and animals closely resemble their parents.
- Many characteristics of an organism are inherited from the parents of the organism, but other characteristics result from an individual's interactions with the environment. Inherited characteristics include the color of flowers and the number of limbs of an animal. Other features, such as the ability to play a musical instrument, are learned through interactions with the environment.

Organisms and their environments concepts

- All animals depend on plants. Some animals eat plants for food. Other animals eat animals that eat the plants.
- An organism's patterns of behavior are related to the nature of that organism's environment, including the kinds and numbers of other organisms present, the availability of food and resources, and the physical characteristics of the environment. When the environment changes, some plants and animals survive and reproduce, and others die or move to new locations.
- All organisms cause changes in the environment where they live. Some of these changes are detrimental to themselves or other organisms, whereas others are beneficial.
- Humans depend on both their natural and their constructed environment. Humans change environments in ways that can either be beneficial or detrimental for other organisms, including the humans themselves.

K–4 Earth and Space Science Standards

Content Standard D—K–4:

All students should develop an understanding of:

- Properties of Earth materials
- Objects in the sky

Properties of Earth materials concepts

- Earth materials are solid rocks and soils, liquid water, and the gases of the atmosphere. These varied materials have different physical and chemical properties. These properties make them useful, for example, as building materials, as sources of fuel, or for growing the plants we use as food. Earth materials provide many of the resources humans use.
- Soils have properties of color and texture, capacity to retain water and ability to support the growth of many kinds of plants, including those in our food supply. Other Earth materials are used to construct buildings, make plastics and provide fuel for generating electricity and operating cars and trucks.
- The surface of the Earth changes. Some changes are due to slow processes, such as erosion and weathering and some changes are due to rapid processes such as land slides, volcanoes, and earthquakes.
- Fossils provide evidence about the plants and animals that lived long ago and nature of the environment at that time.

Objects in the sky concepts

- The sun, moon, stars, clouds, birds, and airplanes all have properties, locations, and movements that can be described and that may change.
- Objects in the sky have patterns of movement. The sun, for example, appears to move across the sky in the same way every day, but its path changes slowly over the seasons. The moon moves across the sky on a daily basis much like the sun. The shape of the moon seems to change from day to day in a cycle that lasts about a month.
- The sun provides the light and heat necessary to maintain the temperature of the Earth.
- Weather can change from day to day and over the season. Weather can be described by measurable quantities, such as temperature, wind direction and speed, precipitation, and humidity.

5–8 Physical Science Standards

Content Standard B—5–8:

All students should develop an understanding of:

- Properties and changes of properties in matter
- Motions and forces
- Transformations of energy

Properties and changes of properties in matter concepts

- Substances have characteristic properties such as density, boiling point, and solubility, which are independent of the amount of the sample. A mixture of substances can often be separated into the original substances by using one or more of these characteristic properties.
- Substances react chemically in characteristic ways with other substances to form new substances (compounds) with different characteristic properties. In chemical reac-

tions the total mass is conserved. Substances are often placed in categories or groups if they react in similar ways, for example, metals.

- Chemical elements do not break down by normal laboratory reactions such as heating, electric current, or reaction with acids. There are more than 100 known elements which combine in a multitude of ways to produce compounds, which account for the living and non living substances that we encounter.

Motions and forces concepts

- The motion of an object can be described by its position, direction of motion, and speed.
- An object that is not being subjected to a force will continue to move at a constant speed and in a straight line.
- If more than one force acts on an object, then the forces can reinforce or cancel one another, depending on their direction and magnitude. Unbalanced forces will cause changes in the speed and/or direction of an object's motion.

Transformations of energy concepts

- Energy exists in many forms, including heat, light, chemical, nuclear, mechanical and electrical. Energy can be transformed from one form to another.
- Heat energy moves in predictable ways, flowing from warmer objects to cooler ones until both objects are at the same temperature.
- Light interacts with matter by transmission (including refraction), absorption, or scattering (including reflection).
- In most chemical reactions energy is released or added to the system in the form of heat, light, electrical, or mechanical energy.
- Electrical circuits provide a means of converting electrical energy into heat, light, sound, chemical or other forms of energy.
- The sun is a major source of energy for changes on the Earth's surface.

5–8 Life Science Standards

Content Standard C—5–8:

All students should develop an understanding of:

- Structure and function in living organisms
- Reproduction and heredity
- Regulation and behavior
- Populations and ecosystems
- Diversity and adaptions of organisms

Structure and function in living systems concepts

- Living systems at all levels of organization demonstrate complementary structure and function. Important levels of organization for structure and function include cells, organs, organ systems, whole organisms, and ecosystems.
- All organisms are composed of cells—the fundamental unit of life. Most organisms are single cells; other organisms, including humans, are multicellular.
- Cells carry on the many functions needed to sustain life. They grow and divide, producing more cells.
- Specialized cells perform specialized functions in multicellular organisms. Groups of specialized cells cooperate to form a tissue, such as a muscle. Different tissues are in turn grouped together to form larger functional units, called organs. Each type of cell, tissue, and organ has a distinct structure and set of functions that serve the organism as a whole. The human organism has systems for digestion, respiration, reproduction, circulation, excretion, movement, control and coordination, and for protection from disease.
- Disease represents a breakdown in structures or functions of an organism. Some diseases are the result of intrinsic failures of the system. Others are the result of infection by other organisms.

Reproduction and heredity concepts

- Reproduction is a characteristic of all living systems; since no individual organism lives forever, it is essential to the continuation of species. Some organisms reproduce asexually. Other organisms reproduce sexually.
- In many species, including humans, females produce eggs and males produce sperm. An egg and sperm unite beginning the development of a new individual. This new individual has an equal contribution of information from its mother (via the egg) and its father (via the sperm). Sexually produced offspring are never identical to either of their parents.
- Each organism requires a set of instructions for specifying its traits. Heredity is the passage of these instructions from one generation to another.
- Hereditary information is contained in genes, located in the chromosomes of each cell. Each gene carries a single unit of information, and an inherited trait of an individual can be determined by either one or many genes. A human cell contains many thousands of different genes.
- The characteristics of an organism can be described in terms of a combination of traits. Some traits are inherited and others result from interactions with the environment.

Regulation and behavior concepts

- All organisms must be able to obtain and use resources, grow, reproduce, and maintain a relatively stable internal environment while living in a constantly changing external environment.
- Regulation of an organism's internal environment involves sensing external changes in the environment and

changing physiological activities to keep within the range required to survive.

- Behavior is one kind of response an organism may make to an internal or environmental stimulus. A behavioral response requires coordination and communication at many levels including cells, organ systems, and whole organisms. Behavioral response is a set of actions determined in part by heredity and in part from past experience.
- An organism's behavior has evolved through adaptation to its environment. How organisms move, obtain food, reproduce, and respond to danger, all are based on the organism's evolutionary history.

Populations and ecosystems concepts

- Populations consist of all individuals of a species that occur together at a given place. All of the populations living together and the physical factors with which they interact compose an ecosystem.
- Populations of organisms can be categorized by the function they serve in an ecosystem. Plants and some micro-organisms are producers—they make their own food. All animals, including humans, are consumers, which obtain food by eating other organisms. Decomposers, primarily bacteria and fungi, are consumers that use waste materials and dead organisms for food. Food webs identify the relationships among producers, consumers, and decomposers in an ecosystem.
- For ecosystems, the major source of energy is sunlight. Energy entering ecosystems as sunlight is converted by producers into stored chemical energy through photosynthesis. It then passes from organism to organism in food webs.
- The number of organisms an ecosystem can support depends on the resources available and abiotic factors such as quantity of light and water, range of temperatures, and the soil composition. Given adequate biotic and abiotic resources and no disease or predators, populations, including humans, increase at very rapid (exponential) rates. Limitations of resources and other factors such as predation and climate limit the growth of population in specific niches in the ecosystem.

Diversity and adaptations of organisms concepts

- There are millions of species of animals, plants, and micro-organisms living today that differ from those that lived in the remote past. Each species lives in a specific and fairly uniform environment.
- Although different species look very different, the unity among organisms becomes apparent from an analysis of internal structures, the similarity of their chemical processes, and the evidence of common ancestry.
- Biological evolution accounts for a diversity of species developed through gradual processes over many genera-

tions. Species acquire many of their unique characteristics through biological adaptation which involves the selection of naturally occurring variations in populations. Biological adaptations include changes in structures, behaviors, or physiology that enhance reproductive success in a particular environment.

- Extinction of a species occurs when the environment changes and the adaptive characteristics of a species do not enable it to survive in competition with its neighbors. Fossils indicate that many organisms that lived long ago are now extinct. Extinction of species is common. Most of the species that have lived on the Earth no longer exist.

5–8 Earth and Space Science Standards

Content Standard D—5–8:

All students should develop an understanding of:
- Structure of the Earth's system
- Earth's history
- Earth in the solar system

Structure of the Earth system concepts

- The solid Earth is layered with a thin brittle crust, hot convecting mantle, and dense metallic core.
- Crustal plates on the scale of continents and oceans constantly move at rates of centimeters per year in response to movements in the mantle. Major geological events, such as earthquakes, volcanoes, and mountain building, result from these plate motions.
- Land forms are the result of a combination of constructive and destructive forces. Constructive forces include crustal deformation, volcanoes, and deposition of sediment, while destructive forces include weathering and erosion.
- Changes in the solid Earth can be described as the rock cycle. Old rocks weather at the Earth's surface, forming sediments that are buried, then compacted, heated, and often recrystallized into new rock. Eventually, these new rocks may be brought to the surface by the forces that drive plate motions, and the rock cycle continues.
- Soil consists of weathered rocks, decomposed organic material from dead plants, animals and bacteria. Soils are often found in layers, with each having a different chemical composition and texture.
- Water, which covers the majority of the Earth's surface, circulates through the crust, oceans, and atmosphere in what is known as the water cycle. Water evaporates from the Earth's surface, rises and cools as it moves to higher elevations, condenses as rain or snow, and falls to the surface where it collects in lakes, oceans, soil, and in rocks underground.

- Water is a solvent. As it passes through the water cycle it dissolves minerals and gases and carries them to the oceans.
- The atmosphere is a mixture of oxygen, nitrogen, and trace gases that include water vapor. The atmosphere has different properties at different elevations.
- Clouds, formed by the condensation of water vapor, affect weather and climate. Some do so by reflecting much of the sunlight that reaches Earth from the sun, while others hold heat energy emitted from the Earth's surface.
- Global patterns of atmospheric movement influence local weather. Oceans have a major effect on climate, because water in the oceans holds a large amount of heat.
- Living organisms have played many roles in the Earth system, including affecting the composition of the atmosphere and contributing to the weathering of rocks.

Earth's history concepts
- The Earth processes we see today, including erosion, movement of crustal plates, and changes in atmospheric composition, are similar to those that occurred in the past. Earth history is also influenced by occasional catastrophes, such as the impact of an asteroid or comet.
- Fossils provide important evidence of how life and environmental conditions have changed.

Earth in the solar system concepts
- The Earth is the third planet from the sun in a system that includes the moon, the sun, eight other planets and their moons, and smaller objects such as asteroids and comets. The sun, an average star, is the central and largest body in the solar system.
- Most objects in the solar system are in regular and predictable motion. These motions explain such phenomena as the day, the year, phase of the moon, and eclipses.
- Gravity is the force that keeps planets in orbit around the sun and governs the rest of the motion in the solar system. Gravity alone holds us to the Earth's surface and explains the phenomena of the tides.
- The sun is the major source of energy for phenomena on the Earth's surface, such as growth of plants, winds, ocean currents, and the water cycle. Seasons result from variations in the amount of the sun's energy hitting the surface, due to the tilt of the Earth's rotation axis.

APPENDIX B Curriculum Projects

The National Science Foundation and other organizations and agencies supported many science curriculum projects during the sixties and seventies. Many were innovative and presented new and different approaches to science education. Some have endured, while others are no longer available in print. In addition, the educational reform movement has brought new curricula into existence. Below you will find a list of the notable projects, complete with short descriptions.

Projects marked with * are currently in development. The date following the asterisk indicates the anticipated year of completion.

Activities to Integrate Mathematics and Science (AIMS)
P.O. Box 7766, Fresno, CA 93747; (209) 291-1766

Activities to Integrate Mathematics and Science publishes elementary and middle school integrated curriculum materials (K–9) that have been produced and tested by teachers. It conducts national leadership training and local workshops and seminars.

Topics include Down to Earth, Fall into Math and Science, Floaters and Sinkers, From Head to Toe, Fun with Foods, Glide into Winter with Math and Science, Hardhatting in a Geoworld, Jawbreakers and Heart Thumpers, Math + Science—A Solution, Our Wonderful World, Out of this World, Overhead and Underfoot, Pieces and Patterns, Popping with Power, Primarily Bears, Seasoning Math and Science: Spring and Summer, Seasoning Math and Science: Fall & Winter, The Sky's the Limit!, Spring into Math & Science, and Water, Precious Water.

AIMS was developed through Fresno Pacific College as an outgrowth of a National Science Foundation project.

Arkansas's Project MAST: Mathematics and Science Together

University of Arkansas, College of Education, Gifted Programs, 2801 South University, Little Rock, AR 72204; (501) 569-3410

This project uses existing materials along with materials developed for the project to introduce integrated science and mathematics instruction in grades 2–6. The program emphasizes critical thinking and utilizes instructional technology. Intensive teacher training focuses on content knowledge and familiarity with the instructional materials.

Bottle Biology

Department of Plant Physiology, University of Wisconsin–Madison, 1630 Linden Drive, Madison, WI 53706; (608) 263-5645

This booklet contains suggestions for activities that use a variety of throwaway containers, primarily plastic beverage bottles, in constructing experiments and life science exploration. Activities can be adapted to all K–12 instructional levels.

Chemical Education for Public Understanding (CEPUP)

Lawrence Hall of Science, University of California, Berkeley, CA 94720; (510) 642-8718

The Chemical Education for Public Understanding project produces modular materials stressing chemical concepts and processes associated with current societal issues and risk assessment. The hands-on orientation addresses topics such as pollution, household chemicals, toxic and municipal waste, and chemicals in foods. The modules contain student materials and laboratory kits for grades 6–8.

Distributors include Addison-Wesley Publishing Company; Lab-Aids, Inc.; Fisher Scientific; Science Kit and Boreal Laboratories; and Sargent-Welsh Scientific Company.

Conceptually Oriented Program in Elementary Science (COPES)

No longer active: materials available on *Science Helper, K–8*

COPES is a general K–6 science program developed around five major conceptual schemes: structural units of the universe, interaction and change, conservation of energy, degradation of energy, and a statistical view of nature.

Conservation for Children

6560 Hanover Drive, San Jose, CA 95129; (408) 725-8376

Conservation for Children consists of activities designed to educate students in grades 1–6 about basic concepts of ecology and conservation through integration with mathematics, social studies, and language arts. The group publishes a curriculum guide and conducts staff development programs.

Curriculum in Human Biology for the Middle Grades

Stanford University, School of Education, Stanford, CA 94305-3096; (415) 723-4662

This two-year human biology course is designed for seventh- and eighth-grade students. The course includes human physiology, anthropology, psychology, and sociology topics that are relevant to adolescent maturation. Videotapes have been developed to provide teachers with background for the print materials. Summer institutes were offered for teachers interested in more assistance with course content.

Delta Science Modules

Delta Education, P.O. Box 3000, Nashua, NH 03061-3000

Delta Science Modules offer a means to accomplish problem-solving goals. Instruction proceeds with children manipulating materials designed to bring out process skills. The modules are clustered around the content areas of life, earth, and physical science. Each module is a self-contained unit of work and includes hands-on materials, a teacher's guide, and a storage system. Most activities are designed to be one class period. The lesson plans for that activity are usually one page in length. Units culminate in application and evaluation sessions. Delta provides experiences for developing inquiry skills, positive science attitudes, and understanding of science concepts.

Denver Audubon Society's Education Project

Denver Audubon Society, 975 Grant Street, Denver, CO 80203; (303) 860-1476

The materials train volunteers to work with small groups of children from a variety of socioeconomic backgrounds. They explore, study, and participate in hands-on experiences with animals and plants that grow in surrounding neighborhoods. The handbook is designed to assist organizations developing similar programs.

Developmental Approaches in Science and Health (DASH)

University of Hawaii, Manoa, College of Education, 1776 University Avenue, Honolulu, HI 96822; (808) 956-6918

This program provides sequential, integrated curricula in science, health, and technology for students in grades K–6. It also offers alternative instructional strategies for teaching a heterogeneous population; its instructional materials require minimal preparation times and are easy to use and to organize. Concepts in biology, physical and earth science, and applications in health and technology are taught through practical and applied situations.

Eco-Inquiry

New York Botanical Garden, Institute of Ecosystem Studies, Box AB, Millbrook, NY 12545-0129; (914) 667-5976

This ecological curriculum features an emphasis on the conceptual underpinnings of ecological literacy (nutrient cycling and energy flow); commitment to demystifying the practices of scientists; and the development of students' inquiry skills and dispositions through modeling the scientific method.

ECO-NET

Institute for Global Communications, 18 DeBoom Street, San Francisco, CA 94107

ECO-NET provides an inexpensive way to access the Internet and literally thousands of resources and e-mail. Special conferences are available on a huge array of environmental issues in addition to environmental education and other topics of interest to both students and educators. Curriculum support materials as well as up-to-the-minute information are available. Requires a computer and modem. A cost is involved for the monthly rate plus connect time charges for prime-time use.

Eighteenth-Century Electricity Kit

The Bakken, 3537 Zenith Avenue South, Minneapolis, MN 55416; (612) 927-6508

These materials use depictions and recreations of eighteenth-century electricity experiments to promote better understanding of physics. They incorporate historical information and can be easily integrated into existing curricula. They were developed for grades 7–12. The kits include laboratory kits, teacher materials, and informational videos.

Distributor: Sargent-Welch Scientific Company

Elementary School Science and Health

Biological Science Curriculum Study, 830 North Tejon, Suite 405, Colorado Springs, CO 80903; (719) 578-1136

This K–6 program divides instructional units among life, health, earth, and physical sciences. Students learn science content and process skills as well as social skills, problem solving, decision making, and use of technology.

Distributor: Kendall/Hunt Publishing Company

Elementary Science Study (ESS)

Education Development Center, Newton, MA 02160; (617) 969-7100

Several modules may be purchased from Delta Education; some activities are available on *Science Helper K–8*.

The Elementary Science Study consists of fifty-six hands-on units that can be used as a complete curriculum or as resource units in a general elementary curriculum. They were extensively revised for commercial use. Revised copies are available through Educational Resource Information Center and Delta Education.

Units include Animal Activity; Animals in the Classroom; Attribute Games and Problems; Balloons and Gases; Behavior of Mealworms; Batteries and Bulbs; Batteries and Bulbs II; Bones; Brine Shrimp; Budding Twigs; Butterflies; Changes; Clay Boats; Colored Solutions; Crayfish; Daytime Astronomy; Drops, Streams, and Containers; Earthworms; Eggs and Tadpoles; Gases and "Airs"; Geo Blocks; Growing Seeds; Heating and Cooling; Ice Cubes; Kitchen Physics; Life of Beans and Peas; Light and Shadows; Mapping; Match and Measure; Microgardening; Mirror Cards; Mobiles; Mosquitoes; Musical Instrument Recipe Book; Mystery Powders; Optics; Pattern Blocks; Peas and Particles; Pendulums; Pond Water; Primary Balancing; Printing; Rocks and Charts; Sand; Senior Balancing; Sink or Float; Small Things; Spinning Tables; Starting from Seeds; Stream Tables; Structures; Tracks; Water Flow; Where is the Moon? and Whistles and Strings.

Explorations in Middle School Science

Jostens Learning Corporation, 6170 Cornerstone Court East 5300, San Diego, CA 92121-3710; (619) 391-9900

This computer-based program provides ninety computer lessons in life, earth, and physical science for students in grades 6–9. The heart of each lesson is a computer-simulated laboratory to improve student achievement, critical thinking, communications and scientific process skills, and attitudes about science. Extension activities provide hands-on learning. The lessons, designed for a networked system, use on-line tools.

Explorations in Science

Roy Beven, Jostens Learning Corporation, 6170 Cornerstone Court East, San Diego, CA 92121; (800) 521-8538 x6372

Explorations in Science provides student lessons in physical, life, and earth science on a CD-ROM and local-area computer network (IBM, Mac, Apple IIGS) for grades 6–9. Computer-simulated laboratories and hands-on activities guide students in acquiring scientific concepts and developing critical-thinking skills. Computer laboratories allow students to conduct experimental activities in physical, earth, and life science that are too dangerous, too difficult, or too time-consuming to be done in the classroom.

Foundation and Challenges to Encourage Technology-based Science (FACETS)

American Chemical Society, 1155 16th Street NW, Washington, DC 20036; (202) 872-6179

This two-year curriculum uses a balanced treatment of science, technology, and society in a hands-on and cooperative learning approach. Topics are studied in the context of problems relevant to middle school students' lives. There is a teacher/administrator training component and a newsletter to network teachers and students using the materials.

Foundational Approaches in Science Teaching (FAST)

Curriculum Research and Development Group, University of Hawaii, 1776 University Avenue, Room UHS 2-202, Honolulu, HI 96822; (808) 948-7863

Foundational Approaches in Science Teaching uses laboratory and field activities to engage students in investigations of physical science, ecology, and relational study. Students use the knowledge gained in studying the environment to develop concepts related to technology, resource management, and conservation. Designed for use in grades 6–8.

Full Option Science System (FOSS)

Lawrence Hall of Science, University of California, Berkeley, CA 94720; (510) 642-8941

Materials include student equipment kits, student print materials, and alternative assessment materials for grades 3–6. All materials are designed to engage students in actively constructing scientific concepts through hands-on laboratory activities. Several types of assessment tools are included as an integral component of instruction. Sixteen modules exist in four topic areas: life science, physical science, earth science, and scientific reasoning and technology.

Current distributor: Encyclopaedia Britannica Educational Corporation

Franklin Activity Kits

Franklin Institute Science Museum, Museum To Go Science Resource Center, 20th and the Parkway, Philadelphia, PA 19103; (215) 448-1297

Two to four kits for each grade level (K–6) provide students with hands-on learning experiences in physical, earth, and life sciences. Both the kits and the eight or ten exercises per kit can be used independently, allowing teachers maximum flexibility in their use, and enabling kits to reach larger numbers of students within a school. Teacher training is provided to increase confidence in the use of science materials.

Distributor: Science Kit and Boreal Laboratories

Great Explorations in Math and Science (GEMS)

Lawrence Hall of Science, University of California, Berkeley, CA 94720; (415) 642-7771

Great Explorations in Math and Science offers twenty-four publications that in-tegrate mathematics with the life, earth, and physical sciences. The materials consist of teacher guides, presentation materials, and exhibit guides. Designed for K–12, the lessons are written for instructors with little knowledge of mathematics and science.

Topics include Animal Defenses; Animals in Action; Bubble-ology; Buzzing a Hive; Chemical Reactions; Convection: A Current Event; Crime Lab Chemistry; Discovering Density; Earth, Moon, and Stars; Fingerprinting; Hide a Butterfly; Hot Water and Warm Homes from Sunlight; Liquid Explorations; The "Magic" of Electricity; Mapping Animal Movements; Mapping Fish Habitats; More than Magnifiers; Oobleck: What Do Scientists Do? Paper Towel Testing; QUIDICE; Shapes, Loops, and Images; Solids, Liquids, and Gases; Vitamin C Testing; and The Wizard's Lab.

GrowLab

National Gardening Association, 180 Flynn Avenue, Burlington, VT 05401; (802) 863-1308

These materials utilize indoor gardening as a vehicle for teaching life science and engaging students in scientific inquiry. A teacher network provides resources for connecting schools to community partners and other educators who are using the materials nationwide. Designed for K–8, the materials include teacher resource books, seed kits, planter equipment, posters, a newsletter, the teacher network, and informational videos.

GREEN (Global Rivers Environmental Education Network)

School of Natural Resources, University of Michigan, Ann Arbor, MI 48109-1115

GREEN provides a variety of curriculum-related resources on water quality. Emphasizing student participation, GREEN also has assistance for international or cross-cultural projects, computer networking, and low-cost equipment. Of particular interest to high school classes is a curriculum guide, *Investigating Streams and Rivers,* and a corresponding *Field Manual for Water Quality Monitoring.* This program is widely acclaimed and international in scope.

Hands-on Elementary Science

Education Department, Hood College, Frederick, MD 21701; (301) 663-3131

The focus of the Hands-on Elementary Science series is on developing science process skills in grades 1–5. Materials include curriculum guides and materials kits.

Dissemination is supported through the National Diffusion Network.

Hands-on Science

Hands-on Science Outreach, 4910 Macon Road, Rockville, MD 20852; (301) 460-5922

Thematically organized materials provide recreational activities in science for use in after-school settings. The kits are organized around three themes: structure and change, patterns, and energy. Required leader training sessions facilitate effective discovery of science by participants at a wide range of ages. Consumable kits promote ownership and mastery of scientific concepts by participants, especially those from economically disadvantaged backgrounds.

Health Activities Project (HAP)

Lawrence Hall of Science, University of California, Berkeley, CA 94702; (415) 642-4193

This project provides elementary students with activities and information relevant to health and safety in their daily lives.

Topics include Action/Reaction; Balance in Movement; Breathing

Fitness; Consumer Health Decisions; Environmental Health and Safety; Flexibility and Strength; Growth Trends; Heart Fitness; Nutritional/ Dental Health; Personal Health Decisions; Sight and Sound; and Skin Temperature.

Horizons Plus

Houston Museum of Natural Science, 1 Hermann Circle Drive, Houston, TX 77030; (713) 639-4632

Horizons Plus consists of kits, including teacher materials and hands-on activity files for grades 1–6, to be used as a vehicle for introducing science concepts and hands-on activities in the context of students' experiences. The storybook design encourages multidisciplinary instruction and science learning in settings outside of school.

Distributor: Silver Burdett and Ginn

Improving Middle School Science: A Collaborative Approach

Education Development Center, Inc., 55 Chapel Street, Newton, MA 02160; (617) 969-7100

This multidisciplinary project for seventh- and eighth-grade students is targeted to the needs of early adolescents in urban environments. Materials integrate life, physical, and earth science within the context of science, society, and technology problems. Materials also include informal science education strategies.

Improving Urban Elementary Science: A Collaborative Approach

Education Development Center, 55 Chapel Street, Newton, MA 02160, (617) 969-7100

Materials in this K–5 project are designed to improve urban students' abilities to think critically, use language, and solve problems using the natural world as an experimental base.

Life, physical, and earth science are balanced, and activities are tied to the urban setting. These activities integrate science with the rest of the elementary curriculum, particularly mathematics and language arts.

Informal Science Study (ISS)

University of Houston, Room 450 Farish Hall, Houston, TX 77004; (713) 749-1692

Through Information Science Study, students investigate physical science concepts demonstrated in such familiar contexts as amusement park rides, sports, and playground activities. Designed for children in grades 5–12, the units consist of materials, equipment, and teacher prompts.

Dissemination is through the National Diffusion Network.

Insights: A Hands-on Elementary Science Curriculum

Education Development Center, 55 Chapel Street, Newton, MA 02160; (800) 225-4276

This elementary science program (K–6) consists of thematic modules that can be used together as a complete curriculum or as individual modules in conjunction with existing programs. They focus on a limited number of concepts and themes in depth and breadth, reflecting a balance of life, physical, and earth sciences, as well as attitudes, skills, knowledge, and values. They support cultural, racial, and linguistic diversity and are designed to be especially responsive to the needs of the urban school.

The Institute for Earth Education

P.O. Box 288, Warrenville, IL 60555

Based on the work of Steve Van Matre, Earth Education is the process of helping people build an understanding of, appreciation for, and harmony with the earth and its life. Publications and programs include *Acclimatization* (1972), *Acclimatizing* (1974), *Sunship Earth* (1979), *Earthkeepers* (1988), *Earth Education: A New Beginning* (1990), Earthwalks and Conceptual Encounters I and II.

JASON Mediterranean Expedition

The JASON Foundation for Education, 395 Totten Pond Road, Waltham, MA 02154; (617) 487-9995

Instructional materials address school science and social science relevant to on-line investigations undertaken by the underwater seeing-eye robot JASON. Materials also stand alone as thematic units about the exploration of sunken vessels in the Mediterranean Sea and the Great Lakes and about life in the Galapagos Islands. The project provides teacher guides, lesson plans, and posters to prepare students and teachers for the JASON downlink to museums.

Junior High/Middle School Life Science Program

Jefferson County Public School, Science Department, 1209 Quail Street, Lakewood, CO 80215; (303) 231-2351

This year-long curriculum in life science emphasizes the understanding and care of the human body as an alternative for educators seeking materials to improve their life science curricula or a resource for educators interested in integrating health topics into their existing life science course.

K–6 Project STARLAB

Young Astronaut Council 1211 Connecticut Avenue NW, Suite 800 Washington, DC 20036 (202) 682–1084

This project consists of science-based learning environments in two K–6 inner-city schools in Washington, DC. The project contains science and math-based curriculum materials, teacher

kits, teacher training, and supplemental activities that can be integrated into all subject areas.

Learning About Plants (LEAP)

Cornell Plantations, Cornell University, One Plantations Road, Ithaca, NY 14850; (607) 255-3020

LEAP is an activity-based life science program for grades K–6. The project integrates classroom and field experiences, emphasizing conceptual development through exploration of plants. The materials consist of four units for each grade.

Life Lab Science Program

1156 High Street, Santa Cruz, CA 95064; (408) 476-7140

Life Lab uses the garden as the basis of this program for grades K–6. Using familiar materials, it provides activities that integrate physical, life, and earth sciences; students then use the knowledge gained to analyze situations involving values and ethical issues. An earlier project was entitled *The Growing Classroom* for grades K–3, and the program contains videodisks.

Distributor: Addison-Wesley Publishing Company for *The Growing Classroom* and Video Discovery for the *Life Lab Science Program.*

Marine Science Project: FOR SEA

17771 Fjord Drive, NE, Poulsbo, WA 98370; (206) 779-5549

This project is designed to supplement existing science programs in grades 2, 4, 6, 7–8, and 9–12.

FOR SEA is disseminated through the National Diffusion Network.

Microcomputer-Based Laboratory Tools

Technical Education Research Center, 2067 Massachusetts Avenue, Boston, MA 02140; (617) 547-0430

Sensors for various physical parameters are interfaced to a computer so that experimental data can be easily gathered and displayed, thus providing K–12 students with a greater opportunity to engage actively in experimentation. Typical detectors include those for motion, temperature, voltage, pH, light, and sound. Instructional materials are included.

Distributor: IBM Educational Systems

Middle School Life Science

Jefferson County Public Schools, Lakewood, CO 80212; (303) 231-2351

This full-year course in life science for grades 6–8 is organized around a series of learning cycles in which students engage in hands-on laboratory activities, apply the concepts learned to other situations, and form connections between this new knowledge and other areas of inquiry. In this program, concepts are learned through active participation, rather than activities merely illustrating concepts discussed in lecture. Its goal is to engage students effectively in the discovery of scientific knowledge through connections to language arts, mathematics, and social sciences.

Distributor: Kendall/Hunt Publishing Company

Model Elementary Science Program

District of Columbia Public Schools, 415 12th Street NW, Washington, DC 20004; (202) 767-8666

This urban project for typical students is designed for teaching based on one hour of science instruction each day, research-based procedure for inquiry teaching, and experiential learning. All students are engaged in science, and interrelationships between science and technology are stressed. In this project, science is a core activity frequently integrated with other content areas, particularly mathematics and language arts.

National Geographic Kids Network

National Geographic Society, Educational Services, Dept. 5397, Washington, DC 20036; (800) 368-2728

Participating students collect scientific data in their home environments and feed the information into a nationwide electronic network, facilitating the discovery of scientific concepts on a national and global scale. Students communicate with other students and practicing scientists across the country. For Apple IIGS, IBM, and Mac.

Study units include Hello, Acid Rain, and Weather.

National SERIES Project

National Series Project, 300 Lakeside Drive, Oakland, CA 94612; (510) 987-0119

High school students lead younger children (ages 9–12) in the discovery of science. Trained by adult mentors, teens guide younger students through six scientific units, addressing such concepts as chemistry and the environment, agriculture, and recycling. Each unit culminates in a community service project, giving students opportunities to apply acquired knowledge to real problems in their own communities.

National Urban League Preschool Science Collaborative

National Urban League, New York, NY 10021; (212) 310-9214

This project consists of physical science activities for preschool children and provides training for parents and teachers of this age group. Materials include a center-based science activities manual, an activities booklet for use by parents, and play areas for science explorations. A promotional videotape highlights various parts of the training and promotes use of the materials.

Naturescope

National Wildlife Federation, 1412 Sixteenth Street, NW, Washington, DC 20036

Naturescope is designed to improve the teaching of natural sciences. It includes hands-on activities and worksheets for elementary grades. Each issue focuses on a specific topic (e.g., birds, trees, geology, pollution, rain forests, weather, oceans, mammals, reptiles, arts and crafts, dinosaurs, astronomy, deserts, wetlands, endangered species, and insects).

Oceanic Education Activities for Great Lakes Schools (OEAGLS)

Ohio Sea Grant Education Program, Ohio State University, 059 Ramseyer Hall, 29 W. Woodruff Avenue, Columbus, OH 43210

Thirty multidisciplinary classroom activities for grades 5–9 focus on the role of the oceans and the Great Lakes in the lives of Ohioans and address economic, political, social, scientific, and technological issues. Computer programs, primary activities, and other publications are also available.

Operation SMART

Operation SMART, 2336 Kahn Street, Port Townsend, WA 98368; (206) 385-7585

This program of out-of-school activities emphasizes hands-on experiences in math, science, and technology for girls ages 6–18. Its activities are aimed at combating existing barriers to participation in science and mathematics by girls through the creation of positive environments for learning, special staff awareness training, and bombardment of girls with information about careers and educational opportunities not traditionally promoted among women.

Outdoor Biology Instructional Strategies (OBIS)

Lawrence Hall of Science, University of California, Berkeley, CA 94720; (415) 642-4193

OBIS consists of ninety-seven modules for students in grades 3–10. The out-of-school environment is used to increase environmental awareness through nontraditional activities such as games, crafts, and experiments. Examples: Ants, Beach Zonation, Creepers and Climbers, Fly a Leaf, Metric Capers, and Roots and Shoots.

Distributor: Delta Education

Project First Step (Science and Technology Education Program)

U.S. Space Foundation, 1551 Vapor Trail, Colorado Springs, CO 80916; (719) 550-1414

This three-year curriculum for grades 6, 7, and 8 features hands-on inquiry learning; use of space and aviation technologies to motivate students to study life, earth, and physical sciences; concrete representations of abstract scientific concepts; and an approach that encourages gender equity and the participation of minorities and the disabled.

Project Learning Tree

American Forest Foundation, 1111 19th Street, N.W., Suite 780, Washington, DC 20036

PLT is a multidisciplinary set of environmental education activities designed to help elementary and secondary students better understand the forest community and its relationship to other environments and the day-to-day lives of people. The materials are available only to individuals who attend a six-hour PLT workshop.

Project STARWALK

Lakeview Museum Planetarium, 1125
    W. Lake Avenue, Peoria, IL 61614;
    (309) 686-6682

This National Diffusion Network–distributed program integrates field trips to a planetarium with classroom lessons about space concepts for grades 3 and 5. Materials include teacher management assistance and training materials.

Project WET (Water Education for Teachers)

201 Culbertson Hall, Montana State
    University, Bozeman, MT 59717;
    (406) 994-5392

Project WET is a national program designed to teach about water issues. The core of the program is a K–12 curriculum and activity guide containing approximately 100 multidisciplinary activities, available through inservice workshops. In addition, a variety of supplementary resources are being developed to complement and extend the guide including modules (e.g., wetlands, watersheds, ground water), demonstration models, children's literature books, and living history materials. All materials reflect a balanced and diverse approach to water issues, incorporate various cultural perspectives, and accommodate many learning styles.

Project WILD

5430 Grosvenor Lane, Bethesda, MD
    20814; (301) 493-5447

Project WILD is an interdisciplinary, supplementary environmental and conservation education program for educators of kindergarten through high school age youth that prepares students to make responsible decisions about wildlife and the environment. It includes a wide variety of instructional strategies that can be incorporated into different subjects. Aquatic Project WILD (1987) focuses on marine and aquatic education. In includes additional WILD activities from the original elementary and secondary WILD guides. These materials are available only through a six-hour workshop.

The Rivers Curriculum

Southern Illinois University
    at Edwardsville, Box 2222,
    Edwardsville, IL 62026-2222

The Rivers Curriculum was written by teachers and designed around six content units for high school students. Each unit is organized around field trips to the river and include curriculum for chemistry, biology, earth science, mathematics, geography, and language arts.

Science Activities for the Visually Impaired/Science Activities for Learners with Physical Handicaps (SAVI/SELPH)

Lawrence Hall of Science, University
    of California, Berkeley, CA 94720;
    (415) 642-8941

SAVI/SELPH activities enable students with special needs to participate successfully in multisensory investigations of physical, life, and earth science. The nine modules work well in many environments and can be taught by teachers with limited science instruction experience.

Units are Communication, Environmental Energy, Environments, Kitchen Interactions, Magnetism and Electricity, Measurement, Mixtures and Solutions, Scientific Reasoning, and Structures of Life.

Science and Technology: Investigating Human Diversity

Biological Sciences Curriculum Study,
    830 North Tejon, Suite 405,
    Colorado Springs, CO 80903;
    (719) 578-1136

This three-year activity-based program is available for students in grades 5–9. The program continues the K–6 materials and focuses on the specific developmental needs of the early adolescent. It also encourages the participation of female and minority students, and students with disabilities; emphasizes reasoning and critical thinking; illustrates careers; and introduces the science, technology, and society theme.

Science and Technology for Children (STC)

National Science Resources Center,
    Arts and Industries Building,
    Room 1201, Smithsonian Institution, Washington, DC 20560;
    (202) 357-2555

The National Science Resources Center provides a four-year elementary science curriculum for grades 1–6 in the areas of physical, life, and earth science. The twenty-four hands-on science teaching units focus on important age-appropriate concepts and skills. The units link science with other subjects including mathematics, language arts, social studies, and art. Each unit includes a teacher's guide, a classroom set of student activity books, a kit of equipment and materials, and an annotated list of science trade books, audiovisual materials, and computer software that can be used to supplement the unit.

Distributor: Carolina Biological Supply Company

Science—A Process Approach (SAPA/SAPA II)

American Association for the
    Advancement of Science,
    Washington, DC, 1333 H Street
    NW, Washington, DC 20005;
    (202) 326-6400

Science—A Process Approach (SAPA), produced by the National Science Foundation during the sixties, focuses heavily on the processes of science rather than on concepts. In both versions, activities form a sequential K–6 program in which mastery of specific skills is predicated on the accumulation of experience.

Distributor: Activities are currently available on *Science Helper K–8* or as revisions from Delta Education.

Science Curriculum Improvement Study (3 versions) (SCIS/SCISII/SCIIS)

Lawrence Hall of Science, University of California, Berkeley, CA 94720; (415) 642-8718

SCIS, in all three versions, focuses on concepts and processes of science for grades K–6. Investigations in physical and life science include exploration, interpretation, and application skills.

SCIS: Beginnings; Communities; Ecosystems; Energy Sources; Environments; Interaction and Systems; Life Cycles; Material Objects; Models: Electric and Magnetic Interactions; Organisms; Populations; Relative Position and Motion; Subsystems and Variables.

SCIS II: Communities; Ecosystems; Energy Sources; Environments; Interaction and Systems; Life Cycles; Material Objects; Modeling Systems; Organisms; Populations; Measurement, Motion, and Change; Subsystems and Variables.

SCIIS/85: Beginnings; Communities; Ecosystems; Energy Sources; Environments; Interaction and Systems; Life Cycles; Material Objects; Scientific Theories; Organisms; Populations; Relative Position and Motion; Subsystems and Variables.

Distributor: Units available on *Science Helper K–8*. All three versions are available through Delta Education.

Science for Life and Living: Integrating Science, Technology, and Health

Biological Sciences Curriculum Study, 830 North Tejon, Suite 405, Colorado Springs, CO 80903; (719) 578-1136

This program is evenly divided among the life, health, earth, and physical sciences. Students learn science content and process skills as well as social skills, problem solving, decision making, and use of technology. Supplementary activities integrate reading, language arts, and mathematics.

Distributor: Kendall/Hunt Publishing Company.

Science Helper K–8

Room 302, Norman Hall, University of Florida, Gainesville, FL 32607; (904) 392-0761

The University of Florida has produced *Science Helper K–8,* a CD-ROM database that provides access to materials developed by the major National Science Foundation curriculum projects of the sixties and seventies. Excerpts from the actual programs are indexed by grade, subject, skill, keyword, and content. A search results in the on-screen image of a page of the document and can be printed. Curriculum projects included are COPES—Conceptually Oriented Program for Elementary Science; ESS—Elementary Science Study (partial); SAPA: Science—A Process Approach; SCIS—Science Curriculum Improvement Study; USMES—Unified Science and Mathematics for Elementary School (partial).

ScienceVision

Interactive Media Science Project, 205 Carothers Hall, Florida State University, Tallahassee, FL 32306; (904) 644-8422

These materials utilize interactive videodisks to provide students (grades 6–8) with the tools and information necessary to solve extended problems in life science, earth and space science, and physical science that are of real-world scope and significance. Videodisks allow students to visit locations, listen to experts, collect data, and reach conclusions without leaving the classroom. Materials include interactive videodisks, computer software (Apple IIGS and Mac),

student log books, teacher's guides, and laboratory activities.

Distributor: Houghton Mifflin Company

The Second Voyage of the *Mimi*

Wings for Learning, 1600 Green Hill Road, P.O. Box 660002, Scotts Valley, CA 95067-0002

A voyage into ancient Mayan civilization serves as a vehicle for teaching interdisciplinary science and mathematics. Twelve 15-minute documentary-format episodes, accompanied by student materials and hands-on activities, engage students in the discovery of mathematics and science. Software learning modules, whose themes are derived from the video series, offer flexible learning opportunities in either science or mathematics to individuals or small groups of students.

Self Help Elementary Level Science (SHELS)

Florida State University, Gainesville, FL 32611; (904) 392-0761

These are videotapes with print materials to be used as a form of staff development for teachers and administrators. The tapes include topics such as strategies for dealing with obstacles to teaching elementary science and techniques for research-based teaching.

TLTG Physical Science/TLTG Math for Science

Texas Learning Technology Group, P.O. Box 2974, Austin, TX 78768-2974; (512) 467-0222

This two-semester physical science course is delivered primarily through interactive videodisk and includes courseware, teacher resources, laboratory exercises, classroom management, testing systems, and a computer tutorial for science-related mathematics for grades 8–10. This full-year physical science course includes units in chemistry, physics, and energy resources of the future.

Distributor: Glencoe Corporation

Terracorps

Upland Unified School District, 904
    West 9th Street, P.O. Box 1239,
    Upland, CA 91786;
    (714) 981-1603

Ecological science materials have been developed for students in grades 6–8; they feature real-life applications and classroom activities. The thirty-six modules represent life, earth, and physical science topics. The units are arranged into three levels of proficiency, each with increasing skills and a higher level of measurement, concept, and knowledge. A videotape teaching-training component is available.

T/S/M (Technology/Science/ Mathematics) Integration Activities

Virginia Polytechnic Institute and
    State University, 144 Smyth Hall,
    Blacksburg, VA 24061-0432;
    (703) 231-6480

These materials for grades 6–9 use design-under-constraint activities, in which students create their own solutions to problems given a fixed set of resources and conditions, to teach concepts in science, mathematics, and technology. Through activities such as trying to harness wind power with any apparatus constructed from provided materials, students create their own learning experiences. Because these problems do not have a single correct answer, each solution offers some opportunity for learning. While these materials require the facilities of a technology or industrial arts class-

room, they are designed to be implemented through technology, science, or mathematics courses.

Unified Science and Mathematics for Elementary Schools

Education Development Center, Newton, MA 02160; (617) 969-7100

Materials can be obtained from ERIC. Partial inclusion has been made on *Science Helper K–8.*

This project provided a series of twenty-three guides for use in grades K–8. The units include a beginning challenge that is investigated by the students through project activity cards and background papers. Teacher instructions are limited as learning is developed through students' independent activities.

Topics include Advertising, Bicycle Transportation, Burglar Alarm Design, Classroom Design, Classroom Management, Consumer Research—Product Testing, Describing People, Designing for Human Proportions, Dice Design, Electromagnet Device Design, Growing Plants, Lunch Lines, Manufacturing, Orientation, Pedestrian Crossings, Play Area Design and Use, School Zoo, Soft Drink Design, Traffic Flow, USMES Design Lab Manual, The USMES Guide, Ways to Learn/Teach, and Weather Predictions.

Wisconsin Fast Plants

Wisconsin Fast Plants Program,
    Department of Plant Pathology,
    University of Wisconsin–Madison,
    1630 Linden Drive, Madison, WI
    53706; (608) 263-2634

These rapid-cycling cabbage-related plants facilitate the study of plant biol-

ogy and genetics at all levels (K–college). The manual contains suggested activities and resources for teachers using Fast Plants. Kits include seeds and instruction in addition to a teacher resource manual.

Distributor: Carolina Biological Supply Company

WOW! The Wonders of Wetlands

Environmental Concern, P.O. Box P,
    St. Michaels, MD 21663;
    (410) 745-9620

This educator's guide provides a range of activities labeled from grades K–12, though most of them can be adapted for several grade levels. WOW! is designed so that lessons may be used individually or as an entire unit with much potential for integration with social studies, language, mathematics and other disciplines.

Zero Population Growth

1400 16th Street, NW, Suite 320,
    Washington, D.C. 20036

ZPG provides a wide variety of population education resource materials, including newsletters, fact sheets, publications, curricula, and videos. Teaching materials are cross-disciplinary, emphasize hands-on learning, and may be used alone or as part of a larger population unit. These include *For Earth's Sake* (6–10), *USA by Numbers* (9–12+), *EdVentures in Population Education* (4–12), *Global 2000 Countdown Kit* (9–12), and *Elementary Population Activities Kit* (K–6). Information and data are also available through Population Reference Bureau, 777 14th Street, NW, Suite 800, Washington, DC 20005.

APPENDIX C

State Education Agencies

Each state has an agency that oversees the educational structure within the state. Below is a listing of these agencies.

Alabama
Alabama State Department of
    Education
Gordon Persons Building
Montgomery, Alabama 36130

Alaska
Alaska State Department of
    Education
P.O. Box F
Juneau, Alaska 99811

Arizona
Arizona Department of Education
1535 West Jefferson Street
Phoenix, Arizona 85007

Arkansas
Arkansas Department of Education
1535 West Jefferson Street
4 State Capitol Mall
Little Rock, Arkansas 72201

Bureau of Indian Affairs
Department of Interior, BIA
1849 C Street NW
Mail Stop 3525, Code 521
MIBWashington, DC 20240

California
State Department of Education
721 Capitol Mall, 3rd Floor
Sacramento, California 95814

Colorado
Colorado Department of Education
201 East Colfax Avenue
Denver, Colorado 80203

Connecticut
State Department of Education
P.O. Box 2219, Room 369
Hartford, Connecticut 06145

Delaware
State Department of Public Instruction
Townsend Building
P.O. Box 1402
Dover, Delaware 19903

District of Columbia
Education Program
D.C. Public Schools
415 12th Street NW, Room 1004
Washington, DC 20004

Florida
Florida Department of Education
Florida Education Center,
    Suite 522
Tallahassee, Florida 32399

Georgia
Georgia Department of Education
1862 Twin Towers East
Atlanta, Georgia 30334

Hawaii
Education Program
189 Lunalilo Home Road, 2nd Floor
Honolulu, Hawaii 96825

Idaho
Idaho Department of Education
Len B. Jordan Office Building
Boise, Idaho 83720

Illinois
Illinois State Board of Education
100 North First Street
Springfield, Illinois 62777-0001

Indiana
Indiana Department of Education
229 State House
Indianapolis, Indiana 46204-2798

Iowa
Iowa Department of Education
Grimes State Office Building
Des Moines, Iowa 50319-0146

Kansas
Kansas Department of Education
120 East 10th Street
Topeka, Kansas 66612-1103

Kentucky
Kentucky Department of
    Education
Capitol Plaza Tower, 17th Floor
Frankfort, Kentucky 40601

Louisiana
State Department of Education
P.O. Box 94064
Baton Rouge, Louisiana 70804-9064

Maine
Maine State Department of Education
State House Station #23
Augusta, Maine 04333

Maryland
Maryland State Department of
    Education
200 West Baltimore Street
Baltimore, Maryland 21201-2595

Massachusetts
Massachusetts Department of
    Education
1385 Hancock Street
Quincy, Massachusetts 02169

Michigan
Michigan Department of Education
P.O. Box 30008
Lansing, Michigan 48909

Minnesota
Minnesota Department of Education
Capitol Square Building, Room 922
St. Paul, Minnesota 55101

Mississippi
State Department of Education
Walter Sillers Building, Suite 501
P.O. Box 771
Jackson, Mississippi 39205-0771

Missouri
Department of Education
Department of Elementary and
   Secondary Education
P.O. Box 480
Jefferson, Missouri 65102

Montana
Office of Public Instruction
State Capitol Building
Helena, Montana 59620

Nebraska
Nebraska Department of Education
P.O. Box 84987
301 Centennial Mall South
Lincoln, Nebraska 68509

Nevada
Nevada Department of Education
Capitol Complex
Carson City, Nevada 89710

New Hampshire
New Hampshire Department of
   Education
101 Pleasant Street
Concord, New Hampshire 03301

New Jersey
New Jersey Department of Education
Division of General Academic
   Education
CN 500
Trenton, New Jersey 08625-0500

New Mexico
State Department of Education
300 Don Gaspar Street
Santa Fe, New Mexico 87501-2786

New York
New York State Education
   Department
Bureau of Professional Career
   Opportunity Programs
Empire State Plaza
Cultural Education Center,
   Room 5C64
Albany, New York 12230

North Carolina
Department of Public Instruction
116 West Edenton Street
Raleigh, North Carolina 27603-1712

North Dakota
Department of Public Instruction
State Capitol
Bismarck, ND 58505

Ohio
Ohio Department of Education
65 South Front Street
Columbus, Ohio 43266-0308

Oklahoma
State Department of Education
2500 North Lincoln Boulevard
Oklahoma City, Oklahoma 73105

Oregon
Oregon Department of Education
700 Pringle Parkway, S.E.
Salem, Oregon 97310

Pennsylvania
Pennsylvania Department of
   Education
333 Market Street, 7th Floor
Harrisburg, Pennsylvania 17126-0333

Puerto Rico
Office of Education
Office 809
Department of Education
Hato Rey, Puerto Rico 00919

Rhode Island
Rhode Island Department of
   Education
22 Hayes Street
Providence, Rhode Island 02908

South Carolina
South Carolina Department of
   Education
Curriculum Section
801 Rutledge Building
Columbia, South Carolina 29201

South Dakota
Division of Education
700 Governors Drive
Pierre, South Dakota 57501-2291

Tennessee
Tennessee Department of Education
4th Floor Northwing
Cordell Hull Building
Nashville, Tennessee 37243-0388

Texas
Texas Education Agency
1701 N. Congress
Austin, Texas 78701

Utah
Utah Department of Education
250 East 500 South
Salt Lake City, Utah 84111

Vermont
Vermont State Department of
   Education
120 State Street
Montpelier, Vermont 05602

Virginia
Virginia Department of Education
P.O. Box 6Q
Richmond, Virginia 23216-2060

Washington
Washington Department of
   Education
P.O. Box 47200
Old Capitol Building, FG-11
Olympia, Washington 98504

West Virginia
West Virginia Department of
    Education
1900 Kanawha Blvd., East,
    Room B-252
Charleston, West Virginia 25305

Wisconsin
Department of Public
    Instruction
125 South Webster Street
P.O. Box 7841
Madison, Wisconsin 53707-7841

Wyoming
State Department of Education
241 Hathaway Building
Cheyenne, Wyoming 82002-0050

Organizations That Support Reform in Science Education

American Association for the Advancement of Science (AAAS)
1333 H Street NW, Washington, DC
    20005; (202) 326-6400

American Business Conference (ABC)
1730 K Street NW, Suite 1200, Washington, DC 20006; (202) 822-9300

American Society for Training and Development (ASTD)
1630 Duke Street, Box 1443, Alexandria, VA 22313; (703) 683-8100

The Business Council
888 Seventeenth Street NW, Washington, DC 20006; (202) 298-7650

The Business Roundtable (BRT)
200 Park Avenue, New York, NY
    10166; (212) 682-6370

Center for Leadership in School Reform
950 Breckenridge Lane, Suite 200, Louisville, KY 40207; (502) 895-1942

Committee for Economic Development (CED)
477 Madison Avenue, New York, NY
    10022; (212) 688-2063

The Conference Board
845 Third Avenue, New York, NY
    10022; (212) 759-0900

Council for Aid to Education
51 Madison Avenue, Suite 2200, New
    York, NY 10010; (212) 689-4200

Educate America
310 South Street, Morristown, NJ
    07960; (201) 285-5200

National Alliance of Business—Center for Excellence in Education
1201 New York Avenue NW, Suite
    700, Washington, DC 20005; (202)
    289-2925

National Assessment of Educational Progress (NAEP)
P.O. Box 6710, Princeton, NJ 08541-
    6710; (609) 734-1624

National Association of Partners in Education (NAPE)
209 Madison Street, Alexandria, VA
    22314; (703) 836-4880

National Board for Professional Teaching Standards
300 River Place, Suite 3600, Detroit,
    MI 48207; (313) 259-0830

National Center on Education and the Economy
39 State Street, Suite 500, Rochester,
    NY 14614; (716) 546-7620

National Center for the Improvement of Science Teaching and Learning (The NETWORK, Inc.)
290 South Main Street, Andover, MA 01810; (617) 470-1080

National Center for Science Teaching and Learning (NCSTL)
Ohio State University, Research Center, 1314 Kinnear Road, Columbus, OH 43212; (614) 292-3339.

National Education Goals Panel
1850 M Street NW, Suite 270, Washington, DC 20036; (202) 632-0952

National Science Foundation (NSF)
4201 Wilson Boulevard, Alexandria, VA 22230; (703) 306-1234

National Science Resources Center (NSRC)
Arts and Industries Building, Room 1201, Smithsonian Institution, Washington, DC 20560; (202) 357-2555

National School Boards Association (NSBA)
1680 Duke Street, Alexandria, VA 22314; (703) 838-6722

Public Education Fund Network
601 13th Street NW, Suite 370 South, Washington, DC 20005-3808; (202) 628-7460

Secretary's Commission on Achieving Necessary Skills (SCANS)
U.S. Department of Labor, 200 Constitution Avenue NW, Washington, DC 20210; (800) 788-SKIL

Triangle Coalition for Science and Technology Education
5112 Berwyn Road, 3d Floor, College Park, MD 20740; (301) 220-0870

United States Chamber of Commerce—Center for Workforce Preparation and Quality Education
1615 H Street NW, Washington, DC 20062; (202) 463-5525

APPENDIX E

Resource Organizations

American Association of Physics Teachers (AAPT)
5112 Berwyn Road, 2d Floor, College Park, MD 20740; (301) 345-4200

The American Association of Physics Teachers offers professional publications, publications for high school students, a periodic newsletter for students and teachers, activities for students and teachers, curriculum development, and career information.

American Astronomical Society
University of Texas at Austin, Austin, TX 78712-1083; (512) 471-1083

The American Astronomical Society sponsors special meetings for precollege science teachers that are held in conjunction with the association's yearly professional conference. The program introduces teachers to modern research in astronomy through special lectures and activities.

American Chemical Society (ACS)

1155 16th Street NW, Washington, DC 20036; (202) 872-6179

The American Chemical Society resources include *Chem Matters*, a publication for high school teachers and students, *Wonder-Science* for elementary students and their parents, professional publications, curriculum development, and career information.

American Geological Institute (AGI)

National Center for Earth Science Education, 4220 King Street, Alexandria, VA 22302; (703) 379-2480

The American Geological Institute focuses on student and teacher activities, curriculum development, professional publications, and newsletters.

American Geophysical Union

2000 Florida Avenue NW, Washington, DC 20009; (202) 462-6903

The American Geophysical Union promotes educational opportunities through its publications.

American Institute of Aeronautics and Astronautics

370 L'Enfant Promenade SW, Washington, DC 20024; (202) 646-7400

Student activity and career information are provided by the American Institute of Aeronautics and Astronautics.

American Institute of Biological Sciences (AIBS)

College of Natural Sciences, University of Northern Iowa, Cedar Falls, IA 50614-0181; (319) 273-2585

The American Institute of Biological Sciences offers student activities, career information, and professional publications.

American Institute of Chemical Engineers

345 East 47th Street, New York, NY 10017; (212) 705-7370

The American Institute of Chemical Engineers provides student programs and career information.

American Institute of Chemists

Northeast Missouri State University, Kirksville, MO 63701; (816) 785-4620

The American Institute of Chemists sustains teacher activities and professional publications.

American Institute of Physics

335 East 45th Street, New York, NY 10017; (212) 661-9404

The American Institute of Physics produces professional publications, newsletters for students and teachers, activities for students and teachers, curriculum development and career information.

American Meteorological Society

Department of Meteorology, University of Wisconsin, Madison, WI 53706; (608) 262-0776

The American Meteorological Society supports student career information and professional publications.

American Nature Study Society

Pocono Environmental Education Center, R.D.1, Box 268, Dingman's Ferry, PA 18328; (717) 828-2319

The educational products of the American Nature Study Society are student and teacher activities and newsletters.

American Nuclear Society

Department of Mechanical and Energy Engineering, University of Lowell, Lowell, MA 01854; (508) 452-5000

The American Nuclear Society dispenses professional publications, a newsletter for students and teachers, and career information and holds workshops for secondary science and social studies teachers on nuclear technology.

American Physical Society

335 East 45th Street, New York, NY 10017; (212) 682-7341

The American Physical Society provides programs for physics teachers, newsletters, and career information.

American Society for Cell Biology (ASCB)

9650 Rockville Pike, Bethesda, MD 20814; (301) 530-7153

ASCB offers a teacher research fellowship for secondary science teachers through summer research work in the laboratories of ASCB for eight to ten weeks. The purpose of the program is to give science teachers the opportunity to participate in a hands-on research experience in cell biology.

American Society for Engineering Education

11 DuPont Circle #200, Washington, DC 20036; (202) 293-7080

Professional publications, newsletters, and career information can be obtained from the American Society for Engineering Education.

American Society for Microbiology

1913 Eye Street NW, Washington, DC 20006; (202) 833-9680

Student and teacher activities and newsletters are supported by the American Society for Microbiology.

Association for the Education of Teachers in Science (AETS)

5040 Haley Center, Auburn University, Auburn, AL 36849-5212; (205) 844-5785

This association makes presentations of interest to teachers as well as teacher educators at the annual National Science Teachers Association meeting. The presentations include demonstrations, panel discussions, and contributed papers.

Association of Science-Technology Centers

1025 Vermont Avenue NW, Suite 500, Washington, DC 20005-3516; (202) 783-7200

Members of this association offer a variety of programs for science and mathematics teachers. These in-service programs include teacher camp-ins, afternoon courses, and summer institutes. Contact your local center for additional offerings.

Association for Supervision and Curriculum Development (ASCD)

125 North West Street, Alexandria, VA 22314-2798; (703) 549-9110

The Association for Supervision and Curriculum Development recognizes and evaluates educational issues. This organization conducts conferences, publishes newsletters, and provides professional growth opportunities.

Association for Women in Science (AWIS)

2401 Virginia Avenue NW, No. 303, Washington, DC 20037; (202) 833-2998

The Association for Women in Science dispenses career information for women.

Biological Science Curriculum Study (BSCS)

830 N. Tejon Street, Suite 405, Colorado Springs, CO 80903; (719) 578-1136

BSCS is active in the production of curriculum materials for grades K–12. See Appendix B for additional information.

Center for Excellence in Education

7710 Old Springhouse Road, Suite 100, McLean, VA 22102; (703) 448-9062

Lectures, mentor programs, and laboratory experiences for outstanding students and teachers are sustained by Center for Excellence in Education.

The Center for Teaching and Learning

University of North Dakota, Box 8158, University Station, Grand Forks, ND 58202; (701) 777-2674

The Center for Teaching and Learning produces educational monographs.

Coalition for Earth Science Education (CESE)

Geological Society of America, 3300 Penrose Place, P.O. Box 9140, Boulder, CO 80301; (303) 447-2020

CESE was established to promote communication among organizations interested in earth science education. More than thirty organizations have joined the coalition.

Council for Elementary Science International (CESI)

Department of Curriculum and Instruction, 212 Townsend Hall, University of Missouri, Columbia, MO 65211; (314) 882-7247

The Council for Elementary Science International promotes and produces books related to elementary science teaching.

Council of State Science Supervisors (CSSS)

c/o Joseph Exline, Virginia Department of Education, P.O. Box 60, Richmond, VA 23216-2060; (804) 371-6198/ 225-2876

This organization composed of state science consultants throughout the United States and its territories develops policy positions and shares information to be disseminated through state education agencies. Each consultant is capable of providing information on science education programs within his or her state. See Appendix B for a complete listing.

The Council of Interracial Books for Children

1841 Broadway, New York, NY 10023; (212) 757-5339

The Council of Interracial Books for Children provides brochures to assist in the selection of racially unbiased reading for children.

Educational Products Information Exchange (EPIE)

P.O. Box 839, Water Mill, NY 11976; (516) 283-4922

Educational Products Information Exchange publishes *The Educational Software Selector (TESS)* and newsletters, *Epiegram* and *Microgram*.

Educational Resources Information Center (ERIC)

Educational Resources Information Centers distribute education-related literature published by the Government Printing Office and by other organizations not necessarily under the direction of the federal government. ERIC can be accessed through most libraries. ERIC has several clearinghouses, including:

ERIC Clearinghouse on Elementary and Early Childhood Education

University of Illinois, College of Education, 805 West Pennsylvania Ave., Urbana, IL 61801-4897

ERIC Clearinghouse on Handicapped and Gifted Children

Council for Exceptional Children, 1920 Association Drive, Reston, VA 22091-3660

ERIC Clearinghouse for Science, Mathematics, and Environmental Education

Ohio State University, 1200 Chambers Road, Room 310, Columbus, OH 43212-1792

ERIC Clearinghouse for Social Studies/Social Science Education

Indiana University Social Studies Development Center, 2805 East 10th Street, Suite 120, Bloomington, IN 47405-2373

Environmental Protection Agency (EPA)

Public Information Center and Library, 401 M Street SW, Washington, DC 20460; (202) 260-2090

The Environmental Protection Agency furnishes information and publications relating to environmental concerns.

Fermilab National Accelerator Laboratory Science Education Center

Fermilab MS 777, Box 500, Batavia, IL 60510; (708) 840-2031

The center provides assistance to schools and/or school districts by providing effective instructional materials and basic science content for educators; modeling effective teaching skills and methods; promoting and modeling the effective use of technology as it relates to science instruction; and providing high-quality precollege science materials for educators in a collection of trade books, curriculum materials, videos, and other multimedia materials.

Foundation for Science and the Handicapped

West Virginia University, Morgantown, WV 26506-6057; (304) 293-5201

This foundation produces professional publications and newsletters relating to science and the disabled.

Girls Clubs of America, Inc.; Operation SMART

30 East 33rd Street, New York, NY 10016; (212) 689-3700

Career materials and programs designed to encourage girls and minorities in science, mathematics, and technology careers are sustained through the efforts of the Girls Clubs of America.

Harvard-Smithsonian Center for Astrophysics

Project STAR, 60 Garden Street, Cambridge, MA 02138; (617) 495-9798

The Harvard-Smithsonian Center for Astrophysics's Project STAR includes study modules, software, films, and teacher support materials relating to the role of science and research in astronomy.

International Technology Education Association (ITEA)

1914 Association Drive, Reston, VA 22901-1502; (703) 860-2100

ITEA serves as a clearinghouse for curriculum materials for technology education. The association conducts an annual conference, workshops, and symposia to advance ideas on teaching and learning technology.

Lawrence Hall of Science (LHS)

University of California, Berkeley, CA 94720; (510) 642-7771

The Lawrence Hall of Science has developed several series of materials related to science or the integration of science and mathematics for grades K–6. See Appendix B for curriculum examples.

Mid-Atlantic Equity Center

American University, School of Education, 5010 Wisconsin Avenue NW, Washington, DC 20016; (202) 885-8517

The Mid-Atlantic Equity Center provides information and materials emphasizing race, sex, and national origin desegregation.

Minority High School Student Research Apprentice Program

National Center for Research Resources, National Institutes of Health, Westwood Building, Room 10All, Bethesda, MD 20892; (301) 496-6743

This agency-sponsored program offers minority teachers or teachers who reach a significant number of minority students the opportunity to gain hands-on research experience, update their skills in modern research techniques, and broaden their scientific concepts through participation in a summer research project at a local university, health professional school, or research organization.

National Aeronautics and Space Administration (NASA)

NASA Headquarters, CODE XEE, Washington, DC 20546; (202) 453-8396

The National Aeronautics and Space Administration Education Division provides educational programs and materials for teachers and students from the elementary to the university level. See Appendix F for a complete listing of NASA educational centers.

National Association for Research in Science Teaching (NARST)

c/o Dr. William Holliday, 402 Teachers College, University of Cincinnati, Cincinnati, OH 45221; (513) 475-2335

NARST provides presentations on research findings at national and regional meetings of the National Science Teachers Association. These presentations include papers, panel discussions, workshops, and demonstrations on a variety of issues such as teaching science through reading and writing, collaborative learning, and assessment.

National Association for Science, Technology, and Society (NASTS)

Pennsylvania State University, 128 Willard Building, University Park, PA 16802; (814) 865-9951

The National Association for Science, Technology, and Society conducts annual meetings and publishes newsletters and journals.

National Association of Biology Teachers (NABT)

11250 Roger Bacon Drive #19, Reston, VA 22090; (703) 471-1134

This national organization for biology teachers publishes activities for teachers and students, related journals, and convenes annual conferences.

National Association of Geology Teachers

1041 New Hampshire Street, P.O. Box 368, Lawrence, KS 66044; (913) 843-1234

The National Association of Geology Teachers produces activities for teacher use, newsletters, and career information.

National Audubon Society

613 Riversville Road, Greenwich, CT 06830; (203) 869-5272

The National Audubon Society publishes *Audubon Adventures*, software, and television specials for children and professional growth workshops for teachers.

National Association for the Professional Advancement of Black Chemists and Chemical Engineers

1265 Main Street, W-6, Waltham, MA 02254; (617) 725-2000

Professional publications, Adopt-A-School Program, and career information are sustained by the National Association for the Professional Advancement of Black Chemists and Chemical Engineers.

National Diffusion Network (NDN)

Office of Educational Research and Improvement, U.S. Department of Education, 555 New Jersey Avenue NW, Washington, DC 20208-1525; (202) 357-6134

The National Diffusion Network (NDN) is a system to identify and provide access to exemplary education programs nationwide. The Network provides a listing of programs and state coordinators.

National Earth Science Teachers Association (NESTA)

Department of Geological Sciences, Michigan State University, East Lansing, MI 48824; (202) 328-5800

The National Earth Science Teachers Association offers activity ideas, background information, and slide sets for earth science.

National Oceanic and Atmospheric Administration (NOAA)

National Weather Service Office of Warning and Forecast, 8060 13th Street, Silver Spring, MD 20910; (301) 443-8910

The National Oceanic and Atmospheric Administration provides pamphlets, booklets, and other information about weather phenomena.

National Science Supervisors Association (NSSA)

Glastonbury Public Schools, 330 Hubbard Street, Glastonbury, CT 06033; (203) 633-5231

NSSA and its Leadership Institute for Science Education (LISE) subsidiary provide programs and publications to improve science education through leadership development. Included are summer leadership institutes, regional workshops, state training programs, directories, handbooks, and other resources.

National Science Teachers Association (NSTA)

1840 Wilson Boulevard, Arlington, VA 22201-3000; (703) 243-7100

This national professional organization for K–college science educators convenes regional and national conferences and publishes journals, including *Science and Children* (elementary), *Science Scope* (middle school) and *The Science Teacher* (high school). Additional publications can be ordered through its catalog.

National Wildlife Federation

1412 16th Street NW, Washington, DC 20036; (202) 790-4360

The National Wildlife Federation produces curriculum materials and magazines, including *Ranger Rick* and *Naturescope*.

Native American Science Education Association (NAESA)

1333 H Street NW, Washington, DC 20005; (202) 371-8100

Curriculum materials for teachers and newsletters relating to Native American initiatives can be obtained from the Native American Science Education Association.

Optical Society of America

1816 Jefferson Place NW, Washington, DC 20036; (202) 233-8130

The Optical Society of America provides staff development activities for physics teachers at its annual professional conference.

Oak Ridge Institute of Science and Education (ORISE)

Science Engineering/Education Division, P.O. Box 117, Oak Ridge, TN 37831-0117; (615) 576-6220

ORISE offers a variety of teacher development programs for teachers of various grade levels. Many of the programs are interdisciplinary, combining various physical and life science with mathematics.

Population Association of America

Center for Demographic Studies, U.S. Bureau of the Census, Building 3, Room 3081, Washington, DC 20233; (202) 429-0891

The Population Association of America offers professional publications, newsletters, and career information.

School Science and Mathematics Association (SSMA)

Bowling Green State University, 126 Life Sciences Building, Bowling Green, OH 43403; (419) 372-7393

Professional journals and newsletters are supplied by the School Science and Mathematics Association. This association convenes an annual national conference.

Smithsonian Institution

Arts and Industries Building, Room 1163, Washington, DC 20560; (202) 357-2425

The Smithsonian Institution sponsors educational programs and special events related to education. The National Science Resources Center is supported by Smithsonian Institution.

Society for Social Studies of Science

Department of Sociology, Louisiana State University, Baton Rouge, LA 70803; (504) 388-1645

The Society for Social Studies of Science supports professional publications and newsletters.

The Society for the Advancement of Chicanos and Native Americans in Science

Thinmann Laboratories, University of California, Santa Cruz, CA 95064; (408) 429-2295

The Society for the Advancement of Chicanos and Native Americans in Science furnishes teacher materials and newsletters.

Soil and Water Conservation Society

7515 Northeast Ankeny Road, Ankeny, IA 50021; (515) 289-2831

The Soil and Water Conservation Society produces professional publications, activities for students, curriculum development, career information, regional workshops, and newsletters.

U.S. Department of Education, Eisenhower Program for Mathematics and Science Education, State Program

600 Independence Avenue, Washington, DC 20202; (202) 401-2000

This federal agency is responsible for facilitating the Dwight D. Eisenhower Program for Mathematics and Science Education. This program provides all schools in the nation with funds for staff development in science and mathematics education.

U.S. Geological Survey

Distribution Branch, Box 25286, Federal Center, Denver, CO 80225; (703) 648-6515

The U.S. Geological Survey offers workshops for teachers at three regional centers located in Reston, VA; Denver, CO; and Menlo Park, CA. Teachers participating are usually located within commuting distance, but teachers nationwide are eligible to attend.

U.S. Metric Association

10245 Andasol Avenue, Northridge, CA 91325; (818) 263-5606

Newsletters, activities for students and teachers and curriculum materials can be obtained from the U.S. Metric Society.

The Wildlife Society

5410 Grosvenor Lane, Bethesda, MD 20814; (301) 897-9770

The Wildlife Society provides curriculum materials and programs related to wildlife conservation.

Young Astronaut Council

Box 65432, 1211 Connecticut Avenue NW, Washington, DC 20036; (202) 682-1986

The Young Astronaut Council facilitates a program of enrichment materials through local chapters.

APPENDIX F

National Aeronautics and Space Administration (NASA) Resources

The National Aeronautics and Space Administration (NASA) Education Division provides educational programs and materials for teachers and students from the elementary to the university level. To help disseminate materials to elementary and secondary educators, the NASA Education Division has established the NASA Teacher Resource Center Network (TRCN). This network comprises Teacher Resource Centers (TRCs), Regional Teacher Resource Centers (RTRCs), and the Central Operation of Resources for Educators (CORE).

Located at the nine NASA research centers, TRCs have a variety of NASA-related educational materials in several formats: videotapes, slides, audiotapes, publications, lesson plans and activities. NASA educational materials can be copied at TRCs.

Regional Teacher Resource Centers (RTRCs)

To offer more educators the opportunity to visit the TRCN, NASA forms partnerships with planetariums, universities, museums, and other nonprofit organizations to serve as RTRCs and plans to have RTRCs as broadly distributed geographically as possible. Teachers may preview NASA materials at these RTRCs or copy the materials.

NASA Central Operation Resources for Education (CORE)

Lorain County Joint Vocational School, 15181 Route 58 South, Oberlin, OH 44074; (216) 774-1051 X293/294

Designed for the national and international distribution of aerospace educational materials to enhance the NASA Teacher Resource Center Network, CORE provides educators with another source for NASA educational audiovisual materials. CORE processes teacher requests by mail for a minimal fee. On school letterhead, educators can request a catalog and order form at the address above.

Teacher Resource Centers, Regional Teacher Resource Centers and other NASA program locations are listed by state:

U.S. Space & Rocket Center
NASA Teacher Resource Center
Huntsville, AL 35807
(205) 544-5812

University of Arkansas-Little Rock
Natural Science Building, Room 215
2801 South University
Little Rock, AK 72204

Lunar and Planetary Lab
NASA Regional Teacher Resource
   Center
University of Arizona
Tucson, AZ 85721

NASA Ames-Dryden Flight Research
   Facility
Public Affairs Office (Trl. 42)
NASA Teacher Resource Center
Edwards AFB, CA 93523
(805) 258-3546

Mail Stop TO-25
NASA Ames Research Center
Moffett Field, CA 94035
(415) 604-5543

Mail Code 180-20 5
Jet Propulsion Laboratory
4800 Oak Grove Drive
Pasadena, CA 91109

U.S. Space Foundation
NASA Regional Teacher Resource
   Center
1525 Vapor Trail
Colorado Springs, CO 80916
(719) 550-1000

Delaware Teacher Center
Claymont Education Campus
NASA Regional Teacher Resource
   Center
3401 Green Street
Claymont, DE 19703
(302) 792-3806

University of the District of
   Columbia
NASA Regional Teacher Resource
   Center
Mail Stop 4201
4200 Connecticut Avenue NW
Washington, DC 20008
(202) 282-7338

National Air and Space Museum
Smithsonian Institution
Education Resource Center,
   P-700
Washington, DC 20560
(202) 786-2109

Mail Code PA-EAB
NASA Kennedy Space Center, FL
   32899
(407) 867-4444

NASA John F. Kennedy Space
   Center
Educators Resources Library
Mail Code ERL
Kennedy Space Center, FL
   32899
(407) 867-4090

University of Idaho at Moscow
NASA Regional Teacher Resource
    Center
ID Space Grant College Fellowship
    Program
College of Education
Moscow, ID 83843
(208) 885-6030

Parks College of St. Louis
    University
NASA Regional Teacher Resource
    Center
Rt. 157 and Falling Springs Road
Cahokia, IL 62206
(618) 337-7500

Chicago Museum of Science and
    Industry
NASA Regional Teacher Resource
    Center
57th Street and Lakeshore Drive
Chicago, IL 60637-2093
(312) 684-1414 X429

University of Evansville
NASA Regional Teacher Resource
    Center
School of Education
1800 Lincoln Ave.
Evansville, IN 47714
(812) 479-2393

University of Northern Iowa
NASA Regional Teacher Resource
    Center
IRTS
Room 222, Schnidler Education
    Center
Cedar Falls, IA 50614-0009

Kansas Cosmosphere and Space
    Center
NASA Regional Teacher Resource
    Center
1100 North Plum
Hutchinson, KS 67501
(316) 662-2305 or (800) 397-0330

Murray State University
NASA Regional Teacher Resource
    Center
Waterfield Library
Murray, KY 42071
(502) 762-4420

Bossier Parish Community College
NASA Regional Teacher Resource
    Center
2719 Airline Drive
Bossier City, LA 71111
(318) 746-7754

Southern University
NASA Regional Teacher Resource
    Center
Downtown Metro Center
610 Texas Street
Shreveport, LA 71101
(318) 674-3444

Public Affairs Office (130)
NASA Goddard Office Space Flight
    Center
Greenbelt, MD 20771
(301) 286-7207

NASA Goddard Space Flight Center
Teacher Resource Laboratory
Mail Code 130.3
Greenbelt, MD 20771
(301) 286-8570

Northern Michigan University
NASA Regional Teacher Resource
    Center
Olson Library Media Center
Marquette, MI 49855
(906) 227-2270

Central Michigan University
NASA Regional Teacher Resource
    Center
Ronan Hall, Room 101
Mount Pleasant, MI 48859
(517) 774-4387

Oakland University
NASA Regional Teacher Resource
    Center
O'Dowd Hall, Room 216
Rochester, MI 48309-4401
(313) 370-2485

Mankato State University
NASA Regional Teacher Resource
    Center
Department of Curriculum and
    Instruction
MSU Box 52/P.O. Box 8400
Mankato, MN 56002-8400
(507) 389-5710 or 1516

St. Cloud State University Center for
    Information Media
NASA Regional Teacher Resource
    Center
St. Cloud, MN 56301
(612) 255-2062

Tri-State Learning Center (SSC-TRC)
NASA Teacher Resource Center
Rt. 72 West Box 508
Iuka, MS 38854
(601) 423-4373

Mississippi Delta Community College
NASA Regional Teacher Resource
    Center
P.O. Box 177
Moorehead, MS 38761
(601) 246-5631

NASA John C. Stennis Space
    Center
Stennis Space Center, MS 39529
(601) 688-3341

NASA Stennis Space Center
Teacher Resource Center
Building 1200
Stennis Space Center, MS 39529
(601) 688-3338

Western Montana College of
    the University of Montana
NASA Regional Teacher Resource
    Center
Carson Library
Dillon, MT 59725
(406) 683-7011

University of Nebraska State
    Museum
NASA Regional Teacher Resource
    Center
14th & U Streets
P.O. Box 880338
Lincoln, NE 68588-0338
(402) 472-8899

University of New Mexico
NASA Regional Teacher Resource
    Center
Continuing Education and
    Community Service
1634 University NE
Albuquerque, NM 87131
(505) 277-3861

New Mexico State University
NASA Regional Teacher Resource
    Center
New Mexico Space Grant
    Consortium
Box 3001, Department SG
Las Cruces, NM 88003-0001
(505) 646-6414

The City College
NASA Regional Teacher Resource
    Center
NAC Building, Room 5224
Convent Avenue at 138th Street
New York, NY 10031
(212) 690-6993

University of North Carolina,
    Charlotte
NASA Regional Teacher Resource
    Center
J. Murray Atkins Library
Charlotte, NC 28223
(704) 547-2559

University of North Dakota
NASA Regional Teacher Resource
    Center
Wayne Peterson Room
Earth Systems Science Building
Space Studies Department
P.O. Box 7306, University Station
Grand Forks, ND 58203-7306
(701) 777-4856 or 1-800-828-4274

Mail Stop 7-4
NASA Lewis Research Center
21000 Brookpark Road
Cleveland OH 44135
(216) 433-5583

NASA Lewis Research Center
Teacher Resource Center
Mail Stop 8-1
21000 Brookpark Road
Cleveland, OH 44135
(216) 433-2017

Oklahoma State University
NASA Regional Teacher Resource
    Center
300 North Cordell
Stillwater, OK 74078-0422
(405) 744-7015

Mid-Atlantic Technology
    Application Center
NASA Regional Teacher Resource
    Center
University of Pittsburgh,
823 William Pitt Union
Pittsburgh, PA 15260
(412) 648-7008

Rhode Island College
NASA Regional Teacher Resource
    Center
Aerospace Education
Providence, RI 02908
(401) 456-8567

Dr. Robert W. Fitzmaurice
Center Education Program Officer
Public Affairs Office (AP-4)
NASA Johnson Space Center
Houston, TX 77058
(713) 483-1257

NASA Johnson Space Center
Teacher Resource Center
Mail Code AP-4
Houston, TX 77058
(713) 483-8696

Weber State University
NASA Regional Teacher Resource
    Center
WSU Center for Science Education
Ogden, UT 66048
(801) 626-6160

Mail Stop 154
NASA Langley Research Center
Hampton, VA 23665-5525
(804) 864-3307/3312

NASA Langley Teacher Research
    Center
Virginia Air and Space Center
600 Settler Landing Road
Hampton, VA 23669
(804) 727-0800

Radford University
NASA Regional Teacher Resource
    Center
P.O. Box 6886
Radford, VA 24142
(703) 831-5127

NASA Wallops Flight Facility
Education Complex Visitor
    Center
NASA Teacher Resource
    Center
Building J-17, P.O. Box 98
Wallops Island, VA 23337
(804) 824-2295

Norwich University
Vermont College Educational
    Resource Center
NASA Regional Teacher
    Resource Center
Schulman Hall
Montpelier, VT 05602
(802) 828-8845

University of Washington
NASA Regional Teacher
    Resource Center
AK-50, c/o Geophysics Dept.
Seattle, WA 98195
(206) 543-1943

Wheeling Jesuit College
NASA Regional Teacher
    Resource Center
220 Washington Ave.
Wheeling, WV 26003
(304) 243-2388

University of Wisconsin
    at LaCrosse
NASA Regional Teacher
    Resource Center
Morris Hall, Room 200
LaCrosse, WI 54601
(608) 785-8148 or 8650

University of Wyoming
NASA Regional Teacher
    Resource Center
Learning Resource Center
P.O. Box 3374 University
    Station
Laramie, WY 82701-3374
(307) 766-2527

Materials and Resource Sources

Acid Rain Foundation
1630 Blackhawk Hills
St. Paul, MN 55122

AIMS Education Foundation
P.O. Box 7766
Fresno, CA 93747

Allyn & Bacon, Inc.
160 Gould Street
Needham Heights, MA 02194

Arbor Scientific
P.O. Box 2750
Ann Arbor, MI 48106

Carolina Biological Supply Co.
2700 York Road
Burlington, NC 27215

Children's Press
1224 West Van Buren Street
Chicago, IL 60607

Connecticut Valley Biological Supply
Co., Inc.
82 Valley Road
P.O. Box 326
Southampton, MA 01073

Dale Seymour Publications
P.O. Box 10888
Palo Alto, CA 94303

Delta Education, Inc.
P.O. Box 950
Hudson, NH 03051

Dover Publications, Inc.
180 Varick Street
New York, NY 10014

Edmund Scientific Co.
101 E. Glouster Pike
Barrington, NJ 08007

ERIC Clearinghouse for Science,
    Mathematics, and Environmental
    Education (ERIC/SMEAC)
1200 Chamber Road, 3rd Floor
Columbus, OH 43212

Flinn Scientific, Inc.
P.O. Box 219
Batavia, IL 60510

Frey Scientific Co.
905 Hickory Lane
Mansfield, OH 44905

Harcourt Brace Jovanovich, Inc.
Five Sampson St.
Saddle Brook, NJ 07662

Harper & Row
10 East 53rd Street
New York, NY 10022

Glencoe
383 Madison Avenue
New York, NY 10017

J. B. Lippincott Company
East Washington Square
Philadelphia, PA 19105

Lab-Aids, Inc.
249 Trade Zone Drive
Ronkonkoma, NY 11779

McGraw-Hill, Inc.
1221 Avenue of the Americas
New York, NY 10020

NASCO
901 Janesville Avenue
Fort Atkinson, WI 53538

PASCO Scientific
1876 Sabre Street
Hayward, CA 94545

Sargeant Welch, Inc.
7300 North Linder Avenue
Skokie, IL 60067

Science Kit, Inc.
777 E. Park Drive
Tonawanda, NY 14150-6781

Silver Burdett & Ginn
250 James Street, CN818
Morristown, NJ 07960

Venier Software
2920 SW 89th Street
Portland, OR 97225

Out-of-School Resources

3-2-1 Contact
Children's Television Workshop, One Lincoln Plaza, New York, NY 10023; (212) 595-3456

Over 220 half-hour award-winning programs, broadcast over seven seasons, designed to stimulate student interest in science. 3-2-1 Contact Action Kits are video clips and activities for use in after-school care facilities. They are designed to be engaging to students and require minimal supervision.

Hands-on-Science
Hands-on-Science Outreach, Inc., 4910 Macon Road, Rockville, MD 20852; (301) 460-5922

Thematically organized materials provide recreational activities in science for use in after-school settings. Required leader training sessions facilitate effective discovery of science by participants at a wide range (K–6) of age levels. Consumable kits promote ownership and mastery of scientific concepts by participants, especially those from economically disadvantaged backgrounds.

National SERIES Project
300 Lakeside Drive, Oakland, CA 94612; (510) 987-0119

High school students lead younger children (ages 9–12) in the discovery of science. Trained by adult mentors, teens guide younger students through six scientific units, addressing such concepts as chemistry and the environment, agriculture, and recycling. Each unit culminates in a community service project, giving students opportunities to apply acquired knowledge to real problems in their own communities.

National Urban League Preschool Science Collaborative
Education Department, 500 East 62nd Street, New York, NY 10021; (212) 310-9214

Materials provide suggestions for physical science activities for use in preschool classrooms. Activities are especially designed to appeal to students from low-income or single-parent households.

Operation SMART
Girls, Inc., 30 E. 33rd Street, New York, NY 10016; (212) 689-3700

This program of out-of-school activities emphasizes hands-on experiences in mathematics, science, and technology for girls ages 6–18. Its activities are aimed at combating existing barriers to participation in science and mathematics by girls, through the creation of positive environments for learning, special staff awareness training, and bombardment of girls with information about careers and educational opportunities not traditionally promoted among women.

Reading Rainbow
GNP, P. O. Box 80669, Lincoln, NE 68501; (800) 228-4630

Books are used as a platform for introducing a wide range of concepts and ideas, including scientific topics, to young viewers (ages 5–9). Videotapes of episodes, booklists, and teacher's guides are available to teachers and librarians across the country to facilitate utilization of the program in schools.

Science-by-Mail
Museum of Science, Science Park, Boston, MA 02114-1099; (800) 729-3300

Three science challenge units per year contain self-explanatory science exploration that may be conducted at home, in community-based activities, or in schools. Solutions to open-ended problems are submitted to scientist mentors, who review and respond to student work.

SuperScience Magazine
Scholastic, Inc., 2931 E. McCarthy Street, P.O. Box 3710, Jefferson City, MO 65102-3710

Student magazines use common scientific topics of interest to students to encourage hands-on activities and discovery of scientific concepts. Activities integrate science learning with reading, mathematics, and social studies. *SuperScience Red:* grades 1–3 and *SuperScience Blue:* grades 4–6.

The Second Voyage of the *Mimi*
Wings for Learning, 1600 Green Hill Road, P. O. Box 660002, Scotts Valley, CA 95067-0002

A voyage into ancient Mayan civilization serves as a vehicle for teaching interdisciplinary science and mathematics. Twelve 15-minute documentary-format episodes, accompanied by student materials and hands-on activities, engage students in the discovery of mathematics and science. Software learning modules whose themes are derived from the video series offer flexible learning opportunities in either science or mathematics to individuals or small groups of students.

References

AAAS (American Association for the Advancement of Science).(1993). *Benchmarks for scientific literacy*. New York: Oxford University Press.

Adeniyi, E. O. (1985). Misconceptions of selected ecological concepts held by some Nigerian students. *Journal of Biological Education, 19* (4), 311–316.

Alfke, D. (1974, April). Asking operational questions. *Science and Children*, pp. 18–19.

Antonouris, G. (1989). Multicultural science. *School Science Review, 70* (252), 97–100.

Appleton, K. (1993). Using theory to guide practice: Teaching science from a constructivist perspective. *School Science and Mathematics, 93* (5), 269–274.

Arbor Scientific Company (ASC). (1996). *Arbor scientific—innovation in science education*. Ann Arbor, MI: Arbor Scientific.

Arnold, D. S., Atwood, R. K., & Rogers, U. M. (1973). An investigation of the relationships among question level, response level, and lapse time. *School Science and Mathematics, 73*, 591–595.

Ausubel, D. P. (1963). Psychology of meaningful verbal learning. New York: Grune and Stratton.

———. (1968). *Educational psychology: A cognitive view*. New York: Holt, Rinehart and Winston.

Baker, D. (1988). Research matters to the science teacher teaching for gender differences. *National Association of Research in Science Teaching*.

Bank Street College of Education. (1995). *The voyages of Mimi I and II*. Pleasantville, NY: Sunburst Communications.

Barnes, C. P. (1978). *Questioning strategies to develop critical thinking skills*. (ERIC Document No. 169486)

Bennett, W. J. (1986). *What works*. Washington, DC: U.S. Department of Education.

Berger, C. F., Lu, C. R., Belzer, S. J., and Voss, B. E. (1994). *Research on the uses of technology in science education*. In D. L. Gabel (Ed.) *Handbook of research on science teaching and learning* (pp. 466–490). New York: Macmillan.

Biddulph, F., & Osborne, R. (1984, February). Children's questions and science teaching: An alternative approach. *Learning in science project* (Working Paper No. 117).

Hamilton, New Zealand: Waikato University, February. (ERIC Reproduction Document No. ED 252400)

Biddulph, F., Symington, D., & Osborn, R. (1986). The place of children's questions in primary science education. *Research in Science and Technological Education, 4* (1) 77–78.

Birnie, H. H., & Ryan, A. (1984, April). Inquiry/discovery revisited. *Science and Children*, p. 31.

Bloom, B. J. (1984). The 2 sigma problem: The search for methods of group instruction as effective as one-to-one tutoring. *Educational Researcher, 13*, 4–16.

Bloom, B. S. (1956). *Taxonomy of educational objectives: The classification of educational goals, handbook I: cognitive domain*. New York: Longman.

Blosser, P. E. (1985). Using questions in science classrooms. In R. Doran (Ed.), *Research matters. . .to the science teacher, 2*. (ERIC Document No. 273490)

———. (1993). *Using cooperative learning in science education*. Columbus, OH: ERIC Clearinghouse for Science, Mathematics, and Environmental Education. (ERIC Reproduction Document No. Ed 351207)

Bredderman, T. (1982, September). Activity science—The evidence shows it matters. *Science and Children*, pp. 39–41.

———. (1984). The influence of activity-based elementary science programs on classroom practices: A quantitative synthesis. *Journal of Research in Science Teaching, 21* (3), 290–303.

Brown, D. R. (1979). Helping handicapped youngsters learn science by doing. In M. B. Rowe (Ed.), *What research says to the science teacher* (Vol. 2, p. 85), Washington, DC: National Science Teachers Association.

Brown, I. D. (1986). Topic 4: Teacher questioning techniques. *Staff development project—Science Grades K–6*. Jackson, MS: Mississippi Association for Teacher Education. (ERIC Document No. ED 285726)

Bruner, J. S. (1961). The act of discovery. *Harvard Educational Review, 31*, 21–32.

———. (1962). *The process of education*. Cambridge, MA: Harvard University Press.

Budavari, S., et al. (1989). *The Merck Index: An encyclopedia of chemicals, drugs, and biologicals* (11th Ed.). (Rahway, NJ: Merck & Co.)

Bybee, R., & Hendricks, P. W. (1972). Teaching science concepts to preschool deaf children to aid language development. *Science Education, 56* (3), 303–310.

Charles, C. M., & Malian, I. M. (1980). *The special student.* St. Louis, MO: C. V. Mosby.

Chaille, C., & Brittain, L. (1991). *The Young Child as Scientist.* New York: HarperCollins.

Chivers, G. (1986). Intervention strategies to increase the proportion of girls and women studying and pursuing careers in technological fields: A West European review. *Journal of Engineering Education, 11* (3), 248.

CHRIS: Hazardous Chemical Data. (1989). U.S. Department of Transportation, Superintendent of Documents. Washington, DC: U.S. Government Printing Office.

Coble, C. R., Levey, B., & Matteis, F. (1985). *Science for learning disabled students.* (ERIC Document No. 258 803)

Cole, J. T., Kitano, M. K., & Brown, L. M. (1981). Concept analysis: A model for teaching basic science concepts to intellectually handicapped students. In M. E. Corrick, Jr. (Ed.), *Teaching handicapped students science: A resource book K–12 teachers* (pp. 51–53). Washington, DC: National Education Association.

College Board. (1987). *Get into the equation: Math and science, parents and children.* (ERIC Document No. 295 785)

Cooper, H. H. (1979). Pygmalion grows up: A model for teacher expectation, communication, and performance influence. *Review of Education Research, 49* 389–410.

Cooperation for Public Broadcasting. (1995). *The Annenberg/CPB math and science project—the guide to math and science reform; EE toolbox, inter-disciplinary education access (IDEA), parks as classrooms* (Computer disc). Available through the Corporation for Public Broadcasting.

Cremin, L. A. (1976). *Public Education.* New York: Basic Books.

Decker, L. E. (1981). *Foundation of community education.* Charlottesville, VA: Mid-Atlantic Center for Community Education.

Denkla, M., in Kantrowitz, B., and Wingert, P. (1989, April 17) How kids learn. *Newsweek,* 53–54.

Dewey, J. (1916). *Democracy and education.* New York: Macmillan.

———. (1937). *Experience and education.* New York: Collier Books.

Dillion, G. (1977). Mimeograph. In Donna L. Hager-Schoeny et al., *Community involvement for classroom teachers* (2nd ed). Charlottesville, VA: Community Collaborators, 27.

Driver, R. (1983). *The pupil as scientist?* Milton Keynes, England: Open University Press.

———. (1994). *Making sense of science.* London: Routledge.

Driver, R., Guensne, E., & Tiberghien, A. (1985). *Children's ideas in science.* Milton Keynes, England: Open University Press.

Duckworth, E., in Kantrowitz, B., & Wingert, P. (1989, April 17). How kids learn. *Newsweek,* p. 55.

Dunn, R., & Dunn, K. (1975). Finding the best fit—learning styles, teaching styles. *NAASP Bulletin, 59,* 37–49.

Elfner, L. E. (1988). *Exemplars: Women in science, engineering, and mathematics.* Columbus, OH: Ohio Academy of Science.

Elliott, D. L., & Carter, K. (1986). *Scientific illiteracy in elementary science textbook programs.* Paper presented at the Annual Meeting of the American Educational Research Association, San Francisco, April. (ERIC Document No. 269257)

Elstgeest, J. (1985). The right question at the right time. In W. Harlen (Ed.), *Primary science: Taking the plunge.* London: Heinemann Educational Books.

ETS (Educational Testing Service).(1989). *A world of differences: An international assessment of mathematics and science.* Princeton, NJ: Center for the Assessment of Educational Progress.

———. (1992). *National assessment of educational progress.* Washington, DC: U.S. Department of Education.

Fathman, A. K., Quinn, M. E., & Kessler, C. (1992). *Teaching science to English learners, grades 4–8.* Washington, DC: National Clearinghouse for Bilingual Education. (ERIC Document Reproduction Service No. ED 349 844)

Fields, S. (1989, April). The scientific teaching method. *Science and Children,* p. 15.

Flick, L. B. (1989). Will the real scientist please stand up! *Science Scope, 13* (3), 6–7.

———. (1993). The meanings of hands-on science. *Journal of Science Teacher Education, 4* (1), 3–4.

Fort, D. C., & Varney, H. L. (1989). How students see scientists: Mostly male, mostly white, and mostly benevolent. *Science and Children, 26* (8), 8–13.

FOSS (1990). *Full option science system.* Berkeley, CA: Lawrence Hall of Science.

Foster, G. W., & Heiting, W. A. (1994). Embedded assessment. *Science and Children, 32* (2), 30–33.

Funk & Wagnalls (1968). *Standard dictionary.* New York: Reader's Digest Association.

Gallagher, J. J., & Aschner, M. J. (1963). A preliminary report on analyses of classroom interaction. *Merrill-Palmer Quarterly, 9,* 183–195.

Gamrell, L. B. (1983). The occurrence of think-time during reading comprehension. *Journal of Educational Research, 75,* 144-148.

Gerlovich, J., and Hartman, K. (1990). *Science safety: A diskette for elementary educators.* Waukee, IA: JaKel.

Gerlovich, J., Hartman, K., & Gerard, T. (1992). *The total science safety system for grades 7–14.,* Waukee, IA: JaKel.

Glencoe Science Professional Series. (1994). *Alternative assessment in the science classroom.* (ERIC Document Reproduction Document Service No. Ed 370 778)

Goldhammer, A., & Isenberg, S. (1984). *Operation: Frog.* (Educational software.) New York: Scholastic.

Good, R. G. (1977). *How children learn science.* New York: Macmillan.

Good, R. G., Wandersee, J. H., & St. Julien, J. (1993). Cautionary notes on the appeal of the new "ism" (constructivism) in science education. In K. Tobin (Ed.) *The practice of constructivism in science education* (pp. 71–87). Washington, DC: AAAS Press.

Gorodetsky, M., Fisher, K. M., & Wyman, B. (1994). Generating connections and learning with Semnet, a tool for constructing knowledge networks. *Journal of Science Education and Technology, 3* (3), 137–144.

Guerra, C. J. (1988, March). Pulling science out of a hat. *Science and Children,* pp. 23–24.

Habecker, J. E. (1976). *An analysis of reading questions in basal reading series based on Bloom's taxonomy.* Unpublished doctoral dissertation, University of Pennsylvania, Philadelphia.

Hager-Schoeny, D. L., & Galbreath, D. (1982). *Utilizing community resources in the classroom: An in-service reference collection.* Charlottesville, VA: University of Virginia, Mid-Atlantic Center for Community Education.

Halloran, J. D. (1970). *Attitude formation and change.* Great Britain: Leicester University Press.

Hamrick, L., & Harty, H. (1987). Influence of resequencing general science content on the science achievement, attitude toward science, and interest in science of sixth grade students. *Journal of Research in Science Teaching, 24* (1), 16.

Hargie, O. D. (1978). The importance of teacher questions in the classroom. *Educational Research, 20,* 99–102.

Harlen, W. (1992). *The teaching of science.* London: David Fulton Publishers.

———. (1993). *Teaching and learning primary science.* London: Paul Chapman Publishing.

Harms, N. (1981). VIII. Project synthesis: Summary and implications for teachers. In N. C. Harms & R. E. Yager (Eds.), *What research says to the science teacher* (Vol. 3). Washington, DC: National Science Teachers Association.

Harris, R. (1981). An audio-tactile approach to science education for visually impaired students. In M. E. Corrick, Jr. (Ed.), *Teaching handicapped students science.* Washington, DC: National Education Association.

Hazen, R. M., & Trefil, J. (1992). *Science matters: Achieving science literacy.* (New York: Doubleday).

Hein, G. E., & Price, S. (1994). *Active assessment for active science: A guide for elementary school teachers.* Portsmouth, NH: Heinemann.

Holdzkom, D., & Lutz, P. B. (1984). *Research within reach: Science education.* Charleston, WV: Research and Development Interpretation Service.

Holt, J. (1971). *How children learn.* London: Penguin Press. 152.

Humrich, E. (1988). Sex differences in the second IEA science study: U.S. results in an international context. Paper presented at the annual meeting of the National Association for Research in Science Teaching. (Education Resource Information Center Document No. ED 292 649)

Hunkins, F. P. (1970). Analysis and evaluation questions: Their effects upon critical thinking. *Educational Leadership, 27,* pp. 697–705.

Hurd, R. D. (Ed.).(1968). *New directions in elementary science teaching.* Belmont, CA: Wadsworth.

Hurd, P. D. (1982). Middle school/junior high science: Changing perspectives. *Middle/Junior High Science Bulletin, 5* 12.

———. (1986, January). Perspectives for the reform of science education. *Phi Delta Kappan,* pp. 353–358.

Iatridis, M. (1981, October). Teaching science to preschoolers. *Science and Children.*

Jelly, S. (1985). Helping children raise questions—and answering them. In W. Harlen (Ed.), *Primary science: Taking the plunge.* (p. 54). London: Heinemann Educational Books.

Johnson, R. T., & Johnson, D. W. (1991). So what's new about cooperative learning in science? *Cooperative Learning, 11* (3), 2–3.

Jones, G. M., Mullis, I. V. S., Raisen, S. A., Weiss, I. R., & Weston, E. A. (1992). *The 1990 science report card, NAEP's assessment of fourth, eighth, and twelfth graders.* Washington, DC: U.S. Department of Education.

Jones, M. G., & Wheatley, J. (1988). Factors influencing the entry of women into science and related fields. *Science Education, 72,* 127–142.

Jones, R. M. (1985, May). Teaming up. *Science and Children,* p. 21.

Kahle, J. B. (1983). Do we make science available for women? In F. K. Brown & D. P. Butts (Eds.), *Science teaching: A profession speaks* (pp.33–36). Washington, DC: National Science Teachers Association.

———. (1990). Why girls don't know. In M. B. Rowe (Ed.), *What research says to the science teacher. Vol. 6: The process of knowing*. Washington, DC: National Science Teachers Association.

Kahle, J. B., & Lakes, M. K. (1983). The myth of equality in science classrooms. *Journal of Research in Science Teaching, 20* (2), 131–140.

Kahle, J. B., & Rennie, L. J. (1993). Ameliorating gender differences in attitudes about science: A cross-national study. *Journal of Science Education and Technology, 2* (1), 321–333.

Karplus, R. (1964). The science curriculum improvement study—Report to the Piaget conference. *Journal of Research in Science Teaching, 2*, 236–240.

Katz, L., in Kantrowitz, B. and Wingert, P. (1989, April 17). How kids learn. *Newsweek*, p. 55.

Kinnear, J. (1994). *What science education really says about communication of science concepts* (Report No. CS508-657). Sydney, New South Wales, Australia: Annual Meeting of the International Communication Association. (ERIC Document Reproduction Service No. ED 372 455)

Knuth, Randy. (1995). *Engaging learning through technology*. Paper presented at the IVLA/IAECT Conference, Chicago, October.

Koran, J. J., & Koran, J. L. (1973). *Validating a teacher behavior by student performance* (Report No. FSDE-730-063). Tallahassee, FL: Florida State Department of Education.

Kroot, N. E. (1976). *An analysis of the responses of four, six, and eight year old children to four kinds of questions*. Unpublished doctoral dissertation, Indiana University, Bloomington.

Kuhn, T. S. (1970). *The structure of scientific revolutions*. (1st edition published in 1962). Chicago: University of Chicago Press.

Langrehr, J. (1993). Getting thinking into science questions. *Australian Science Teacher Journal, 39* (4), 36.

Levin, T., & Long, R. (1981). *Effective instruction*. Washington, DC: Association for Supervision and Curriculum Development.

Levine, D. U., & Ornstein, A. C. (1983). Sex differences in ability and achievement. *Journal of Research and Development in Education, 16* (2), 62–66.

Los Angeles Unified School District. (1977). Title IV-D: Effects of teacher expectation on student learning project. In *The Reflector*. Los Angeles: Unified School District Office of Instruction.

Loucks-Horsley, S. (Ed.).(1990). *Elementary school science for the '90s*. Andover, MA: The NETWORK.

Martin, R., Wood, G., & Stevens, E. (1988). *An introduction to teaching: A question of commitment*. Boston: Allyn and Bacon.

Martin, R. E. (1984). *The credibility principle and teacher attitudes toward science*. New York: Peter Lang.

McCracken, M. (1986). *Turnabout children*. Boston: Little, Brown.

McIntyre, M. (1984). *Early childhood and science*. Washington, DC: National Science Teachers Association.

McLeod, R. J. (1979, October). Selecting a textbook for good science teaching. *Science and Children*, pp. 14–15.

Mechling, K. R., & Oliver, D. L. (1983a). *Characteristics of a good elementary science program, handbook III*. Washington, DC: National Science Teachers Association.

———. (1983b). *Science teaches basic skills, handbook 1*. Washington, DC: National Science Teachers Association.

———. (1983c). Activities not textbooks: What research says about science programs. *Principal, 43*.

Meyer, L. A., Greer, E. A., & Crummey, L. (1986). *Elementary science textbooks: Their contents, text characteristics, and comprehensibility*. (Technical Report No. 386). Champaign, IL: University of Illinois. (ERIC Document No. 278947)

Mullins, I. V. S., & Jenkins, L. B. (1988). *The science report card: Elements of risk and recovery*. Princeton, NJ: Educational Testing Service.

Munson, B. H. (1994). Ecological misconceptions. *Journal of Environmental Education, 24* (4), 30–34.

Murphy, N. (1994). Helping preservice teachers master authentic assessment for the learning cycle model. In L. E. Schafer (Ed.), *Behind the methods class door: Educating elementary and middle school science teachers*. Columbus, OH: ERIC Clearinghouse for Science, Mathematics and Environmental Education.

National Curriculum Council. (1989). *Science: Non-statutory guidance*. London: NCC.

National Geographic Society. (1995). *National Geographic Kids Network*. Washington, DC: National Geographic Society.

National Research Council. (1992). *National Science Education Standards: A sampler*. Washington, D.C.: National Research Council.

National Research Council (NRC). (1996) *National Science Education Standards*. Washington, DC: National Academy Press.

National Science Board Commission on Precollege Education in Mathematics, Science, and Technology. (1983). *A revised and intensified science and technology curriculum for grades K–12 is urgently needed for our future.* (ERIC Document No. 239 847)

National Science Teachers Association. (1982). *Science-technology-society: Science education for the 1980's: Position statement.* Washington, DC: NSTA.

———. (1983). *Conditions for good science teaching in secondary schools.* Washington, DC: NSTA.

———. (1991, October–November). *An NSTA position statement: Multicultural science education.*

Nickerson, R. S. (1995). Can technology help teach for understanding? In Perkins, D. N., Schwartz, J. L., West, M. M., and Wiske, M. S. (Eds.). *Software goes to school—teaching for understanding new technologies.* New York: Oxford University Press.

North Carolina Museum of Life and Science. (1992). Science in the classroom. In Triangle Coalition for Science and Technology Education, *A guide for planning a volunteer program for science, mathematics, and technology education* (p. 59). College Park, MD: Triangle Coalition.

Novak, J. D. (1979). *A theory of education.* Ithaca, NY: Cornell University Press.

———. (1991, October). Clarify with concept maps. *Science Teacher,* p. 45.

Novak, J., & Gowin, D. B. (1986). *Learning how to learn.* New York: Cambridge University Press.

Osborne, R. & Freyberg, P. (1990). *Learning in science: The implications of children's science.* In S. Loucks-Horsley (Ed.), *Elementary school science for the '90s,* (p. 49). Andover, MA: The Network.

Oskamp, S. (1977). *Attitudes and opinions.* Englewood Cliffs, NJ: Prentice-Hall.

Ostlund, K. L. (1992, March). Sizing up social skills. *Science Scope,* pp. 31–33.

Padilla, M., Muth, D., & Lund Padilla, R. (1991). Science and reading: Many process skills in common. In C. M. Santa & D. E. Alvermann (Eds.), *Science learning: Processes and applications* (pp. 14–19). Newark, DE: International Reading Association.

Pearlman, S., & Pericak-Spector, K. (1992, October). Expect the unexpected question. *Science and Children,* pp. 36–37.

Peterson, P., & Knapp, P. (1993). Inventing and reinventing ideas: Constructivist teaching and learning in mathematics. In G. Cawletti (Ed.), *Challenges and achievements of American education.* Alexandria, VA: Association for Supervision and Curriculum Development.

Petty, R. E., & Cacioppa, J. T. (1981). *Attitudes and persuasion: Classic and contemporary approaches.* Dubuque, IA: William C. Brown.

Phillips, W. C. (1991). Earth science misconceptions. *Science Teacher, 58* (2), 21–23.

Piaget, J. (1954). *The construction of reality in the child.* New York: Basic Books.

Piburn, M., & Enyeart, M. (1985). *A comparison of the reasoning ability of gifted and mainstreamed science students.* (ERIC Document No. 255 379).

Pollina, A. (1995). Gender balance: Lessons from girls in science and mathematics. *Educational Leadership, 53* (1), 30–33.

Prather, J. P. (1991, April). Speculative philosophical analysis of priorities for research in science education. Research report presented at the 64th Annual Meeting of the National Association for Research in Science Teaching, Fontana, WI.

Price, S., & Hein, G. E. (1994, October). Scoring active assessments. *Science and Children,* pp. 26–29.

Project Technology Engineering Application of Mathematics and Science. (1992). Tips for teachers working with volunteers. In Triangle Coalition for Science and Technology Education, *A guide for planning a volunteer program for science, mathematics, and technology education.* College Park, MD: Triangle Coalition.

Puckett-Cliatt, M J., & Shaw, J. M. (1985, November–December). Open questions, open answers. *Science and Children,* pp. 14–16.

Raizen, S. A., & Kaser, J. S. (1989, May). Assessing science learning in elementary school: Why, what and how? *Phi Delta Kappan,* May, 718–722.

Rakow, S. J. (1986). *Teaching science as inquiry.* Bloomington, IN: Phi Delta Kappa.

———. (1989, November–December). Safety supplement. *Science Scope.*

Reichel, A. G. (1994). Performance assessment: Five practical approaches. *Science and Children, 32* (2), 21–25.

Reichert, B. (1989, November–December). What did he say? Science in the multilingual classroom. *Science Scope,* pp. 10–11.

Renner, J. W., & Marek, E. A. (1988). *The learning cycle and elementary school science teaching.* Portsmouth, NH: Heinemann.

Rennie, L., & Parker, L. (1986). A comparison of mixed-sex and single-sex grouping in year 5 science lessons. Paper presented at the Annual Meeting of the American Educational Research Association, San Francisco. (ERIC Document No. ED 273 443)

Rice, J. R. (1983, January). A special science fair: LD children learn what they can do. *Science and Children,* pp. 15–16.

Riley, J. P. (1986). The effects of teachers wait-time and knowledge comprehension questioning on science achievement. *Journal of Research in Science Teaching, 23* (4), 335–342.

Risner, G. P. (1987). *Cognitive levels of questioning demonstrated by test items that accompany selected fifth-grade science textbooks.* (ERIC Document No. 291752)

Risner, G. P., Skeel, D. J., & Nicholson, J. L. (1992, September). A closer look at textbooks. *Science and Children,* pp. 42–45, 73.

Roberts, R. M. (1989). *Serendipity: Accidental discoveries in science.* New York: Wiley.

Rodriguez, I., & Bethel, L. J. (1983). An inquiry approach to science and language teaching. *Journal of Research in Science Teaching, 20* (4), 291–296.

Rogers, D. L., Martin, Jr., R. E., & Kousaleos, S. (1988). Encouraging science through playful discovery. *Day Care and Early Education, 16* (1), 21.

Rosenshine, B. (1976). Classroom instruction. In W. L. Gage (Ed.), *The psychology of teaching methods.* Chicago: University of Chicago Press.

———. (1979). Content, time, and direct instruction. In P. L. Peterson & H. C. Walberg (Eds.), *Research on teaching: Concepts, findings, and implications.* Berkeley, CA: McCutcheon.

———. (1986, April). Synthesis of research on explicit teaching. *Educational Leadership,* pp. 60–69.

Rothkopf, E. Z. (1972). Variable adjunct question schedules, interperson interaction, and incidental learning from written material. *Journal of Educational Psychology, 63,* 87–92.

Rowe, M. B. (1970). Wait-time and rewards as instructional variables: Influence on inquiry and sense of fate control. *New Science in the Inner City.* New York: Teachers College, Columbia University.

———. (1973). *Teaching science as continuous inquiry.* New York: McGraw-Hill.

———. (1974). Wait-time and rewards as instructional variables, their influence on language, logic, and fate control: Part I–wait time. *Journal of Research in Science Teaching, 13* (2), 81–94; Part II–rewards. *Journal of Research in Science Teaching, 13* (4), 291–308.

Rutherford, F. J., & Ahlgren, A. (1988). Rethinking the science curriculum. In R. S. Brandt (Ed.), *Content of the curriculum.* Alexandria, VA: Association for Supervision and Curriculum Development.

———. (1990). *Science for all Americans.* New York: Oxford University Press.

Sabar, N. (1979). Science, curriculum, and society: Trends in science curriculum. *Science Education, 63* (2), 257–269.

Sadker, D., Sadker, M., & Thomas, D. (1981). Sex equity and special education. *Pointer, 26* (1), 33.

Safran, D. (1974). *Preparing teachers for parent involvement.* Menlo Park, California: Center for the Study of Parent Involvement.

Sargent-Welch Scientific Co. *Equipment catalogue.* Skokie, IL: Sargent-Welch Scientific.

Schlichter, C. L. (1983, February). The answer is in the question. *Science and Children,* p. 10.

Schwartz, J. L. (1985). *Sir Isaac Newton's Games* (Educational software). Pleasantville, NY: Sunburst Communications.

———. (1995). Shuttling between the particular and the general: Reflections on the role of conjecture and hypothesis in the generation of knowledge in science and mathematics. In Perkins, D. N., Schwartz, J. L., West, M. M., & Wiske, M. S., *Software goes to school—teaching for understanding new technologies.* (pp. 7–22). New York: Oxford University Press.

Shapiro, B. (1994). *What children bring to light: A constructivist perspective on children's learning in science.* New York: Teachers College Press.

Shavelson, R. J., & Baxter, G. P. (1992, May). What we've learned about assessing hands-on science. *Educational Leadership,* pp. 20–25.

Shaw, K. L., & Etchberger, M. L. (1993). Transitioning into constructivism: A vignette of a fifth grade teacher. In K. Tobin (Ed.), *The practice of constructivism in science education* (pp. 259–266). Washington, DC: AAAS Press.

Shaw, K. L., & Jakubowski, E. H. (1991). Teachers changing for changing times. *Focus on learning problems in mathematics, 13* (4), 13–20.

Shepardson, D. P., & Pizzini, E. L. (1992). Gender bias in female elementary teachers' perceptions of the scientific ability of students. *Science Education, 76* (2), 147–153.

Shrigley, R. L. (1987, May). Discrepant events: Why they fascinate students. *Science and Children,* p. 25.

Shymansky, J. A., Hedges, L., & Woodworth, G. (1990). A reassessment of the effects of inquiry-based science curricula of the 60's on student performance. *Journal of Research on Science Teaching, 27* (2), 127–144.

Shymansky, J. A., Kyle, Jr., W. C., & Allport, J. M. (1982, November–December). How effective were the hands-on programs of yesterday? *Science and Children,* pp. 14–15.

Slavin, R. L. (1995). *Cooperative learning.* Boston: Allyn and Bacon.

Smith, D. D., & Luchasson, R. (1992). *Introduction to special education.* Boston: Allyn and Bacon.

Smith, P. G. (1995, September). Reveling in rubrics. *Science Scope,* pp. 34–36.

Snir, J., Smith, C., and Grosslight, L. (1995) Conceptually enhanced simulations: A computer tool for science teaching. In Perkins, D. N., Schwartz, J. L., West, M. M., &

Wiske, M. S., (Eds.), *Software goes to school—teaching for understanding new technologies* (pp. 106–129). New York: Oxford University Press.

Spady, W. G. (1994). Choosing outcomes of significance. *Educational Leadership, 51* (6), 18–22.

State of Iowa. (1988). *School code of Iowa.* Des Moines, IA.

Staver, J. R., & Bay, M. (1987). Analysis of the project synthesis goal cluster orientation and inquiry emphasis of elementary science textbooks. *Journal of Research in Science Teaching, 23* (7), 629–643.

Stefanich, G. P. (1985). *Addressing orthopedic handicaps in the science classroom.* (Educational Resource Document No. 258 802)

Stone, C. L. (1982). *A meta-analysis of advance-organizer studies.* Paper presented at the Annual Meeting of the American Educational Research Association, New York. (ERIC Document No. 220476)

Styer, S. (1984, March). Books that ask the right questions. *Science and Children,* pp. 40–42.

Suchman, J. R. (1962). *The elementary school training program in scientific inquiry.* Report to the U.S. Office of Education, Project Title VII. Urbana: University of Illinois.

———. (1971). Motivation inherent in the pursuit of meaning: Or the desire to inquire. In H. I. Day, D. E. Berlyne, & D. E. Hunt (Eds.), *Intrinsic motivation: A new direction in education.* Toronto: Holt, Rinehart, & Winston.

Sumrall, W. J. (1995). Reasons for the perceived images of scientists by race and gender of students in grades 1–7. *School Science and Mathematics, 95* (2), 83–90.

Taba, H., Levine, S., & Elsey, F. F. (1964). *Thinking in elementary school children* (U.S. Office of Education Cooperative Research Project No. 1574). San Francisco: San Francisco State College.

Tobin, K. (1984). Effects of extended wait-time on discourse characteristics and achievement in middle school grades. *Journal of Research in Science Teaching, 21* (8) 779–791.

Tobin, K. G., & Capie, W. (1982). *Wait-time and learning in science.* AETS Outstanding Paper for 1981. (ERIC Document No. ED 221353)

Tobin, K., Tippins, D. J., & Gallard, A. J. (1994). Research on instructional strategies for teaching science. In D. L. Gabel, (Ed.), *Handbook on research on science teaching.* New York: Macmillan.

Triangle Coalition for Science and Technology Education. (1991). *A guide for building an alliance for science, mathematics and technology education.* College Park, MD: Triangle Coalition for Science and Technology Education.

———. (1992). *A guide for planning a volunteer program for science, mathematics and technology education.* College Park,

MD: Triangle Coalition for Science and Technology Education.

U.S. Office of Education. (1977). Education of handicapped children: Assistance to the states: Procedures for evaluating specific learning disabilities. *Federal Register, Part III. December 29.* Washington, DC: U.S. Department of Health, Education, and Welfare.

Valentino, C. (1985). *Question of the week.* Palo Alto, CA: Dale Seymore Publications.

Victor, E. (1985). *Science for the elementary school.* New York: Macmillan.

Von Glaserfeld, E. (1993). Questions and answers about radical constructivism. In Tobin, K. (Ed.), *The practice of constructivism in science education.* (Washington, DC: AAAS Press), p. 23–38.

Vygotsky, L. S. (1978). *Mind and society: The development of higher mental processes.* Cambridge, MA: Harvard University Press.

Wadsworth, B. J. (1996). *Piaget's theory of cognitive and affective development.* White Plains, NY: Longman Publishers.

Watson, S. B. (1992, February). Cooperative methods. *Science and Children,* pp. 30–31.

Weiss, I. R. (1978). *Report of the 1977 National Survey of Science, Mathematics, and Social Studies Education* (SE 78-72). Prepared for the National Science Foundation Directorate for Science Education. Research Triangle Park, NC: Center for Educational Research and Evaluation.

Western Regional Environmental Education Council. (1992). *Project WILD and Aquatic Project WILD.* Golden, CO.

Western Regional Environmental Education Council. (1994). *Project Learning Tree.* Golden, CO.

———. (1995). *Project WET.* Golden, CO.

Wheeler, G., & Sherman, T. F. (1983). Readability formulas revisited. *Science and Children, 20* (7), 38–40.

Wilen, W. (1986). *Questioning skills for teachers.* Washington, DC: National Education Association.

Wilen, W. W., & Ambrose, Jr., A. C. (1986) Effective questions and questioning: A research review. *Theory and Research in Social Education, 14* (2), pp. 153–161.

Willert, M. K., & Kamii, C. (1985, May). Reading in kindergarten: Direct vs. indirect teaching. *Young Children,* p. 3.

Williams, C. K., & Kamii, C. (1986, November). How do children learn by handling objects? *Young Children,* p. 26.

Williams, I. W. (1984). Chemistry. In A. Craft & G. Bardell (Eds.), *Curriculum opportunities in a multicultural society* (pp. 133–146). New York: Harper & Row.

Williams-Norton, M., Reisdorf, M., & Spees, S. (1990, March). Home is where the science is. *Science and Children,* pp. 13–15.

Willis, S. (1995a). Reinventing science education. *Curriculum update* (Summer), 2. Association for Supervision and Curriculum Development, Alexandria, VA.

———. (1995b). Reinventing science education: Reformers promote hands-on, inquiry-based learning. ASCD *Curriculum update,* Summer.

Windram, M. P. (1988, March). Getting at reading through science inquiries. *Roeper Review,* 150–152.

Wiser, M. (1995). Use of history of science to understand and remedy students' misconceptions about heat and temperature. In Perkins, D. N., Schwartz, J. L., West, M. M., & Wiske, M. S. (Eds.), *Software goes to school—teaching for understanding new technologies.* (pp. 23–28). New York: Oxford University Press.

Wolfinger, D. M. (1984). *Teaching science in the elementary school.* Boston: Little, Brown.

Wright, D. (1980). A report on the implications for the science community of three NSF-supported studies of the state of precollege science education. In H. A. Smith (Ed.), *What are the needs in precollege science, mathematics, and social science education? Views from the field.* Washington, DC: National Science Foundation.

Yager, R. E. (1983). The importance of terminology in teaching K–12 science. *Journal of Research in Science Teaching, 20* (6), 577–588.

———. (1984). The major crisis in science education. *School Science and Mathematics, 84* (3), 196.

Yager, R. E., & Penick, J. E. (1987, October). New concerns for affective outcomes in science. *Educational Leadership* p. 93.

Yager, R. (1991, September). The constructivist learning model. *Science Teacher,* pp. 52–57.

Zimmerman, B. J., & Pike, E. O. (1972). Effects of modeling and reinforcement on the acquisition and generalization of question-asking behavior. *Child Development, 43,* 892–907.

Index